Lecture Notes in Computer Science 11254

Commenced Publication in 1973
Founding and Former Series Editors:
Gerhard Goos, Juris Hartmanis, and Jan van Leeuwen

More information about this series at http://www.springer.com/series/7408

Tiago Massoni · Mohammad Reza Mousavi (Eds.)

Formal Methods: Foundations and Applications

21st Brazilian Symposium, SBMF 2018
Salvador, Brazil, November 26–30, 2018
Proceedings

 Springer

Editors
Tiago Massoni (ID)
Federal University of Campina Grande
Campina Grande, Brazil

Mohammad Reza Mousavi (ID)
University of Leicester
Leicester, UK

ISSN 0302-9743   ISSN 1611-3349 (electronic)
Lecture Notes in Computer Science
ISBN 978-3-030-03043-8   ISBN 978-3-030-03044-5 (eBook)
https://doi.org/10.1007/978-3-030-03044-5

Library of Congress Control Number: 2018958772

LNCS Sublibrary: SL2 – Programming and Software Engineering

This Springer imprint is published by the registered company Springer Nature Switzerland AG
The registered company address is: Gewerbestrasse 11, 6330 Cham, Switzerland

Preface

Welcome to the proceedings of the 21st Brazilian Symposium on Formal Methods (SBMF 2018), held during November 26–30, 2018, in Salvador, Brazil. This volume contains the papers accepted for presentation at SBMF 2018. For this edition of SBMF, we received 30 full submissions from 15 different countries. An international Program Committee comprising 56 leading scientists from 13 countries reviewed the papers thoroughly, providing a minimum of three and a maximum of five review reports for each paper. We ended up accepting 14 submissions, which translates into 47% of all submissions. The program included three invited talks by the following world-renowned computer scientists:

- Prof. José Meseguer, University of Illinois at Urbana-Champaign, USA
- Prof. Alexandre Mota, Federal University of Pernambuco, Brazil
- Prof. Jim Davies, University of Oxford, UK

We thank the Brazilian Computer Society (SBC), the Federal University of Bahia, and the Organizing Committee, for having provided various facilities and for their generous support. We are also grateful to our Program Committee (and additional reviewers) for their professional and hard work in providing expert review reports and thorough discussions leading to a very interesting and strong program. Many thanks for the sponsorship of the Federal University of Bahia (UFBA) and CAPES, and Springer for agreeing to publish the proceedings as a volume of *Lecture Notes of Computer Science*. We also acknowledge the facilities provided by the EasyChair system, which were crucial in managing the process of submission, selection, revision, and publication of the manuscripts included in this volume.

September 2018

Tiago Massoni
Mohammad Reza Mousavi

Organization

Program Committee

Aline Andrade	Universidade Federal da Bahia, Brazil
Luis Barbosa	University of Minho, Portugal
Harsh Beohar	Universität Duisburg-Essen, Germany
Christiano Braga	Universidade Federal Fluminense, Brazil
Michael Butler	University of Southampton, UK
Sergio Campos	UFMG, Brazil
Ana Cavalcanti	University of York, UK
Simone André Da Costa Cavalheiro	Universidade Federal de Pelotas, Brazil
Matteo Cimini	University of Massachusetts Lowell, USA
Márcio Cornélio	UFPE, Brazil
Andrea Corradini	Università di Pisa, Italy
Pedro R. D'Argenio	Universidad Nacional de Córdoba, Argentina
Jim Davies	University of Oxford, UK
Ana De Melo	University of São Paulo, Brazil
David Deharbe	ClearSy, France
Ewen Denney	RIACS/NASA, USA
Clare Dixon	University of Liverpool, UK
Rachid Echahed	CNRS and University of Grenoble, France
José Luiz Fiadeiro	Royal Holloway, University of London, UK
Alysson Filgueira	UEPB, Brazil
Luciana Foss	Universidade Federal de Pelotas, Brazil
Rohit Gheyi	Universidade Federal de Campina Grande, Brazil
Jan Friso Groote	Eindhoven University of Technology, The Netherlands
Stefan Hallerstede	Aarhus University, Denmark
Reiko Heckel	University of Leicester, UK
Rob Hierons	The University of Sheffield, UK
Hossein Hojjat	Rochester Institute of Technology, USA
Juliano Iyoda	Universidade Federal de Pernambuco, Brazil
Thierry Lecomte	ClearSy, France
Michael Leuschel	University of Düsseldorf, Germany
Patricia Machado	Federal University of Campina Grande, Brazil
Rodrigo Machado	Universidade Federal do Rio Grande do Sul, Brazil
Marcelo Maia	Universidade Federal de Uberlândia, Brazil
Narciso Marti-Oliet	Universidad Complutense de Madrid, Spain
Anamaria Martins Moreira	Universidade Federal do Rio de Janeiro, Brazil
Tiago Massoni	Universidade Federal de Campina Grande, Brazil
Alvaro Moreira	Federal University of Rio Grande do Sul, Brazil

Alexandre Mota	Universidade Federal de Pernambuco, Brazil
Arnaldo Moura	Universidade Estadual de Campinas, Brazil
Mohammad Mousavi	University of Leicester, UK
David Naumann	Stevens Institute of Technology, USA
Minh Ngo	Inria, France
Daltro Jose Nunes	Institute of Informatics, Federal University of Rio Grande do Sul, Brazil
Jose Oliveira	University of Minho, Portugal
Marcel Vinicius Medeiros Oliveira	Universidade Federal do Rio Grande do Norte, Brazil
Fernando Orejas	Universitat Politècnica de Catalunya, Spain
Arend Rensink	University of Twente, The Netherlands
Leila Ribeiro	Universidade Federal do Rio Grande do Sul, Brazil
Jan Oliver Ringert	University of Leicester, UK
Augusto Sampaio	Federal University of Pernambuco, Brazil
Leila Silva	Universidade Federal de Sergipe, Brazil
Adenilso Simao	Universidade de São Paulo, Brazil
Neeraj Singh	INPT-ENSEEIHT/IRIT, University of Toulouse, France
Ana Sokolova	University of Salzburg, Austria
Sofiene Tahar	Concordia University, Canada
Jim Woodcock	University of York, UK

Additional Reviewers

Beohar, Harsh	Nikouei, Mohammad
Dezani, Mariangiola	Rashid, Adnan
Gazda, Maciej	Ribeiro, Pedro
Klein Galli, Jaqueline	Siddique, Umair
Laveaux, Maurice	Stolz, Volker
Milanez, Alysson	Tuosto, Emilio
Neele, Thomas	Varshosaz, Mahsa

Contents

The Pragmatic Dimension of Formal Methods: Towards Building a Sound Synthesiser

Alexandre Mota[(✉)]

Centro de Informática, Universidade Federal de Pernambuco, Recife, Brazil
acm@cin.ufpe.br

Formal methods are mathematically based languages, tools and techniques for the specification, development and verification of systems [12]. Although most effort is being spent on specifying systems and verifying their properties, a final goal of most formal methods is achieving correct code from formal specifications. In this direction we find two representative strategies: (i) one is based on proposing refinements until a certain concrete design is achieved and then an almost direct mapping from mathematical elements to the source code of some programming language is made [17]; and (ii) another is using some refinement calculus in which specification and programming constructs are available in a single language and code is achieved by removing the specification elements by applying specific refinement rules [9]. Both strategies depend on developers experience.

In a complementary direction to the previous strategies, we can find automatic program synthesis. Program synthesis typically perform some form of search over the space of programs to generate a program that is consistent with a variety of constraints (for instance, input-output examples, specifications, and partial programs-or sketches). Program synthesis is considered the holy grail of Computer Science since the beginning of Artificial Intelligence in the 1950s. Automatic program synthesis is gaining attention nowadays thanks to the advances in SAT/SMT theories and efficient solvers. With such tools, it is now possible to solve very complex logical expressions in reasonable time. Thus the goal of automatic program synthesis is to automatically find a program in some programming language that satisfies a (formal) specification [3]; this is known as deductive synthesis. In the last decade, several applications of synthesis in the field of programming by examples have been deployed in mass-market industrial products (this is known as inductive synthesis), where the formal specification is replaced by a set of test cases. Using examples instead of specifications is an inherited Artificial Intelligence culture.

In this paper we present a clear and elegant formulation of program synthesis as an Alloy*[1] specification by applying its model finder (the Alloy* Analyzer) to search for a program that satisfies a contract in terms of pre and post-conditions [10]. Alloy* is a variant of the original Alloy tailored for synthesis, where a counterexample-guided inductive synthesis (CEGIS [14]) algorithm

---

[1] https://aleksandarmilicevic.github.io/hola/.

© Springer Nature Switzerland AG 2018
T. Massoni and M. R. Mousavi (Eds.): SBMF 2018, LNCS 11254, pp. 1–4, 2018.
https://doi.org/10.1007/978-3-030-03044-5_1

is implemented in the Alloy* Analyzer. Our proposal embeds in Alloy* both the syntax and the denotational semantics of Winskel's IMP(erative) language. This encoding makes this synthesiser more abstract than others found in literature and thus easily adaptable to handle different scenarios. Another significant difference is that this synthesiser can find programs, similar to the ones found in the work reported in [15], instead of just expressions. We illustrate our approach by synthesising Euclid's greatest common divisor algorithm. In addition, Alloy* provides us a great platform for the rapid development of a synthesiser. We show that this synthesiser can be easily adapted to deal with examples instead of specifications, and thus obtaining a programming by example synthesiser, to consider template of the final programs, named sketches, as well as to reuse previous synthesised code to improve its search process in a single solution. We briefly discuss the advantages and disadvantages of using all these facilities.

A difficulty all synthesisers have is in the amount of input the user has to provide. To become even more productive, we propose a system that envelops this synthesiser around the concepts of genetic algorithms to minimise the amount of user input. The proposed system has helped to synthesize seven programs (IntSQRT, Maj5, Maj8, Max4, Modu, Fact, and Fib) found in the SyGuS competition, iJava and IntroClass, and Genetic programming communities.

This work on program synthesis follows a trend since the early days I and my colleagues contribute to formal methods. We have created several solutions this way that were applied from INPE[2] (the Brazilian Institute for Space Research) [11] to Embraer[3] [2]. In general several of our contributions use a transformational approach where we propose a language L_P whose semantics is given in terms of a mature formal language L_B, which has available tool support. Thus we define a mapping from L_P to L_B in a algebraic style and prove its soundness and completeness. This is indeed a similar approach used by the Alloy Analyzer [6] and many other formal tools, except that no mapping is formally defined as no soundness and correctness theorems are presented.

As the formal methods tools, which we have based our own work, were developed as any software system, that is, in an ad hoc (and sometimes, semi-formally) way, we intend to recreate the foundation of our program synthesiser using a formal approach. Here we do not pretend to follow the full path as reported in [7] because in this direction we have to prove that the hardware circuits are correct and so on. To propose a feasible scope, in this work we assume that a few tools are trustworthy enough and close to code so that we can use them to create a solution we can convince others and ourselves it is worthy using Formal Methods. Similar to the LTL model checker reported in the work [1], we intend to create a relational model finder [16] with the capabilities of Alloy* [5,8] using a theorem prover, where the code is correct with respect to the specification as reported in the work [4]. Indeed such a kind of tool development can even be applied to a theorem prover itself, which instead of just coding directly in a programming language as reported in the work [13], one can formally specify

---

what is a theorem prover and generate code automatically. Moreover, as this code generation is directly related to the functions bodies stated in the theorem prover itself, a program synthesiser can be used to alleviate the burden of creating these functions bodies directly.

Acknowledgements. I would like to thank my colleagues Augusto Sampaio, Juliano Iyoda, Márcio Cornélio, Ana Cavalcanti, and Jim Woodcock for our collaborations. And to CNPq, grant 302170/2016-2, for supporting my research.

References

1. Esparza, J., Lammich, P., Neumann, R., Nipkow, T., Schimpf, A., Smaus, J.-G.: A fully verified executable LTL model checker. In: Sharygina, N., Veith, H. (eds.) CAV 2013. LNCS, vol. 8044, pp. 463–478. Springer, Heidelberg (2013). https://doi.org/10.1007/978-3-642-39799-8_31
2. Gomes, A., Mota, A., Sampaio, A., Ferri, F., Watanabe, E.: Constructive model-based analysis for safety assessment. Int. J. Softw. Tools Technol. Transf. **14**(6), 673–702 (2012)
3. Gulwani, S., Polozov, O., Singh, R.: Program synthesis. Found. Trends Program. Lang. **4**(1–2), 1–119 (2017)
4. Hupel, L., Nipkow, T.: A verified compiler from Isabelle/HOL to CakeML. In: Ahmed, A. (ed.) ESOP 2018. LNCS, vol. 10801, pp. 999–1026. Springer, Cham (2018). https://doi.org/10.1007/978-3-319-89884-1_35
5. Jackson, D.: Boolean compilation of relational specifications. Technical report, Cambridge, MA, USA (1998)
6. Jackson, D.: Software Abstractions: Logic, Language, and Analysis. The MIT Press, Cambridge (2006)
7. Leroy, X.: A formally verified compiler back-end. J. Autom. Reason. **43**(4), 363 (2009)
8. Milicevic, A., Near, J.P., Kang, E., Jackson, D.: Alloy*: a general-purpose higher-order relational constraint solver. Form. Methods Syst. Des., 1–32 (2017). https://doi.org/10.1007/s10703-016-0267-2
9. Morgan, C.: Programming from Specifications. Prentice Hall International Series in Computer Science, 2nd edn. Prentice Hall, Upper Saddle River (1994)
10. Mota, A., Iyoda, J., Maranhão, H.: Program synthesis by model finding. Inf. Process. Lett. **116**(11), 701–705 (2016)
11. Mota, A., Sampaio, A.: Model-checking CSP-Z: strategy, tool support and industrial application. Sci. Comput. Program. **40**(1), 59–96 (2001)
12. O'Regan, G.: Concise Guide to Software Engineering: From Fundamentals to Application Methods. UTCS. Springer, Cham (2017). https://doi.org/10.1007/978-3-319-57750-0
13. Paulson, L.C.: Designing a theorem prover. In: Handbook of Logic in Computer Science, vol. 2, pp. 415–475. Oxford University Press Inc., New York (1992)
14. Solar-Lezama, A., Tancau, L., Bodik, R., Seshia, S., Saraswat, V.: Combinatorial sketching for finite programs. SIGOPS Oper. Syst. Rev. **40**(5), 404–415 (2006)
15. Srivastava, S., Gulwani, S., Foster, J.S.: From program verification to program synthesis. In: Proceedings of the 37th Annual ACM SIGPLAN-SIGACT Symposium on Principles of Programming Languages, POPL 2010, pp. 313–326. ACM (2010)

16. Torlak, E., Jackson, D.: Kodkod: a relational model finder. In: Grumberg, O., Huth, M. (eds.) TACAS 2007. LNCS, vol. 4424, pp. 632–647. Springer, Heidelberg (2007). https://doi.org/10.1007/978-3-540-71209-1_49
17. Woodcock, J., Davies, J.: Using Z: Specification, Refinement, and Proof. Prentice-Hall Inc., Upper Saddle River (1996)

Formal Design of Cloud Computing Systems in Maude

José Meseguer[✉]

Department of Computer Science,
University of Illinois at Urbana-Champaign, Urbana, USA
meseguer@illinois.edu

Abstract. Cloud computing systems are complex distributed systems whose design is challenging for two main reasons: (1) since they are distributed systems, a correct design is very hard to achieve by testing alone; and (2) cloud computing applications have high availability and performance requirements; but these are hard to measure before implementation and hard to compare between different implementations. This paper summarizes our experience in using formal specification in Maude and model checking analysis to quickly explore the design space of a cloud computing system to achieve a high quality design that: (1) has verified correctness guarantees; (2) has better performance properties than other design alternatives so explored; (3) can be achieved before an actual implementation; and (4) can be used for both rapid prototyping and for automatic code generation.

Keywords: Specification and verification of distributed systems
Cloud computing · Rewriting logic · Maude

1 The Challenge of Cloud Computing

Cloud computing systems are used massively and need to meet high performance requirements such as high availability and throughput, and low latency, even with network congestion and faults, and during software and hardware upgrades. Furthermore, for both high availability and fault tolerance, data has to be replicated. However, the *CAP theorem* [12] shows that it is impossible to simultaneously have high availability and strong consistency in replicated data stores. This means that, depending on the application, different tradeoffs need to be found in the design of a cloud computing system between consistency and performance. For example, for a social network a weak consistency notion such as "eventual consistency" may be acceptable in exchange for high performance, whereas a medical information system will clearly require stronger consistency notions, even at the cost of some losses in performance. Indeed, as explained in [13], there is a wide spectrum of consistency models to choose from. One of the most crucial tasks in the design of a cloud computing system is to achieve

© Springer Nature Switzerland AG 2018
T. Massoni and M. R. Mousavi (Eds.): SBMF 2018, LNCS 11254, pp. 5–19, 2018.
https://doi.org/10.1007/978-3-030-03044-5_2

a good balance between good performance and consistency guarantees that are sufficient for the kinds of applications intended for the given system.

With some notable exceptions (see, e.g., [33]), in practice, cloud computing systems are often designed and built using only informal designs and only with the aid of testing techniques. Also, only after a system has been for the most part built, do experimental evaluations become possible. Since furthermore, these distributed systems can be quite large (for example, Cassandra has about 345,000 lines of code) and fairly complex, all this means that: (i) subtle bugs can easily pass undetected; (ii) it may not be entirely clear what consistency and correctness guarantees can be given for the system; and (iii) it can be very costly to explore other design alternatives, since the cost of implementing them is too high.

All this also means that there is a good opportunity for formal methods to provide much needed analytic and predictive power for exploring cloud computing system designs *before they are built*. However, this is also a challenge since:

1. The formal methods employed must naturally support distributed system design and analysis.
2. The formal notations used should be easy to understand by system designers. Furthermore, they should be simple and concise enough to precisely capture design ideas at a high level in specifications orders of magnitude shorter than code. This then makes it easy to express alternative designs and to explore the practical impact of various design choices.
3. They should be able to analyze correctness properties, if possible automatically, and to provide counterexamples when such properties are violated.
4. Since for these systems high performance is as important as correctness, the formal specification and analysis methods should also be able to provide not just "yes" or "no" answers to logical correctness questions, but also *quantitative* answers to performance questions.

It is worth stressing that point (2) is of great importance: only after having arrived at a good design is it meaningful to spend further efforts verifying in depth its properties. To put it perhaps more sharply, the exploration of a system's design and that of its logical and performance properties should happen *simultaneously* and, once a good design has thus been identified, its formal analysis should increase in depth. Also, all this should be done *before* actually building the systems, so that: (a) costly design errors are caught as early as possible; and (b) as much as possible is known about such a design, including its logical correctness properties and its estimated performance, before it is built.

2   Rewriting Logic and Maude

A rewrite theory $\mathcal{R} = (\Sigma, E, R)$ specifies is a *concurrent system*, whose *states* are the elements of the algebraic data type $T_{\Sigma/E}$, and whose *concurrent transitions* are specified by the rewrite rules R. We have found rewriting logic particularly well suited for specifying cloud computing systems. Such systems can be naturally specified as configurations of distributed objects, often clients and servers, which communicate with each other through message passing. The sending and receiving of messages by such objects has a very natural formalization by means of simple rewrite rules. In our experience, the rewrite rule formalism is easy to understand by network engineers and distributed system designers.

Maude [14] is a language implementing rewriting logic. Since a program in Maude is just a rewrite theory, Maude is a very simple language. However, Maude is both highly expressive and versatile and very high level, affording a very direct and concise representation of the concurrent system being modeled.

Maude is also a high-performance language. For example, in a recent detailed benchmarking of 15 well-known algebraic, functional and object-oriented languages by Hubert Garabel and his collaborators at INRIA Rhône-Alpes, Haskell and Maude were the two languages showing the highest overall performance [18].

For the purposes of this paper, the main points to emphasize are that, once a distributed system designed has been expressed in Maude as a rewrite theory:

- Such a system design can be *simulated* using Maude's `frewrite` command.
- Its reachability properties, including both failures of invariants and monitoring of consistency and other properties can be exhaustively analyzed by breadth first search using Maude's `search` command.
- Provided that the set of states reachable from a given initial state is finite, its LTL temporal logic properties can be analyzed using Maude's LTL model checker [14].
- To specify the system's real-time aspects and model check its real-time temporal logic properties the Real-Time Maude language and system can be used [34].
- Expressing the system's probabilistic aspects as a *probabilistic rewrite theory* [1], its quantitative performance aspects can be analyzed by statistical model checking using the PVeStA tool [2].

In all these ways, Maude supports a style of formal specification and analysis of cloud computing systems that effectively meets the challenge to formal methods that such systems pose, as explained in Sect. 1. In fact, to the best of my knowledge it seems fair to say that rewriting logic as supported by Maude is the first formally based approach in which both correctness and performance aspects of cloud computing systems have been systematically analyzed.

3 Specifying and Analyzing Cloud Computing Systems

The work on specifying and analyzing cloud computing systems in Maude has focused on two main areas: (i) formal specification and analysis of cloud storage systems; and (ii) some security aspects of cloud computing.

3.1   Formal Specification and Analysis of Cloud Storage Systems

Only a short summary of work in this area is possible here. I refer to the survey [11], from which the summary of the work on systems (1)–(3) is drawn, for a detailed account. My summary of (4) is based on [35], and that of (5)–(6) on [29,30]. The cloud storage systems that have been specified and analyzed in Maude include:

1. **Apache Cassandra** [22] is an open-source industrial key-value data store having about 345,000 lines of code that only guarantees *eventual consistency*. To the best of our knowledge, before our work no formal specification of Cassandra existed and, although believed to guarantee eventual consistency, no verification of that property had been carried out. After studying Cassandra's code, we first developed a 1,000-line Maude specification with just 20 rewrite rules [31], that captured the system's main components such as data partitioning strategies, consistency levels, and timestamp policies for ordering multiple versions of data. Standard model checking allowed us to confirm that Cassandra does support eventual consistency and to analyze under what conditions Cassandra can guarantee strong consistency. To also analyze Cassandra's performance features and those of a design alternative, we then develop a probabilistic model of Cassandra in [26]. By modifying a single function in our Maude model we obtained a model of our proposed design alternative. The statistical model checking analysis of the original Cassandra model and our alternative Cassandra-like design in PVeStA indicated that the proposed design alternative did *not* improve Cassandra's performance. But this left open the question of how reliable these analyses were. To answer this question we modified the Cassandra code to obtain an implementation of the alternative design, and executed both the original Cassandra code and the new system on representative workloads. These experiments showed that PVeStA statistical model checking provides reliable performance estimates.

2. **Megastore** [10] is a key part of Google's cloud infrastructure. Megastore's trade-off between consistency and efficiency is to guarantee consistency only for transactions that access a single *entity group* (e.g., "John's email" or "books on formal verification"). Megastore's code is not publicly available, and only a short high-level description has been given in [10]. To fully understand the Megastore algorithms Jon Grov and Peter Ölveczky first developed in [19] a sufficiently detailed executable formal specification of Megastore in Real-Time Maude based on the description in [10]. This is the first publicly available formalization and reasonably detailed description of Megastore. It contains 56 rewrite rules, of which 37 deal with fault tolerance features.

To analyze both the correctness and the performance of Megastore's Maude model two additional models were developed: (i) since in the original real-time model only those behaviors that are possible *within the given timing parameters* are analyzed, to exhaustively analyze all possible system behaviors *irrespective* of particular timing parameters, an *untimed* model was also developed; and (ii) for *performance estimation* purposes, a real-time model in which certain parameters, such as the messaging delays between two nodes, are selected probabilistically according to a given probability distribution was also developed.

Furthermore, Jon Grov had an idea on how to extend Megastore so that it would also guarantee strong consistency for certain transactions accessing *multiple* entity groups *without* sacrificing performance. This led to the design of *Megastore-CGC*. The key observation is that a Megastore site replicating a set of entity groups participates in all updates of these entity groups, and should therefore be able to maintain an ordering on those updates. The idea behind the Megastore-CGC extension is that, by making this ordering explicit, such an "ordering site" can validate transactions [20]. Since Megastore-CGC exploits the implicit ordering of updates during Megastore commits, it *piggybacks* ordering and validation onto Megastore's commit protocol and therefore does not require additional messages for validation and commit. A *failover* protocol deals with failures of the ordering sites. Both simulations (to discover performance bottlenecks) and Maude model checking were extensively used during the development of Megastore-CGC, whose formalization contains 72 rewrite rules. The performance estimated for Megastore and Megastore-CGC using randomized simulations in Real-Time Maude indicated that both system designs had about the same performance. That is, a design with considerably stronger consistency guarantees was obtained without sacrificing performance.

3. **RAMP.** Read-Atomic Multi-Partition (RAMP) transactions were proposed by Peter Bailis *et al.* [9] to offer light-weight multi-partition transactions that guarantee one of the fundamental consistency levels, namely, *read atomicity*: either all updates or no updates of a transaction are visible to other transactions. The paper [9] gives hand proofs of correctness properties and proposes a number of variations of RAMP without giving details. We used Maude to: (i) check whether RAMP indeed satisfies the guaranteed properties, and (ii) develop detailed specifications of the different variations of RAMP and check which properties they satisfy. Specifically, in [25,28] we used reachability analysis to analyze whether the different variants of RAMP satisfy the following properties (from [9]):

   - *Read atomic isolation*: either all updates or no updates of a transaction are visible to other transactions.
   - *Companions present*: if a version is committed, then each of the version's sibling versions are present on their respective partitions.
   - *Synchronization independence*: each transaction will eventually commit or abort.
   - *Read your writes*: a client's writes are visible to her subsequent reads.

We analyzed these properties for our seven versions of RAMP. Our analysis results agree with the theorems and conjectures in [9]: all versions satisfy the above properties, except that: (i) RAMP without 2PC only satisfies synchronization independence; and (ii) RAMP with one-phase writes does not satisfy read-your-writes.

Furthermore, in [27] we used statistical model checking to analyze whether the different variants of RAMP offer the expected performance (only two of the versions were implemented by the RAMP developers for performance analysis). Our statistical model checking performance results: (a) were consistent with the experimental evaluations of the two implemented designs; (b) were also consistent with conjectures made by the RAMP developers for other unimplemented designs; and (c) have uncovered some promising new designs that seem attractive for some applications.

4. **P-Store** [38] P-Store is a data store that combines wide-area replication, data partition, some fault tolerance, serializability, and limited use of atomic multicast. It has influenced other recent data store designs that can be seen as extensions of its design. P-Store uses atomic multicast to order concurrent transactions and group communication for atomic commit. As pointed out for example in [4], both atomic multicast and group communication commit seem to be key building blocks in cloud storage systems. However such features were not formalized in previous work. Indeed, Ölveczky's paper on P-Store [35] describes the formalization and formal analysis of P-Store in Maude and, as part of its main contributions, specifies group communication commitment, and defines an abstract Maude model of atomic multicast that allows any possible ordering of message reception consistent with atomic multicast. Besides providing a Maude formal model of two versions of P-Store, the work in [35] performed model checking analysis. This analysis uncovered some significant errors in the supposedly-verified P-Store algorithm, like read-only transactions never getting validated in certain cases. One of the authors of the original P-Store paper [38] did confirm that a nontrivial mistake had been found in their algorithm and suggested a way of correcting the mistake. The Maude analysis of the corrected algorithm did not find any errors. Furthermore, the analysis showed that a crucial assumption was missing from the original P-Store paper, and that a key definition was very easy to misunderstand because of how it was phrased in English. All this showed that there is a clear need for formal specification and analysis beyond the standard prose-cum-pseudo-code descriptions and informal correctness proofs.

5. **Walter** [41] is a distributed partially replicated data store providing Parallel Snapshot Isolation (PSI), an important consistency property that offers attractive performance while ensuring adequate guarantees for certain kinds of applications. Walter is a very good opportunity for formal methods, because no formal system specification existed at all before our work in [30], and there was no formal (or even informal) verification that it guarantees PSI. Furthermore, Walter is also a good stepping stone towards placing the design of cloud-based transaction systems in a formally-based modular framework. In this sense, Walter has been a key missing design in the spectrum, so that its study complements and enriches the general picture that has been obtained in the formal modeling and analysis studies on Cassandra, Megastore, RAMP, P-Store, and ROLA discussed above in (1)–(4) and below on (6).

In [30] we have:
- Given in Maude the first formal executable specification of Walter.
- Formalized the SI and PSI properties and formally analyzed for the first time whether the Walter design satisfies either of these properties. This analysis has been achieved by: (a) providing a parametric method to generate all initial states for given parameters; and (b) performing model checking analysis to verify the SI and PSI properties for all initial states for various parameter choices. Our analysis shows that the Walter design does indeed satisfy the PSI property for all our initial states but fails to satisfy the SI property;
- Extended the Maude model of Walter from a rewrite theory to a probabilistic rewrite theory by adding time and probability distributions for message delays to the original specification. We then carried out a systematic statistical model checking analysis of the key performance metric, transaction throughput, under a wide range of workloads. The results of this analysis confirm that the performance estimates thus obtained are consistent with those obtained experimentally for the Walter implementation in [41]; and they furthermore provide new insights about Walter's performance beyond the limited ranges for which such information was available by experimental evaluation in [41].

6. **ROLA** [29] is a new distributed transaction protocol that has been designed and analyzed using Maude from the very beginning. Different applications require negotiating the consistency vs. performance trade-offs in different ways. The point of ROLA is to explore a specific such tradeoff not studied before. The key issue is the required degree of consistency for a given application, and how to meet its consistency requirements with high performance. Cerone et al. [13] survey a hierarchy of consistency models for distributed transaction protocols including (in increasing order of strength): (i) read atomicity (RA): either all or none of a distributed transactions updates are visible to another transaction (that is, there are no fractured reads); (ii) causal consistency (CC): if transaction T2 is causally dependent on transaction T1, then if another transaction sees the updates by T2, it must also see the updates of T1 (e.g., if A posts something on a social media, and C sees Bs comment on As post, then C must also see As original post); (iii) parallel snapshot isolation (PSI): like CC but without lost updates; and so on, all the way up to the well-known serializability guarantees. A key property of transaction protocols is the prevention of lost updates (PLU). The weakest consistency model in [13] satisfying both RA and PLU is PSI. However, PSI, and the already discussed Walter protocol [41] implementing PSI, also guarantee CC. Cerone et al. conjecture that a system guaranteeing RA and PLU without guaranteeing CC should be useful, but up to now we are not aware of any such protocol. The point of ROLA is exactly to fill this gap: guaranteeing RA and PLU, but not CC. Two key questions are then: (a) are there applications needing high performance where RA plus PLU provide a sufficient degree of consistency? and (b) can a new design meeting RA plus PLU outperform existing designs, like Walter, meeting PSI?

Regarding question (a), an example of a transaction that requires RA and PLU but not CC is the becoming friends transaction on social media. Bailis et al. [8] point out that RA is crucial for this operation: If Edinson and Neymar become friends, then Unai should not see a fractured read where Edinson is a friend of Neymar, but Neymar is not a friend of Edinson. An implementation of becoming friends must obviously guarantee PLU: the new friendship between Edinson and Neymar should not be lost. Finally, CC could be sacrificed for the sake of performance: Assume that Dani is a friend of Neymar. When Edinson becomes Neymar's friend, he sees that Dani is Neymar's friend, and therefore also becomes a friend of Dani. The second friendship therefore causally depends on the first one. However, it does not seem crucial that others are aware of this causality: If Unai sees that Edinson and Dani are friends, then it is not necessary that he knows that (this happened because) Edinson and Neymar are friends.

Regarding question (b), the work in [29] compared the performance of ROLA with that of Walter. To model time and performance issues, ROLA has been specified in Maude as a probabilistic rewrite theory. ROLA's RA and PLU requirements were then analyzed by standard model checking disregarding time issues. To estimate ROLA's performance, and to compare it with that of Walter, the specification of Walter in Maude was used, and the Maude models of both ROLA and Walter were analyzed by statistical model checking analysis using the PVeStA tool. The results of this analysis showed that ROLA outperforms Walter in all performance requirements for all read/write transaction rates. To the best of our knowledge this is the first demonstration that, by a suitable use of formal methods, a completely new distributed transaction protocol can be designed and thoroughly analyzed, as well as be compared with other designs, very early on, before its implementation.

3.2 Some Security Aspects of Cloud Computing Systems

The work on using formal specification and analysis in Maude for cloud computing security is less developed than that on storage systems, but it can give a taste for what is possible. A common theme through both of the studies that I summarize below is that cloud computing, while giving rise to new security vulnerabilities, does also offer the possibility of arriving at system designs that take advantage of cloud computing to increase system security. My summary of (1) is based on material in [15], and that of (2) on [11,39]

1. **Achieving Stable Availability in the Face of DoS Attacks**. Availability is a crucial security property for cloud-based systems. It can be compromised by distributed Denial of Service (DoS) attacks. In [15] two Maude-based formal patterns (in the sense of [32]), and their combination into the ASV+SR pattern were presented. Used in their ASV+SR combination, they can effectively defend cloud-based systems against DoS attacks. The key notion proposed is that of *stable availability*, meaning that, with very high probability, service quality remains very close to a chosen threshold, regardless of how

bad the DoS attack can get. This notion is a good example of how cloud computing can be used to enhance security, in this case defenses against DoS attacks. The two most basic formal patterns used as defenses against DoS attacks were: (i) the Adaptive Selective Verification (ASV) pattern, which enhances a communication protocol with a defense mechanism, and (ii) the Server Replicator (SR) pattern, which exploits cloud computing's flexibility to provision additional resources based on perceived congestion. However, ASV achieves availability without stability, and SR cannot achieve stable availability at a reasonable cost. As a main result the work in [15] shows, by statistical model checking with the PVeStA tool, that (iii) the ASV+SR composition of both patterns yields a new pattern which guarantees stable availability at a reasonable cost.

The key problem addressed is that DoS defense mechanisms that help maintaining availability can nevertheless show performance degradation as a DoS attack worsens. Thus, a key goal in [15] is to design DoS security adaptive measures that can achieve stable availability, which means that with very high probability service quality remains very close to a chosen constant quantity, which does not change over time, regardless of how bad the DoS attack can get. Cloud Computing, by offering the possibility of dynamic resource allocation, can be used to leverage stable availability when combined with DoS defense mechanisms.

The ASV protocol [3,24] is a well-known defense against DoS attacks in the typical situation that clients and attackers use a shared channel where neither the attacker nor the client have full control over the communication channel [24]. The ASV protocol adapts to increasingly severe DoS attacks and provides improved availability. However, it cannot provide stable availability. By replicating servers one can dynamically provision more resources to adapt to high demand situations and achieve stable availability; but the cost of provisioned servers drastically increases in a DoS attack situation. These two patterns are modeled in Maude and then formally composed to obtain the new ASV+SR pattern. As a main result the work in [15] shows, by analyzing the quantitative properties of ASV+SR with the statistical model checker PVeStA, that ASV+SR guarantees stable availability at a reasonable cost. The key idea of ASV+SR is relatively easy to explain. As a DoS attack gets worse, ASV servers randomly drop an increasing number of messages from clients, and honest clients increase their resending of messages based on their perceived latency to get a server's response. ASV ensures that messages from honest clients *will* eventually get through, but performance is degraded. ASV+SR pattern avoids this performance degradation. However, *much fewer additional servers* need to be provisioned than if a naive approach based only on SR were used. Actually, in ASV+SR the threshold for provisioning new servers is itself a chosen parameter: one can settle for a small, constant factor in performance degradation at the expense of substantial savings in the provisioning of new servers.

2. **Building a Group Key Management Service on top of ZooKeeper**.
Zookeeper [23] is a fault-tolerant distributed key/value data store that provides reliable distributed coordination. The work in [39] investigated whether a useful group key management service can be built using ZooKeeper using Maude and statistical model checking in PVeStA.

Group key management is the management of cryptographic keys for secure communication between multiple authorized entities. A central group key controller can fulfill this need by: (a) authenticating/admitting authorized users into the group, and (b) generating a *group key* and distributing it to authorized group members [42]. In settings with a centralized group controller, its failure can impact both group dynamics and periodic key updates, leaving the group key vulnerable. This is especially significant when designing a cloud-based group key management service, since such a service will likely manage many groups.

The work in [39] investigated whether a fault-tolerant cloud-based group key management service could be built by leveraging existing coordination services commonly available in cloud infrastructures and if so, how to design such a system. In particular, we: (a) designed a group key management service built using Zookeeper [23], a reliable distributed coordination service supporting Internet-scale distributed applications, (b) developed a rewriting logic model of our design in Maude [14], based on [21], where key generation is handled by a centralized key management server and key distribution is offloaded to a ZooKeeper cluster and where the group controller stores its state in ZooKeeper to enable quick recovery from failure, and (c) analyzed our model using the PVeStA [2] statistical model checking tool. The analysis centered on two key questions: (1) can a ZooKeeper-based group key management service handle faults more reliably than a traditional centralized group key manager, and (2) can it scale to a large number of concurrent clients with a low enough latency to be useful?

Our analysis consisted of two experiments. Both were run hundreds of times via PVeStA and average results were collected. The first experiment was designed to test whether saving snapshots of the group key manager's state in the ZooKeeper store could increase the overall reliability of the system.

In the first experiment we compared the average key manager availability (i.e., the time it is available to distribute keys to clients) between a single key manager and two key managers where they share a common state saved in the ZooKeeper store. We observed an availability improvement from 65% to 85%. Our second experiment was designed to examine whether using ZooKeeper to distribute shared keys is efficient and scalable enough for real-world use. The experiment measured the variations in: (a) the percentage of keys successfully received by group members, and (b) the key distribution latency, as increasing numbers of clients joined a group per second. We analyzed our original model and a slightly modified model where we added a 2 s wait time between key updates from the key manager. While our initial experiments show that naively using ZooKeeper as a key distribution agent works well, at high client join rates, the key reception rate leveled out around

96%. This occurs because ZooKeeper can apply key updates internally more quickly then clients can download them. By adding extra latency between key updates, the ZooKeeper servers are forced to wait enough time for the correct keys to propagate to clients, the slightly modified design achieved a 99% key reception in all cases. On the other hand, key distribution latency remained relatively constant, at around half a second, regardless of the join rate because ZooKeeper can distribute keys at a much higher rate than a key manager can update them [23].

In essence, our analysis confirmed that a scalable and fault-tolerant key-management service can indeed be built using ZooKeeper, settling various doubts raised about the effectiveness of ZooKeeper for key management by an earlier, but considerably less-detailed, model and analysis [16]. This result is not particularly surprising, especially considering that many man-hours would be needed to optimize an actual system. More interestingly, the analysis also showed that system designs may suffer from performance bottlenecks not readily apparent in the original description—highlighting the power of formal modeling and analysis as a method to explore the design space.

4   Limitations and Some Future Directions

One important limitation of this extended abstract is that there is no room for a careful comparison with related work. Fortunately, a quite up to date such comparison has been given in the survey [11], to which I refer for a discussion of other work in this area. Two other current limitations pointing to future research directions are: (1) the absence at the moment of full verification by theorem proving for the systems that I have discussed; and (2) the current status of Maude executable specifications as *prototypes* useful for simulation and analysis, but not used for the moment for distributed implementations.

Regarding limitation (1), the obvious thing to say is that theorem proving is a natural next step. I have emphasized earlier—and the various systems I have discussed have further stressed—that perhaps the first and most valuable service that Maude executable specifications can render to cloud computing is not verification per se, but rather *fast design exploration*. It makes no sense to model check the *wrong* design. And, due to the labor intensive nature of theorem proving, it makes even less sense to perform theorem proving verification on such a wrong design, particularly since theorem provers are not that good at finding counterexamples and, furthermore, in this area logical correctness is only part of the story: performance matters quite as much. Theorem proving is, as I said, a complementary next step: after having arrived at a good system design and having thoroughly analyzed its logical correctness properties—resp. its performance—by standard model checking—resp. by statistical model checking—for representative initial states, the next step is to fully verify the systems key logical properties for *all initial states* by theorem proving. For Maude specifications of distributed systems, three related approaches, one based on symbolic model checking and two based on theorem proving, seem particularly well suited:

- The *Logical Model Checking* approach in [5–7,17] is in some sense halfway between model checking and theorem proving: it allows full verification of temporal logic properties for *infinite-state systems* and for *infinite sets of initial states*.
- The deductive verification of invariants and other safety properties by the unification methods supported by Maude's *Invariant Analyzer* tool [36,37] is also directly relevant and can be a useful tool for verifying invariants.
- The *Constructor-Based Reachability Logic* for rewrite theories presented in [40] is a third attractive alternative. Reachability logic generalizes Hoare logic and can express many Hoare-like partial correctness properties, including invariants. Although its tool is still under development, it has already been applied to the deductive verification of some distributed systems.

Regarding limitation (2) there are two main things to say. First, thanks to Maude's support for TCP-IP sockets as built-in objects [14], Maude programs can be easily distributed. The basic idea is that objects in a distributed system written in Maude can be executed in different machines, with sockets used to support message passing communication across machines. What is needed, however, is to make the passage from a Maude model to its distributed implementation as simple and as efficient as possible. Current, as yet unpublished, research is advancing this direction. In particular, distributed storage systems are among the examples we are experimenting with. Second, this direction is particularly important to arrive at system implementations that are *correct by construction*. In fact, this dovetails very nicely with the effort in overcoming limitation (1), since all this should make it possible to generate correct by construction distributed implementations from Maude-based formal specifications of system designs that have already been submitted to both model checking and theorem proving verification.

Acknowledgements. As the references make clear, most these ideas have been developed in joint work with a large number of collaborators and former or present students, including: Musab AlTurki, Rakesh Bobba, Jonas Eckhardt, Jatin Ganhotra, Jon Grov, Indranil Gupta, Si Liu, Tobias Mühlbauer, Son Nguyen, Peter Csaba Ölveczky, Muntasir Raihan Rahman, Stephen Skeirik, and Martin Wirsing. Furthermore, in some of the work I report on, such as [19,20,35], I have not been involved. These projects were partially supported by the Air Force Research Laboratory and the Air Force Office of Scientific Research, under agreement number FA8750-11-2-0084, the National Science Foundation under Grant Nos. NSF CNS 1409416 and NSF CNS 1319527, and the Naval Research Laboratory under contract number NRL N00173-17-1-G002. I thank the organizers of SBMF 2018 for giving me the opportunity of presenting these ideas at the meeting in Salvador.

References

1. Agha, G., Meseguer, J., Sen, K.: PMaude: rewrite-based specification language for probabilistic object systems. Electr. Notes Theor. Comput. Sci. **153**(2), 213–239 (2006)
2. AlTurki, M., Meseguer, J.: PVESTA: a parallel statistical model checking and quantitative analysis tool. In: Corradini, A., Klin, B., Cîrstea, C. (eds.) CALCO 2011. LNCS, vol. 6859, pp. 386–392. Springer, Heidelberg (2011). https://doi.org/10.1007/978-3-642-22944-2_28
3. AlTurki, M., Meseguer, J., Gunter, C.: Probabilistic modeling and analysis of DoS protection for the ASV protocol. Electr. Notes Theor. Comput. Sci. **234**, 3–18 (2009)
4. Ardekani, M.S., Sutra, P., Shapiro, M.: G-DUR: a middleware for assembling, analyzing, and improving transactional protocols. In: Proceedings of the 15th International Middleware Conference, pp. 13–24. ACM (2014)
5. Bae, K., Escobar, S., Meseguer, J.: Abstract logical model checking of infinite-state systems using narrowing. In: Rewriting Techniques and Applications (RTA 2013). LIPIcs, vol. 21, pp. 81–96. Schloss Dagstuhl-Leibniz-Zentrum fuer Informatik (2013)
6. Bae, K., Meseguer, J.: Infinite-state model checking of LTLR formulas using narrowing. In: Escobar, S. (ed.) WRLA 2014. LNCS, vol. 8663, pp. 113–129. Springer, Cham (2014). https://doi.org/10.1007/978-3-319-12904-4_6
7. Bae, K., Meseguer, J.: Predicate abstraction of rewrite theories. In: Dowek, G. (ed.) RTA 2014. LNCS, vol. 8560, pp. 61–76. Springer, Cham (2014). https://doi.org/10.1007/978-3-319-08918-8_5
8. Bailis, P., Fekete, A., Ghodsi, A., Hellerstein, J.M., Stoica, I.: Scalable atomic visibility with RAMP transactions. ACM Trans. Database Syst. **41**(3), 15:1–15:45 (2016)
9. Bailis, P., Fekete, A., Hellerstein, J.M., Ghodsi, A., Stoica, I.: Scalable atomic visibility with RAMP transactions. In: Proceedings of the SIGMOD 2014. ACM (2014)
10. Baker, J., et al.: Megastore: providing scalable, highly available storage for interactive services. In: CIDR 2011 (2011). www.cidrdb.org
11. Bobba, R., et al.: Design, formal modeling, and validation of cloud storage systems using Maude. Technical report, University of Illinois Computer Science Department, June 2017. http://hdl.handle.net/2142/96274. Campbell, R.H., et al. (eds.) Assured Cloud Computing, J. Wiley (2018, to appear)
12. Brewer, E.A.: Towards robust distributed systems (abstract). In: Proceedings of the Nineteenth Annual ACM Symposium on Principles of Distributed Computing, p. 7. ACM (2000)
13. Cerone, A., Bernardi, G., Gotsman, A.: A framework for transactional consistency models with atomic visibility. In: Proceedings of the 26th International Conference on Concurrency Theory, CONCUR 2015. LIPIcs, vol. 42, pp. 58–71. Schloss Dagstuhl - Leibniz-Zentrum fuer Informatik (2015)
14. Clavel, M., et al.: All About Maude - A High-Performance Logical Framework. LNCS, vol. 4350. Springer, Heidelberg (2007). https://doi.org/10.1007/978-3-540-71999-1
15. Eckhardt, J., Mühlbauer, T., AlTurki, M., Meseguer, J., Wirsing, M.: Stable availability under denial of service attacks through formal patterns. In: de Lara, J., Zisman, A. (eds.) FASE 2012. LNCS, vol. 7212, pp. 78–93. Springer, Heidelberg (2012). https://doi.org/10.1007/978-3-642-28872-2_6

16. Eckhart, J.: Security analysis in cloud computing using rewriting logic. Master's thesis, Ludwig-Maximilans-Universität München (2012)
17. Escobar, S., Meseguer, J.: Symbolic model checking of infinite-state systems using narrowing. In: Baader, F. (ed.) RTA 2007. LNCS, vol. 4533, pp. 153–168. Springer, Heidelberg (2007). https://doi.org/10.1007/978-3-540-73449-9_13
18. Garavel, H., Tabikh, M.A., Arrada, I.S.: Benchmarking implementations of term rewriting and pattern matching in algebraic, functional, and object-oriented languages: the 4th rewrite engines competition. In: Rusu, V. (ed.) WRLA 2018. LNCS, vol. 11152, pp. 1–25. Springer, Cham (2018). https://doi.org/10.1007/978-3-319-99840-4_1
19. Grov, J., Ölveczky, P.C.: Formal modeling and analysis of Google's Megastore in Real-Time Maude. In: Iida, S., Meseguer, J., Ogata, K. (eds.) Specification, Algebra, and Software. LNCS, vol. 8373, pp. 494–519. Springer, Heidelberg (2014). https://doi.org/10.1007/978-3-642-54624-2_25
20. Grov, J., Ölveczky, P.C.: Increasing consistency in multi-site data stores: Megastore-CGC and its formal analysis. In: Giannakopoulou, D., Salaün, G. (eds.) SEFM 2014. LNCS, vol. 8702, pp. 159–174. Springer, Cham (2014). https://doi.org/10.1007/978-3-319-10431-7_12
21. Gupta, J.: Available group key management for NASPInet. Master's thesis, Univeristy of Illinois at Champaign-Urbana (2011)
22. Hewitt, E.: Cassandra: The Definitive Guide. O'Reilly Media, Sebastopol (2010)
23. Hunt, P., Konar, M., Junqueira, F., Reed, B.: ZooKeeper: wait-free coordination for internet-scale systems. In: USENIX ATC, vol. 10 (2010)
24. Khanna, S., Venkatesh, S.S., Fatemieh, O., Khan, F., Gunter, C.A.: Adaptive selective verification. In: INFOCOM, pp. 529–537. IEEE (2008)
25. Liu, S., Ganhotra, J., Rahman, M.R., Nguyen, S., Gupta, I., Meseguer, J.: Quantitative analysis of consistency in NoSQL key-value stores. LITES 4(1), 03:1–03:26 (2017)
26. Liu, S., Nguyen, S., Ganhotra, J., Rahman, M.R., Gupta, I., Meseguer, J.: Quantitative analysis of consistency in NoSQL key-value stores. In: Campos, J., Haverkort, B.R. (eds.) QEST 2015. LNCS, vol. 9259, pp. 228–243. Springer, Cham (2015). https://doi.org/10.1007/978-3-319-22264-6_15
27. Liu, S., Ölveczky, P.C., Ganhotra, J., Gupta, I., Meseguer, J.: Exploring design alternatives for RAMP transactions through statistical model checking. In: Duan, Z., Ong, L. (eds.) ICFEM 2017. LNCS, vol. 10610, pp. 298–314. Springer, Cham (2017). https://doi.org/10.1007/978-3-319-68690-5_18
28. Liu, S., Ölveczky, P.C., Rahman, M.R., Ganhotra, J., Gupta, I., Meseguer, J.: Formal modeling and analysis of RAMP transaction systems. In: Proceedings of the 31st Annual ACM Symposium on Applied Computing, Pisa, Italy, 4–8 April 2016, pp. 1700–1707. ACM (2016)
29. Liu, S., Ölveczky, P.C., Santhanam, K., Wang, Q., Gupta, I., Meseguer, J.: ROLA: a new distributed transaction protocol and its formal analysis. In: Russo, A., Schürr, A. (eds.) FASE 2018. LNCS, vol. 10802, pp. 77–93. Springer, Cham (2018). https://doi.org/10.1007/978-3-319-89363-1_5
30. Liu, S., Ölveczky, P.C., Wang, Q., Meseguer, J.: Formal modeling and analysis of the Walter transactional data store. In: Rusu, V. (ed.) WRLA 2018. LNCS, vol. 11152, pp. 136–152. Springer, Cham (2018). https://doi.org/10.1007/978-3-319-99840-4_8

31. Liu, S., Rahman, M.R., Skeirik, S., Gupta, I., Meseguer, J.: Formal modeling and analysis of Cassandra in Maude. In: Merz, S., Pang, J. (eds.) ICFEM 2014. LNCS, vol. 8829, pp. 332–347. Springer, Cham (2014). https://doi.org/10.1007/978-3-319-11737-9_22

32. Meseguer, J.: Taming distributed system complexity through formal patterns. Sci. Comput. Program. **83**, 3–34 (2014)

33. Newcombe, C., Rath, T., Zhang, F., Munteanu, B., Brooker, M., Deardeuff, M.: How Amazon Web Services uses formal methods. Commun. ACM **58**(4), 66–73 (2015)

34. Ölveczky, P.C., Meseguer, J.: Semantics and pragmatics of Real-Time Maude. High.-Order Symb. Comput. **20**(1–2), 161–196 (2007)

35. Ölveczky, P.C.: Formalizing and validating the P-Store replicated data store in Maude. In: James, P., Roggenbach, M. (eds.) WADT 2016. LNCS, vol. 10644, pp. 189–207. Springer, Cham (2017). https://doi.org/10.1007/978-3-319-72044-9_13

36. Rocha, C., Meseguer, J.: Proving safety properties of rewrite theories. In: Corradini, A., Klin, B., Cîrstea, C. (eds.) CALCO 2011. LNCS, vol. 6859, pp. 314–328. Springer, Heidelberg (2011). https://doi.org/10.1007/978-3-642-22944-2_22

37. Rocha, C., Meseguer, J.: Mechanical analysis of reliable communication in the alternating bit protocol using the Maude invariant analyzer tool. In: Iida, S., Meseguer, J., Ogata, K. (eds.) Specification, Algebra, and Software. LNCS, vol. 8373, pp. 603–629. Springer, Heidelberg (2014). https://doi.org/10.1007/978-3-642-54624-2_30

38. Schiper, N., Sutra, P., Pedone, F.: P-Store: genuine partial replication in wide area networks. In: Proceedings of the 29th IEEE Symposium on Reliable Distributed Systems (SRDS 2010), pp. 214–224. IEEE Computer Society (2010)

39. Skeirik, S., Bobba, R.B., Meseguer, J.: Formal analysis of fault-tolerant group key management using ZooKeeper. In: 13th IEEE/ACM International Symposium on Cluster, Cloud, and Grid Computing (CCGrid 2013). IEEE Computer Society (2013)

40. Skeirik, S., Stefanescu, A., Meseguer, J.: A constructor-based reachability logic for rewrite theories. In: Fioravanti, F., Gallagher, J.P. (eds.) LOPSTR 2017. LNCS, vol. 10855, pp. 201–217. Springer, Cham (2018). https://doi.org/10.1007/978-3-319-94460-9_12

41. Sovran, Y., Power, R., Aguilera, M.K., Li, J.: Transactional storage for geo-replicated systems. In: Proceedings of the 23rd ACM Symposium on Operating Systems Principles 2011, SOSP 2011, pp. 385–400. ACM (2011)

42. Wong, C.K., Gouda, M.G., Lam, S.S.: Secure group communications using key graphs. IEEE/ACM Trans. Netw. **8**(1), 16–30 (2000)

Source Code Analysis with a Temporal Extension of First-Order Logic

David Come[✉], Julien Brunel, and David Doose

ONERA, Toulouse, France
{david.come,julien.brunel,david.doose}@onera.fr

Abstract. Formal methods and static analysis are widely used in software development, in particular in the context of safety-critical systems. They can be used to prove that the software behavior complies with its specification: the software correctness. In this article, we address another usage of these methods: the verification of the quality of the source code, *i.e.*, the compliance with guidelines, coding rules, design patterns.

Such rules can refer to the structure of the source code through its Abstract Syntax Tree (AST) or to execution paths in the Control Flow Graph (CFG) of functions. AST and CFGs offer complementary information and current methods are not able to exploit both of them simultaneously. In this article, we propose an approach to automatically verifying the compliance of an application with specifications (coding rules) that reason about both the AST of the source code and the CFG of its functions. To formally express the specification, we introduce FO^{++}, a logic defined as a temporal extension of many-sorted first-order logic. In our framework, verifying the compliance of the source code comes down to the model-checking problem for FO^{++}. We present a correct and complete model checking algorithm for FO^{++} and establish that the model checking problem of FO^{++} is PSPACE-complete. This approach is implemented into Pangolin, a tool for analyzing C++ programs. We use Pangolin to analyze two middle-sized open-source projects, looking for violations of six coding rules and report on several detected violations.

1 Introduction

In today's complex systems, software is often a central element. It must be correct (because any miscalculation can have severe consequences in human or financial terms) but also meet other criteria in term of quality such as readability, complexity, understandability, uniformity .... Whereas formal methods and static analysis (such as abstract interpretation, (software) model checking or deductive methods) are effective means to ensure software correctness, code quality is often dealt with by *manual peer-review*, which is a slow and costly process as it requires to divert one or several programmers to perform the review. However, formal methods and static analysis can also be used to improve code quality. They can perform automatic and exhaustive code queries, looking for

T. Massoni and M. R. Mousavi (Eds.): SBMF 2018, LNCS 11254, pp. 20–38, 2018.
https://doi.org/10.1007/978-3-030-03044-5_3

bug-prone situations that hinder quality [4], enforcing the use of API functions in Linux code [16] or statically estimating test coverage [3].

It is essential that end-users can specify what they are looking for since each project has conventions, norms, and specificity that must be taken into account. There are many existing formalisms to specify queries, and they either use the *Abstract Syntax Tree* (AST) as their source of information [4,10,12,14,20] or the *Control Flow Graph* (CFG) of functions [6]. However, each one provides additional and complementary information. CFGs provide an over-approximation of the possible executions of a function as some paths may never be taken. Conversely, the AST allows finding additional *structural* properties that are not present in the CFG. These structural properties can be about a function (its name, its declared return type, possible class membership, ...) but they can also be related to classes and objects of the software (inheritance relationship, class attributes, global variables, ...). However, there is currently no framework for reasoning simultaneously and adequately over these two sources of information.

This is why we propose an approach to verifying the compliance of source code with user properties that refer both to the CFG of functions and to structural information, which is related to the AST. To formally express the user properties, we introduce in Sect. 2 the logic FO^{++}. It is a temporal extension of many-sorted first-order logic. On the one hand, many-sorted first-order logic is used to handle structural information. The use of a sorted logic makes it easier to manipulate the variety of possible structural elements that may be found (classes, attributes, types, ...). On the other hand, temporal logics are used to specify properties on the ordering of statements in the different paths within the CFGs of functions. Each statement description within a temporal formula, *i.e.*, each atom of a temporal formula, is a *syntactic* pattern of a statement (no value analysis is addressed).

The source code verification procedure is then reduced to the FO^{++} model-checking problem on an FO^{++} interpretation structure extracted from the source code to analyze.

Illustrating Example. To illustrate our approach, we consider the C++ source code shown in Listing 1.1 which represents a monitoring system (Fig. 1).

In this source code, the values of the attributes are recorded and formatted through objects of type Log, which have a log function. We want to make sure that for each class that has an attribute of type Log, each private attribute is logged in each public function, and not modified after being logged. Property 1 expresses this requirement more precisely, in natural language.

Property 1 (Correct usage of logger). For each class C *that has an attribute of type* Log, there <u>is a single function</u> that <u>logs all</u> *private attributes*. *That function* <u>must always be called in</u> *each public function*, <u>and</u> *the attributes* <u>must not be modified later on.</u>

In Property 1, the text in italics refers to aspects of the property that are related to the AST whereas aspects related to paths within the CFG of functions are underlined.

```
1  class A{};
2  class B{
3   public:
4   void serA(int n)
      {
5     a += n;
6     store();
7   }
8   void serB(
9           string s)
        {
10    store();
11    if(s == "reset
      "){
12    b = "";
13    }
14  }
15  private:
16  void store(){
17    logger.log(a);
18    logger.log(b);
19  }
20  int a; string b;
21  Log logger;
22 }
```

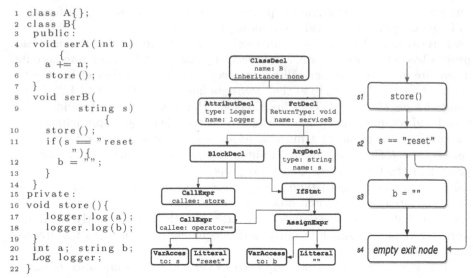

Listing 1.1. snippet for monitoring   **Fig. 1.** Extract of the AST of B   **Fig. 2.** CFG of serB

Notice that in Listing 1.1, class A does not have a Log attribute and thus is not concerned by the property, whereas B does. In B, store fulfills the requirements of logging all privates attributes (namely a and b), and serA is compliant with the property. However, serB is not because b can be reset after the call to store. This is clearly visible on Fig. 2, which illustrates serB's CFG. Indeed, on the control flow path $s1$-$s2$-$s3$, b is assigned in $s3$ whereas store was called in $s1$. We show in this article that FO^{++} allows the user to express formally Property 1 in a natural way, and Pangolin is then able to detect automatically that Listing 1.1 is not compliant.

Article Layout. The rest of the article is organized as follows: Sect. 2 defines the syntax and semantics of FO^{++}. Section 3 presents a model checking algorithm for FO^{++} and establishes its correctness and termination. The model checking problem for FO^{++} is also proved to be PSPACE-complete. Section 4 details FO^{++} specialization for C++ and Sect. 5 presents the architecture of our prototype Pangolin. Then Sect. 6 details the result of some experiments we conducted with Pangolin and Sect. 7 details the related work.

2 FO^{++} Definition

FO^{++} is defined as a temporal extension of many-sorted first-order logic. Two temporal logics are available within FO^{++}: Linear Temporal Logic (LTL) and Computation-Tree Logic (CTL). LTL considers discrete linear time whereas CTL is a discrete branching time logic (at each instant, it is possible to quantify over the paths that leave the current state). Both are well-established logics and tackle different issues. CTL is natural over graph-like structure as it offers path quantification, whereas LTL offers a path-sensitive analysis, and its ability to refer to the past of an event is convenient.

The extension is done through a process close to parametrization [8]. Intuitively, the parametrization of a formal logic L_1 by a formal logic L_2 consists of using complete L_2 formulas as atoms for L_1. When evaluating L_1 formulas, L_2 atoms are evaluated according to L_2 rules. Here, the process is more complicated since some of the elements in the first-order domain (intuitively, the functions in the source code) are associated with interpretation structures for temporal formulas (intuitively, the CFGs of functions). Syntactically, the temporal extension is done by adding two specific binary predicates models$_{\text{LTL}}$and models$_{\text{CTL}}$. If f is a first-order variable and φ is an LTL formula (resp. a CTL formula) then models$_{\text{LTL}}(f, \varphi)$ (resp. models$_{\text{CTL}}(f, \varphi)$) is true if f denotes a function in the source code and if the CFG of f satisfies the formula φ according to LTL (resp. CTL) semantic rules. This yields a very modular formalism as it is easy to incorporate new logics for specifying properties over CFGs.

2.1   Syntax

Terms. Let S_i be a collection of sorts, V a finite set of variables, and F a set of function[1] symbols. Each variable and constant belongs to a unique sort and each function symbol f has a profile $S_1, \times \ldots \times S_n \to S_{n+1}$, where n is the arity of f (a 0-arity function is a constant) and each S_i is a sort.

The set T_S of FO^{++} terms of sort S is defined inductively as follows: if x is a variable of sort S then $x \in T_S$; if $f \in$ F has the profile $S_1, \times \ldots \times S_n \to S$, and for each $i \in 1..n, t_i \in T_{S_i}$ then $f(t_1, \ldots, t_n) \in T_S$. The set $T = \bigcup T_{S_i}$ denotes all FO^{++} terms.

Atoms. The set P of predicate symbols consists of (1) classical predicate symbols, each of which is associated with a profile $S_1, \times \ldots \times S_n$, where n is the arity of the predicate and each S_i is a sort, and (2) two special 2-arity predicates symbols: models$_{\text{LTL}}$ and models$_{\text{CTL}}$. An *atom* in FO^{++} consists of either a usual predicate applied to FO^{++} terms, or the special predicate models$_{\text{LTL}}$ (resp. models$_{\text{CTL}}$) applied to an FO^{++} term and an LTL (resp. CTL) formula. Considering the latter case, *i.e.*, models$_{\text{LTL}}$ and models$_{\text{CTL}}$, the first argument of both predicates is a term (in practice: a variable representing a function in the source code under analysis). The second argument of models$_{\text{LTL}}$ (resp. models$_{\text{CTL}}$) is an LTL (resp. CTL) formula as defined in Sect. 2.2.

Formulas. FO^{++} formulas are defined as follows: $\top, \bot$ are formulas, if a is an atom then a is also a formula; if S is a sort and Q is a formula, then $\neg Q, Q \vee Q, Q \wedge Q, Q \iff Q, Q \implies Q, \forall x \colon S\ Q, \exists x \colon S\ Q$ are also formulas.

A sentence is an FO^{++} formula without free-variable. In the rest of the paper, all formulas are sentences.

---

[1] Not to be confused with functions in the software under study.

Semantics

Interpretation Structure. An FO^{++} formula is interpreted over a structure $M = (\mathcal{D}, \mathcal{EKS}, \text{eks}, \text{has\_eks}, I_F, I_P)$. The domain $\mathcal{D}$ is a set in which terms are interpreted. It is partitioned into disjoint sub-domains $\mathcal{D}_S$, one for each sort S; $\mathcal{EKS}$ is a set of Enhanced Kripke Structures (EKS) as defined in Sect. 2.2, which are used to interpret temporal formulas. $\text{has\_eks}(x): \mathcal{D} \to \{\text{true}, \text{false}\}$ is a function, which indicates whether a value in the domain has an associated EKS. $\text{eks}: \mathcal{D} \to \mathcal{EKS}$ is a partial function, which maps some elements of $\mathcal{D}$ to an EKS[2]. I_F defines an interpretation for functions in F such that if $f \in$ F has a profile $S_1 \times \ldots \times S_n \to S_{n+1}$ then $I_F(f): \mathcal{D}_{S_1} \times \ldots \times \mathcal{D}_{S_n} \to \mathcal{D}_{S_{n+1}}$. I_P defines an interpretation for predicates in P such that if $p \in$ P has a profile $S_1 \times \ldots \times S_n$ then $I_p(p) \subseteq \mathcal{D}_{S_1} \times \ldots \times \mathcal{D}_{S_n}$ is the set of all tuples of domain values for which p is true.

I_F and I_P are specific to the programming language used for the project under analysis, whereas $\mathcal{D}$ and $\mathcal{EKS}$ are even specific to the program itself.

Environment. An environment is a partial function from the set V of variables to the domain $\mathcal{D}$. If σ is an environment, x a variable in V and d a value in $\mathcal{D}$, then $\sigma[x \leftarrow d]$ denotes the environment σ_1 where $\sigma_1(x) = d$ and for every $x \neq y, \sigma_1(y) = \sigma(y)$.

From an environment σ and an interpretation I_F for functions, we define an interpretation $K_\sigma : \text{T} \to \mathcal{D}$ for terms in the following way: for each variable x in $V, K_\sigma(x) = \sigma(x)$ and for an arbitrary term $f(t_1, \ldots, t_n)$, $K_\sigma(f(t_1, \ldots, t_n)) = I_F(f)(K_\sigma(t_1), \ldots, K_\sigma(t_n))$

Satisfaction Rules. Let M be an interpretation structure, σ an environment and K_σ an interpretation for terms according to this environment. We define the satisfaction relation of FO^{++} as follows[3]:

$M, K_\sigma \models \neg Q$ iff $M, K_\sigma \not\models Q$

$M, K_\sigma \models Q_1 \wedge Q_2$ iff $M, K_\sigma \models Q_1$ and $M, K_\sigma \models Q_2$

$M, K_\sigma \models \exists x \colon S\ Q$ iff there is an $a \in \mathcal{D}_S$ such that $M, K_{\sigma[x \leftarrow a]} \models Q$

$M, K_\sigma \models p(t_1, \ldots, t_1)$ iff $(K_\sigma(t_1), \ldots, K_\sigma(t_n)) \in I_P(p)$

$M, K_\sigma \models \text{models}_{\text{CTL}}(x, \psi)$ iff $\text{has\_eks}(x)$ and $\text{eks}(x), K_\sigma \models_{CTL} \psi$

$M, K_\sigma \models \text{models}_{\text{LTL}}(x, \psi)$ iff $\text{has\_eks}(x)$ and $\text{eks}(x), K_\sigma \models_{LTL} \psi$

If Q is a formula without any free variable, we write $M \models Q$ for $M, K_\emptyset \models Q$ where $\emptyset$ denotes an empty environment.

2.2   Temporal Formulas

Syntax. The syntax of LTL and CTL slightly differs from their standard definition, in which atoms are atomic propositions (see, *e.g.*, [19]). Here, since we are

---

[2] For any $x \in \mathcal{D}$ if $\text{has\_eks}(x)$ if and only if $\text{eks}(x)$ is defined.

[3] For conciseness, we only provide the semantics of a minimal set of Boolean connectives.

in a first-order context, an atom is a predicate in a set PREDEKS (disjoint from P) applied to terms. We call TATOMS the set of atoms of temporal formulas. The predicates in PREDEKS describe *syntactic* properties of the statements within a CFG (whereas predicates in P denotes (static) structural properties about the source code under study). For instance, in order to reason about the fact the current statement of a CFG contains a call to a certain function, we can define a predicate call($\cdot$) in PREDEKS, such that call(x) is true if there is a call to the function denoted by the first-order variable x in the current statement of the CFG.

The syntax of LTL is inductively defined as follows: TATOMS are valid LTL formula. If ψ_1, ψ_2 are valid LTL formulas, so are $\psi_1 \circ \psi_2$, $\neg\psi_1$, $\mathbf{X}\psi_1$, $\mathbf{G}\,\psi_1$, $\mathbf{F}\,\psi_1$, $\psi_1\,\mathbf{U}\,\psi_2$, $\mathbf{Y}\psi_1$, $\mathbf{O}\,\psi_1$, $\mathbf{H}\,\psi_1$ and $\psi_1\,\mathbf{S}\,\psi_2$ where $\circ$ is a binary Boolean connective.

CTL syntax is similar to LTL syntax, except that the temporal operators are $\mathbf{A}\circ-$, $\mathbf{E}\circ-$, $\mathbf{A}[-\,\mathbf{U}\,-]$, $\mathbf{E}[-\,\mathbf{U}\,-]$ with $\circ \in \{\mathbf{X}, \mathbf{F}, \mathbf{G}\}$.

Semantics. The slight change of formalism is reflected into the interpretation structures used. Instead of using traditional Kripke structures, FO^{++} uses *Enhanced Kripke structures*. An Enhanced Kripke structure is simply a Kripke structure where the valuation function associates each state with the interpretation of predicates in PREDEKS, instead of a set of atomic propositions.

EKS Formal Definition. Let $B = (S, \to, I_{\text{EKS}}, [\![\,]\!])$ be an EKS. S is a set of states, $\to \subseteq S \times S$ is the transition relation between states (written $\circ \to \circ$), $I_{\text{EKS}} \subseteq S$ is the set of initial states and $[\![\,]\!] : \text{PREDEKS} \times S \to P(\mathcal{D}^n)$ associates a predicate p of arity n with its interpretation in a state s, denoted $[\![p]\!]_s$ (*i.e.*, the set of all tuples of concrete values for which the predicate is true).

Interpretation Rules for Temporal Formulas. The satisfaction of LTL and CTL formulas is defined in the standard way (see, *e.g.*, [19]), except for atoms, which are built from predicates instead of atomic propositions, as explained above. Given an environment σ, an interpretation K_σ, a predicate $p \in$ PREDEKS, a state s and some terms $v_1, \ldots, v_n$, the satisfaction relation for temporal atoms is defined as follows[4]:

$$s, K_\sigma \models p(v_1, \ldots, v_n) \text{ iff } (K_\sigma(v_1), \ldots, K_\sigma(v_n)) \in [\![p]\!]_s \qquad (1)$$

An example of FO^{++} formula is given in Sect. 4.3.

Remark 1 (Difference with FO-CTL and FO-LTL). Notice that a more classical way of combining first-order and temporal logics results in FO-LTL [15] and FO-CTL [5]. Intuitively, FO-LTL allows a free combination of LTL and first-order symbols and is evaluated on a succession of states on which the value of some variables depends. FO-LTL adds to LTL the possibility to quantify on the values that variables in a given state. FO-CTL is used to specify property on a single first-order Kripke structures. These structures have transitions with

---

[4] It applies to both $\models_{\text{LTL}}$ and $\models_{\text{CTL}}$ and is thus simply denoted with $\models$.

conditional assignments and FO-CTL offers to quantify over the variable used in those conditional assignments.

Strictly speaking, we cannot compare their expressive power with respect to FO^{++} because the interpretation structures are different. The main difference is due to the mapping of some domain elements to temporal interpretation structures, which is called eks in FO^{++} semantics. In FO^{++}, a quantification over the elements that are mapped to temporal interpretation structures comes to an indirect quantification over these temporal interpretation structures, which is not possible in the case of FO-LTL and FO-CTL. On the other hand, for pragmatic reasons, we restrict FO^{++} syntax not to allow quantifiers in the scope of temporal operators, whereas they are allowed in FO-CTL and FO-LTL.

3 FO^{++} Model Checking

In this section, we investigate the *model checking* problem for FO^{++}.

3.1   Model Checking Algorithm

Given an FO^{++} formula ϕ and an interpretation structure M, the model checking algorithm $\mathrm{MC}^{++}(M, \phi)$ returns `true` if M satisfies ϕ, and `false` otherwise. To do so, we chose to rely on an approach that is similar to rewriting systems. This way, we can decouple the basic steps of the algorithm (rewriting rules) from the way these steps are ordered (the strategy). This offers a flexible and modular presentation of the algorithm. In our implementation, we also took advantage of this structure to log the different steps of the algorithm for a potential offline review. Notice, however, that we are not strictly in the scope of higher-order rewriting systems such as defined in [18] because some of our rules include conditions that refer to the interpretation structure.

MC^{++} **Terms.** The terms that are handled by the algorithm MC^{++}, called MC^{++} terms, are similar to FO^{++} formulas but include elements of the semantic domain, which are useful for quantifier unfolding. The FO^{++} formula ϕ is first translated into an FO^{++} term, which is then successively rewritten until reaching `true` or `false`.

For each sort S, any element $d \in D_S$ is considered as a constant of sort S. Then, if p is a predicate symbol of profile S and $d \in D_S$ is an element of the semantic domain associated with S in M, then $p(d)$ is a valid MC^{++} term. Besides, a quantified formula is represented by a term in which all values that are necessary for the quantifier unfolding are listed. For example, considering a sort S with an associated semantic domain $D_S = \{d_1, \ldots, d_n\}$, the formula $\forall x : s\ Q$ is represented by the term $\mathtt{all_D}(x.Q, < d_1, \ldots, d_n >)$, and the formula $\exists x : s\ Q$ is represented by the term $\mathtt{some_D}(x.Q, < d_1, \ldots, d_n >)$.

Rewriting First-Order Terms. The rewriting rules for the first-order part of the logic are split into three categories: the rules related to the evaluation of

FO^{++} functions and non temporal predicates, the rules that perform unfolding of quantifiers and the rules that evaluate Boolean connectives.

Functions and Predicates. Functions and predicates are evaluated once all their arguments are domain constants. The values are determined by their respective interpretation functions. The rewriting rules are $p(t_1, \ldots t_n) \rightsquigarrow$ **true** if $(t_1, \ldots, t_n) \in P(p)$, $p(t_1, \ldots t_n) \rightsquigarrow$ **false** if $(t_1, \ldots, t_n) \notin P(p)$ and $f(t_1, \ldots t_n) \rightsquigarrow I(f)(t_1, \ldots, t_n)$, where each t_i denotes a value in the domain D_{S_i}.

Unfolding Quantifiers. Unfolding a universal quantifier (respectively an existential one) transforms the quantified expression $x.Q$ into a conjunction (respectively disjunction) of an expression where the bounded variable x is replaced by a constant d of the domain which has not been considered yet (denoted $Q[x/d]$), and the original quantified expression without d_1 in the list of values to consider. Quantifiers with an empty list of values are treated in a classical way. Formally, the following four rules are defined:

$\text{all}_\text{S}(x.Q, < d, Y >) \rightsquigarrow Q[x/d] \wedge \text{all}_\text{S}(x.Q, < Y >)$ $\text{all}_\text{S}(x.Q, < >) \rightsquigarrow$ **true**
$\text{some}_\text{S}(x.Q, < d, Y >) \rightsquigarrow Q[x/d] \vee \text{some}_\text{S}(x.Q, < Y >)$ $\text{some}_\text{S}(x.Q, < >) \rightsquigarrow$ **false**

Constant Propagation. Boolean constants **true** and **false** are propagated upward also in classical manner. *And, Or* and *Imply* connectives are evaluated in short-circuit manner from left to right and if short-circuit evaluation is not conclusive, then the term is rewritten into its right subterm. Rules for equivalence connective only applies if both subterms are boolean constants and so do rules for negations.

Rewriting Temporal Predicates. Rewriting a temporal predicate $\text{models}_\text{LTL}(f, \psi)$ or $\text{models}_\text{CTL}(f, \psi)$ into a Boolean value is done in two steps:

1. a reduction algorithm generates a classical temporal model checking problem out of f and ψ;
2. the application of a model checking algorithm to this new problem.

Reduction Algorithm. For generating an equivalent model checking problem from $\text{models}_\text{LTL}(f, \psi)$ or $\text{models}_\text{CTL}(f, \psi)$ (when f has an EKS), the reduction algorithm operates in three steps:

1. for each call to a predicate in PREDEKS with a unique set of parameters, it generates an atomic proposition. For instance, for $p \in$ PREDEKS, $t_1: \mathcal{D}, \ldots, t_n: \mathcal{D}$, a call to $p(t_1, \ldots, t_n)$ gives an atomic proposition $id(p, t_1, \ldots, t_n)$. Notice that at this step, because of previous rewriting rules, the parameters of these predicates are necessarily constants (corresponding to values in the domain) and not first-order variables;
2. a classical interpretation structure for temporal logic formulas M_f (a transition system, the states of which are labeled with atomic propositions) is built out of eks (f), the CFG associated with f. The structure of M_f copies the graph from eks (f), with an extra final state that loops back to itself. For a

state s in eks (f), if $(t_1, \ldots, t_n) \in \llbracket p \rrbracket_s$, its dual in M_f is labeled with the atomic proposition $id(p, t_1, \ldots, t_n)$;

3. the new formula ϕ' to analyze over M_f is ϕ where each call $p(t_1, \ldots, t_n)$ is substituted by $id(p, t_1, \ldots, t_n)$.

Strategy Used. The algorithm MC^{++} uses a *leftmost-outermost* strategy to rewrite the formula, which can be described as follows. (1) Try to apply some rule to the toplevel term. (2) If it is not possible then recursively apply the strategy to the leftmost subterm (considered as the new toplevel term), and then (3) try again to apply a rule to the toplevel term. If it is still not possible then apply a rule to the right-hand side subterm.

3.2   Correctness and Termination

In this section, we establish that the algorithm MC^{++} is correct and terminates.

Proposition 1 (Correctness). *Let M be an interpretation structure and ϕ an FO^{++} formula. If $\mathrm{MC}^{++}(M, \phi)$ returns* **true** *then $M \models \phi$, and if $\mathrm{MC}^{++}(M, \phi)$ returns* **false** *then $M \nvDash \phi$.*

Proof (sketch). It is straightforward to define a semantics for MC^{++} terms similarly to FO^{++} formulas. Then, we can easily prove that each rewriting rule preserves the semantics of MC^{++} terms.   □

Proposition 2 (Termination). *Let M be an interpretation structure and ϕ an FO^{++} formula. $\mathrm{MC}^{++}(M, \phi)$ terminates and returns either* **true** *or* **false**.

Proof. We show that any application of the first-order logic evaluation rules ends (which therefore stands for the chosen strategy). To do so, we consider the following function s as defined in Eq. (2), the value of which decreases with each application of the rules.

$$s(\phi) \begin{cases} (s(\psi) + 1)^{n+1} & \text{if } \phi = \circ(x.\psi, [d_1, \ldots, d_n]) \text{ for } \circ \in \{\texttt{all}_S, \texttt{some}_S\} \\ s(\psi_1) + s(\psi_2) & \text{if } \phi = \psi_1 \circ \psi_2, \text{for any binary } \circ \text{ operator} \\ s(\psi) + 1 & \text{if } \phi = \neg\psi \\ 1 + \sum_{i=1}^n s(d_i) & \text{if } \phi = f(d_1, \ldots, d_n), f \text{ either a function or predicate} \\ 1 & \text{otherwise} \end{cases}$$
(2)

Proof (sketch). For conciseness, we only show the demonstration for the evaluation of functions and predicates (Eq. (3)), as well as for quantifiers unfolding (Eqs. (4) and (5)). Other cases are similar and straightforward. First of all, notices that s is minored by 1.

$$s(p(d_1, \ldots, d_n)) = 1 + \sum_{i=1}^n s(d_i) > 1 = s(\texttt{false}) = s(\texttt{true})$$

$$s(f(d_1, \ldots, d_n)) = 1 + \sum_{i=1}^n s(d_i) > 1 = s(I(f)(d_1, \ldots, d_1))$$
(3)

The second inequality holds because $I(f)(d_1, \ldots, d_1)$ is a constant for the domain and its value by s is 1. By similarity between all_S and some_S for unfolding the quantifiers, we only consider the case of all_S.

$$
\begin{aligned}
s(\text{all}_S(x.P, < d_1, d2, \ldots, d_n >)) &= (s(P) + 1)^{n+1} \\
&= s(P)(s(P) + 1) + (s(P) + 1)^n \\
&> s(P[x/d_1]) + (s(P) + 1)^n \\
&= s(P[x/d_1] \wedge \text{all}_S(x.P, < d_2, \ldots, d_n >))
\end{aligned}
\tag{4}
$$

$$
s(\text{all}_S(x.P, < >)) = (s(P) + 1)^1 > 1 = s(\text{true})
\tag{5}
$$

Moreover, generating the equivalent classical temporal model checking problem ends, just as its evaluation with a classical temporal model checking algorithm. This proves that the algorithm ends. Besides, since for every MC^{++} term different from $\texttt{true}$ and $\texttt{false}$, some rewriting rule is applicable (this can be proved by induction on MC^{++} terms) then MC^{++} terminates either with $\texttt{true}$ or with $\texttt{false}$.   □

The completeness directly follows from Proposition 1 and Proposition 2.

Corollary 1 (Completeness). *Let M be an interpretation structure and ϕ an FO^{++} formula. If $M \models \phi$ then $\text{MC}^{++}(M, \phi) = \texttt{true}$ and if $M \nvDash \phi$ then $\text{MC}^{++}(M, \phi) = \texttt{false}$.*

3.3   Complexity

Proposition 3. *The model checking problem of FO^{++} is PSPACE-complete.*

Proof. Hardness: FO^{++} subsumes first-order logic, whose model-checking problem (also called query evaluation) is PSPACE-complete [22]. Hence FO^{++} model-checking is at least as hard as FO model-checking FO^{++} model (*i.e.* FO^{++} model-checking is PSPACE-hard).

Membership: Let us consider the algorithm MC^{++} presented above with inputs M (an interpretation structure) and ϕ (an FO^{++} formula). We consider n as the size of the problem input, *i.e.*, the size of ϕ (number of connectives, FO^{++} terms and atoms) plus the size of M (size of the domain, of predicate and function interpretation, plus the number of nodes of the different EKS). The size of the initial MC^{++} term is in $O(n)$. An application of an unfolding rule to an MC^{++} term introduces a larger MC^{++} term and increases the memory space by at most n. Indeed, at most n new memory is required for the new expression ($Q[x/d]$ in the unfolding rules). All other rules decrease the memory consumption as they reduce the number of MC^{++} terms. By using the leftmost-outermost strategy and our two unfolding rules the algorithm unfolds the quantifiers in depth-first manner. Let k be the maximum number of nested quantifiers. The algorithm uses at most $(k + 1) * n$ space to represent "unfolded" terms before reaching a term where all the first-order variables are substituted by a domain constant. For such a term, the only possible applicable rewriting rules are either the rules for Boolean connectives (which decrease the space needed to represent the term) or the rule for functions and predicates. Functions and non temporal predicates required a constant space to be evaluated. Evaluating temporal predicates is a two steps process. The first step is the reduction algorithm that produces a classical temporal model-checking problem. Its overall size m is smaller than n as both the Kripke structure and the temporal formula mimics the inputs of reduction algorithm and as their respective sizes are components of n. Evaluating this problem is done with a polynomial amount of memory with respect to m (and therefore with respect to n) since model checking for CTL (resp. LTL) is PTIME-complete (resp. PSPACE-complete). Therefore, the space needed for the whole algorithm is polynomial in n, hence the result.   □

4   Application to C++ Source Code Analysis

FO^{++} construction remains generic as it does not mention any particular programming language. To be used as a specification language, it must be instantiated for a specific programming language. This means defining appropriate sets for sorts, functions and predicate symbols, as well as a method for extracting an interpretation structure (including interpretation for functions and predicates) from the source code. In this section, we detail the instantiation of FO^{++} for C++.

4.1 FO^{++} for C++

Sort. The sorts indicate the nature of the different structural elements we can reason about. In a C++ program, the different structural elements are *declarations* such as functions, classes, variables or types. Both *classes* and *types* have their own sort. Within functions, we distinguish between *free functions* and *member functions*, and operate a further distinction for *constructors* and *destructors*. We also operate a distinction on variables between *attributes*, *local variables*, and *global variables*. Hence, FO^{++} for C++ has a total of 9 *sorts*.

Functions and Non Temporal Predicates. FO^{++} functions are used to designate an element in the code from another related element, such as the unqualified version of a *const*-qualified type or the class in which an attribute was defined. Non-temporal predicates are used to query information about the structural elements. This includes for instance parenthood relationship between elements (*i.e.* an attribute a belongs to class c), visibility, inheritance relationship between classes, types and their qualification (*const* or *volatile* for instance). The semantics of functions and non-temporal predicates complies with the C++ standard [1]. Table 1 lists some functions and predicates with their informal semantics. The full list of functions and predicates is available on the Pangolin repository[5].

---

[5] https://gitlab.com/Davidbrcz/Pangolin.

Table 1. Small subset of structural predicates in the FO^{++} instantiation for C++

Predicate	Informal semantics
$isAttributeOf(a, c)$	true iff a refers to a field of c
$isMemFctOf(f, c)$	true iff f is a member function within c
$isPrivate(f), isPublic(f)$	true iff f is private (resp. public) within its class
$type(a, T)$	true iff the type of a is T

4.2 Extracting an Interpretation Structure

Domain. Extracting the domain $\mathcal{D}$ from an AST consists of traversing the AST and collecting the various declarations in order to know the sort of each domain element. Figure 3a shows domain $\mathcal{D}$ obtained from the source code shown in Listing 1.1, partitioned into four sub-domains (one for each relevant sort).

Generating $\mathcal{EKS}$. If the full definition of a C++ function f is present in the AST of the C++ source code, then has_eks(f) is true and eks(f) is defined in the following manner. We consider the CFG of f, where each node only contain a single statement (a basic block is not included into a node, but is split into a succession of nodes instead). The EKS states and transitions of eks(f) are then directly taken from the nodes and edges of the CFG of f, except that the state corresponding to the exit node of the CFG has an infinite loop on itself to ensure infinite traces and comply with LTL and CTL semantics. Function calls are considered like any other statement, hence there is neither interprocedural analysis nor specific recursive calls handling. In each state of the EKS, the valuation of the predicates in PREDEKS directly follows from the syntax of the statement that is in this state. Notice that some paths of the EKS may never be taken by the program execution, because, *e.g.*, a condition of a while loop is always evaluated to false during execution. Since we do not perform value analysis, our method still considers such paths. This is in accordance with our

A, B	CLASS
serviceA serviceB store	int std::string class A class B
MEMFCT	**TYPE**
n, s	a, b, logger
LOCALVAR	**ATTR**

(a) Domain $\mathcal{D}$ for listing 1.1. Elements in the partitions are typeseted, sorts are capitalized. Empty partitions are not shown.

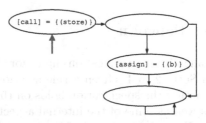

(b) Enhanced Kripke structure for serB with two predicates *call* and *assign*. The valuation are shown only when non empty. The bold arrow denotes the initial state

Fig. 3. Semantic domain partially illustrated

objective to analyze the quality of the code, instead of checking its semantic correctness.

Figure 3b shows the EKS for serB with two elements from PREDEKS: *call*, and *assign*. The predicate $call(x)$ is true on states such that there is a call to function x (the arguments do not matter) and $assign(x)$ is true on states such that there is an assignment to x (*i.e.* $x = \dots$).

4.3   Example: Formalizing Log Correct Usage

To illustrate concretely FO^{++} for C++, we formalize Property 1 in Eq. (6). The universal quantification on c indicates that the property applies to all classes. We then look for a private attribute l whose type is *Log*. (The symbol *Log* is here an FO^{++} constant.) We then look at all attributes of class c, and if there is one whose type is *Log*, then we look for a function s such that

- Each private attribute a from class c (whose type is not *Log*) is logged in s (*i.e.* there is a call to log on l with a as argument in s). The formalization of this relies on the predicate *call_log* of PREDEKS such that *call_log*(x, y) is true on a CFG state if there is call of the shape x.log(y) in this state. The CTL formula $\mathbf{AF}$ *call_log*(l, a) states that in all paths within the CFG of s, there is finally a state in which *call_log*(l, a) is true.
- For all public functions f, in all paths in the CFG of f, there is at some point a call to s, and the attribute a is no longer assigned after this call.

$$
\begin{aligned}
&\forall c\colon \text{CLASS } \forall l\colon \text{ATTR } \big(isAttributeOf(l, c) \wedge type(l, Log) \implies \\
&\exists s\colon \text{MEMFCT } (isMemFctOf(s, c) \wedge name(s, \texttt{store}) \wedge \\
&\forall a\colon \text{ATTR } (isAttributeOf(a, c) \wedge isPrivate(a) \wedge \neg type(a, \texttt{Log}) \implies \\
&\qquad \text{models}_{\text{CTL}}(s, \mathbf{AF}\, call\_log(l, a)) \wedge \\
&\forall f\colon \text{MEMFCT } (isMemFctOf(f, c) \wedge isPublic(f) \implies \\
&\qquad \text{models}_{\text{CTL}}(f, \mathbf{AF}\, call(s) \wedge \mathbf{AG}(call(s) \implies \mathbf{AXAG}\neg assign(a)))))))
\end{aligned}
$$
(6)

5   Pangolin

Pangolin[6] is a verification engine for C++ programs based on the ideas developed in Sects. 2 to 4. Given a rule as a formula in FO^{++} for C++, Pangolin checks whether the specification holds on the program. Figure 4 illustrates this process as well as some of the internal aspects of Pangolin.

From the user point of view, the specification is written in a concrete syntax of FO^{++} for C++ as it is presented in Sect. 4.1. The code to analyze must compile in order to be examined as Pangolin needs to traverse the code AST to extract an FO^{++} interpretation structure. This implies that a simple extract of code taken

---

[6] Pangolin is available at https://gitlab.com/Davidbrcz/Pangolin.

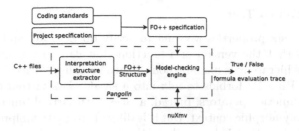

Fig. 4. Pangolin overview

out of its context cannot be analyzed. For each formula and each file, Pangolin returns true if the formula holds on the file and false otherwise. It also prints a complete trace of the evaluation process that can be reviewed. If the formula does not hold, it is possible to find with this trace the values of the quantified variables that explain algorithm output, hence providing a counter-example. It also increases the user's confidence in the correctness of the implementation.

From an internal point of view, Pangolin consists of two parts: an interpretation structure extractor and a model checking engine. The extractor follows the specification given Sect. 4.2, and is based on Clang and its API libtooling [17]. Clang provides an up-to-date and complete support for C++, direct access to the code AST and facilitates the computation of the CFG of a function. Pangolin implements the model checking algorithm presented in Sect. 3, and it relies on nuXmv [9] for evaluating model checking problems resulting from the reduction algorithm. However, because of short-circuit evaluation of logical connectives, the model-checking algorithm stops at the first counter-example found. With this algorithm, to find the next counter-example, it is necessary either to change the formula to exclude the counter-example that was found, or to correct the code and then start over the analysis. To find all the possible counter-examples, Pangolin also implements an alternative algorithm where quantifiers are unfolded less efficiently, so that all the values for the different quantifiers are explored, which makes it possible to find all the counter-examples at once.

6   Experiments

We study the conformity of two open-source projects with respect to six generic properties that address good programming practices accepted for C++. The first project is *ZeroMQ*, a high-performance asynchronous messaging framework. The second is *MiniZinc* [21], a solver agnostic modeling language for combinatorial satisfaction and optimization problems. We picked these two projects because they are active popular C++ projects with a middle size code base (around 50k SLOC each).

6.1 Properties to Test

Table 2 lists the six properties we want to verify on ZeroMQ and Minizinc. P1 mainly ensures that the version of a function that can be executed from anywhere in a class hierarchy is unambiguous, hence bringing clarity for maintainers and reviewers. Rule P2 forbids to mix into a single class virtual functions and overloaded arithmetic operators. Indeed, a class with virtual functions is meant to be used in polymorphic context. But it is difficult to write foolproof and useful arithmetic operators that behave coherently in a polymorphic context.

P3 ensures that there no unused private elements (function and attributes) within a class. Indeed, they are only accessible from within the class, and unused private elements are either superfluous (and hindering code quality) or symptom of a bug. P4 must be enforced because the C++ programming language specifies that virtual function resolution is not performed within constructors and destructors. Hence, when there is a call to a virtual function in either the constructors or destructors, the callee is likely not to be the intended function.

The last two rules are to enforce *const-correctness*. The driving idea behind the *const correctness* is to prevent the developer from modifying by accident a variable or an object because it would result in a compilation error. Variables marked as *const* are immutable whereas *const* member functions cannot alter the internal state of an object. Thus, any non-constant element must be justified: a variable assigned at most once must be constant (P5), and objects with only calls to constant member functions must also be constant as well (P6).

For the sake of conciseness, we only show (in Eq. (7)) the formal translation of property P5[7]. The rule uses the word *modified*, whose meaning must be specified by the formalization. Here, we say that a variable x is *modified* when it is to the left of a binary operator (*i.e.* x $= where $ is (eventually) one operator among ^, +, -, \, *, &, |, <<, >>) or is the argument of an unary operator among increment, decrement or addressof (*i.e.* x++, ++x, x--, --x, &x). For clarity, in Eq. (7), $modified(x)$ is an abbreviation for a disjunction of 15 predicates (one for each operator). Also, the formalization is done in a "negative" way: we look for a function f in which a not constant variable v is modified at least once (the first **AF** ... part) and never again afterwards **AG** ... $\implies$ **AXAG**¬....

$$\exists f: \textsc{FreeFct}\Big(\exists v: \textsc{LocalVar}\big(locallyDeclared(v, f) \wedge \neg isConst(v)\wedge$$

$$\text{models}_{\text{CTL}}(f, \mathbf{AF}\,modified(v) \wedge \mathbf{AG}(modified(v) \implies \mathbf{AXAG}\neg modified(v))))\Big)$$

$$(7)$$

6.2 Results and Analysis

Table 3 summarizes the experiments on *ZeroMQ* and *MiniZinc*. For each rule and each project, columns *CE* shows the total number of counter-examples found and column *Timing* the average time over 10 runs with its standard deviation, both in seconds.

---

[7] But all rules are available in Pangolin repository.

Table 2. Properties to verify

Name	Definition
P1	A virtual function shall not be defined more than once in an inheritance hierarchy
P2	A class should not have virtual functions and overloaded arithmetic operators
P3	In all classes, there are neither unused private attributes nor private functions
P4	In all classes, no virtual functions shall be invoked from any destructor or constructors
P5	In all functions, all local variables modified at most once must be marked as constant
P6	In all functions, any locally declared object on which only const member functions are called must also be marked as constant

Defects Found. For property P1, all counter-examples found are real violations of the rule. Pangolin found no counter-example for property P2. Regarding P3, Pangolin found for ZeroMQ 3 unused attributes and 1 for MiniZinc. Many of the functions that Pangolin found, many were, in fact, called. Two were virtual and inherited from a parent class but with reduced visibility as it is allowed by C++. They were therefore called from a function of the parent class. The rest of the functions were used but not as specified. For instance, they were used as callbacks or called on an object of the same type as the class (this is allowed in C++ because between 2 objects of the same type, there is no encapsulation). Concerning P4, Pangolin found one counter-example on MiniZinc, which was a true violation. Many of the results for rules P5 and P6 are real counter-examples for the specification but are legitimate code. Indeed, for P5 does not take into account that a variable may change through a pointer or a reference, while rule P6 does not take into account public attributes of a class that may change.

Table 3. Summary of the defects found in ZeroMQ and MiniZinc with the average required time to perform the analysis

Property	Project	CE	Timing	Property	Project	CE	Timing (s)
P1	ZeroMQ	7	36 (2.30)	P4	ZeroMQ	0	821 (210.2)
	MiniZinc	8	44 (1.31)		MiniZinc	1	104 (12.39)
P2	ZeroMQ	0	90 (6.4)	P5	ZeroMQ	59	225 (2.9)
	MiniZinc	0	64 (1.5)		MiniZinc	170	13136 (321.4)
P3 (attributes)	ZeroMQ	3	2015 (110.2)	P6	ZeroMQ	2	176 (5.9)
	MiniZinc	1	910 (10.2)		MiniZinc	12	942 (16.31)
P3 (functions)	ZeroMQ	105	2778 (138)				
	MiniZinc	2	780 (19.2)				

With hindsight, these false alarms could have been removed with a more precise rule. For instance, for property P6, there two approaches to design a more precise rule. On the one hand, one could exclude classes with public attributes from the property (*i.e. in all functions, any locally declared object whose class does not have public attributes and on which only const member functions are called must also be marked as constant*). On the other hand, one could into account the public attributes for determining if an object should be constant (*In all functions, any locally declared object on which only const member functions are called and no public attributes are changed must also be marked as constant*).

Performance. The tests were performed on *Intel(R) Xeon(R) CPU E5-1607 v3 @ 3.10 GHz* with 32 GB of memory. Properties involving temporal properties are slower than sheer structural properties. Indeed, there is an overhead to evaluate temporal predicates. This overhead is the sum of the time spent to evaluate of the classical model-checking problem on the one hand and of communication time on the other hand. The former varies with the complexity of the formula and of the EKS, whereas the latter is constant. The execution time of P5 and P6 is radically different between the 2 projects (despite a comparable size) because a particular Minizinc function contains more than 3000 lines and temporal predicates are long to evaluate over it. This shows that Pangolin can scale and find defects in real code bases.

7   Related Work

There are many existing code representations and associated formalisms to specify queries. A more detailed comparison of existing code query technologies can be found in [2] or in [11]. ASTLOG [10] is a project for examining directly a program AST with a Prolog-based language. Thus, it allows to directly examine the very structure of the AST, whereas our approach exploits the AST to gain information and does not directly analyze it. In [20], the authors generate UML models from the AST of the code and use Object Constraint Language [7] to perform queries. HERCULES/PL [14] is a pattern specification language for C and Fortran programs on top of the HERCULES framework. It uses the target language and HERCULES specific compiler annotations (such as *pragma* in C) for specifying the code to match. In [12], the authors define TGraphs, a graph representation of the whole AST of the program, and they define GReQL, a graph querying language for performing queries. QL [4] uses a special relational database that contains a representation of the program extracted from its AST. Queries are expressed in a programming language similar to SQL, and are compiled to Datalog. Like all these methods (expect ASTLOG), our method works with a code representation that is built from the AST outside the functions. However, unlike all the above-mentioned methods, in addition to the AST, our approach also examines the body of functions through paths within their CFG, and allows for sophisticated reasoning about these paths through temporal logics.

On the other hand, Coccinelle [6] focuses on the CFG of a C function instead of its AST. It uses CTL-VW (a variant of FO-CTL) to describe and retrieve a sequence of statements within a CFG. This reasoning about execution paths within a CFG was an inspiration for the temporal aspect of FO^{++}. But, unlike Coccinelle, FO^{++} can specify a property about several functions through the first-order reasoning over the code AST. However, Coccinelle has a code transformation feature, which FO^{++} does not offer.

In [13], the authors detect design patterns described in formalism based on a combination of predicate logic and Allen's interval-based temporal logic. The complete formalism is latter translated into Prolog to effectively search the design pattern. However, its semantic model is not provided (especially how functions are handled). FO^{++} offers a more modular combination mechanism for logics and integrates two discrete temporal logics (CTL and LTL), which we think are more natural to use than the Allen's temporal logic, given that the statements are discrete events.

8   Conclusion

This paper presents a formal approach to source code verification in which the requirements can simultaneously refer to execution paths in the CFG of functions and to structural information that comes from the source code AST. To formalize the requirements, we introduce the logic FO^{++}, which is a temporal extension of many-sorted first-order logic. We propose a model checking algorithm for FO^{++} and prove its correctness, termination and that FO^{++} model checking problem is PSPACE complete. This approach has been implemented in Pangolin, a tool for analyzing C++ programs. With it, we analyzed two middle-sized open-source projects (ZeroMQ and MiniZinc), looking for violations of 6 good-practice coding-rules and found several occurrences of them.

As future works, there are two directions: user interaction, and expressive power. An input language closer to real code and better user feedback would improve user interaction. The expressive power of the method would be increased with interprocedural and multi-file analysis and the adequate specification formalism to handle it.

References

1. ISO International Standard ISO/IEC 14882:2014(E) Programming Language C++
2. Alves, T.L., Hage, J., Rademaker, P.: A comparative study of code query technologies. In: Proceedings - 11th IEEE International Working Conference on Source Code Analysis and Manipulation, SCAM 2011, pp. 145–154 (2011)
3. Alves, T.L., Visser, J.: Static estimation of test coverage. In: 2009 Ninth IEEE International Working Conference on Source Code Analysis and Manipulation, pp. 55–64, September 2009
4. Avgustinov, P., De Moor, O., Jones, M.P., Schäfer, M.: QL: object-oriented queries on relational data. In: Ecoop 2016, pp. 1–25 (2016)

5. Bohn, J., Damm, W., Grumberg, O., Hungar, H., Laster, K.: First-order-CTL model checking. In: Arvind, V., Ramanujam, S. (eds.) FSTTCS 1998. LNCS, vol. 1530, pp. 283–294. Springer, Heidelberg (1998). https://doi.org/10.1007/978-3-540-49382-2_27

6. Brunel, J., Doligez, D., Hansen, R.R., Lawall, J.L., Muller, G.: A foundation for flow-based program matching. ACM SIGPLAN Not. **44**(1), 114 (2009)

7. Cabot, J., Gogolla, M.: Object Constraint Language (OCL): a definitive guide. In: Bernardo, M., Cortellessa, V., Pierantonio, A. (eds.) SFM 2012. LNCS, vol. 7320, pp. 58–90. Springer, Heidelberg (2012). https://doi.org/10.1007/978-3-642-30982-3_3

8. Caleiro, C., Sernadas, C., Sernadas, A.: Parameterisation of logics. In: Fiadeiro, J.L. (ed.) WADT 1998. LNCS, vol. 1589, pp. 48–63. Springer, Heidelberg (1999). https://doi.org/10.1007/3-540-48483-3_4

9. Cavada, R., et al.: The NUXMV symbolic model checker. In: Biere, A., Bloem, R. (eds.) CAV 2014. LNCS, vol. 8559, pp. 334–342. Springer, Cham (2014). https://doi.org/10.1007/978-3-319-08867-9_22

10. Crew, R.F.: ASTLOG: a language for examining abstract syntax trees. In: Proceedings of the Conference on Domain-Specific Languages on Conference on Domain-Specific Languages (DSL), DSL 1997, p. 18. USENIX Association, Berkeley (1997)

11. Dit, B., Revelle, M., Gethers, M., Poshyvanyk, D.: Feature location in source code: a taxonomy and survey. J. Softw. Evol. Process. **25**(1), 53–95 (2013)

12. Ebert, J., Bildhauer, D.: Reverse engineering using graph queries. In: Engels, G., Lewerentz, C., Schäfer, W., Schürr, A., Westfechtel, B. (eds.) Graph Transformations and Model-Driven Engineering. LNCS, vol. 5765, pp. 335–362. Springer, Heidelberg (2010). https://doi.org/10.1007/978-3-642-17322-6_15

13. Huang, H., Zhang, S., Cao, J., Duan, Y.: A practical pattern recovery approach based on both structural and behavioral analysis. J. Syst. Softw. **75**(1–2), 69–87 (2005)

14. Kartsaklis, C., Hernandez, O.R.: HERCULES/PL: the pattern language of HERCULES. In: Proceedings of the 1st Workshop on Programming Language Evolution, pp. 5–10 (2014)

15. Kuperberg, D., Brunel, J., Chemouil, D.: On finite domains in first-order linear temporal logic. In: Artho, C., Legay, A., Peled, D. (eds.) ATVA 2016. LNCS, vol. 9938, pp. 211–226. Springer, Cham (2016). https://doi.org/10.1007/978-3-319-46520-3_14

16. Lawall, J.L., Muller, G., Palix, N.: Enforcing the use of API functions in Linux code. In: Proceedings of the 8th Workshop on Aspects, Components, and Patterns for Infrastructure Software - ACP4IS 2009, p. 7 (2009)

17. Lopes, B.C., Rafael, A.: Getting Started with LLVM Core Libraries (2014)

18. van Raamsdonk, F.: Higher-order rewriting. In: Narendran, P., Rusinowitch, M. (eds.) RTA 1999. LNCS, vol. 1631, pp. 220–239. Springer, Heidelberg (1999). https://doi.org/10.1007/3-540-48685-2_17

19. Huth, M., Ryan, M.: Logic in Computer Science (2004)

20. Seifert, M., Samlaus, R.: Static source code analysis using OCL. Electron. Commun. EASST **15** (2008)

21. Stuckey, P.J., Feydy, T., Schutt, A., Tack, G., Fischer, J.: The MiniZinc challenge 2008–2013. AI Mag. **35**(2), 55–60 (2014)

22. Vardi, M.Y.: The complexity of relational query languages (extended abstract). In: Proceedings of the Fourteenth Annual ACM Symposium on Theory of Computing, STOC 1982, pp. 137–146. ACM, New York (1982)

A Type-Directed Algorithm to Generate Well-Typed Featherweight Java Programs

Samuel S. Feitosa[1]([⊠]), Rodrigo Geraldo Ribeiro[2],
and Andre Rauber Du Bois[1]

[1] PPGC, Universidade Federal de Pelotas, Pelotas, RS, Brazil
{samuel.feitosa,dubois}@inf.ufpel.edu.br
[2] PPGCC, Universidade Federal de Ouro Preto, Ouro Preto, MG, Brazil
rodrigo@decsi.ufop.br

Abstract. Property-based testing of compilers or programming languages semantics is difficult to accomplish because it is hard to design a random generator for valid programs. Most compiler test tools do not have a well-specified way of generating type-correct programs, which is a requirement for such testing activities. In this work, we formalize a type-directed procedure to generate random well-typed programs in the context of Featherweight Java, a well-known object-oriented calculus for the Java programming language. We implement the approach using the Haskell programming language and verify it against relevant properties using QuickCheck, a library for property-based testing.

Keywords: Featherweight Java · QuickCheck · Property-based testing

1 Introduction

Currently, Java is one of the most popular programming languages [22]. It is a general-purpose, concurrent, strongly typed, class-based object-oriented language. Since its release in 1995 by Sun Microsystems, and acquired by Oracle Corporation, Java has been evolving over time, adding features and programming facilities in its new versions. For example, in a recent major release of Java, new features such as lambda expressions, method references, and functional interfaces, were added to the core language, offering a programming model that fuses the object-oriented and functional styles [11].

The adoption of the Java language is growing for large projects, where many applications have reached a level of complexity for which testing, code reviews, and human inspection are no longer sufficient quality-assurance guarantees. This problem increases the need for tools that employ analysis techniques, aiming to explore all possibilities in an application to guarantee the absence of unexpected behaviors [7]. The use of formal subsets of languages helps in the understanding of the problem, and allows the use of automatic tools, since a certain degree of abstraction is applied, and only properties of interest are used, providing a degree of confidence that cannot be reached using informal approaches.

© Springer Nature Switzerland AG 2018
T. Massoni and M. R. Mousavi (Eds.): SBMF 2018, LNCS 11254, pp. 39–55, 2018.
https://doi.org/10.1007/978-3-030-03044-5_4

Creating tests for programming languages or compilers is difficult since several requirements should be respected to produce a valid and useful test case [2,4]. When a person is responsible for this task, tests could be limited by human imagination, the creator can make assumptions about the implementation, impacting in the quality of the test cases, and the maintenance of such tests is also an issue when the language evolves. Because of this, there is a growing research community studying random test generation, which is not an easy task, since the generated programs should respect the constraints of the programming language compiler, such as the correct syntax, or the type-system requirements in a statically-typed language.

In this context, this work provides the formal specification of a type-directed procedure for generating Java programs, using the typing rules of Featherweight Java (FJ) [12] to generate only well-typed programs. FJ is a small core calculus with a rigorous semantic definition of the main core aspects of Java. The motivations for using the specification of FJ are that it is very compact, so we can specify our generation algorithm in a way that it can be extended with new features, and its minimal syntax, typing rules, and operational semantics fit well for modeling and proving properties for the compiler and programs. As far as we know, there is no formal specification of well-typed test generators for an object-oriented calculus like FJ. This work aims to fill this gap, providing the description of a generation procedure for FJ programs by using a syntax directed judgment for generating random type-correct FJ programs, adapting the approach of Palka et al. [18] in terms of QuickCheck [5]. We are aware that using only automated testing is not sufficient to ensure safety or correctness, but it can expose bugs before using more formal approaches, like formalization in a proof assistant.

Specifically, we made the following contributions:

– We provided a type-directed [16] formal specification for constructing random programs. We proved that our specification is sound with respect to FJ type system, i.e. it generates only well-typed programs.
– We implemented an interpreter[1] for FJ and the type-directed algorithm to generate random FJ programs following our formal specification using the Haskell programming language.
– We used 'javac' as an oracle to compile the random programs constructed through our type-directed procedure. We also used QuickCheck as a proof of concept to check type-soundness proofs using the interpreter and the generated programs[2].

The remainder of this text is organized as follows: Sect. 2 summarizes the FJ proposal. Section 3 presents the process of generating well-typed random programs in the context of FJ. Section 4 proves that our generation procedure is

---

[1] The source-code for our Haskell interpreter and the complete test suite is available at: https://github.com/fjpub/fj-qc/.

[2] Details of implementation and experiments are presented in our technical report, which can be found at: https://github.com/fjpub/fj-qc/raw/master/tr.pdf.

sound with respect to FJ typing rules. Section 5 shows how the results of testing type-safety properties of FJ with QuickCheck. Section 6 discusses some related works. Finally, we present the final remarks in Sect. 7.

2 Featherweight Java

Featherweight Java [12] is a minimal core calculus for Java, in the sense that as many features of Java as possible are omitted, while maintaining the essential flavor of the language and its type system. Nevertheless, this fragment is large enough to include many useful programs. A program in FJ consists of the declaration of a set of classes and an expression to be evaluated, that corresponds to the Java's main method.

FJ is to Java what λ-calculus is to Haskell. It offers similar operations, providing classes, methods, attributes, inheritance and dynamic casts with semantics close to Java's. The Featherweight Java project favors simplicity over expressivity and offers only five ways to create terms: object creation, method invocation, attribute access, casting and variables [12].

FJ semantics provides a purely functional view without side effects. In other words, attributes in memory are not affected by object operations [19]. Furthermore, interfaces, overloading, call to base class methods, null pointers, base types, abstract methods, statements, access control, and exceptions are not present in the language. As the language does not allow side effects, it is possible to formalize the evaluation just using the FJ syntax, without the need for auxiliary mechanisms to model the heap [19].

The abstract syntax of FJ is given in Fig. 1.

In the syntactic definitions L represents classes, K defines constructors, M stands for methods, and e refers to the possible expressions. The metavariables A, B, C, D, E, and F can be used to represent class names, f and g range over field names, m ranges over method names, x and y range over variables, d and e range

Syntax

$L ::=$	class declarations
$\quad$ class C extends D $\{\overline{C}\ \overline{f}; K\ \overline{M}\}$	
$K ::=$	constructor declarations
$\quad C(\overline{C}\ \overline{f})$ $\{$super$(\overline{f})$; this.$\overline{f} = \overline{f};\}$	
$M ::=$	method declarations
$\quad C$ m$(\overline{C}\ \overline{x})$ $\{$ return $e;\}$	
$e ::=$	expressions
$\quad x$	variable
$\quad e.f$	field access
$\quad e.$m$(\overline{e})$	method invocation
$\quad$ new $C(\overline{e})$	object creation
$\quad (C)\ e$	cast

Fig. 1. Syntactic definitions for FJ.

over expressions. We let $\varphi : L \to C$ denote a function that returns a class name
(C) from a given class declaration (L). Throughout this paper, we write $\overline{C}$ as
shorthand for a possibly empty sequence $C_1, ..., C_n$ (similarly for $\overline{f}$, $\overline{x}$, etc.). An
empty sequence is denoted by $\bullet$, and the length of a sequence $\overline{x}$ is written $\#\overline{x}$. The
inclusion of an item x in a sequence $\overline{X}$ is denoted by $x : \overline{X}$, following Haskell's
notation for lists. We consider that a finite mapping M is just a sequence of
key-value pairs. Notation $M(K) = V$ if $K\,V \in M$. Following common practice,
we let the metavariable Γ denote an arbitrary typing environment which consists
of a finite mapping between variables and types.

A class table CT is a mapping from class names, to class declarations L, and
it should satisfy some conditions, such as each class C should be in CT, except
Object, which is a special class; and there are no cycles in the subtyping relation.
Thereby, a program is a pair (CT, e) of a class table and an expression. The FJ
authors presented rules for subtyping and auxiliary definitions (functions *fields*,
mtype, and *mbody*), which are omitted from this text for space reasons.

Figure 2 shows the typing rules for FJ expressions.

$$\frac{}{\Gamma \vdash \text{x}:\ \Gamma(\text{x})} \text{ [T-Var]}$$

$$\frac{\Gamma \vdash e_0:\ C_0 \qquad \textit{fields}(C_0) = \bar{C}\ \bar{f}}{\Gamma \vdash e_0.f_i:\ C_i} \text{ [T-Field]}$$

$$\frac{\textit{mtype}(\text{m},\ C_0) = \bar{D} \to C \qquad \Gamma \vdash e_0:\ C_0 \qquad \Gamma \vdash \bar{e}:\ \bar{C} \qquad \bar{C} <:\ \bar{D}}{\Gamma \vdash e_0.\text{m}(\bar{e}):\ C} \text{ [T-Invk]}$$

$$\frac{\textit{fields}(C) = \bar{D}\ \bar{f} \qquad \Gamma \vdash \bar{e}:\ \bar{C} \qquad \bar{C} <:\ \bar{D}}{\Gamma \vdash \text{new } C(\bar{e}):\ C} \text{ [T-New]}$$

$$\frac{\Gamma \vdash e_0:\ D \qquad D <:\ C}{\Gamma \vdash (C)\ e_0:\ C} \text{ [T-UCast]}$$

$$\frac{\Gamma \vdash e_0:\ D \qquad C <:\ D \qquad C \neq D}{\Gamma \vdash (C)\ e_0:\ C} \text{ [T-DCast]}$$

$$\frac{\Gamma \vdash e_0:\ D \qquad C \not<:\ D \qquad D \not<:\ C \qquad \textit{stupid warning}}{\Gamma \vdash (C)\ e_0:\ C} \text{ [T-SCast]}$$

Fig. 2. Expression typing.

The typing judgment for expressions has the form $\Gamma \vdash e:$ C, meaning that in
the environment Γ, expression e has type C. The typing rules are syntax directed,
with one rule for each form of expression, save that there are three rules for casts.
The rule T-Var results in the type of a variable x according to the context Γ. If
the variable x is not contained in Γ, the result is undefined. Similarly, the result

is undefined when calling the functions $fields$, $mtype$, and $mbody$ in cases when the target class or the methods do not exist in the given class. The rule T-Field applies the typing judgment on the subexpression e_0, which results in the type C_0. Then it obtains the *fields* of class C_0, matching the position of f_i in the resultant list, to return the respective type C_i. The rule T-Invk also applies the typing judgment on the subexpression e_0, which results in the type C_0, then it uses *mtype* to get the formal parameter types $\bar{D}$ and the return type C. The formal parameter types are used to check if the actual parameters $\bar{e}$ are subtypes of them, and in this case, resulting in the return type C. The rule T-New checks if the actual parameters are a subtype of the constructor formal parameters, which are obtained by using the function *fields*. There are three rules for casts: one for *upcasts*, where the subject is a subclass of the target; one for *downcasts*, where the target is a subclass of the subject; and another for *stupid casts*, where the target is unrelated to the subject. Even considering that Java's compiler rejects as ill-typed an expression containing a stupid cast, the authors found that a rule of this kind is necessary to formulate type soundness proofs[3].

Figure 3 shows the rules to check if methods and classes are well-formed.

Method typing

$$\frac{\begin{array}{c} \bar{x} \colon \bar{C}, \text{this} \colon C \vdash e_0 \colon E_0 \qquad E_0 <: C_0 \\ \text{class C extends D } \{...\} \\ \text{if } mtype(\text{m, D}) = \bar{D} \to D_0, \\ \text{then } \bar{C} = \bar{D} \text{ and } C_0 = D_0 \end{array}}{C_0 \text{ m}(\bar{C} \ \bar{x}) \ \{ \text{ return } e_0; \ \} \text{ OK in C}}$$

Class typing

$$\frac{K = C(\bar{D} \ \bar{g}, \ \bar{C} \ \bar{f}) \ \{ \text{ super}(\bar{g}); \text{ this}.\bar{f} = \bar{f}; \ \} \\ fields(D) = \bar{D} \ \bar{g} \qquad \bar{M} \text{ OK in C}}{\text{class C extends D } \{ \ \bar{C} \ \bar{f}; \text{ K } \bar{M} \ \} \text{ OK}}$$

Fig. 3. Method and class typing.

The rule for *method typing* checks if a method declaration M is well-formed when it occurs in a class C. It uses the expression typing judgment on the body of the method, with the context Γ containing the special variable **this** with type C, and the variables from the formal parameters with their declared types. The rule for *class typing* checks if a class is well-formed, by checking if the constructor applies super to the fields of the superclass and initializes the fields declared in this class, and that each method declaration in the class is well-formed.

The authors also presented the semantic rules for FJ, which are omitted here, but can be found in the original paper [12]. FJ calculus is intended to be a starting point for the study of various operational features of object-oriented programming in Java-like languages, being compact enough to make rigorous proof

---

[3] A detailed explanation about *stupid casts* can be found in p. 260 of [19].

feasible. Besides the rules for evaluation and type-checking rules, the authors presented proofs of type soundness for FJ as another important contribution, which will be explored by our test suite in the next sections.

3   Program Generation

The creation of tests for a programming language semantics or compiler is time-consuming. First, because it should respect the programming language requirements, in order to produce a valid test case. Second, if the test cases are created by a person, it stays limited by human imagination, where obscure corner cases could be overlooked. If the compiler writers are producing the test cases, they can be biased, since they can make assumptions about their implementation or about what the language should do. Furthermore, when the language evolves, previous test cases could be an issue, considering the validity of some old tests may change if the language semantics is altered [1].

Considering the presented problem, there is a growing research field exploring random test generation. However, generating good test programs is not an easy task, since these programs should have a structure that is accepted by the compiler, respecting some constraints, which can be as simple as a program having the correct syntax, or more complex such as a program being type-correct in a statically-typed programming language [18].

For generating random programs in the context of FJ, we follow two distinct phases, expression and class generation, generalizing the approach of [18] considering that FJ has a nominal type system instead of a structural one. In this way, we have specified a generation rule inspired by each typing rule, both for expression generation and class table generation.

3.1   Expression Generation

We assume that a class table CT is a finite mapping between names and its corresponding classes. We let $dom(\text{CT})$ denote the set of names in the domain of the finite mapping CT. The generation algorithm uses a function $\xi : [a] \to a$, which returns a random element from an input list. We slightly abuse notation by using set operations on lists (sequences) and its meaning is as usual.

The expression generation is represented by the following judgment:

$$\text{CT} ; \Gamma ; \text{C} \to \text{e} \tag{1}$$

There CT is a class table, Γ is a typing environment, C is a type name and e is the produced expression.

For generating *variables*, we just need to select a name from the typing environment, which has a type C.

$$\frac{}{\text{CT} ; \Gamma ; \text{C} \to \xi \left(\{ \text{x} \mid \Gamma(\text{x}) = \text{C} \} \right)} \text{ [G-Var]}$$

For *fields access*, we first need to generate a list of candidate type names for generating an expression with type C' which has at least one field whose type is C. We name such list $\overline{C_c}$:

$$\overline{C_c} = \{C_1 | C_1 \in dom(\text{CT}) \wedge \exists x.Cx \in fields(C_1)\}$$

Now, we can build a random expression by using a type randomly chosen from it.

$$C' = \xi(\overline{C_c})$$
$$\text{CT} ; \Gamma ; C' \to e$$

Since type C' can have more than one field with type C, we need to choose one of them (note that, by construction, such set is not empty).

$$C\ f = \xi(\{Cx | Cx \in fields(C')\})$$

The rule `G-Field` combines these previous steps to generate a field access expression:

$$\frac{\begin{array}{c}\overline{C_c} = \{C_1 \mid C_1 \in dom(\text{CT}) \wedge \exists\ x.\ C\ x \in fields(C_1)\} \\ C' = \xi(\overline{C_c}) \\ \text{CT} ; \Gamma ; C' \to e \\ C\ f = \xi(\{C\ x \mid C\ x \in fields(C')\}) \end{array}}{\text{CT} ; \Gamma ; C \to e.f} \quad [\text{G-Field}]$$

For *method invocations*, we first need to find all classes which have method signatures with return type C. As before, we name such candidate class list as $\overline{C_c}$.

$$\overline{C_c} = \{C_1 | C_1 \in dom(\text{CT}) \wedge \exists m\bar{D}.mtype(m, C_1) = \bar{D} \to C\}$$

Next, we need to generate an expression e_0 from a type chosen from $\overline{C_c}$, we name such type as C'.

$$C' = \xi(\overline{C_c})$$
$$\text{CT} ; \Gamma ; C' \to e_0$$

From such type C', we need to chose which method with return type C will be called. For this, we select a random signature from its list of candidate methods.

$$\overline{M_c} = \{(m, \bar{D} \to C) \mid \exists\ m.\ mtype(m, C') = \bar{D} \to C\}$$
$$(m', \bar{D}' \to C) = \xi(\overline{M_c})$$

Next, we need to generate arguments for all formal parameters of method m'. For this, since arguments could be of any subtype of the formal parameter type, we need to choose it from the set of all candidate subtypes.

First, we define a function called subtypes, which return a list of all subtypes of some type.

$$subtypes(\text{CT}, \text{Object}) = \{\text{Object}\}$$
$$subtypes(\text{CT}, C) = \{C\} \cup subtypes(\text{CT}, D), \text{ if class C extends D} \in \text{CT}$$

Using this function, we can build the list of arguments for a method call.

$$\bar{a} = \{e | D \in \bar{D}' \wedge CT; \Gamma; \xi(subtypes(CT, D)) \rightarrow e\}$$

The rule **G-Invk** combines all these previous steps to produce a method call.

$$
\frac{
\begin{array}{c}
\overline{C_c} = \{C_1 \mid C_1 \in dom(CT) \wedge \exists\, m\, \bar{D}.\ mtype(m, C_1) = \bar{D} \rightarrow C\} \\
C' = \xi(\overline{C_c}) \\
CT\ ;\ \Gamma\ ;\ C' \rightarrow e_0 \\
\overline{M_c} = \{(m, \bar{D} \rightarrow C) \mid \exists\, m.\ mtype(m, C') = \bar{D} \rightarrow C\} \\
(m', \bar{D}' \rightarrow C) = \xi(\overline{M_c}) \\
\bar{a} = \{e \mid D \in \bar{D}' \wedge CT;\ \Gamma;\ \xi(subtypes(CT, D)) \rightarrow e\}
\end{array}
}{
CT\ ;\ \Gamma\ ;\ C \rightarrow e_0.m'(\bar{a})
}
\quad \text{[G-Invk]}
$$

The generation of a random *object creation* expression is straightforward: First, we need to get all field types of the class C and produce arguments for C's constructor parameters, as demonstrated by rule **G-New**.

$$
\frac{
\begin{array}{c}
\bar{F} = \{C' \mid C'\ f \in fields(C)\} \\
\bar{a} = \{e \mid F \in \bar{F} \wedge CT\ ;\ \Gamma\ ;\ \xi(subtypes(CT, F)) \rightarrow e\}
\end{array}
}{
CT\ ;\ \Gamma\ ;\ C \rightarrow new\ C(\bar{a})
}
\quad \text{[G-New]}
$$

We construct *upper casts* expressions for a type C using the **G-UCast** rule.

$$
\frac{
\begin{array}{c}
\bar{D} = subtypes(CT, C) \\
CT\ ;\ \Gamma\ ;\ \xi(\bar{D}) \rightarrow e
\end{array}
}{
CT\ ;\ \Gamma;\ C \rightarrow (C)\ e
}
\quad \text{[G-UCast]}
$$

Although we do not start a program with *downcasts* or *stupid casts*, because expressions generated by these typing rules can reduce to *cast unsafe* terms [12], we defined the generation process in the rules **G-DCast** and **G-SCast**, since they can be used to build inner subexpressions.

For generating downcasts, first we need the following function, which returns the set of super types of a given class name C.

$supertypes(CT, Object) = \bullet$

$supertypes(CT, C) = \{D\} \cup supertypes(CT, D)$, if class C extends $D \in CT$

Then, we can produce the rule **G-DCast** to generate a downcast expression.

$$
\frac{
\begin{array}{c}
\bar{D} = supertypes(CT,C) \\
CT\ ;\ \Gamma\ ;\ \xi(\bar{D}) \rightarrow e
\end{array}
}{
CT\ ;\ \Gamma\ ;\ C \rightarrow (C)\ e
}
\quad \text{[G-DCast]}
$$

The generation of stupid casts has a similar process, except that it generates a list of unrelated classes, as we can see in the first line of the rule **G-SCast**.

$$
\frac{
\begin{array}{c}
\bar{C} = dom(CT) - (subtypes(CT,C) \cup supertypes(CT,C)) \\
CT\ ;\ \Gamma\ ;\ \xi(\bar{C}) \rightarrow e
\end{array}
}{
CT\ ;\ \Gamma\ ;\ C \rightarrow (C)\ e
}
\quad \text{[G-SCast]}
$$

Considering the presented generation rules, we are able to produce well-typed expressions for each FJ's definitions.

3.2   Class Table Generation

To generate a class table, we assume the existence of an enumerable set $\overline{C_n}$ of class names and $\overline{V_n}$ of variable names. The generation rules are parameterized by an integer n which determines the number of classes that will populate the resulting table, a limit m for the number of members in each class and a limit p for the number of formal parameters in the generated methods. This procedure is expressed by the following judgment:

$$\mathrm{CT} ; \mathrm{n} ; \mathrm{m} ; \mathrm{p} \to \mathrm{CT}'$$

It is responsible to generate n classes using as input the information in class table CT (which can be empty), each class will have up to m members. As a result, the judgment will produce a new class table CT'. As expected, this judgment is defined by recursion on n:

$$\frac{}{\mathrm{CT} ; 0 ; \mathrm{m} ; \mathrm{p} \to \mathrm{CT}} \;\; [\text{CT-Base}]$$

$$\frac{\mathrm{CT} ; \mathrm{m} ; \mathrm{p} \to \mathrm{L} \quad \varphi(L)\, \mathrm{L} : \mathrm{CT} ; \mathrm{n} ; \mathrm{m} ; \mathrm{p} \to \mathrm{CT}'}{\mathrm{CT} ; \mathrm{n} + 1 ; \mathrm{m} ; \mathrm{p} \to \mathrm{CT}'} \;\; [\text{CT-Step}]$$

Rule **CT-Base** specifies when the class table generation procedure stops. Rule **CT-Step** uses a specific judgment to generate a new class, inserts it in the class table CT, and generate the next n classes using the recursive call $\varphi(L)\, L : CT$; n ; m ; p $\to CT'$. The following judgment presents how classes are generated:

$$\mathrm{CT} ; \mathrm{m} ; \mathrm{p} \to \mathrm{C}$$

It generates a new class, with at most m members, with at most p formal parameters in each method, using as a starting point a given class table. First, we create a new name which is not in the domain of the input class table, using:

$$\mathrm{C} = \xi(\overline{C_n} - (dom(\mathrm{CT}) \cup \{Object\}))$$

This rule selects a random class name from the set $\overline{C_n}$ excluding the names in the domain of CT and **Object**. Next, we need to generate a valid super class name, which can be anyone of the set formed by the domain of current class table CT and **Object**:

$$\mathrm{D} = \xi(dom(\mathrm{CT}) \cup \{Object\})$$

After generating a class name and its super class, we need to generate its members. For this, we generate random values for the number of fields and methods, named **fn** and **mn**, respectively. Using such parameters we build the fields and methods for a given class.

Field generation is straightforward. It proceeds by recursion on n, as shown below. Note that we maintain a set of already used attribute names $\overline{U_n}$ to avoid duplicates.

$$\frac{}{\mathrm{CT} ; 0 ; \overline{U_n} \to \bullet} \;\; [\text{G-Fields-Base}]$$

$$\frac{\begin{array}{c} C = \xi(dom(\mathrm{CT}) \cup \{\mathrm{Object}\}) \\ \mathrm{f} = \xi(\overline{V_n} - \overline{U_n}) \\ \mathrm{CT} \; ; \; \mathrm{n} \; ; \; \mathrm{f} : \overline{U_n} \to \bar{\mathrm{C}} \; \bar{\mathrm{f}} \end{array}}{\mathrm{CT} \; ; \; \mathrm{n} + 1 \; ; \; \overline{U_n} \to \mathrm{C} \; \mathrm{f} : \bar{\mathrm{C}} \; \bar{\mathrm{f}}} \quad \text{[G-Fields-Step]}$$

Generation of the method list proceeds by recursion on m, as shown below. We also maintain a set of already used method names $\overline{U_n}$ to avoid method overload, which is not supported by FJ. The rule **G-Method-Step** uses a specific judgment to generate each method, which is described by rule **G-Method**.

$$\frac{}{\mathrm{CT} \; ; \; \mathrm{C} \; ; \; 0 \; ; \; \mathrm{p} \; ; \; \overline{U_n} \to \bullet} \quad \text{[G-Methods-Base]}$$

$$\frac{\begin{array}{c} \mathrm{x} = \xi(\overline{V_n} - \overline{U_n}) \\ \mathrm{CT} \; ; \; \mathrm{C} \; ; \; \mathrm{p} \; ; \; \mathrm{x} \to \mathrm{M} \\ \mathrm{CT} \; ; \; \mathrm{C} \; ; \; \mathrm{m} \; ; \; \mathrm{p} \; ; \; \mathrm{x} : \overline{U_n} \to \bar{\mathrm{M}} \end{array}}{\mathrm{CT} \; ; \; \mathrm{C} \; ; \; \mathrm{m} + 1 \; ; \; \mathrm{p} \; ; \; \overline{U_n} \to \mathrm{M} : \bar{\mathrm{M}}} \quad \text{[G-Methods-Step]}$$

The rule **G-Method** uses an auxiliary judgment for generating formal parameters (note that we can generate an empty parameter list). To produce the expression, which defines the method body, we build a typing environment using the formal parameters and a variable **this** to denote this special object. Also, such expression is generated using a type that can be any of the possible subtypes of the method return type C_0.

$$\frac{\begin{array}{c} \mathrm{n} = \xi([0..(\mathrm{p} - 1)]) \\ \mathrm{CT} \; ; \; \mathrm{n} \; ; \; \bullet \to \bar{\mathrm{C}} \; \bar{\mathrm{x}} \\ \mathrm{C}_0 = \xi(dom(\mathrm{CT}) \cup \{\mathrm{Object}\}) \\ \varGamma = \bar{\mathrm{C}} \; \bar{\mathrm{x}}, \mathrm{this} : \mathrm{C} \\ \bar{\mathrm{D}} = subtypes(\mathrm{CT},\mathrm{C}_0) \\ \mathrm{E}_0 = \xi(\bar{\mathrm{D}}) \\ \mathrm{CT} \; ; \; \varGamma \; ; \; \mathrm{E}_0 \to \mathrm{e} \end{array}}{\mathrm{CT} \; ; \; \mathrm{C} \; ; \; \mathrm{p} \; ; \; \mathrm{m} \to (\mathrm{C}_0 \; \mathrm{m} \; (\bar{\mathrm{C}} \; \bar{\mathrm{x}}) \; \{\mathrm{return} \; \mathrm{e};\})} \quad \text{[G-Method]}$$

We create the formal parameters for methods using a simple recursive judgment that keeps a set of already used variable names $\overline{U_n}$ to ensure that all variables produced are distinct.

$$\frac{}{\mathrm{CT} \; ; \; 0 \; ; \; \overline{U_n} \to \bullet} \quad \text{[G-Param-Base]}$$

$$\frac{\begin{array}{c} C = \xi(dom(\mathrm{CT}) \cup \{\mathrm{Object}\}) \\ \mathrm{x} = \xi(\overline{V_n} - \overline{U_n}) \\ \mathrm{CT} \; ; \; \mathrm{n} \; ; \; \mathrm{x} : \overline{U_n} \to \bar{\mathrm{C}} \; \bar{\mathrm{x}} \end{array}}{\mathrm{CT} \; ; \; \mathrm{n} + 1 \; ; \; \overline{U_n} \to (\mathrm{C} \; \mathrm{x} : \bar{\mathrm{C}} \; \bar{\mathrm{x}})} \quad \text{[G-Param-Step]}$$

Finally, using the generated class name and its super class, we build its constructor definition using the judgment:

$$CT ; \mathrm{C} ; \mathrm{D} \to \mathrm{K}$$

Rule **G-Constr** represents the process to generate the constructor.

$$\frac{\begin{array}{c} \bar{D}\ \bar{g} = \mathit{fields}(D) \\ \bar{C}\ \bar{f} = \mathit{fields}(C) \text{ - } \bar{D}\ \bar{g} \end{array}}{CT\ ;\ C\ ;\ D \to (\ C\ (\bar{D}\ \bar{g},\ \bar{C}\ \bar{f})\ \{\ super(\bar{g})\ ;\ this.\bar{f} = \bar{f}\ \}\ )}\ [\text{G-Constr}]$$

The process for generating a complete class is summarized by rule **G-Class**, which is composed by all previously presented rules.

$$\frac{\begin{array}{c} C = \xi(\overline{C_n} \text{ - } (\mathit{dom}(CT) \cup \{\text{Object}\})) \\ D = \xi(\mathit{dom}(CT) \cup \{\text{Object}\}) \\ \text{fn} = \xi([1..m]) \\ \text{mn} = \xi([1..(m \text{ - fn})]) \\ CT' = C\ (\text{class } C \text{ extends } D\ \{\})\ :\ CT \\ CT'\ ;\ \text{fn}\ ;\ \bullet \to \bar{C}\ \bar{f} \\ CT'' = C\ (\text{class } C \text{ extends } D\ \{\bar{C}\ \bar{f}\})\ :\ CT \\ CT''\ ;\ C\ ;\ \text{mn}\ ;\ p\ ;\ \bullet \to \bar{M} \\ CT'\ ;\ C\ ;\ D \to K \end{array}}{CT\ ;\ m\ ;\ p \to (\text{class } C \text{ extends } D\ \{\ \bar{C}\ \bar{f};\ K\ \bar{M}\ \})}\ [\text{G-Class}]$$

Considering the presented generation rules, we are able to fill a class table with well-formed classes in respect to FJ typing rules.

4 Soundness of Program Generation

The generation algorithm described in the previous section produces only well-typed FJ programs.

Lemma 1 (Soundness of expression generation). *Let* CT *be a well-formed class table. For all* Γ *and* $C \in dom$ *(CT), if* CT $;\ \Gamma\ ;\ C \to e$ *then exists* D, *such that* $\Gamma \vdash e : D$ *and* $D <: C$.

Proof. The proof proceeds by induction on the derivation of $CT\ ;\ \Gamma\ ;\ C \to e$ doing a case analysis on the last rule used to deduce $CT\ ;\ \Gamma\ ;\ C \to e$. We show some cases of the proof.

Case (G-Var): Then, e = x, for some variable x. By rule **G-Var**, $x = \xi(\{y \mid \Gamma(y) = C\})$ and from this we can deduce that $\Gamma(x) = C$ and the conclusion follows by rule **T-Var**.

Case (G-Invk): Then, $e = e_0.m(\bar{e})$ for some e_0 and $\bar{e}$; $CT\ ;\ \Gamma\ ;\ C' \to e_0$, for some C'; there exists $(m, \bar{D}' \to C)$, such that $\mathit{mtype}(m, C') = \bar{D} \to C$ and for all $e' \in \bar{e},\ D \in \bar{D}',\ CT\ ;\ \Gamma\ ;\ \xi(\mathit{subtypes}(CT, D)) \to e'$. By the induction hypothesis, we have that: $\Gamma \vdash e_0 : D',\ D' <: C'$, for all $e' \in \bar{e},\ D \in \bar{D}'.\ \Gamma \vdash e' : B,\ B <: D$ and the conclusion follows by the rule **T-Invk** and the definition of subtyping relation.

Lemma 2 (Soundness of subtypes). *Let* CT *be a well-formed class table and* $C \in dom(\text{CT})$. *For all* D. *if* $D \in subtypes(\text{CT}, C)$ *then* $C <: D$.

Proof. Straightforward induction on the structure of the result of *subtypes* (CT, C).

Lemma 3 (Soundness of method generation). *Let* CT *be a well-formed class table and* $C \in dom(\text{CT}) \cup \{\texttt{Object}\}$. *For all p and m, if* CT ; C ; p ; m $\rightarrow C_0$ m $(\bar{C}\bar{x})$ { return e; } *then* C_0 m $(\bar{C}\bar{x})$ { return e; } *OK in C.*

Proof. By rule G-Method, we have that:

- $\bar{C} \subseteq dom(\text{CT})$
- $\Gamma = \{\bar{C} \; \bar{x}, \texttt{this} : C\}$
- $C_0 = \xi(dom(\text{CT}) \cup \{\texttt{Object}\})$
- $\bar{D} = subtypes(\text{CT}, C_0)$
- $CT ; \Gamma ; E_0 \rightarrow e$
- $E_0 = \xi(\bar{D})$

By Lemma 2, we have that for all $D \in \bar{D}$, $C_0 <: D$.
By Lemma 1, we have that $\Gamma \vdash e : E'$ and $E' <: E_0$.
Since CT is well-formed, then $mtype(\text{m}, C) = \bar{C} \rightarrow C_0$ and the conclusion follows by rule *method typing* and the definition of the subtyping relation.

Lemma 4 (Soundness of class generation). *Let* CT *be a well-formed class table. For all m, p, if* CT ; m ; p $\rightarrow$ CD *then* CD OK.

Proof. By rule G-Class, we have that:

- CD = class C extends D { $\bar{C}$ $\bar{f}$; K $\bar{M}$ }
- C = $\xi(\overline{C_n}$ - $(dom(\text{CT}) \cup \texttt{Object}))$
- D = $\xi(dom(\text{CT}) \cup \texttt{Object})$
- fn = $\xi([1..m])$
- mn = $\xi([1..(m - fn)])$
- $CT' = C$ (class C extends D {}) : CT
- CT' ; fn $\rightarrow \bar{C}$ $\bar{f}$
- $CT'' = C$ (class C extends D { $\bar{C}$ $\bar{f}$; }) : CT
- CT'' ; C ; mn ; p ; $\bullet \rightarrow \bar{M}$
- CT' ; C ; D $\rightarrow$ K

By Lemma 3, we have that for all m. m $\in \bar{M}$, m OK.
By rule (G-Constr) we have that K = C ($\bar{D}$ $\bar{g}$, $\bar{C}$ $\bar{f}$) {super($\bar{g}$); this.$\bar{f}$ = $\bar{f}$;}, where $\bar{D}$ $\bar{g}$ = fields(D).
The conclusion follows by rule *class typing*.

Lemma 5. *Let* CT *be a well-formed class table. For all n, m and p, if* CT ; n ; m ; p $\rightarrow$ CT' *then for all C, D* $\in$ *dom*(CT'), *if C* $<:$ *D and D* $<:$ *C then* CT(C) $=$ CT(D).

Proof. By induction on n.

Case n = 0: We have that $CT' = CT$. Conclusion follows by the fact that CT is a well-formed class table.

Case n = n' + 1: Suppose C, D $\in$ *dom*(CT'), C <: D and D <: C.By the induction hypothesis we have that for all CT_1, C', D' $\in CT_1$, if C' <: D' and D' <: C' then C' = D', whereCT ; n ; m ; p $\rightarrow CT_1$. Let L be a class such CT ; m ; p $\rightarrow L$. By Lemma 4, we have L OK in CT. By the induction hypothesis on $\varphi(L)$ L: CT; n; p $\rightarrow CT'$ and rule CT-Step we have the desired conclusion.

Lemma 6 (Soundness of class table generation). *Let* CT *be a well-formed class table. For all n, m and p, if* CT ; n ; m ; p $\rightarrow$ CT' *then* CT' *is a well-formed class table.*

Proof. By induction on n.

Case n = 0: We have that $CT' = CT$ and the conclusion follows.

Case n = n' + 1: By rule CT-Step we have that:

- CT ; m ; p $\rightarrow$ L
- $\varphi(L)$ L : CT ; n ; m ; p $\rightarrow CT'$

By Lemma 4, we have that L OK. By the induction hypothesis we have that CT' is a well-formed class table. By Lemma 5, we have that subtyping in CT' is antisymmetric. Conclusion follows by the definition of a well-formed class table.

Theorem 1 (Soundness of program generation). *For all n, m and p, if* • ; n ; m ; p $\rightarrow$ CT *then:*

(1) CT *is a well-formed class table.*
(2) *For all C* $\in$ CT, *we have C OK.*

Proof. Corollary of Lemmas 4, 5 and 6.

5   Quick-Checking Semantic Properties

As a proof of concept we have implemented an interpreter following the semantics of FJ and used random generated programs to test this interpreter against some properties[4], including those for type-soundness presented in the FJ original paper. The properties were specified and tested using QuickCheck [3]. Besides progress and preservation of the interpreter, we also used QuickCheck to verify if all generated class tables are well-formed, and also if all generated expressions are well-typed and cast-safe. Furthermore, our tests cases were generated into Java files, and compiled using the Oracle's standard 'javac' compiler (the closest implementation of Java Language Specification) to validate our generator algorithm. After compiling and running many thousands of well-succeeded tests, we

---

[4] More details about using QuickCheck for testing the semantic properties of FJ are in our technical report at: https://github.com/fjpub/fj-qc/raw/master/tr.pdf.

gain a high-degree of confidence in our type-directed procedure for generating programs.

As a way to measure the quality of the generated test cases, we used the Haskell Program Coverage tool [9] to check how much of the interpreter code base was covered by our test suite. Results of code coverage for each module (evaluator, type-checker, auxiliary functions, and total, respectively) are presented in Fig. 4.

Top Level Definitions		Alternatives		Expressions	
%	covered / total	%	covered / total	%	covered / total
100%	2/2	85%	18/21	92%	165/179
100%	3/3	52%	22/42	68%	163/237
100%	6/6	77%	27/35	91%	98/107
100%	11/11	68%	67/98	81%	426/523

Fig. 4. Test coverage results.

Although not having 100% of code coverage, the proposed generation algorithm was capable to verify the main safety properties present in FJ paper. After analyzing test coverage results, we could observe that code not reached by test cases consisted of error control when evaluating the semantics or when dealing with expressions that are not well-typed.

6 Related Work

Property-based testing is a technique for validating code against an executable specification by automatically generating test-data, typically in a random and/or exhaustive fashion [3]. However, the generation of random test-data for testing compilers represents a challenge by itself, since it is hard to come up with a generator of valid test data for compilers, and it is difficult to provide a specification that decides what should be the correct behavior of a compiler [18]. As a consequence of this, random testing for finding bugs in compilers and programming language tools received some attention in recent years.

The testing tool Csmith [23] is a generator of programs for language C, supporting a large number of language features, which was used to find a number of bugs in compilers such as GCC, LLVM, etc. Le et al. [14] developed a methodology that uses differential testing for C compilers. Lindig [15] created a tool for testing the C function calling convention of the GCC compiler, which randomly generates types of functions. There are also efforts to generate test cases for other languages [8]. All of these projects rely on informal approaches, while ours is described formally and applied to property-based testing.

More specifically, Daniel et al. [6], Soares et al. [21] and Mongiovi et al. [17] generate Java programs to test refactoring engines, some of them applied in Eclipse and NetBeans IDEs. Gligoric et al. [10] presented an approach for describing tests using non-deterministic test generation programs applying in the Java context. Klein et al. [13] generated random programs to test an object-oriented library. Silva, Sampaio and Mota [20] used program generation to verify transformations in Java programs. Allwood and Eisenbach [1] also used FJ as a basis to define a test suite for the mainstream programming language in question, testing how much of coverage their approach was capable to obtain. These projects are closely related to ours since they are generating code in the object-oriented context. The difference of our approach is that we generated randomly complete classes and expressions, and proved that both are well-formed and well-typed. Another difference is that we also used property-based testing to check that the properties of the FJ semantics hold by using the generated programs.

The work of Palka, Claessen and Hughes [18] also used the QuickCheck library in their work aiming to generate λ-terms to test the GHC compiler. Our approach was somewhat inspired by theirs, in the sense we also used QuickCheck and the typing rules for generating well-typed terms. Unlike their approach, we provided a standard small-step operational semantics to describe our generation algorithm.

7 Conclusion

In this work, we presented a syntax directed judgment for generating random type correct FJ programs, proving soundness with respect to FJ typing rules, and using property-based testing to verify it. The lightweight approach provided by QuickCheck allows to experiment with different semantic designs and implementations and to quickly check any changes. During the development of this work, we have changed our definitions many times, both as a result of correcting errors and streamlining the presentation. Ensuring that our changes were consistent was simply a matter of re-running the test suite. Encoding the type soundness properties as Haskell functions provides a clean and concise implementation that helps not only to fix bugs but also to improve understanding the meaning of the presented semantic properties.

As future work, we intend to use Coq to provide formally certified proofs for our generation procedure, as well as for the FJ semantics, showing that they do enjoy safety properties. We can also to explore the approach used in our test suite for other FJ extensions, besides using other tools like QuickChick (a random testing plug-in for Coq) with the same purpose.

References

1. Allwood, T.O.R., Eisenbach, S.: Tickling Java with a feather. Electron. Notes Theor. Comput. Sci. **238**(5), 3–16 (2009). http://dx.doi.org/10.1016/j.entcs.2009.09.037
2. Bazzichi, F., Spadafora, I.: An automatic generator for compiler testing. IEEE Trans. Softw. Eng. **4**, 343–353 (1982)
3. Blanco, R., Miller, D., Momigliano, A.: Property-based testing via proof reconstruction work-in-progress. In: LFMTP 17: Logical Frameworks and Meta-Languages: Theory and Practice (2017)

4. Celentano, A., Reghizzi, S.C., Vigna, P.D., Ghezzi, C., Granata, G., Savoretti, F.: Compiler testing using a sentence generator. Softw. Pract. Experience **10**(11), 897–918 (1980)
5. Claessen, K., Hughes, J.: QuickCheck: a lightweight tool for random testing of Haskell programs. In: Proceedings of the Fifth ACM SIGPLAN International Conference on Functional Programming, ICFP 2000, pp. 268–279 (2000). http://doi.acm.org/10.1145/351240.351266
6. Daniel, B., Dig, D., Garcia, K., Marinov, D.: Automated testing of refactoring engines. In: Proceedings of the the the 6th Joint Meeting of the European Software Engineering Conference and the ACM SIGSOFT Symposium on The Foundations of Software Engineering, ESEC-FSE 2007, pp. 185–194 (2007). http://doi.acm.org/10.1145/1287624.1287651
7. Debbabi, M., Fourati, M.: A formal type system for Java. J. Object Technol. **6**(8), 117–184 (2007)
8. Drienyovszky, D., Horpácsi, D., Thompson, S.: Quickchecking refactoring tools. In: Proceedings of the 9th ACM SIGPLAN Workshop on Erlang, Erlang 2010, pp. 75–80 (2010). http://doi.acm.org/10.1145/1863509.1863521
9. Gill, A., Runciman, C.: Haskell program coverage. In: Proceedings of the ACM SIGPLAN Workshop on Haskell Workshop, Haskell 2007, pp. 1–12 (2007). http://doi.acm.org/10.1145/1291201.1291203
10. Gligoric, M., Gvero, T., Jagannath, V., Khurshid, S., Kuncak, V., Marinov, D.: Test generation through programming in Udita. In: Proceedings of the 32nd ACM/IEEE International Conference on Software Engineering, vol. 1, pp. 225–234. ACM (2010)
11. Gosling, J., Joy, B., Steele, G., Bracha, G., Buckley, A.: The Java language specification, Java SE 8 edition (Java series) (2014)
12. Igarashi, A., Pierce, B.C., Wadler, P.: Featherweight Java: A minimal core calculus for Java and GJ. ACM Trans. Program. Lang. Syst. **23**(3), 396–450 (2001). http://doi.acm.org/10.1145/503502.503505
13. Klein, C., Flatt, M., Findler, R.B.: Random testing for higher-order, stateful programs. In: Proceedings of the ACM International Conference on Object Oriented Programming Systems Languages and Applications, OOPSLA 2010, pp. 555–566 (2010). http://doi.acm.org/10.1145/1869459.1869505
14. Le, V., Afshari, M., Su, Z.: Compiler validation via equivalence modulo inputs. SIGPLAN Not. **49**(6), 216–226 (2014). http://doi.acm.org/10.1145/2666356.2594334
15. Lindig, C.: Random testing of C calling conventions. In: Proceedings of the Sixth International Symposium on Automated Analysis-driven Debugging, AADEBUG 2005, pp. 3–12 (2005). http://doi.acm.org/10.1145/1085130.1085132
16. McBride, C.: Djinn, monotonic. In: PAR@ ITP, pp. 14–17 (2010)
17. Mongiovi, M., Mendes, G., Gheyi, R., Soares, G., Ribeiro, M.: Scaling testing of refactoring engines. In: 2014 IEEE International Conference on Software Maintenance and Evolution (ICSME), pp. 371–380. IEEE (2014)
18. Palka, M.H., Claessen, K., Russo, A., Hughes, J.: Testing an optimising compiler by generating random lambda terms. In: Proceedings of the 6th International Workshop on Automation of Software Test, AST 2011, pp. 91–97 (2011). http://doi.acm.org/10.1145/1982595.1982615
19. Pierce, B.C.: Types and Programming Languages, 1st edn. The MIT Press (2002)
20. da Silva, T.D., Sampaio, A., Mota, A.: Verifying transformations of java programs using alloy. In: Cornélio, M., Roscoe, B. (eds.) SBMF 2015. LNCS, vol. 9526, pp. 110–126. Springer, Cham (2016). https://doi.org/10.1007/978-3-319-29473-5_7
21. Soares, G., Gheyi, R., Massoni, T.: Automated behavioral testing of refactoring engines. IEEE Trans. Softw. Eng. **39**(2), 147–162 (2013)

22. tiobe.com: TIOBE Index, April 2018. https://www.tiobe.com/tiobe-index/. Accessed 09 Apr 2018
23. Yang, X., Chen, Y., Eide, E., Regehr, J.: Finding and understanding bugs in C compilers. SIGPLAN Not. **46**(6), 283–294 (2011). http://doi.acm.org/10.1145/ 1993316.1993532

Programming Language Foundations in Agda

Philip Wadler[(✉)]

University of Edinburgh, Edinburgh, UK
wadler@inf.ed.ac.uk

Abstract. One of the leading textbooks for formal methods is *Software Foundations* (SF), written by Benjamin Pierce in collaboration with others, and based on Coq. After five years using SF in the classroom, I have come to the conclusion that Coq is not the best vehicle for this purpose, as too much of the course needs to focus on learning tactics for proof derivation, to the cost of learning programming language theory. Accordingly, I have written a new textbook, *Programming Language Foundations in Agda* (PLFA). PLFA covers much of the same ground as SF, although it is not a slavish imitation.

What did I learn from writing PLFA? First, that it is possible. One might expect that without proof tactics that the proofs become too long, but in fact proofs in PLFA are about the same length as those in SF. Proofs in Coq require an interactive environment to be understood, while proofs in Agda can be read on the page. Second, that constructive proofs of preservation and progress give immediate rise to a prototype evaluator. This fact is obvious in retrospect but it is not exploited in SF (which instead provides a separate normalise tactic) nor can I find it in the literature. Third, that using raw terms with a separate typing relation is far less perspicuous than using inherently-typed terms. SF uses the former presentation, while PLFA presents both; the former uses about 1.6 as many lines of Agda code as the latter, roughly the golden ratio.

The textbook is written as a literate Agda script, and can be found here: http://plfa.inf.ed.ac.uk.

Keywords: Agda · Coq · Lambda calculus · Dependent types

1 Introduction

The most profound connection between logic and computation is a pun. The doctrine of Propositions as Types asserts that a certain kind of formal structure may be read in two ways: either as a proposition in logic or as a type in computing. Further, a related structure may be read as either the proof of the proposition or as a programme of the corresponding type. Further still, simplification of proofs corresponds to evaluation of programs.

Accordingly, the title of this paper, and the corresponding textbook, *Programming Language Foundations in Agda* (hence, PLFA) also has two readings. It may be parsed as "(Programming Language) Foundations in Agda" or

© Springer Nature Switzerland AG 2018
T. Massoni and M. R. Mousavi (Eds.): SBMF 2018, LNCS 11254, pp. 56–73, 2018.
https://doi.org/10.1007/978-3-030-03044-5_5

"Programming (Language Foundations) in Agda"—specifications in the proof assistant Agda both describe programming languages and are themselves programmes.

Since 2013, I have taught a course on Types and Semantics for Programming Languages to fourth-year undergraduates and masters students at the University of Edinburgh. An earlier version of that course was based on *Types and Programming Languages* by Pierce [2002], but my version was taught from its successor, *Software Foundations* (hence, SF) by Pierce et al. [2010], which is based on the proof assistance Coq (Huet et al. 1997). I am convinced by the claim of Pierce [2009], made in his ICFP Keynote *Lambda, The Ultimate TA*, that basing a course around a proof assistant aids learning.

However, after five years of experience, I have come to the conclusion that Coq is not the best vehicle. Too much of the course needs to focus on learning tactics for proof derivation, to the cost of learning the fundamentals of programming language theory. Every concept has to be learned twice: e.g., both the product data type, and the corresponding tactics for introduction and elimination of conjunctions. The rules Coq applies to generate induction hypotheses can sometimes seem mysterious. While the `notation` construct permits pleasingly flexible syntax, it can be confusing that the same concept must always be given two names, e.g., both `subst N x M` and N [x := M]. Names of tactics are sometimes short and sometimes long; naming conventions in the standard library can be wildly inconsistent. *Propositions as types* as a foundation of proof is present but hidden.

I found myself keen to recast the course in Agda (Bove et al. 2009). In Agda, there is no longer any need to learn about tactics: there is just dependently-typed programming, plain and simple. Introduction is always by a constructor, elimination is always by pattern matching. Induction is no longer a mysterious separate concept, but corresponds to the familiar notion of recursion. Mixfix syntax is flexible while using just one name for each concept, e.g., substitution is _[_:=_] . The standard library is not perfect, but there is a fair attempt at consistency. *Propositions as types* as a foundation of proof is on proud display.

Alas, there is no textbook for programming language theory in Agda. *Verified Functional Programming in Agda* by (Stump 2016) covers related ground, but focuses more on programming with dependent types than on the theory of programming languages.

The original goal was to simply adapt *Software Foundations*, maintaining the same text but transposing the code from Coq to Agda. But it quickly became clear to me that after five years in the classroom I had my own ideas about how to present the material. They say you should never write a book unless you cannot *not* write the book, and I soon found that this was a book I could not not write.

I am fortunate that my student, Wen Kokke, was keen to help. She guided me as a newbie to Agda and provided an infrastructure that is easy to use and produces pages that are a pleasure to view. The bulk of the book was written January–June 2018, while on sabbatical in Rio de Janeiro.

This paper is a personal reflection, summarising what I learned in the course of writing the textbook. Some of it reiterates advice that is well-known to some members of the dependently-typed programming community, but which deserves to be better known. The paper is organised as follows.

Section 2 outlines the topics covered in PLFA, and notes what is omitted.

Section 3 compares Agda and Coq as vehicles for pedagogy. Before writing the book, it was not obvious that it was even possible; conceivably, without tactics some of the proofs might balloon in size. In fact, it turns out that for the results in PLFA and SF, the proofs are of roughly comparable size, and (in my opinion) the proofs in PLFA are more readable and have a pleasing visual structure.

Section 4 observes that constructive proofs of progress and preservation combine trivially to produce a constructive evaluator for terms. This idea is obvious once you have seen it, yet I cannot find it described in the literature. For instance, SF separately implements a `normalise` tactic that has nothing to do with progress and preservation.

Section 5 claims that raw terms should be avoided in favour of inherently-typed terms. PLFA develops lambda calculus with both raw and inherently-typed terms, permitting a comparison. It turns out the former is less powerful—it supports substitution only for closed terms—but significantly longer—about 1.6 times as many lines of code, roughly the golden ratio.

I will argue that Agda has advantages over Coq for pedagogic purposes. My focus is purely on the case of a proof assistant as an aid to *learning* formal semantics using examples of *modest* size. I admit up front that there are many tasks for which Coq is better suited than Agda. A proof assistant that supports tactics, such as Coq or Isabelle, is essential for formalising serious mathematics, such as the Four-Colour Theorem (Gonthier 2008), the Odd-Order Theorem (Gonthier et al. 2013), or Kepler's Conjecture (Hales et al. 2017), or for establishing correctness of software at scale, as with the CompCert compiler (Kästner et al. 2017; Leroy 2009) or the SEL4 operating system (Klein et al. 2009; O'Connor et al. 2016).

2   Scope

PLFA is aimed at students in the last year of an undergraduate honours programme or the first year of a master or doctorate degree. It aims to teach the fundamentals of operational semantics of programming languages, with simply-typed lambda calculus as the central example. The textbook is written as a literate script in Agda. As with SF, the hope is that using a proof assistant will make the development more concrete and accessible to students, and give them rapid feedback to find and correct misaprehensions.

The book is broken into two parts. The first part, Logical Foundations, develops the needed formalisms. The second part, Programming Language Foundations, introduces basic methods of operational semantics. (SF is divided into books, the first two of which have the same names as the two parts of PLFA, and cover similar material.)

Each chapter has both a one-word name and a title, the one-word name being both its module name and its file name.

Part I, Logical Foundations

Naturals: Natural Numbers. Introduces the inductive definition of natural numbers in terms of zero and successor, and recursive definitions of addition, multiplication, and monus. Emphasis is put on how a tiny description can specify an infinite domain.

Induction: Proof by Induction. Introduces induction to prove properties such as associativity and commutativity of addition. Also introduces dependent functions to express universal quantification. Emphasis is put on the correspondence between induction and recursion.

Relations: Inductive Definitions of Relations. Introduces inductive definitions of less than or equal on natural numbers, and odd and even natural numbers. Proves properties such as reflexivity, transitivity, and anti-symmetry, and that the sum of two odd numbers is even. Emphasis is put on proof by induction over evidence that a relation holds.

Equality: Equality and Equational Reasoning. Gives Martin Löf's and Leibniz's definitions of equality, and proves them equivalent, and defines the notation for equational reasoning used throughout the book.

Isomorphism: Isomorphism and Embedding. Introduces isomorphism, which plays an important role in the subsequent development. Also introduces dependent records, lambda terms, and extensionality.

Connectives: Conjunction, Disjunction, and Implication. Introduces product, sum, unit, empty, and function types, and their interpretations as connectives of logic under Propositions as Types. Emphasis is put on the analogy between these types and product, sum, unit, zero, and exponential on naturals; e.g., product of numbers is commutative and product of types is commutative up to isomorphism.

Negation: Negation, with Intuitionistic and Classical Logic. Introduces logical negation as a function into the empty type, and explains the difference between classical and intuitionistic logic.

Quantifiers: Universals and Existentials. Recaps universal quantifiers and their correspondence to dependent functions, and introduces existential quantifiers and their correspondence to dependent products.

Decidable: Booleans and Decision Procedures. Introduces booleans and decidable types, and why the latter is to be preferred to the former.

Lists: Lists and Higher-order Functions. Gives two different definitions of reverse and proves them equivalent. Introduces map and fold and their properties, including that fold left and right are equivalent in a monoid. Introduces predicates that hold for all or any member of a list, with membership as a specialisation of the latter.

Part II, Programming Language Foundations

Lambda: Introduction to Lambda Calculus. Introduces lambda calculus, using a representation with named variables and a separate typing relation. The language used is PCF (Plotkin 1977), with variables, lambda abstraction, application, zero, successor, case over naturals, and fixpoint. Reduction is call-by-value and restricted to closed terms.

Properties: Progress and Preservation. Proves key properties of simply-typed lambda calculus, including progress and preservation. Progress and preservation are combined to yield an evaluator.

DeBruijn: Inherently Typed de Bruijn Representation. Introduces de Bruijn indices and the inherently-typed representation. Emphasis is put on the structural similarity between a term and its corresponding type derivation; in particular, de Bruijn indices correspond to the judgment that a variable is well-typed under a given environment.

More: More Constructs of Simply-Typed Lambda Calculus. Introduces product, sum, unit, and empty types as well as lists and let bindings are explained. Typing and reduction rules are given informally; a few are then give formally, and the rest are left as exercises for the reader. The inherently typed representation is used.

Bisimulation: Relating Reduction Systems. Shows how to translate the language with "let" terms to the language without, representing a let as an application of an abstraction, and shows how to relate the source and target languages with a bisimulation.

Inference: Bidirectional Type Inference. Introduces bidirectional type inference, and applies it to convert from a representation with named variables and a separate typing relation to a representation de Bruijn indices with inherent types. Bidirectional type inference is shown to be both sound and complete.

Untyped: Untyped Calculus with Full Normalisation. As a variation on earlier themes, discusses an untyped (but inherently scoped) lambda calculus. Reduction is call-by-name over open terms, with full normalisation (including reduction under lambda terms). Emphasis is put on the correspondence between the structure of a term and evidence that it is in normal form.

Discussion

PLFA and SF differ in several particulars. PLFA begins with a computationally complete language, PCF, while SF begins with a minimal language, simply-typed lambda calculus with booleans. PLFA does not include type annotations in terms, and uses bidirectional type inference, while SF has terms with unique types and uses type checking. SF also covers a simple imperative language with

Hoare logic, and for lambda calculus covers subtyping, record types, mutable references, and normalisation—none of which are treated by PLFA. PLFA covers an inherently-typed de Bruijn representation, bidirectional type inference, bisimulation, and an untyped call-by-name language with full normalisation—none of which are treated by SF.

SF has a third volume, written by Andrew Appel, on Verified Functional Algorithms. I'm not sufficiently familiar with that volume to have a view on whether it would be easy or hard to cover that material in Agda. And SF recently added a fourth volume on random testing of Coq specifications using QuickChick. There is currently no tool equivalent to QuickChick available for Agda.

There is more material that would be desirable to include in PLFA which was not due to limits of time. In future years, PLFA may be extended to cover additional material, including mutable references, normalisation, System F, pure type systems, and denotational semantics. I'd especially like to include pure type systems as they provide the readers with a formal model close to the dependent types used in the book. My attempts so far to formalise pure type systems have proved challenging, to say the least.

3   Proofs in Agda and Coq

The introduction listed several reasons for preferring Agda over Coq. But Coq tactics enable more compact proofs. Would it be possible for PLFA to cover the same material as SF, or would the proofs balloon to unmanageable size?

As an experiment, I first rewrote SF's development of simply-typed lambda calculus (SF, Chapters Stlc and StlcProp) in Agda. I was a newbie to Agda, and translating the entire development, sticking as closely as possible to the development in SF, took me about two days. I was pleased to discover that the proofs remained about the same size.

There was also a pleasing surprise regarding the structure of the proofs. While most proofs in both SF and PLFA are carried out by induction over the evidence that a term is well typed, in SF the central proof, that substitution preserves types, is carried out by induction on terms for a technical reason (the context is extended by a variable binding, and hence not sufficiently "generic" to work well with Coq's induction tactic). In Agda, I had no trouble formulating the same proof over evidence that the term is well typed, and didn't even notice SF's description of the issue until I was done.

The rest of the book was relatively easy to complete. The closest to an issue with proof size arose when proving that reduction is deterministic. There are 18 cases, one case per line. Ten of the cases deal with the situation where there are potentially two different reductions; each case is trivially shown to be impossible. Five of the ten cases are redundant, as they just involve switching the order of the arguments. I had to copy the cases suitably permuted. It would be preferable to reinvoke the proof on switched arguments, but this would not pass Agda's termination checker since swapping the arguments doesn't yield a recursive call on structurally smaller arguments. I suspect tactics could cut down the proof

Progress

We would like to show that every term is either a value or takes a reduction step. However, this is not true in general. The term

```
`zero · `suc `zero
```

is neither a value nor can take a reduction step. And if `s : `N → `N` then the term

```
s · `zero
```

cannot reduce because we do not know which function is bound to the free variable `s`. The first of those terms is ill-typed, and the second has a free variable. Every term that is well-typed and closed has the desired property.

Progress: If `∅ ⊢ M : A` then either `M` is a value or there is an `N` such that `M → N`.

To formulate this property, we first introduce a relation that captures what it means for a term `M` to make progess.

```
data Progress (M : Term) : Set where

  step : ∀ {N}
    → M → N
      -----------
    → Progress M

  done :
      Value M
      -----------
    → Progress M
```

A term `M` makes progress if either it can take a step, meaning there exists a term `N` such that `M → N`, or if it is done, meaning that `M` is a value.

Fig. 1. PLFA, Progress (1/2)

significantly. I tried to compare with SF's proof that reduction is deterministic, but failed to find that proof.

SF covers an imperative language with Hoare logic, culminating in code that takes an imperative programme suitably decorated with preconditions and post-conditions and generates the necessary verification conditions. The conditions are then verified by a custom tactic, where any questions of arithmetic are resolved by the "omega" tactic invoking a decision procedure. The entire exercise would be easy to repeat in Agda, save for the last step: I suspect Agda's automation would not be up to verifying the generated conditions, requiring tedious proofs by hand. However, I had already decided to omit Hoare logic in order to focus on lambda calculus.

To give a flavour of how the texts compare, I show the proof of progress for simply-typed lambda calculus from both texts. Figures 1 and 2 are taken from PLFA, Chapter Properties, while Figs. 3 and 4 are taken from SF, Chapter

If a term is well-typed in the empty context then it satisfies progress.

```
progress : ∀ {M A}
  → ∅ ⊢ M ⦂ A
    ----------
  → Progress M
progress (⊢` ())
progress (⊢ƛ ⊢N)                             =  done V-ƛ
progress (⊢L · ⊢M) with progress ⊢L
... | step L→L'                              =  step (ξ-·1 L→L')
... | done VL with progress ⊢M
...   | step M→M'                            =  step (ξ-·2 VL M→M')
...   | done VM with canonical ⊢L VL
...     | C-ƛ _                              =  step (β-ƛ VM)
progress ⊢zero                               =  done V-zero
progress (⊢suc ⊢M) with progress ⊢M
... | step M→M'                              =  step (ξ-suc M→M')
... | done VM                                =  done (V-suc VM)
progress (⊢case ⊢L ⊢M ⊢N) with progress ⊢L
... | step L→L'                              =  step (ξ-case L→L')
... | done VL with canonical ⊢L VL
...   | C-zero                               =  step β-zero
...   | C-suc CL                             =  step (β-suc (value CL))
progress (⊢μ ⊢M)                             =  step β-μ
```

We induct on the evidence that M is well-typed. Let's unpack the first three cases.

* The term cannot be a variable, since no variable is well typed in the empty context.

* If the term is a lambda abstraction then it is a value.

* If the term is an application L · M , recursively apply progress to the derivation that L is well-typed.

  ◦ If the term steps, we have evidence that L → L' , which by ξ-·1 means that our original term steps to L' · M

  ◦ If the term is done, we have evidence that L is a value. Recursively apply progress to the derivation that M is well-typed.

    ▪ If the term steps, we have evidence that M → M' , which by ξ-·2 means that our original term steps to L · M' . Step ξ-·2 applies only if we have evidence that L is a value, but progress on that subterm has already supplied the required evidence.

    ▪ If the term is done, we have evidence that M is a value. We apply the canonical forms lemma to the evidence that L is well typed and a value, which since we are in an application leads to the conclusion that L must be a lambda abstraction. We also have evidence that M is a value, so our original term steps by β-ƛ .

The remaining cases are similar. If by induction we have a step case we apply a ξ rule, and if we have a done case then either we have a value or apply a β rule. For fixpoint, no induction is required as the β rule applies immediately.

Fig. 2. PLFA, Progress (2/2)

Progress

The *progress* theorem tells us that closed, well-typed terms are not stuck: either a well-typed term is a value, or it can take a reduction step. The proof is a relatively straightforward extension of the progress proof we saw in the Types chapter. We'll give the proof in English first, then the formal version.

```
Theorem progress : ∀ t T,
  empty |- t ∈ T →
  value t ∨ ∃ t', t ==> t'.
```

Proof: By induction on the derivation of $|- t \in T$.

- The last rule of the derivation cannot be `T_Var`, since a variable is never well typed in an empty context.

- The `T_True`, `T_False`, and `T_Abs` cases are trivial, since in each of these cases we can see by inspecting the rule that t is a value.

- If the last rule of the derivation is `T_App`, then t has the form $t_1\ t_2$ for some t_1 and t_2, where $|- t_1 \in T_2 \to T$ and $|- t_2 \in T_2$ for some type T_2. By the induction hypothesis, either t_1 is a value or it can take a reduction step.

  - If t_1 is a value, then consider t_2, which by the other induction hypothesis must also either be a value or take a step.

    - Suppose t_2 is a value. Since t_1 is a value with an arrow type, it must be a lambda abstraction; hence $t_1\ t_2$ can take a step by `ST_AppAbs`.

    - Otherwise, t_2 can take a step, and hence so can $t_1\ t_2$ by `ST_App2`.

  - If t_1 can take a step, then so can $t_1\ t_2$ by `ST_App1`.

- If the last rule of the derivation is `T_If`, then t = if t_1 then t_2 else t_3, where t_1 has type `Bool`. By the IH, t_1 either is a value or takes a step.

  - If t_1 is a value, then since it has type `Bool` it must be either `true` or `false`. If it is `true`, then t steps to t_2; otherwise it steps to t_3.

  - Otherwise, t_1 takes a step, and therefore so does t (by `ST_If`).

Fig. 3. SF, Progress (1/2)

StlcProp. Both texts are intended to be read online, and the figures were taken by grabbing bitmaps of the text as displayed in a browser.

PLFA puts the formal statements first, followed by informal explanation. PLFA introduces an auxiliary relation `Progress` to capture progress; an exercise (not shown) asks the reader to show it isomorphic to the usual formulation with a disjunction and an existential. Layout is used to present the auxiliary relation in inference rule form. In Agda, any line beginning with two dashes is treated as a comment, making it easy to use a line of dashes to separate hypotheses from conclusion in inference rules. The proof of proposition `progress` (the different case making it a distinct name) is layed out carefully. The neat indented structure emphasises the case analysis, and all right-hand sides line-up in the same column. My hope as an author is that students will read the formal proof first, and use it as a tabular guide to the informal explanation that follows.

SF puts the informal explanation first, followed by the formal proof. The text hides the formal proof script under an icon; the figure shows what appears when

```
Proof with eauto.
  intros t T Ht.
  remember (@empty ty) as Gamma.
  induction Ht; subst Gamma...
  - (* T_Var *)
    (* contradictory: variables cannot be typed in an
       empty context *)
    inversion H.

  - (* T_App *)
    (* t = t₁ t₂.  Proceed by cases on whether t₁ is a
       value or steps... *)
    right. destruct IHHt1...
  + (* t₁ is a value *)
    destruct IHHt2...
    * (* t₂ is also a value *)
      assert (∃ x₀ t₀, t₁ = tabs x₀ T₁₁ t₀).
      eapply canonical_forms_fun; eauto.
      destruct H₁ as [x₀ [t₀ Heq]]. subst.
      ∃ ([x₀:=t₂]t₀)...

    * (* t₂ steps *)
      inversion H₀ as [t₂' Hstp]. ∃ (tapp t₁ t₂')...

  + (* t₁ steps *)
    inversion H as [t₁' Hstp]. ∃ (tapp t₁' t₂)...

  - (* T_If *)
    right. destruct IHHt1...

  + (* t₁ is a value *)
    destruct (canonical_forms_bool t₁); subst; eauto.

  + (* t₁ also steps *)
    inversion H as [t₁' Hstp]. ∃ (tif t₁' t₂ t₃)...
Qed.
```

Fig. 4. SF, Progress (2/2)

the icon is expanded. As a teacher I was aware that students might skip it on a first reading, and I would have to hope the students would return to it and step through it with an interactive tool in order to make it intelligible. I expect the students skipped over many such proofs. This particular proof forms the basis for a question of the mock exam and the past exams, so I expect most students will actually look at this one if not all the others.

(For those wanting more detail: In PLFA, variables and abstractions and applications in the object language are written ` x and λ x ⇒ N and L · M. The corresponding typing rules are referred to by ⊢` () and ⊢λ ⊢N and ⊢L · ⊢M, where ⊢L, ⊢M, ⊢N are the proofs that terms L, M, N are well typed, and '()' denotes that there cannot be evidence that a free variable is well typed in the empty context. It was decided to overload infix dot for readability, but not other symbols. In Agda, as in Lisp, almost any sequence of characters is a name, with spaces essential for separation.)

(In SF, variables and abstractions and applications in the object language are written `tvar x` and `tabs x t` and `tapp t`$_1$ `t`$_2$. The corresponding typing rules are referred to as T_Var and T_Abs and T_App.)

Both Coq and Agda support interactive proof. Interaction in Coq is supported by Proof General, based on Emacs, or by CoqIDE, which provides an interactive development environment of a sort familiar to most students. Interaction in Agda is supported by an Emacs mode.

In Coq, interaction consists of stepping through a proof script, at each point examining the current goal and the variables currently in scope, and executing a new command in the script. Tactics are a whole sublanguage, which must be learned in addition to the language for expressing specifications. There are many tactics one can invoke in the script at each point; one menu in CoqIDE lists about one hundred tactics one might invoke, some in alphabetic submenus. A Coq script presents the specification proved and the tactics executed. Interaction is recorded in a script, which the students may step through at their leisure. SF contains some prose descriptions of stepping through scripts, but mainly contains scripts that students are encouraged to step through on their own.

In Agda, interaction consists of writing code with holes, at each point examining the current goal and the variables in scope, and typing code or executing an Emacs command. The number of commands available is much smaller than with Coq, the most important ones being to show the type of the hole and the types of the variables in scope; to check the code; to do a case analysis on a given variable; or to guess how to fill in the hole with constructors or variables in scope. An Agda proof consists of typed code. The interaction is *not* recorded. Students may recreate it by commenting out bits of code and introducing a hole in their place. PLFA contains some prose descriptions of interactively building code, but mainly contains code that students can read. They may also introduce holes to interact with the code, but I expect this will be rarer than with SF.

SF encourages students to interact with all the scripts in the text. Trying to understand a Coq proof script without running it interactively is a bit like understanding a chess game by reading through the moves without benefit of a board, keeping it all in your head. In contrast, PLFA provides code that students can read. Understanding the code often requires working out the types, but (unlike executing a Coq proof script) this is often easy to do in your head; when it is not easy, students still have the option of interaction.

While students are keen to interact to create code, I have found they are reluctant to interact to understand code created by others. For this reason, I suspect this may make Agda a more suitable vehicle for teaching. Nate Foster suggests this hypothesis is ripe to be tested empirically, perhaps using techniques similar to those of Danas et al. [2017].

Neat layout of definitions such as that in Fig. 2 in Emacs requires a monospaced font supporting all the necessary characters. Securing one has proved tricky. As of this writing, we use FreeMono, but it lacks a few characters (⸢ and □) which are loaded from fonts with a different width. Long arrows are necessarily more than a single character wide. Instead, we compose reduction

$\longrightarrow$ from an em dash — and an arrow $\rightarrow$. Similarly for reflexive and transitive closure $\longrightarrow\!\!\!\!\rightarrow$.

4 Progress + Preservation = Evaluation

A standard approach to type soundness used by many texts, including SF and PLFA, is to prove progress and preservation, as first suggested by Wright and Felleisen [1994].

Theorem 1 (Progress). *Given term M and type A such that $\emptyset \vdash M : A$ then either M is a value or $M \longrightarrow N$ for some term N.*

Theorem 2 (Preservation). *Given terms M and N and type A such that $\emptyset \vdash M : A$ and $M \longrightarrow N$, then $\emptyset \vdash N : A$.*

A consequence is that when a term reduces to a value it retains the same type. Further, well-typed terms don't get stuck: that is, unable to reduce further but not yet reduced to a value. The formulation neatly accommodates the case of non-terminating reductions that never reach a value.

One useful by-product of the formal specification of a programming language may be a prototype implementation of that language. For instance, given a language specified by a reduction relation, such as lambda calculus, the prototype might accept a term and apply reductions to reduce it to a value. Typically, one might go to some extra work to create such a prototype. For instance, SF introduces a `normalize` tactic for this purpose. Some formal methods frameworks, such as Redex (Felleisen et al. 2009) and K (Roşu and Şerbănuţă 2010), advertise as one of their advantages that they can generate a prototype from descriptions of the reduction rules.

I was therefore surprised to realise that any constructive proof of progress and preservation *automatically* gives rise to such a prototype. The input is a term together with evidence the term is well-typed. (In the inherently-typed case, these are the same thing.) Progress determines whether we are done, or should take another step; preservation provides evidence that the new term is well-typed, so we may iterate. In a language with guaranteed termination, we cannot iterate forever, but there are a number of well-known techniques to address that issue; see, e.g., Bove and Capretta [2001], Capretta [2005], or McBride [2015]. We use the simplest, similar to McBride's *petrol-driven* (or *step-indexed*) semantics: provide a maximum number of steps to execute; if that number proves insufficient, the evaluator returns the term it reached, and one can resume execution by providing a new number.

Such an evaluator from PLFA is shown in Fig. 5, where (inspired by cryptocurrencies) the number of steps to execute is referred to as *gas*. All of the example reduction sequences in PLFA were computed by the evaluator and then edited to improve readability; in addition, the text includes examples of running the evaluator with its unedited output.

By analogy, we will use the name *gas* for the parameter which puts a bound on the number of reduction steps. Gas is specified by a natural number.

```
data Gas : Set where
  gas : N → Gas
```

When our evaluator returns a term `N`, it will either give evidence that `N` is a value or indicate that it ran out of gas.

```
data Finished (N : Term) : Set where

  done :
    Value N
    ----------
  → Finished N

  out-of-gas :
    ----------
    Finished N
```

Given a term `L` of type `A`, the evaluator will, for some `N`, return a reduction sequence from `L` to `N` and an indication of whether reduction finished.

```
data Steps (L : Term) : Set where

  steps : ∀ {N}
    → L —↠ N
    → Finished N
    ----------
    → Steps L
```

The evaluator takes gas and evidence that a term is well-typed, and returns the corresponding steps.

```
eval : ∀ {L A}
  → Gas
  → ∅ ⊢ L ⦂ A
    ----------
  → Steps L
eval {L} (gas zero)    ⊢L                                   = steps (L ∎) out-of-gas
eval {L} (gas (suc m)) ⊢L with progress ⊢L
... | done VL                                               = steps (L ∎) (done VL)
... | step L—→M with eval (gas m) (preserve ⊢L L—→M)
...     | steps M—↠N fin                                    = steps (L —→⟨ L—→M ⟩ M—↠N) fin
```

Fig. 5. PLFA, Evaluation

It is immediately obvious that progress and preservation make it trivial to construct a prototype evaluator, and yet I cannot find such an observation in the literature nor mentioned in an introductory text. It does not appear in SF, nor in Harper [2016]. A plea to the Agda mailing list failed to turn up any prior mentions. The closest related observation I have seen in the published literature is that evaluators can be extracted from proofs of normalisation (Berger 1993; Dagand and Scherer 2015).

(Late addition: My plea to the Agda list eventually bore fruit. Oleg Kiselyov directed me to unpublished remarks on his web page where he uses the name eval for a proof of progress and notes "the very proof of type soundness can be used to evaluate sample expressions" (Kiselyov 2009).)

5 Inherent Typing Is Golden

The second part of PLFA first discusses two different approaches to modelling simply-typed lambda calculus. It first presents raw terms with named variables and a separate typing relation and then shifts to inherently-typed terms with de Bruijn indices. Before writing the text, I had thought the two approaches complementary, with no clear winner. Now I am convinced that the inherently-typed approach is superior.

Figure 6 presents the raw approach. It first defines Id, Term, Type, and Context, the abstract syntax of identifiers, raw terms, types, and contexts. It then defines two judgements, $\Gamma \ni x : A$ and $\Gamma \vdash M : A$, which hold when under context Γ the variable x and the term M have type A, respectively.

Figure 7 presents the inherent approach. It first defines Type and Context, the abstract syntax of types and contexts, of which the first is as before and the second is as before with identifiers dropped. In place of the two judgements, the types of variables and terms are indexed by a context and a type, so that $\Gamma \ni A$ and $\Gamma \vdash A$ denote variables and terms, respectively, that under context Γ hae type A. The indexed types closely resemble the previous judgements: we now represent a variable or a term by the proof that it is well-typed. In particular, the proof that a variable is well-typed in the raw approach corresponds to a de Bruijn index in the inherent approach.

The raw approach requires more lines of code than the inherent approach. The separate definition of raw terms is not needed in the inherent approach; and one judgement in the raw approach needs to check that $x \not\equiv y$, while the corresponding judgement in the inherent approach does not. The difference becomes more pronounced when including the code for substitution, reductions, and proofs of progress and preservation. In particular, where the raw approach requires one first define substitution and reduction and then prove they preserve types, the inherent approach establishes substitution at the same time it defines substitution and reduction.

Stripping out examples and any proofs that appear in one but not the other (but could have appeared in both), the full development in PLFA for the raw approach takes 451 lines (216 lines of definitions and 235 lines for the proofs) and the development for the inherent approach takes 275 lines (with definitions and proofs interleaved). We have $451/235 = 1.64$, close to the golden ratio.

The inherent approach also has more expressive power. The raw approach is restricted to substitution of one variable by a closed term, while the inherent approach supports simultaneous substitution of all variables by open terms, using a pleasing formulation due to McBride [2005], inspired by Goguen and McKinna [1997], Altenkirch and Reus [1999] and described in Allais et al. [2017]. In fact,

```
Id : Set
Id = String

data Term : Set where
  `_    : Id → Term
  λ_⇒_  : Id → Term → Term
  _·_   : Term → Term → Term

data Type : Set where
  _⇒_   : Type → Type → Type
  `ℕ    : Type

data Context : Set where
  ∅     : Context
  _,_⦂_ : Context → Id → Type → Context

data _∋_⦂_ : Context → Id → Type → Set where

  Z : ∀ {Γ x A}
      ------------------
    → Γ , x ⦂ A ∋ x ⦂ A

  S : ∀ {Γ x y A B}
    → x ≢ y
    → Γ ∋ x ⦂ A
      ------------------
    → Γ , y ⦂ B ∋ x ⦂ A

data _⊢_⦂_ : Context → Term → Type → Set where

  ⊢` : ∀ {Γ x A}
    → Γ ∋ x ⦂ A
      --------------
    → Γ ⊢ ` x ⦂ A

  ⊢λ : ∀ {Γ x N A B}
    → Γ , x ⦂ A ⊢ N ⦂ B
      ---------------------
    → Γ ⊢ λ x ⇒ N ⦂ A ⇒ B

  _·_ : ∀ {Γ L M A B}
    → Γ ⊢ L ⦂ A ⇒ B
    → Γ ⊢ M ⦂ A
      --------------
    → Γ ⊢ L · M ⦂ B
```

Fig. 6. Raw approach in PLFA

I did manage to write a variant of the raw approach with simultaneous open substitution along the lines of McBride, but the result was too complex for use in an introductory text, requiring 695 lines of code—more than the total for the other two approaches combined.

The text develops both approaches because the raw approach is more familiar, and because placing the inherent approach first would lead to a steep

```
data Type : Set where
  _⇒_ : Type → Type → Type
  `ℕ  : Type

data Context : Set where
  ∅   : Context
  _,_ : Context → Type → Context

data _∋_ : Context → Type → Set where

  Z : ∀ {Γ A}
      ---------
    → Γ , A ∋ A

  S_ : ∀ {Γ A B}
    → Γ ∋ A
      ---------
    → Γ , B ∋ A

data _⊢_ : Context → Type → Set where

  `_ : ∀ {Γ} {A}
    → Γ ∋ A
      -------
    → Γ ⊢ A

  ƛ_ : ∀ {Γ} {A B}
    → Γ , A ⊢ B
      ---------
    → Γ ⊢ A ⇒ B

  _·_ : ∀ {Γ} {A B}
    → Γ ⊢ A ⇒ B
    → Γ ⊢ A
      ---------
    → Γ ⊢ B
```

Fig. 7. Inherent approach in PLFA

learning curve. By presenting the more long-winded but less powerful approach first, students can see for themselves the advantages of de Bruijn indices and inherent types.

There are actually four possible designs, as the choice of named variables vs de Bruijn indices, and the choice of raw vs inherently-typed terms may be made independently. There are synergies between the two. Manipulation of de Bruijn indices can be notoriously error-prone without inherent-typing to give assurance of correctness. In inherent typing with named variables, simultaneous substitution by open terms remains difficult.

The benefits of the inherent approach are well known to some. The technique was introduced by Altenkirch and Reus [1999], and widely used elsewhere, notably by Chapman [2009] and Allais et al. [2017]. I'm grateful to David Darais for bringing it to my attention.

6   Conclusion

I look forward to experience teaching from the new text, and encourage others to use it too. Please comment!

Acknowledgement. A special thank you to my coauthor, Wen Kokke. For inventing ideas on which PLFA is based, and for hand-holding, many thanks to Conor McBride, James McKinna, Ulf Norell, and Andreas Abel. For showing me how much more compact it is to avoid raw terms, thanks to David Darais. For inspiring my work by writing SF, thanks to Benjamin Pierce and his coauthors. For comments on a draft of this paper, an extra thank you to James McKinna, Ulf Norell, Andreas Abel, and Benjamin Pierce. This research was supported by EPSRC Programme Grant EP/K034413/1.

References

Allais, G., Chapman, J., McBride, C., McKinna, J.: Type-and-scope safe programs and their proofs. In: Proceedings of the 6th ACM SIGPLAN Conference on Certified Programs and Proofs, pp. 195–207. ACM (2017)

Altenkirch, T., Reus, B.: Monadic presentations of lambda terms using generalized inductive types. In: Flum, J., Rodriguez-Artalejo, M. (eds.) CSL 1999. LNCS, vol. 1683, pp. 453–468. Springer, Heidelberg (1999). https://doi.org/10.1007/3-540-48168-0_32

Berger, U.: Program extraction from normalization proofs. In: Bezem, M., Groote, J.F. (eds.) TLCA 1993. LNCS, vol. 664, pp. 91–106. Springer, Heidelberg (1993). https://doi.org/10.1007/BFb0037100

Bove, A., Capretta, V.: Nested general recursion and partiality in type theory. In: Boulton, R.J., Jackson, P.B. (eds.) TPHOLs 2001. LNCS, vol. 2152, pp. 121–125. Springer, Heidelberg (2001). https://doi.org/10.1007/3-540-44755-5_10

Bove, A., Dybjer, P., Norell, U.: A brief overview of agda – a functional language with dependent types. In: Berghofer, S., Nipkow, T., Urban, C., Wenzel, M. (eds.) TPHOLs 2009. LNCS, vol. 5674, pp. 73–78. Springer, Heidelberg (2009). https://doi.org/10.1007/978-3-642-03359-9_6

Capretta, V.: General recursion via coinductive types. Log. Methods Comput. Sci. **1**(2:1), 1–28 (2005)

Chapman, J.M.: Type checking and normalisation. PhD thesis, University of Nottingham (2009)

Dagand, P.-É., Scherer, G.: Normalization by realizability also evaluates. In: Vingt-sixièmes Journées Francophones des Langages Applicatifs (JFLA 2015) (2015)

Danas, N., Nelson, T., Harrison, L., Krishnamurthi, S., Dougherty, D.J.: User studies of principled model finder output. In: Cimatti, A., Sirjani, M. (eds.) SEFM 2017. LNCS, vol. 10469, pp. 168–184. Springer, Cham (2017). https://doi.org/10.1007/978-3-319-66197-1_11

Felleisen, M., Findler, R.B., Flatt, M.: Semantics engineering with PLT Redex. By Press (2009)

Goguen, H., McKinna, J.: Candidates for substitution. Technical report, Laboratory for Foundations of Computer Science, University of Edinburgh (1997)

Gonthier, G.: The four colour theorem: engineering of a formal proof. In: Kapur, D. (ed.) ASCM 2007. LNCS (LNAI), vol. 5081, pp. 333–333. Springer, Heidelberg (2008). https://doi.org/10.1007/978-3-540-87827-8_28

Gonthier, G., et al.: A machine-checked proof of the odd order theorem. In: Blazy, S., Paulin-Mohring, C., Pichardie, D. (eds.) ITP 2013. LNCS, vol. 7998, pp. 163–179. Springer, Heidelberg (2013). https://doi.org/10.1007/978-3-642-39634-2_14

Hales, T., et al.: A formal proof of the Kepler conjecture. In: Forum of Mathematics, Pi, vol. 5. Cambridge University Press (2017)

Harper, R.: Practical Foundations for Programming Languages. Cambridge University Press (2016)

Huet, G., Kahn, G., Paulin-Mohring, C.: The Coq proof assistant a tutorial. Rapport Technique, 178 (1997)

Kästner, D., Leroy, X., Blazy, S., Schommer, B., Schmidt, M., Ferdinand, C.: Closing the gap-the formally verified optimizing compiler compcert. In: SSS 2017: Safety-critical Systems Symposium 2017, pp. 163–180. CreateSpace (2017)

Kiselyov, O.: Formalizing languages, mechanizing type-soundess and other meta-theoretic proofs (2009, unpublished manuscript). http://okmij.org/ftp/formalizations/index.html

Klein, G., et al.: sel4: formal verification of an OS kernel. In: Proceedings of the ACM SIGOPS 22nd Symposium on Operating Systems Principles, pp. 207–220. ACM (2009)

Leroy, X.: Formal verification of a realistic compiler. Commun. ACM 52(7), 107–115 (2009)

McBride, C.: Type-preserving renaming and substitution (2005, unpublished manuscript). https://personal.cis.strath.ac.uk/conor.mcbride/ren-sub.pdf

McBride, C.: Turing-completeness totally free. In: Hinze, R., Voigtländer, J. (eds.) MPC 2015. LNCS, vol. 9129, pp. 257–275. Springer, Cham (2015). https://doi.org/10.1007/978-3-319-19797-5_13

O'Connor, L., et al.: Refinement through restraint: Bringing down the cost of verification. In: ICFP, pp. 89–102 (2016)

Pierce, B.C.: Types and Programming Languages. MIT press (2002)

Pierce, B.C.: Lambda, the ultimate TA. In: ICFP, pp. 121–122 (2009)

Pierce, B.C.: Software foundations (2010). http://www.cis.upenn.edu/bcpierce/sf/current/index.html

Plotkin, G.D.: LCF considered as a programming language. Theoret. Comput. Sci. 5(3), 223–255 (1977)

Roşu, G., Şerbănuţă, T.F.: An overview of the K semantic framework. J. Log. Algebr. Program. 79(6), 397–434 (2010)

Stump, A.: Verified Functional Programming in Agda. Morgan & Claypool (2016)

Wright, A.K., Felleisen, M.: A syntactic approach to type soundness. Inf. Comput. 115(1), 38–94 (1994)

Formal Verification of n-bit ALU Using Theorem Proving

Sumayya Shiraz and Osman Hasan[⊠]

School of Electrical Engineering and Computer Science,
National University of Sciences and Technology (NUST), Islamabad, Pakistan
{sumayya.shiraz,osman.hasan}@seecs.nust.edu.pk

Abstract. Automatic verification techniques, like automated theorem proving and model checking, cannot analyze large circuits due to the heavy requirements of memory and computational power. On the other hand, we can verify generic circuits, with universally quantified variables, using interactive theorem provers and thus overcome the above-mentioned limitations but at the cost of significant user guidance in the proof process. To facilitate this process and thus reduce the user involvement in the proofs, we recently proposed a higher-order-logic formalization of all the commonly used combinational circuits, like basic gates, adders, multiplier, multiplexers, demultiplexers, decoders and encoders, using the HOL4 theorem prover. In this project's paper, we describe this formally verified library and illustrate its utilization by verifying an n-bit arithmetic logic unit (ALU).

1 Introduction

Verification of digital designs is of utmost importance due to their extensive usage in safety-critical domains, such as health and transportation, where the cost of an undetected system bug is quite high. Traditionally, digital designs are verified using simulation, which ascertains the correctness of the design by observing the behavior of the circuit under a subset of all possible inputs only. Formal verification [15] is an accurate alternative to simulation that overcomes its limitations by proving or disproving the correctness of the given design against its desired properties mathematically. The main principle behind formal analysis of a digital circuit is to construct a computer-based mathematical model of the given circuit and formally verify, within a computer, that this model meets rigorous specifications of intended behavior. Thus, the engineer working with a formal methods-based verification tool has to develop a formal model of the given circuit and the formal specification of the desired properties. Moreover, she may be involved in the verification task as well.

There are some formal verification tools, mainly based on model checking [10] and automated theorem proving techniques [14], that accept Verilog models [2] and automatically translate them to the corresponding formal models and also automatically verify the relationship between the formal model and its corresponding specification. Thus, the verification engineer has to be involved in the

T. Massoni and M. R. Mousavi (Eds.): SBMF 2018, LNCS 11254, pp. 74–89, 2018.
https://doi.org/10.1007/978-3-030-03044-5_6

formal specification of the properties only. These kind of tools, such as FormalPro by Mentor Graphics, Conformal by Cadence, Synopsys Hector, Calypto's SLEC and Formality by Synopsys, are quite well-suited for the industrial setting and are thus widely accepted by the industry as well. However, model checking is generally limited to sequential circuits and also suffers from the well-known state-space explosion problem. Similarly, automated theorem provers cannot cope with the verification problems of large designs as well, due to an exponential increase in computations with an increase in the number of variables and intermediate nodes. Interactive theorem provers [14], using the expressive higher-order logic, can overcome these shortcomings but at the cost of explicit user involvement. The verification engineer needs to manually construct a logical model of the system and then verify the desired properties while guiding the theorem proving tool. This could be a very rigorous process and the user needs to be an expert in both system design and theorem proving skills. This drawback limits the usage of higher-order-logic theorem proving in the mainstream hardware industry where the engineers prefer to have push-button type tools.

To minimize the user involvement in using an interactive theorem prover for the verification of combinational circuits, we recently proposed a library of combinational circuits [27], consisting of formally verified generic circuits of commonly used components, such as various implementations of n-bit Adders, n-bit multiplier, n:1 Multiplexers, 1:n Demultiplexers, $n:2^n$ Decoders, $2^n:n$ Encoders and n-bit logic gates. The verification of these generic components was done interactively but the availability of this library greatly facilitates the verification of more complex designs. The user of the proposed approach has to just provide the structure of the combinational circuit to be verified in terms of its sub-components, based on the existing components in the proposed library, and its desired behavior in the language supported by the HOL4 theorem prover. The relationship between the structural view and the behavior of the given circuit can then be verified using the library of formally verified generic circuits in a very straightforward manner.

In this project's paper, we describe all the main components of this library [27] and illustrate its effectiveness in formally verifying generic circuits by formally verifying an n-bit arithmetic logic unit (ALU) with very minimal user interaction. The main motivation of this paper is to illustrate the utilization of our formally verified library [27] in verifying more complex combination circuits. We have used the HOL4 theorem prover for this work, mainly because the existing library of formal combinational components [27] has been developed in HOL4.

2 Related Work

The first-order-logic theorem prover ACL2 has been used to verify different hardware designs, including register-transfer level (RTL) models of floating-point hardware [8] and pipeline machines using first-order quantification [24]. Similarly, a framework is proposed for the mechanized certification of secure hardware systems using ACL2 [23]. However, these verifications are done for specific operand widths of the components. In order to alleviate this problem, ACL2 has been used in conjunction with symbolic simulation for verifying hardware [11] and VIA nano microprocessor components [32]. However, using symbolic simulation compromises the completeness of the analysis and thus accuracy. Similarly, ACL2 has also been used with IBM's SixthSense model checker [16,17] to develop a hybrid verification framework for digital hardware. But the scalability of this technique is a major concern since the state transition checks grow exponentially for large circuits and thus the automatic verification capability is compromised.

Interactive theorem provers, using higher-order logic, can overcome the limited expressiveness problem of ACL2. Thus, PVS has been used for the verification of some large designs, including some FPGA designs [9] and the floating point unit used in the VAMP processor [3], which supports addition, subtraction, multiplication, division, comparison, and conversions. Similarly, a hardware verification tool, called PROVERIFIC [28], allows Property Specification Language (PSL) assertions to be used with PVS. All the above-mentioned works require detailed user guidance in the proof process. Moreover, these formalizations are dedicated towards a particular circuit and are thus not generic.

The PVS theorem prover has been used along with decision procedures and BDD-based propositional simplification to automatically verify combinational circuits [7]. However, this proof strategy tackles each circuit verification from scratch whereas our approach is modular as we utilize the formally verified models of commonly used combinational circuits to verify more complex circuits. This kind of modularity makes the verification approach more scalable. A library of basic circuits is also implemented and verified in PVS [4] that is quite similar to the one presented in this paper. However, this work is just focused towards the verification of microprocessor designs. Secondly, the formalization and verification details of the components, reported in this work, are not openly available. Thus, our idea is mainly inspired from this work but we have developed recursive definitions for all the commonly used combinational circuits and have formally verified them using the HOL4 theorem prover [27]. To the best of our knowledge, these kinds of generic recursive definitions of combinational circuits have never been presented and used to verify more complex combinational circuits in the literature before.

The Coq theorem prover is based on the Calculus of (Co)Inductive Constructions (CiC) and features dependent types, which are quite helpful in creating reliable circuit models as errors can be caught earlier by type checking [5]. Braibant [5] created a library in Coq to facilitate modeling and verifying hardware circuits. Although dependent types, available in this library, are helpful in creating reliable definitions, the library still requires the user to guide the proof tools, which somewhat limits the scope of this work for industrial usage. A step-by-step procedure for the formal verification of a multiplier in CiC is given in [22]. But this work also requires extensive user interaction for verifying new designs and is specific for one example only.

The HOL theorem prover has been used for the verification of the SPW Datastrobe (DS) encoding [21] and multiway decision graphs (MDG) components library [6]. Both of these works are application specific. A hardware platform for a gate level electronic control unit has been implemented and interactively verified in HOL [31]. Similarly, the HOL Light theorem prover has been used for the verification of floating-point algorithms for division, square root and transcendental functions [13]. However, the verification does not involve the gate level implementations and requires significant user interaction.

Many hybrid techniques, based on the idea of exploiting the strengths of interactive theorem proving and automatic verification tools, have been developed as well. The HOL theorem prover has been integrated with MDG for hardware verification [19]. Similarly, the Pipelined Double-Precision IEEE Floating-Point Multiplier is verified by the Voss hardware verification system using a combination of theorem proving and model checking [1]. The Floating point divider unit of an Intel IA-32 microprocessor [18] and large-scale industrial trials on data-path-dominated hardware [25] are formally verified using the Forte framework, which uses the ThmTac theorem-prover and the symbolic trajectory model checker. However, the verification in the Forte framework requires significant user interaction and thus is not very easy to work with. The Isabelle/HOL theorem prover has been used along with the nuSMV model checker and SAT solvers for verifying some basic combinational circuits and the simple sequential DLX processor at the gate level [30]. However, all these works are focused on one or a subset of combinational circuits. Similarly, due to their hybrid nature, they also suffer from the state-space explosion problem.

Based on the above-mentioned review, it is observed that all of the interactive theorem proving-based verification approaches for combinational logic circuits require the formalization of the circuit to be verified from scratch and require considerable user guidance during the proof process. In order to alleviate these issues, a library of formally verified commonly used combinational circuits is created [27]. The definitions of these formally verified combinational circuits can be readily built upon to formalize almost any other combinational circuit. Moreover, the formally verified expressions of the combinational circuits in this library allow us to verify proof goals of any other combinational circuit in a very straightforward manner involving simple rewriting steps. It is important to note that the development of the library involved human guidance and interactive reasoning but, once developed, this library greatly facilitates the formalization and verification process for more complex combinational circuits. The effectiveness of the library can be estimated with the help of formal verification of generic n-bit ALU, verified in this paper, which is done with minimal user involvement.

3 Formal Verification of Generic Combinational Circuits

This section gives a brief introduction to the formally verified generic library [27] of the commonly used combinational components. This formalization, mainly inspired by the seminal work on digital circuit verification done at the University of Cambridge, UK [12], is the core component for verifying generic combinational circuits. The main idea is to model generic (arbitrary-input) circuit diagrams (implementations) of combinational circuits in a recursive manner, as shown in Fig. 1, by using the logical sub-components of the given circuit and their interconnections. The inputs and outputs of these circuits are modelled as lists of booleans to allow generic definitions. We have used the big endian format for representing these lists of booleans, i.e., 4 bit input data list a is represented as [a4;a3;a2;a1], with a4 being the most-significant bit. The primary inputs and outputs of these definitions are universally quantified while the internal connection points, hidden from the external world, are introduced using existential quantifiers. The behavior, or specifications, of these combinational circuits is represented in terms of their desired input-output relationships. The relationships between the implementations and their corresponding specifications are then verified using induction on the input variables within the sound core of a theorem prover. Any combinational circuit using the formally verified components of this library can then be verified by simply using the above-mentioned formally verified relationships with a very minimal user interaction.

Now, we explain the formally verified components of our library one by one.

3.1 Logic Gates

All of the primitive logic gates i.e., NOT, AND, NAND, OR, XOR, NOR and XNOR, are formally defined in the library [27]. All of these definitions, except the inverter, are generic and thus can be used to model the respective gate with any number of inputs.

3.2 Multiplexer

The n:1 Multiplexer (Mux) [20] passes the signal of any one of the n input data lines to the one bit output line depending upon the $\log_2 n$ input select lines. Figure 1(a) provides the recursive implementation of a generic n:1 Mux, where n is the width of data input lines a, k is the width of select input lines s and b is a boolean output signal. The relation between the width of select and data input lines can be specified by the equation $k = \log_2 n$, or in other words $n = 2^k$. The primitive 2:1 Mux can be implemented using basic logic gates [26]. The n:1 mux is formally verified in Theorem 1, where implementation and specification for n:1 mux is formally defined [27] as mux_imp_n a s b and mux_spec_n a s b respectively.

Theorem 1. $\vdash \forall$a s b.$(\neg$(s = []) $\land$ (LENGTH a = 2 EXP LENGTH s))
$\qquad\qquad \Rightarrow$ (mux_imp_n a s b = mux_spec_n a s b)

where assumptions ensure that at least one select line is required to ensure a valid MUX, and define the relationship between the input data and select lines. Verification of Theorem 1 is primarily based on induction on variable s. The proof script for the formal reasoning about Theorem 1 consists of about 400 lines of HOL code [26].

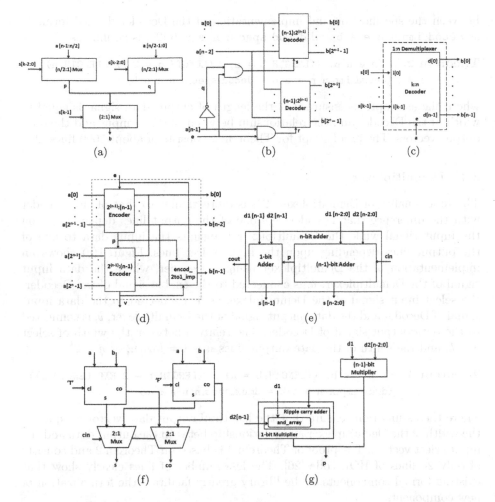

Fig. 1. Recursive Implementations (a) n:1 Mux (b) n:2^n Decoder (c) 1:n Demultiplexer (d) 2^n:n Encoder (e) n-bit Adder (f) 1-bit Carry Select Adder (g) n-bit Multiplier

3.3 Decoder

The recursive implementation of a $n : 2^n$ Decoder [20], shown in Fig. 1(b), is implemented using using two $(n-1) : 2^{(n-1)}$ Decoders having input of tail of the data input line, i.e., $a[n-2:0]$. Head of the data input line, i.e., $a[n-1]$, in conjunction with a global enable input e enables either of the two Decoders, which then sets the bits of the output signal depending upon the binary number represented by the input data vector. Here n is the width of the output data line and is used for the recursive implementation of the circuit. The relationship between the specification and implementation of the Decoder defined formally as decod_imp_n n e a b and decod_spec_n n e a b [27] is verified as:

Theorem 2. ⊢ ∀n e a b. ((LENGTH b = n) ∧ (LENGTH b = 2 EXP LENGTH a))
                    ⇒ (decod_imp_n n e a b = decod_spec_n n e a b)

where the assumptions ensure that the length of output data signal is equal to width of the Decoder and the relationship between the data input and the data output vectors. The proof script for Theorem 2 consists of about 1000 lines [26].

3.4   Demultiplexer

The functionality of Demultiplexer [20] is quite similar to that of the Decoder with the difference that Decoder sets one of the output lines depending upon the input signal while the Demultiplexer transmits the input data to one of the output lines depending upon the input select lines. Figure 1(c) shows an implementation of the Demultiplexer using a Decoder, where the data input signal of the Demultiplexer, a, is connected to the enable signal of the Decoder, the select input signal of the Demultiplexer, s, is connected to the data input signal of Decoder and the data output signal of the Demultiplexer, b, is connected to the data output signal of Decoder. The relation between the width of select line k, and the width of the data output lines n is $k = \log_2 n$, or $n = 2^k$.

Theorem 3. ⊢ ∀ n a s b. ((LENGTH b = n) ∧ (LENGTH b = 2 EXP LENGTH s))
                    ⇒ (dmux_imp_n n a s b = dmux_spec_n n a s b)

where the assumptions ensure that the length of output data vector is equal to the width of the Demultiplexer and relationship between the output data and the input select vectors. The proof of Theorem 3 is based on Theorem 2 and consists of only 20 lines of HOL code [26]. The less number of lines clearly show that existing formal components of the library greatly facilitate the formalization of new components.

3.5   Encoder

The Encoder [20] generates a binary output code for one bit of input True at a time. There are two discrepancies that may happen with the Encoders, i.e., the output behavior is non-deterministic in the case when more than one input bits are True at a time or all input bits are zero. Priority Encoder [20] resolves these issues, by encoding output on the basis of priority and by using a valid output bit, respectively. Figure 1(d) presents a recursive implementation of a $2^n : n$ Priority Encoder, using two $2^{n-1} : (n-1)$ Encoders, which encodes on the basis of the highest priority of the input signal, i.e., all other bits of the input data signal are ignored if the most significant bit of the data input signal is True. Where n specifies the width of the output data signal b, e is the enable input signal of the Encoder, p is connected with the valid output signal of the first Encoder and is used to enable the second Encoder, when the top half of the input data vector contains all False elements, v is the valid output signal, which indicates the validity of the encoded output data signal, and the function `encod_2to1_imp` computes the head of the output data signal using NOT, AND gates and a 2:1 Mux [26]. The relationship between the specification and implementation of the Encoder formally defined as `encod_spec_n n e a b v` and `encod_imp_n n e a b v` [27], is formally verified in HOL as following theorem.

Theorem 4. ⊢ ∀ n e a b v. (LENGTH a = 2 EXP LENGTH b) ∧ (LENGTH b = n)
⇒ (encod_imp_n n e a b v = encod_spec_n n e a b v)

where the assumptions ensure that the length of output data vector is equal to the width of the Encoder and relationship between the input data and the output data vectors. The proof script of Theorem 4 consists of about 900 lines of HOL code [26].

3.6 Ripple Carry Adder

A recursive implementation of n-bit Ripple Carry Adder [20] is shown in Fig. 1(e), where *d1* and *d2* are the two data input vectors which are required to be added, *cin* is the boolean carry input, *cout* is the boolean carry output and *s* is the sum output vector of the adder. One bit adder is implemented using the basic logic gates, i.e., XOR, AND and OR gates [26]. Using 1-bit adder, the structure of the n-bit adder can be formalized as `adder_imp_n n d1 d2` [27]. The variable of recursion n specifies the width of the adder. The behavior can be formalized as `adder_spec_n n d1 d2 cin` [27]. The relationship between the implementation and specification is proved as a theorem, where the assumptions ensure that the lengths of both input vectors is equal to width of the adder. The proof script consists of about 2000 lines [26].

Theorem 5. ⊢ ∀ n d1 d2 cin. (LENGTH d1 = n) ∧ (LENGTH d2 = n) ⇒
(xadder_imp n d1 d2 cin = adder_spec_n n d1 d2 cin)

3.7 Carry Select Adder

The formalization of the Carry Select Adder [20] is quite similar to that of the Ripple Carry Adder since both share the same recursive implementation, shown in Fig. 1(e). The main difference is the implementation of the 1-bit adder, which is implemented using a Mux and full adder as shown in Fig. 1(f). The idea is to obtain the addition for 1-bit data using two full adders working in parallel for both cases of the carry input, i.e., 'T' and 'F'. The final values for sum and carry-out are chosen based on the input value of carry using a Mux. The formal definitions and theorems of the implementation and specification of the n-bit Carry Select Adder are almost same as for the Ripple Carry Adder. The proof script for the formal reasoning consists of about 200 lines of HOL code [26].

3.8 Multiplier

The recursive implementation of a n-bit Multiplier [20] is shown in Fig. 1(g), where each bit of the multiplicand, *d2*, is multiplied one-by-one with the multiplier *d1*, making partial products, which are then added using a Ripple Carry Adder. The 1-bit Multiplier is implemented using a Ripple Carry Adder and arrays of AND gates and_array [26]. Implementation and specification of n-bit multiplier formalized as mult_imp d1 d2 and mult_spec d1 d2 [27] are formally verified as following theorem

Theorem 6. $\vdash \forall$ d1 d2. mult_imp d1 d2 = mult_spec_n d1 d2

The proof script for Theorem 6 consists of about 2000 lines of HOL code [26].

The main advantage of the results presented in this section, i.e., the formal verification of the universally quantified theorems for the correctness of generic combinational circuits with arbitrary inputs, is the ability to use them for verifying a wide range of combinational circuits in a very straightforward manner. This benefit is attained at the cost of extensive user-effort spent in guiding the HOL theorem prover for verifying these theorems. The formalization, presented in this section, took around 7000 lines of HOL code and approximately 12 man-months [27]. These lines and effort include a number of general list and arithmetic theory proofs that are built upon to reason about Theorems 1 to 6. A significant amount of time was also spent on identifying the generic implementations of the common combinational circuits that can be expressed recursively as well.

4 Formal Verification of n-bit ALU

In this section, we use the library of formally verified combinational circuits, described in the previous section, to formally verify an n-bit arithmetic logic unit (ALU), shown in Fig. 2(a). It takes three n-bit inputs, *a*, *b* and *c*, which can be optionally inverted depending upon the signals *nega*, *negb* and *negc*. These signals along with other enable signals, *enab* and *enc*, generate different outputs of the ALU: $a.b$, $-a.b$, $a.b+c$, $a.b-c$, $-a.b+c$, $-a.b-c$, etc. This ALU has been recently formally verified for operand widths ranging form 4 to 256 bits taking 0.01 to 34.66 s [33]. We extend this work by formally verifying this ALU design for n-bit operands.

The first step is the formalization of the implementation of the given circuit, which can be defined using the pre-verified components of the library as follows:

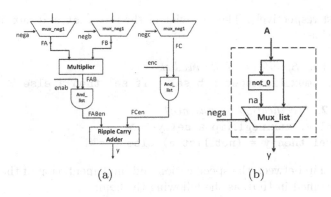

Fig. 2. Implementations (a) n-bit ALU (b) `mux_neg1_imp`

```
∀ n a b c nega negb negc enab enc y co. alu n a b c nega
negb negc enab enc y co = ∃  FA FB FC FAB FABen FCen.
mux_neg1_imp a nega FA  ∧ mux_neg1_imp b negb FB
∧ mux_neg1_imp c negc FC   ∧ mult_imp_n FA FB FAB
∧ and_list_imp FAB enab FABen  ∧ and_list_imp FC
enc FCen  ∧ Adder_imp_n (n + n) FABen (make_list_F n   ++
FCen) F y co
```

Where, the variable n represents the operand widths for variables a, b and c and co denote the carry out signal. The function `Adder_imp_n` and `mult_imp_n` are the formally verified ripple carry adder and multiplier of the generic library, respectively. The function `mux_neg1_imp` represents a combination of a multiplexer and a not gate, shown in Fig. 2(b), such that it allows to select between a given arbitrary-width input and its inverted signal depending upon the select signal *nega*. The implementation and specification of mux_neg1 is formally defined below:

Definition 1. *Implementation of mux_neg1*
    ⊢ ∀ a sel y. mux_neg1_imp a sel y <=>
            mux_list_imp (not_list a) a sel y

Definition 1a. *Implementation of mux_list*
⊢ ∀ a b sel.(mux_list_0 [] b sel= []) ∧(mux_list_0 (h::t) b sel =
        mux_0_imp h (HD b) sel::mux_list_0 t (TL b) sel)
⊢ ∀ a b sel y. mux_list_imp a b sel y = (y = mux_list_0 a b sel)

where `not_list` returns the list by inverting all of its input data elements, the expression `mux_0_imp` is 2:1 mux, defined as `nand (nand in2 (not sel))` `(nand sel in1)` and the HOL function `HD` and `TL` returns the head and tail of the input list respectively. The behavior of the `mux_list` and `mux_neg1` is formally defined as:

Definition 1b. *Specification of mux_list*
⊢ ∀ a b sel. mux_list_spec a b sel = if sel then a else b

Definition 2. *Specification of mux_neg1*
  ⊢ ∀ a sel y. mux_neg1_imp a sel y<=>
      if sel then y = (not_list a) else y = a

The relationship between the specification and implementation of the mux_neg1 is formally verified in HOL as the following theorem:

Theorem 7. *Formal Verification of mux_neg1*
  ⊢ ∀ a b sel y. (mux_neg1_imp a b sel y <=> mux_neg1_spec a b sel y)

Similarly, the component `and_list` is used for either transferring the input data list or list of all false elements. The implementation and specification of this component is formally defined below:

Definition 3. *Implementation of and_list*
  ⊢ ∀ a b sel. (and_list_0 [] en = []) ∧
  (and_list_0 (h::t) en = (and [h;en]::(and_list_0 t en)))
  ⊢ ∀ a en out. and_list_imp a en out = (out = and_list_0 a en)

where the function **and** recursively performs the logical and between all the elements of a boolean list [27] and the function **and_list_0** models a series of AND gates for performing the logical conjunction of a single bit signal *en* with all elements of input list *a* individually. The function **and_list_imp** represents an and_list component in the predicate form.

Definition 4. *Specification of and_list*
  ⊢ ∀ a en. and_list_spec a en = if (en) then a
          else make_list_F (LENGTH a)`;

where the expression (`make_list_F n`) returns a list of *n* false elements [26]. The relationship between the specification and implementation of the and_list is formally verified as:

Theorem 8. *Formal Verification of and_list*
  ⊢ ∀ a en. (and_list_0 a en <=> and_list_spec a en)

The behaviour of the ALU is formally defined by carrying the binary subtraction using the 1's complement of the desired input, i.e., BV_n *(not_list a)*, where **BV_n** converts its argument boolean list into a number [27].

```
(if (enab) then
if (enc) then
if (~nega /\ ~negb /\ ~negc) then
(co::y) = (num_BV_f(SUC (n + n))((BV_n a* BV_n b)+BV_n c))
else if (~nega /\ ~negb /\ negc) then
(co::y)=(num_BV_f(SUC (n + n))((BV_n a*BV_n b)+(BV_n (not_list c))))
else if (~nega /\ negb /\ ~negc) then
(co::y)=(num_BV_f(SUC (n + n))((BV_n a*(BV_n (not_list b)))+BV_n c))
else if (~nega /\ negb /\ negc) then
(co::y) = (num_BV_f(SUC (n + n))
((BV_n a*(BV_n (not_list b)))+(BV_n (not_list c))))
else if (nega /\ ~negb /\ ~negc) then
(co::y)=(num_BV_f(SUC (n + n))(((BV_n (not_list a))*BV_n b)+BV_n c))
else if (nega /\ ~negb /\ negc) then
(co::y) = (num_BV_f(SUC (n + n))
(((BV_n (not_list a))*BV_n b)+(BV_n (not_list c))))
else if (nega /\ negb /\ ~negc) then
(co::y) =  (num_BV_f(SUC (n + n))
(((BV_n (not_list a))*(BV_n (not_list b)))+BV_n c))
else
(co::y) = (num_BV_f (SUC (n + n))
(((BV_n (not_list a))*(BV_n (not_list b))) + (BV_n (not_list c))))
else
if (~nega /\ ~negb) then ((co::y)  = (num_BV_f (SUC (n + n))
(BV_n a * BV_n b)))
else if (~nega /\ negb) then ((co::y)  = (num_BV_f (SUC (n + n))
(BV_n a * (BV_n (not_list b)))))
else if (nega /\ ~negb) then ((co::y)  = (num_BV_f (SUC (n + n))
((BV_n (not_list a)) * BV_n b)))
else ((co::y)  = (num_BV_f (SUC (n + n))
((BV_n (not_list a))*(BV_n (not_list b)))))
else
if (~enc /\ ~negc) then ((co::y)  = (F::make_list_F (n+n)))
else if (~enc /\ negc) then ((co::y)  = (F::make_list_F (n+n)))
else if (enc /\ ~negc) then ((co::y)  =
(num_BV_f (SUC (n + n)) (BV_n c)))
else ((co::y)  = (num_BV_f (SUC (n + n)) (BV_n (not_list c)))))
```

where num_BV_f converts a number into a list with n booleans [27] and the expression SUC n represents the successor of the variable n. The equivalence between the formal implementation and specification of the given circuit is verified as the following theorem.

Theorem 9. *Formal Verification of n-bit ALU*

⊢ ∀ n a b c nega negb negc enab enc y co.
 (LENGTH a = n) ∧ (LENGTH b = n) ∧ (LENGTH c = n) ∧ n > 0 ⇒
  (ALU_n_imp n a b c nega negb negc enab enc y co <=>
  ALU_n_spec n a b c nega negb negc enab enc y co)

where the assumptions ensure that the length of all input data vectors is equal
to the width of the ALU and that should be greater than zero. The proof script
of Theorem 9 is very straightforward and its first part is given below:

```
e (REPEAT STRIP_TAC THEN RW_TAC bool_ss [ALU_n_spec] THEN
RW_TAC std_ss[ALU_n_imp,AND_LIST_THM,and_list_spec,
and_list_imp,mult_imp_n,MULT_N_THM,mult_spec_n,
mux_neg1_thm,mux_neg1_spec,make_list_F,not_0,
LENGTH,Adder_imp_n,ADDER_RIPPLE_N,Adder_spec_n,
BV_n_make_list_F_a,LENGTH_make_list_F,
LENGTH_APPEND,BV,LENGTH_num_BV_f,
LENGTH_not_0,BV_n_make_list_F]);
```

The verification process mainly involves rewriting with the already verified
theorems in a very straightforward manner involving very little user interaction.
The first step is the removal of universal quantifiers using STRIP_TAC. This is
followed by rewriting with the specification definition using RW_TAC bool_ss,
which produces 16 subgoals depending upon the conditional statements used
in the specification of the circuit. The verification of these 16 subgoals is not
shown above due to space limitations but it involves simple rewriting with all
definitions and theorems for the components of library used in the given subgoal using (RW_TAC std_ss). So we merely had to plug-in the definitions of the
specifications and the names of the definitions and theorems for the components
used in the subgoal to be verified in the rewriting tactics. The proof script is
around 800 lines long and required about a couple of hours of development tme.
Hence, use of the library of formally verified components made the verification
process almost automatic, i.e., with very minimal user interaction. Moreover, it
is important to note that based on this formally verified equivalence theorem
with universally quantified input variables, we are able to verify corresponding equivalence relationships for any width size by appropriately instantiating
Theorem 9, which clearly indicates the strength of the proposed methodology in
verifying combinational circuits.

5   Conclusions

In this paper, we have presented our efforts in developing a framework for the
formal verification of generic combinational circuits using a higher-order-logic
theorem prover HOL4 while minimizing the user interactive efforts. The main
idea is to develop a higher-order-logic library of all commonly used combinational circuits that includes their generic circuit implementations, their generic

specifications and the proof of their equivalences. Since, these formalizations are done for arbitrary n-bit circuits so they can be used in turn to formalize and verify other n-bit combinational circuits. In this paper, we used this methodology to verify an n-bit ALU and the user effort in proof guidance was found to be very little. Moreover, the user did not need to have an extensive knowledge of theorem proving for using this library. This ALU is now part of our library and can be further used to verify more complex blocks.

The proposed work opens the door to many interesting future directions of research. The formally verified library of circuits needs to be enhanced and advanced components like, Wallace Tree, Booth multipliers and components of floating-point arithmetic units may be added. More case studies for evaluation purposes are also underway. As long term goals, we plan to integrate a model checker with the proposed methodology to verify both combinational and sequential circuits within the same framework. Our work can also be combined with the recently proposed theorem proving-based analog circuit verification approach [29] to form a theorem proving-based Analog and Mixed Signal (AMS) circuit analysis framework.

Acknowledgement. This work was supported by the National Research Program for Universities grant (number 1543) of Higher Education Commission (HEC), Pakistan.

References

1. Aagaard, M.D., Seger, C.J.H.: The formal verification of a pipelined double-precision IEEE floating-point multiplier. In IEEE/ACM International Conference on Computer-Aided Design, pp. 7–10. IEEE Computer Society (1995)
2. Andraus, Z.S., Sakallah, K.A.: Automatic abstraction and verification of verilog models. In: Design Automation Conference, pp. 218–223. ACM (2004)
3. Berg, C., Jacobi, C.: Formal verification of the VAMP floating point unit. In: Margaria, T., Melham, T. (eds.) CHARME 2001. LNCS, vol. 2144, pp. 325–339. Springer, Heidelberg (2001). https://doi.org/10.1007/3-540-44798-9_26
4. Berg, C., Jacobi, C., Kroening, D.: Formal verification of a basic circuits library. In: IASTED International Conference on Applied Informatics. ACTA Press (2001)
5. Braibant, T.: Coquet: a Coq library for verifying hardware. In: Jouannaud, J.-P., Shao, Z. (eds.) CPP 2011. LNCS, vol. 7086, pp. 330–345. Springer, Heidelberg (2011). https://doi.org/10.1007/978-3-642-25379-9_24
6. Curzon, P., Tahar, S., Ait-Mohamed, O.: Verification of the MDG components library in HOL. In: Theorem Proving in Higher-Order Logics: Emerging Trends, pp. 31–46 (1998)
7. Cyrluk, D., Rajan, S., Shankar, N., Srivas, M.K.: Effective theorem proving for hardware verification. In: Theorem Provers in Circuit Design - Theory, Practice and Experience, Second International Conference, TPCD 1994, Bad Herrenalb, Germany, pp. 203–222 (1994)
8. Russinoff, D., Kaufmann, M., Smith, E., Sumners, R.: Formal Verification of floating-point RTL at AMD using the ACL2 theorem prover. In: IMACS World Congress: Scientific Computation, Applied Mathematics and Simulation (2005)
9. Deng, H.: Formal verification of FPGA based systems. MS Thesis. McMaster University, Canada (2011)

10. Clarke, E.M., Grumberg, O., Peled, D.: Model Checking. MIT press (1999)
11. Sammane, G.Al., Schmaltz, J., Toma, D., Ostier, P., Borrione, D.: TheoSim: combining Symbolic Simulation and Theorem Proving for Hardware Verification. In: Integrated Circuits and System Design, pp. 60–65. ACM (2004)
12. Camilleri, A., Gordon, M., Melham, T.F.: Hardware verification using Higher-order Logic. Technical report IUCAM-CL-TR-91, Computer Laboratory, University of Cambridge, Cambridge, UK (1986). www.cl.cam.ac.uk/techreports/UCAM-CL-TR-91.pdf
13. Harrison, J.: Formal verification at Intel. In: Logic in Computer Science, pp. 45–54. IEEE Computer Society (2003)
14. Harrison, J.: Handbook of Practical Logic and Automated Reasoning. Cambridge University Press (2009)
15. Hasan, O., Tahar, S.: Formal Verification Methods. Encyclopedia of Information Science and Technology, IGI Global, pp. 7162–7170 (2015)
16. Sawada, J., Reeber, E.: ACL2SIX: a hint used to integrate a theorem prover and an automated verification tool. In: Formal Methods in Computer Aided Design, pp. 161–170. IEEE (2006)
17. Sawada, J., Sandon, P., Paruthi, V., Baumgartner, J., Case, M., Mony, H.: Hybrid verification of a hardware modular reduction engine. In: Formal Methods, Computer-Aided Design, pp. 207–214 (2011)
18. Kaivola, R., Aagaard, M.D.: Divider circuit verification with model checking and theorem proving. In: Aagaard, M., Harrison, J. (eds.) TPHOLs 2000. LNCS, vol. 1869, pp. 338–355. Springer, Heidelberg (2000). https://doi.org/10.1007/3-540-44659-1_21
19. Kort, S., Tahar, S., Curzon, P.: Hierarchical formal verification using a hybrid tool. Softw. Tools Technol. Transfer 4(3), 313–322 (2003)
20. Lala, P.K.: Principles of Modern Digital Design. Wiley (2007)
21. Li, L., Liu, L., Guan, Y., Zhang, Y., Zhang, J., Tao, L.: A formal method for verifying the implementation of SPW data-strobe-encoding by applying theorem proving. In: SpaceWire Test and Verification, pp. 247–253 (2010)
22. Paulin-Mohring, C.: Circuits as streams in Coq: verification of a sequential multiplier. In: Berardi, S., Coppo, M. (eds.) TYPES 1995. LNCS, vol. 1158, pp. 216–230. Springer, Heidelberg (1996). https://doi.org/10.1007/3-540-61780-9_72
23. Ray, S., Hunt, W.A.: Mechanized certification of secure hardware designs. In: Microprocessor Test and Verification Common Challenges and Solutions. IEEE Computer Society (2007)
24. Ray, S., Hunt, W.A.: Deductive verification of pipelined machines using first-order quantification. In: Alur, R., Peled, D.A. (eds.) CAV 2004. LNCS, vol. 3114, pp. 31–43. Springer, Heidelberg (2004). https://doi.org/10.1007/978-3-540-27813-9_3
25. Seger, C.-J.H.: An industrially effective environment for formal hardware verification. IEEE Trans. Comput. Aided Design Integr. Circ. Syst. 24(9), 1381–1405 (2005)
26. Shiraz, S.: Automatic formal verification of generic combinational circuits (2018). http://save.seecs.nust.edu.pk/projects/HLHV
27. Shiraz, S., Hasan, O.: A HOL library for hardware verification using theorem proving. IEEE Trans. Comput. Aided Design Integr. Circ. Syst. 37(2), 512–516 (2018)
28. Sule, P., Kim, Y., Mansouri, N.: PROVERIFIC: experiments in employing (PSL) standard assertions in theorem-proving-based verification. In: Midwest Symposium on Circuits and Systems, pp. 112–115 (2005)

29. Taqdees, S.H., Hasan, O.: Formalization of laplace transform using the multivariable calculus theory of HOL-light. In: McMillan, K., Middeldorp, A., Voronkov, A. (eds.) LPAR 2013. LNCS, vol. 8312, pp. 744–758. Springer, Heidelberg (2013). https://doi.org/10.1007/978-3-642-45221-5_50
30. Tverdyshev, S.: Combination of Isabelle/HOL with automatic tools. In: Gramlich, B. (ed.) FroCoS 2005. LNCS (LNAI), vol. 3717, pp. 302–309. Springer, Heidelberg (2005). https://doi.org/10.1007/11559306_18
31. Tverdyshev, S.: A verified platform for a gate-level electronic control unit. In: Formal Methods in Computer-Aided Design, pp. 164–171. IEEE (2009)
32. Hunt Jr., W.A.: Verifying via nano microprocessor components. In: Formal Methods in Computer-Aided Design, pp. 3–10 (2010)
33. Yu, C., Brown, W., Ciesielski,M.: Verification of arithmetic datapath designs using word-level approach: a case study. In: Circuits and Systems, pp. 1862–1865 (2015)

The Scallina Grammar
Towards a Scala Extraction for Coq

Youssef El Bakouny$^{(\boxtimes)}$ (iD) and Dani Mezher

CIMTI, ESIB - Saint-Joseph University, Beirut, Lebanon
{Youssef.Bakouny,Dany.Mezher}@usj.edu.lb

Abstract. In response to the challenges associated with a Coq-based extraction of readable and traceable Scala code, the Scallina project defines a grammar delimiting a common subset of Gallina and Scala along with an optimized translation strategy for programs conforming to the aforementioned grammar. The Scallina translator shows how these contributions can be transferred into a working prototype. A typical application features a user implementing a functional program in Gallina, the core language of Coq, proving this program's correctness with regards to its specification and making use of Scallina to synthesize readable Scala components.

Keywords: Functional programming · Code generation · Coq · Scala

1 Introduction

Coq [16] and Isabelle/HOL [18] are currently two of the world's leading proof assistants; they enable users to implement a program, prove its correctness with regards to its specification and extract a verified implementation[1] expressed in a given functional programming language. Coq has been successfully used to implement CompCert, the world's first formally verified C compiler [12]; whereas Isabelle/HOL has been successfully used to implement seL4, the world's first formally verified general-purpose operating system kernel [10]. The languages that are currently supported by Coq's extraction mechanism are OCaml, Haskell and Scheme [15], while the ones that are currently supported by Isabelle/HOL's extraction mechanism are OCaml, Haskell, SML and Scala [7].

The code generation capabilities of these proof assistants enable the synthesis of verified programs. However, they do not fully address the verification needs of existing software programs[2]. This need is covered by other initiatives such as Leon [3,11], Why3 [4] and Sireum Logika[3]. Leon and Logika allow the automatic

---

[1] An implementation extracted from a program which is proven-correct in a proof assistant can be considered correct when one *assumes* that the proof assistant itself and its corresponding extraction mechanism are correct.

[2] Unless these programs are rewritten from scratch and manually proven using the proof assistant.

[3] http://logika.sireum.org.

© Springer Nature Switzerland AG 2018
T. Massoni and M. R. Mousavi (Eds.): SBMF 2018, LNCS 11254, pp. 90–108, 2018.
https://doi.org/10.1007/978-3-030-03044-5_7

verification of Scala programs. Leon can also resort to Isabelle/HOL machine-checked proofs when its automatic verification mechanism fails to give a timely answer. Similarly, Why3 allows the automatic verification of OCaml programs with the option of resorting to Coq on failure.

The Scala programming language [20] is considerably adopted in the industry. It is the implementation language of many important frameworks, including Apache Spark, Kafka, and Akka. It also provides the core infrastructure for sites such as Twitter, Coursera and Tumblr. A distinguishing feature of this language is its practical fusion of the functional and object-oriented programming paradigms. Its type system is, in fact, formalized by the calculus of Dependent Object Types (DOT) which is largely based on path-dependent types [1]; a limited form of dependent types where types can depend on variables, but not on general terms.

The Coq proof assistant, on the other hand, is based on the calculus of inductive constructions; a Pure Type System (PTS) which provides fully dependent types, i.e. types depending on general terms [5]. This means that Gallina, the core language of Coq, allows the implementation of programs that are not typable in conventional programming languages. A notable difference with these languages is that Gallina does not exhibit any syntactic distinction between terms and types [16].

To cope with the challenge of extracting programs written in Gallina to languages based on the Hindley-Milner [8,17] type system such as OCaml and Haskell[4], Coq's native extraction mechanism implements a theoretical function that identifies and collapses Gallina's logical parts and types; producing untyped λ-terms with inductive constructions that are then translated to the designated target ML-like language, i.e. OCaml or Haskell. During this translation process, a type-checking phase approximates Coq types into ML ones, inserting unsafe type casts where ML type errors are identified [14]. For example, these unsafe type casts are currently inserted when extracting Gallina records with path-dependent types. However, as mentioned in Sect. 3.2 of [15], this specific case can be improved by exploring advanced typing aspects of the target languages. Indeed, if Scala were a target language for Coq's extraction mechanism, a type-safe extraction of such examples could be done by an appropriate use of Scala's path-dependent types.

It is precisely this Scala code extraction feature for Coq that constitutes the primary aim of the Scallina project. Given the advances in both the Scala programming language and the Coq proof assistant, such a feature would prove both interesting and beneficial for both communities. A typical application features a user implementing a functional program in Coq, proving this program's correctness with regards to its specification and making use of Scallina to synthesize Scala components which can then be integrated into larger Scala or Java applications. In fact, since Scala is also interoperable with Java, such a feature would open the door for a significantly larger community of programmers to benefit from the Coq proof assistant.

---

[4] Scheme will not be considered in this paper since it is not statically typed.

However, Scala's type system, which is based on DOT, significantly differs from that of OCaml and Haskell. For instance, Scala sacrifices Hindley-Milner type inference for a richer type system with remarkable support for subtyping and path-dependent types [1]. So, on the one hand, Scala's type system requires the generation of significantly more type information but, on the other hand, can type-check some constructs that are not typable in OCaml and Haskell.

Furthermore, Coq's native extraction mechanism aims to produce readable code; keeping in mind that confidence in programs also comes via the readability of their sources, as demonstrated by the Open Source community. For this purpose, Coq's extraction sticks, as much as possible, to a straightforward translation and emphasizes the production of readable interfaces with the goal of facilitating the integration of the extracted code into larger developments [13]. Scallina also aims to produce readable code; adopting a straightforward translation strategy which favors the synthesis of idiomatic Scala code that is traceable back to the source Gallina code representing its formal specification. This traceability of the generated Scala code clarifies and facilitates potential adaptations of the corresponding formal specification to the needs of the larger Scala or Java application.

In response to the challenges associated with a Coq-based extraction of readable and traceable Scala code, the Scallina project defines a grammar delimiting a common subset of Gallina and Scala; facilitating the reasoning about the fragment of Gallina that is translatable to readable Scala code using a relatively straightforward translation strategy. This subset is based on an ML-like fragment that includes both inductive types and a polymorphism similar to the one found in Hindley-Milner type systems. This fragment was then augmented by introducing the support of Gallina records, which correspond to first-class modules. In this extended fragment, the support of Gallina dependent types is limited to path-dependent types; enabling types to depend on variables, but not on general terms [1].

This paper exposes the Scallina grammar in an incremental fashion. Through the same notation system as Coq's reference manual [16], it elaborates each part of the delimited Gallina subset by providing the corresponding grammar productions followed by pertinent examples of Gallina to Scala translations; illustrating the validity of the underlying translation strategy. This exposition of the Scallina grammar is organized into two main parts: the syntax of terms described in Sect. 2 and the syntax of sentences described in Sect. 3. The Scala code samples exhibited in this paper were all synthesized by an experimental implementation of the Scallina translator which is available online[5]. This prototype facilitates the incremental and iterative development of the Scallina grammar by providing a practical way to test different experimental translation strategies. It also shows how our contributions can be successfully transferred into a working tool.

---

[5] https://github.com/JBakouny/Scallina/tree/v0.5.0.

2   The Syntax of Terms

Since Gallina is based on the calculus of inductive constructions, it does not exhibit any syntactic distinction between terms and types[6] [16]; implying that the syntax of terms in its grammar is used to represent both value and type terms. This contrasts with conventional typed programming languages where a clear distinction is drawn between type terms and value terms. When it comes to its translation to Scala, a given Gallina term should therefore be processed differently depending on whether or not it is a type. For example, a term application "x y" should be translated as a Scala function application "x (y)" if it represents a value or as a Scala generic type application "x [y]" if it represents a type. This difference is reflected in the Scallina grammar which, in contrast with the unrestricted Gallina grammar, distinguishes the syntax of value terms, portrayed in Sect. 2.1, from the syntax of type terms, portrayed in Sect. 2.2.

2.1   Value Terms

The syntax of value terms is given below. Each of the depicted productions is detailed thereafter; demonstrating the expressiveness of the supported subset along with its straightforward Scala translation strategy.

```
term      ::= anonymousFunction
       |     letInDefs
       |     ifExpression
       |     termApplication
       |     infixOperation
       |     patternMatch
       |     recordProjection
       |     qualid
       |     num
       |     tuple
       |     parens
```

Qualids. Qualids, or qualified identifiers, are the simplest form of values. Most qualids are therefore translated using the identity function.

```
qualid    ::=   ident
       | qualid .  ident
```

Shallow Embedding. The few qualids that are not translated using the identity function pertain to Coq library entities which are identified with the corresponding Scala standard library equivalents. For example, a reference to the Gallina list monad is translated to its equivalent Scala standard library List class. This is known as shallow embedding; a concept heavily used by Isabelle's code

---

[6] Except that types cannot start by an abstraction or a constructor.

generation mechanism [6] and Leon's Isabelle extension [9]. Although shallow embedding does carry the risk of semantic mismatches, it has the advantage of improving the reusability of the generated Scala code; facilitating its integration into larger applications. Indeed, a synthesized Scala component which reuses Scala's standard library List class can integrate better with conventional applications when compared with a Scala component that uses a Coq-generated Scala list class.

As of this writing, Coq's extraction mechanism does not use shallow embedding by default but provides Extract commands enabling a user-defined customization of Coq's extraction that allows the mapping of Gallina constants and inductives to target language equivalents. However, this implies that the user is trusted with the relatively error-prone task of correctly identifying Coq library entities with target language equivalents. Instead, Scallina proposes shallow embedding by default similarly to what is done by Isabelle's code generation mechanism; improving both the reusability and the correctness of the synthesized Scala code. This feature could easily be integrated in future versions of Coq's extraction mechanism as an additional flag representing a sensible default which can be set or unset depending on the user's preferences. In such a case, the user would not have to configure the shallow embedding of Gallina entities manually but would just set a flag in Coq's extraction mechanism triggering a pre-configured shallow embedding for each target language. When it comes to the Scala language, this pre-configured shallow embedding is already implemented into the Scallina prototype.

Practically, to cope with the name differences between Gallina and Scala, the Scallina prototype provides a set of predefined name aliases constituting a central part of the Scallina standard library; a dependency which should be included when compiling the synthesized Scala code. For example, when mapping Gallina list functions to Scala list methods, Scallina provides Scala list functions matching the names of the corresponding Coq functions while delegating their work to the appropriate Scala standard library method. An example of such a Scala function is given in Listing 1, it portrays the list append function. In addition to conserving the traceability of the output code, this approach conforms with Coq's Extract commands which generate such aliases. Future versions of Scallina are, in fact, expected to be integrated into Coq's extraction mechanism and should, therefore, provide support for Coq's Extract commands enabling the user to modify these pre-configured defaults.

Listing 1. The app Scallina standard library function

```
def app[A](l1: List[A], l2: List[A]): List[A] = l1 ++ l2
def app[A] = (l1: List[A]) => (l2: List[A]) => l1 ++ l2
```

Note that, in Listing 1, both a curried and an uncurried version of the function are provided, this allows the support of a mixture of both curried and uncurried Scala code. Note also that the curried append function is written as an anonymous function to allow the Scala compiler to distinguish it from its uncurried equivalant. Scallina's curried translation is described in a subsequent section.

Numbers. Gallina's mathematical integers, denoted Z, are mapped to Scala's BigInt which implements integers that are not subject to overflows. This conforms with Isabelle's code generation mechanism that also maps integer types to Scala's BigInt. Furthermore, Leon also recommends the use of BigInt to represent mathematical integers in its supported Hindley-Milner based fragment of the Scala language, dubbed as "Pure Scala"[7].

Natural Numbers. When natural numbers are used in Isabelle's source code, they are mapped, by default, to a generated Scala nat datatype which conforms with Isabelle's internal Peano representation of natural numbers. Section 4 of [9] also mentions a Pure Scala implementation of natural numbers which is mapped to Isabelle's nat type. Similarly, Scallina maps Coq's Peano natural numbers to a Scala Nat datatype included in Scallina's standard library. A large portion of this Nat implementation, available online[8], was itself generated, using the Scallina prototype, from Coq's proven-correct Coq.Init.Nat library. This is congruent with Coq's native extraction mechanism which generates a nat datatype when a program referencing Coq's natural numbers is recursively extracted to OCaml or Haskell.

To facilitate the integration of the extracted code into larger OCaml developments, some Coq users might use the Extract Inductive command for the purpose of mapping Coq's nat type to OCaml's int type. This approach also improves the readability of the generated code since numbers would no longer be represented by repetitive calls to nat's successor constructor. So, for example, the output OCaml code will no longer use S (S (S (S (S O)))) to represent 5. On the other hand, as explained in Sect. 23.2.4 of [16], the resulting OCaml code could eventually suffer from integer overflows if a given Coq nat value exceeds OCaml's max_int. When it comes to Scala, the integer overflow issue can easily be resolved by mapping Coq's nat to Scala's BigInt instead of Scala's Int type. However, this mapping of natural numbers to integers does not take into account the semantic difference between these two types: natural numbers exclude negative values while integers include them. *How can one conserve the semantics of the source Gallina program in the generated Scala code while preserving its readability and reusability in larger Scala or Java developments?* A solution proposed by Scallina consists in providing implicit conversions between Nat and BigInt; making good use of Scala's implicits in Scallina's standard library. This solutions produces an output Scala code that conserves the Nat type but avoids the unreadable representation of numbers as a succession of constructors. It also caters for a better interoperability with regular Scala or Java code since all natural numbers can implicitly be converted to BigInt values and back-again[9].

---

[7] More information about Leon's Pure Scala is available in paragraph 3 of [3] and in the documentation section of http://leon.epfl.ch.

[8] https://github.com/JBakouny/Scallina/blob/master/src/main/resources/scala/of/coq/lang/PeanoNat.scala.

[9] Note that BigInt values can, in turn, easily be converted to Java BigInteger values.

In the latter case, a runtime check is required to signal an error if the regular code ever attempts to implicitly convert negative values to natural numbers.

Value Binders Value binders are not mentioned by the previously exhibited grammar productions but they are indirectly referenced by them. As shown below, the Scallina grammar uses the keyword `binder` to reference value binders which are distinct from the type binders detailed in Sect. 2.2. This distinction highlights the fact that value binders are translated to Scala value parameters and type binders are translated to Scala type parameters, also known as generics.

```
binders   :: =   binder ... binder

binder    :: =   ( ident ... ident : type )
```

In common Scala developments, value parameters are, for the most part, explicitly specified by the user while generic type parameters are usually inferred when applying a given function or method. This is reflected in Scallina's grammar where it is recommended to specify value binders as explicit and type binders as implicit; paving the way for the establishment of coding conventions for Gallina developers that intend to extract traceable Scala code. In this way, a simple value binder (x : Z) with Gallina's mathematical integer is translated to an equivalent Scala parameter (x: BigInt) with the BigInt type.

Anonymous Functions. In contrast with Gallina's standard grammar, the binders supported by Scallina's anonymous function syntax are restricted to value binders. This reflects the limitations of Hindley-Milner based languages, such as OCaml and Haskell, where universal quantifiers must be scoped over the entire type. Section 3.1.5 of [14] gives the classical distr_pair example portraying this limitation: as shown by Listings 2 and 3, the distr_pair function cannot be translated to typable OCaml code. Similarly, Scala anonymous functions support only value parameters [19]; as reflected by the below grammar productions.

```
anonymousFunction :: = fun anonFunBinders => term

anonFunBinders :: = anonFunBinder ... anonFunBinder

anonFunBinder :: = binder | ident
```

Listing 2. The distrPair example

```
Definition distrPair : (∀ X:Set, X → X) → nat*bool :=
  fun f => (f nat O, f bool true).
```

Listing 3. The OCaml extraction of the distrPair example

```
let distrPair f =
  Pair ((Obj.magic f __ O), (Obj.magic f __ True))
```

Currying. Listings 4 and 6 show two Gallina anonymous functions that are translated to the same Scala anonymous function exhibited in Listing 5. This example portrays the generation of curried Scala code recommended by the Scallina translation strategy; conforming with functional programming languages, like OCaml and Gallina, which solely rely on unary functions. In fact, the Gallina function in Listing 6 is mere syntactic sugar for the one in Listing 4.

Listing 4. An addition anonymous function

```
fun (x : Z) => fun (y : Z) => x + y
```

Listing 5. The Scala translation of the addition anonymous function

```
(x: BigInt) => (y: BigInt) => x + y
```

Listing 6. An alternate notation for the addition anonymous function

```
fun (x y : Z) => x + y
```

This default production of curried Scala code facilitates the traceable translation of Gallina programs including higher-order functions or partial applications such as the one in Listing 7. The curried Scala translation portrayed in Listing 8 demonstrates the traceability and readability of the code compared to the tupled alternatives where a code similar to `(aa: BigInt)=> (ba: BigInt)=>` `plus(aa, ba)` would be used to pass the `plus` function to the `higherOrder` function.

Listing 7. A Gallina program including higher-order functions and partial applications

```
Definition plus (a b : nat) : nat := a + b.
Definition higherOrder (f: nat → nat → nat) (a b : nat) : nat := f a b.
Definition plusAgain : nat → nat → nat := higherOrder plus.
```

Listing 8. The curried translation of the higher-order function and partial application

```
def plus(a: Nat)(b: Nat): Nat = a + b
def higherOrder(f: Nat => Nat => Nat)(a: Nat)(b: Nat): Nat = f(a)(b)
def plusAgain: Nat => Nat => Nat = higherOrder(plus)
```

Technical Note. Nevertheless, since most Scala developers are used to writing tupled code as highlighted by Isabelle's code generation mechanism [6], the Scallina prototype does provide an uncurried translation strategy which can be activated through the "--uncurrify" command line option. However, the current implementation of this uncurried strategy is quite experimental and its use is not recommended.

Let-In Definitions and Pattern Matches. In congruence with Isabelle's code generation mechanism, let-in definitions are translated to Scala's **val** declarations.

```
letInDefs :: =  let ident [binders] [: type ] := term in term
           |  let ( [name , ... , name] ) := term in term
           |  let ' pattern := term in term
```

As shown by Listings 9 and 10, let-in definitions pertaining to the same expression are translated to equivalent **val** declarations in the same block.

Listing 9. A function calculating the square of the distance between 2 points

```
Require Import ZArith.
Open Scope Z_scope.

Definition squareDistance (a b: Z * Z) : Z :=
let (x1, y1) := a in
let ' pair x2 y2 := b in
let square (u: Z) := u * u in
let x := x2 - x1 in
let y := y2 - y1 in
(square x) + (square y).
```

Listing 10. The translation of the function calculating the square of the distance

```
def squareDistance(a: (BigInt, BigInt))(b: (BigInt, BigInt)):
    BigInt = {
  val (x1, y1) = a
  val Tuple2(x2, y2) = b
  val square = (u: BigInt) => u * u
  val x = x2 - x1
  val y = y2 - y1
  square(x) + square(y)
}
```

Note that "**let** ' pattern" are translated to Scala **val** declarations which also support patterns. As shown by the translation of pair to Tuple2, these patterns are subject to the previously described shallow embedding. The syntax of patterns, along with that of pattern matches, is given below. A simple translation of a pattern match is portrayed by Listings 11 and 12.

```
patternMatch :: = match term , ... , term with
                 [[|] equation | ... | equation] end

equation :: = multPattern | ... | multPattern => term
multPattern :: = pattern , ... , pattern

pattern    ::= qualid pattern ... pattern
       |    qualid
       |    _
       |    num
       |    ( orPattern , ... , orPattern )

orPattern     ::= pattern | ... | pattern

name    ::= ident
       |    _
```

Other Terms. Although Coq's native extraction mechanism translates if expressions to pattern matches, Scallina proposes a more traceable translation strategy, similar to that of Isabelle, which produces Scala if expressions.

```
ifExpression :: = if term then term else term
```

As shown by Listings 7 and 8, term applications are translated to Scala curried function applications while the + infix operator remains unchanged thanks to Scallina's overloading of this operator for the Nat Scala class.

```
termApplication :: = term ... term

infixOperation :: = term infixOp term
infixOp :: = + | - | * | / | > | < | = | <=? | <= | >= | <? | =? | ::

recordProjection ::= term .( qualid )
```

Record projections are translated to Scala field selections, as explained by Sect. 3.4. Finally, below is the syntax of parenthesis and tuples; both of which are translated to Scala using the identity function.

```
tuple :: = ( term , ... , term )
parens :: = ( term )
```

2.2   Type Terms

The syntax of type terms is giving below. Each of the depicted productions is detailed thereafter; demonstrating the Scallina grammar's clear separation of types from terms; in accordance with conventional programming languages.

```
type   ::= typeApplication
     |   arrowType
     |   pathDependentType
     |   qualid
     |   tupleType
```

Type Applications. As previously mentioned, Gallina type applications, like
`list nat`, are translated to Scala generic type applications such as `List[Nat]`.

```
typeApplication    ::= type ... type
                     | @ qualid type ... type
```

Arrow Types. As explained in Sect. 2.1, Scallina prohibits the use of anonymous function type binders; actively restricting product types to non-dependent
product types, or arrow types. This complies with Coq's type extraction function
where the "prod2" rule in Sect. 3.3.5 of [14] transforms potentially dependent
products types to arrow types; adequately replacing "∀" by "→".

```
arrowType   ::= type → type
```

Path-Dependent Types. As mentioned in Sect. 1, Gallina supports fully
dependent types while Scala supports a limited form of dependent types known
as path-dependent types. This practically means that Gallina allows types to
depend on general terms while Scala only supports types that depend on variables referencing an object containing a type field. Although Scala's support of
dependent types is considerably limited compared to that of Gallina, it nevertheless enables a considerable improvement of Coq's Record extraction described in
Sect. 3.4.

```
pathDependentType    ::= ident .( ident )
```

Tuple Types. As portrayed by Listings 9 and 10, Gallina tuple types, like
`z * z`, are translated to Scala tuple types such as `(BigInt, BigInt)`.

```
tupleType ::= type * ... * type
```

Type Binders. The Scallina grammar uses the keyword `typeBinder` to reference type binders which are clearly distinguishable from the previously detailed
value binders. As explained in Sect. 2.1, and shown by Listings 11 and 12, these
implicit Gallina type binders are translated to Scala's generics.

```
typeBinders    ::= typeBinder âŁ¦ typeBinder

typeBinder     ::= { ident âŁ¦ ident : Set }
               |   { ident }
```

3   The Syntax of Sentences

```
sentence   ::= definition
       |   typeDef
       |   record
       |   recordInstance
       |   inductive
       |   fixpoint
       |   function
```

As explained in Sect. 1.3 of [16], the Vernacular is Gallina's language of commands. It is constituted of sentences beginning with a capital letter and ending with a dot. A significant part of these sentences are commands that extend the environment by defining new types and declaring new constructs. Scallina proposes an optimized Scala translation of a subset of these sentences.

3.1   Function Definitions

Since Gallina's **Definition**, **Fixpoint** and **Function** are all used to represent Coq function definitions, their translation produces Scala **def** declarations. While Scala supports unrestricted recursion, Coq imposes strict requirements on the termination of recursive functions:

- **Fixpoint** enables a primitive form of recursion on a structurally decreasing inductive argument; as described in Sect. 1.3.4 of [16]
- The **Function** plugin [2] is a generalization of **Fixpoint** that supports advanced recursive definitions on non-structurally decreasing arguments; requiring a proof of termination, as mentioned in Sect. 2.3 of [16].
- **Definition** can be used to define non-recursive functions.

```
definition :: = Definition ident [typeBinders] [binders] : type := term .

fixpoint :: =    Fixpoint fixBody .
fixBody :: = ident [typeBinders] binders [fixAnnotation] : type := term
fixAnnotation :: = { struct ident }

function :: = Function functionBody . [proof]
functionBody :: = ident [typeBinders] binders funcAnnotation : type := term
funcAnnotation :: = fixAnnotation | { measure ( anonymousFunction ) ident }
```

As explained in Sect. 2.1 and exhibited by Listings 11 and 12, Scallina produces *curried* Scala code from Gallina function definitions.

Listing 11. A tail recursive Gallina definition of the length function

```
Function lenTailrec {A} (xs : list A) (n : nat)
{ measure (fun xs => length(xs)) xs } : nat :=
match xs with
| nil => n
| _ :: ys => lenTailrec ys (1 + n)
end.
Proof.
  intros.
  simpl.
  omega.
Qed.
```

Listing 12. The Scala translation of the tail recursive length function

```
def lenTailrec[A](xs: List[A])(n: Nat): Nat =
  xs match {
    case Nil     => n
    case _ :: ys => lenTailrec(ys)(1 + n)
  }
```

Perspective. The current version of the Scallina prototype requires Gallina function prototypes to be explicitly typed by specifying the parameter and return types; a limitation which should be alleviated once Scallina is integrated into Coq's native extraction mechanism. Notably, Coq's type inference algorithms, such as the M' algorithm described in Sect. 3.2.3 of [14], could potentially be adapted to Scala with the notable benefit of supporting the extraction of all Gallina constructs through the insertion of unsafe type casts in constructs that are not typable in Scala. In this regards, the Scallina grammar could potentially guide this implementation by providing insight on the Gallina subset that is translatable to Scala using a relatively straightforward translation strategy.

3.2 Type Definition.

In accordance with the "def1" in Sect. 3.3.5 of [14], Gallina type definitions, like "**Definition** total_map (A:**Type**) : **Type** := nat → A.", are translated to Scala type definitions such as "**type** total_map[A] =Nat =>A".

```
typeDef :: = Definition ident [typeDefBinders] : Set := type .
typeDefBinders = typeDefBinder ... typeDefBinder
typeDefBinder :: = typeBinder
    |    ( ident ... ident : Set )
    |    ident
```

3.3 Inductive Definition

Coq supports the implementation of Algebraic Data Types (ADT) using Gallina's inductive definitions.

```
inductive   :: = Inductive indBody .

indBody :: = ident [typeDefBinders] [: Type] : =
        [[|] indBodyItem | ... | indBodyItem]

indBodyItem :: = ident [typeBinders] [binders]
```

Listing 13. A Gallina binary tree ADT

```
Inductive Tree A := Leaf | Node (v: A) (l r: Tree A).
```

Listing 14. The translation of the binary tree ADT

```scala
sealed abstract class Tree[+A]
case object Leaf extends Tree[Nothing]
case class Node[A](v: A, l: Tree[A], r: Tree[A]) extends Tree[A]
object Node {
  def apply[A] =
    (v: A) => (l: Tree[A]) => (r: Tree[A]) => new Node(v, l, r)
}
```

As exhibited by Listings 13 and 14, Scallina emulates ADTs by Scala case classes. This conforms with Scala best practices [21] and is already adopted by both Isabelle/HOL and Leon [9]. However, note that Scallina optimizes the translation of ADTs by generating a **case object** instead of a **case class** where appropriate; as demonstrated by Leaf. Note also that this optimization makes good use of Scala's variance annotations and Nothing bottom type in accordance with the best practices implemented by Scala standard library data structures such as List[+A] and Option[+A]. Last but not least, the curried construction of case classes is enabled by the generation of a helper object with a curried apply method for every **case class** with multiple constructor arguments, such as Node.

3.4   Record Definition and Instantiation

Scallina proposes the translation of Gallina records to Scala functional object-oriented code with support for path-dependent types.

```
record  ::= recordKeyword ident [typeBinders] [: Type] :=
        [ident] { [field ; ... ; field] } .
recordKeyword   ::= Record | Structure | Inductive

field   ::= typeField | valueField

typeField   ::= ident : Type
    |    ident : Type := type
valueField ::= ident [binders] : type
    |    ident [binders] : type := term
```

Since the objective of the Scallina project is not to redefine the Coq extraction process but to extend it with readable Scala code generation, it assumes that a prior removal of logical parts and fully dependent types was already performed by Coq's theoretical extraction function and subsequent type-checking phase; catering for a future integration of the Scallina translation strategy into Coq's native extraction mechanism. In this context, Scallina proposes some modification to the latter with regards to the typing of records with path-dependent types. These modifications were explicitly formulated as possible future works through the aMonoid example in [15]. Listing 15 shows a slight modification of the aMonoid example which essentially removes its logical parts. While, as explained in [15], the current extraction of this example produces unsafe type casts in both OCaml and Haskell; Scallina manages to translate this example to the well-typed Scala code exhibited in Listing 16.

Listing 15. The aMonoid Gallina record with its logical parts removed

```
Record aMonoid : Type := newMonoid {
  dom : Type;
  zero : dom;
  op : dom → dom → dom
}.
Definition natMonoid := newMonoid nat 0 (fun (a: nat) (b: nat) => a + b).
```

Listing 16. The proposed Scala extraction of the aMonoid Gallina record

```
trait aMonoid {
  type dom
  def zero: dom
  def op: dom => dom => dom
}
def newMonoid[dom](zero: dom)(op: dom => dom => dom): aMonoid = {
  type aMonoid_dom = dom
  def aMonoid_zero = zero
  def aMonoid_op = op
  new aMonoid {
    type dom = aMonoid_dom
    def zero: dom = aMonoid_zero
    def op: dom => dom => dom = aMonoid_op
  }
}
def natMonoid = newMonoid[Nat](0)((a: Nat) => (b: Nat) => a + b)
```

In accordance with their Scala representation given in [1], record definitions are translated to Scala traits and record instances are translated to Scala objects. Alternatively to using the newMonoid record constructor shown in Listings 15 and 16, Gallina record instances can be created using the below named fields syntax.

```
recordInstance ::=
    Definition ident [typeBinders] [binders] : type :=
    {| [fieldImpl ; ... ; fieldImpl] |} .

fieldImpl   ::= ident [binders] := term
```

In this case, as portrayed by Listings 17 and 18, record instances are translated to Scala conventional object definitions provided the recordInstance definition omits typeBinders and binders.

Listing 17. The instantiation of a record without any binders

```
Definition intMonoid : aMonoid := {|
  dom := Z;
  zero := 0;
  op := fun (a: Z) (b: Z) => a + b
|}.
```

Listing 18. The translation of the instantiation of a record without any binders

```
object intMonoid extends aMonoid {
  type dom = BigInt
  def zero: dom = 0
  def op: dom => dom => dom = (a: BigInt) => (b: BigInt) => a+b
}
```

As portrayed by Listings 19 and 20, if typeBinders or binders are specified by the recordInstance definition, record instances are translated to Scala anonymous class instances; in congruence with the representation of record instances in [1].

Listing 19. The instantiation of a record with binders

```
Definition genMonoid {A} (z: A) (f: A → A → A) : aMonoid := {|
  dom := A;
  zero := z;
  op a b := f a b
|}.
```

Listing 20. The translation of the instantiation of a record with binders

```
def genMonoid[A](z: A)(f: A => A => A): aMonoid = new aMonoid
    {
    type dom = A
    def zero: dom = z
    def op: dom => dom => dom = (a: dom) => (b: dom) => f(a)(b)
}
```

A complete and well-commented example of a significant Gallina record translation to conventional Scala object definitions is available online[10]. This example also contains a proof showing the equivalent behavior, with regards to a given program, of two Scala objects implementing the same trait.

4 Conclusion and Perspectives

In conclusion, the Scallina project enables the translation of a significant subset of Gallina to readable and traceable Scala code. As exhibited by this paper, the Scallina grammar, along with its proposed translation strategy, facilitates the reasoning about the fragment of Gallina that is translatable to conventional programming languages such as Scala. This strategy embodies several optimizations such as shallow embedding, implicit Nat conversions, an improved record translation and the generation of curried Scala code while leveraging the language's variance annotations and Nothing bottom type during the translation ADTs. The Scallina prototype shows how these contributions can be successfully transferred into a working tool. It also allows the practical Coq-based synthesis of Scala components that can be integrated into larger applications; opening the door for Scala and Java programmers to benefit from the Coq proof assistant.

Future versions of Scallina[11] are expected to be integrated into Coq's extraction mechanism by re-using the expertise acquired through the development of the current Scallina prototype. In this context, an experimental patch for the Coq extraction mechanism[12] was implemented in 2012 but has since become incompatible with the latest version of Coq's source code. The implementation of Scallina's translation strategy into Coq's extraction mechanism could potentially benefit from this existing patch; updating it with regards to the current state of[13] the source code. During this process, the external implementation of the Scallina prototype, which relies on Gallina's stable syntax independently from Coq's source code, could be used to guide the aforementioned integration; providing samples of generated Scala code as needed.

Acknowledgement. The authors would like to thank the National Council for Scientific Research in Lebanon (CNRS-L) for their funding, as well as Murex S.A.S for providing financial support.

---

[10] https://github.com/JBakouny/Scallina/tree/v0.5.0/packaged-examples/v0.5.0/list-queue.
[11] http://www.cnrs.edu.lb/.
[12] http://proofcafe.org/wiki/en/Coq2Scala.
[13] https://www.murex.com/.

References

1. Amin, N., Grütter, S., Odersky, M., Rompf, T., Stucki, S.: The essence of dependent object types. In: Lindley, S., McBride, C., Trinder, P., Sannella, D. (eds.) A List of Successes That Can Change the World. LNCS, vol. 9600, pp. 249–272. Springer, Cham (2016). https://doi.org/10.1007/978-3-319-30936-1_14
2. Barthe, G., Forest, J., Pichardie, D., Rusu, V.: Defining and reasoning about recursive functions: a practical tool for the coq proof assistant. In: Hagiya, M., Wadler, P. (eds.) FLOPS 2006. LNCS, vol. 3945, pp. 114–129. Springer, Heidelberg (2006). https://doi.org/10.1007/11737414_9
3. Blanc, R., Kuncak, V., Kneuss, E., Suter, P.: An overview of the leon verification system: verification by translation to recursive functions. In: Proceedings of the 4th Workshop on Scala, SCALA 2013, pp. 1:1–1:10. ACM, New York (2013). https://doi.org/10.1145/2489837.2489838
4. Filliâtre, J.-C., Paskevich, A.: Why3 — where programs meet provers. In: Felleisen, M., Gardner, P. (eds.) ESOP 2013. LNCS, vol. 7792, pp. 125–128. Springer, Heidelberg (2013). https://doi.org/10.1007/978-3-642-37036-6_8
5. Guallart, N.: An overview of type theories. Axiomathes **25**(1), 61–77 (2015). https://doi.org/10.1007/s10516-014-9260-9
6. Haftmann, F., Bulwahn, L.: Code generation from Isabelle/HOL theories, October 2017. https://isabelle.in.tum.de/dist/Isabelle2017/doc/codegen.pdf
7. Haftmann, F., Nipkow, T.: Code generation via higher-order rewrite systems. In: Blume, M., Kobayashi, N., Vidal, G. (eds.) FLOPS 2010. LNCS, vol. 6009, pp. 103–117. Springer, Heidelberg (2010). https://doi.org/10.1007/978-3-642-12251-4_9
8. Hindley, R.: The principle type-scheme of an object in combinatory logic. Trans. Am. Math. Soc. **146**, 29–60 (1969)
9. Hupel, L., Kuncak, V.: Translating Scala programs to Isabelle/HOL. In: Olivetti, N., Tiwari, A. (eds.) IJCAR 2016. LNCS (LNAI), vol. 9706, pp. 568–577. Springer, Cham (2016). https://doi.org/10.1007/978-3-319-40229-1_38
10. Klein, G., et al.: sel4: formal verification of an OS kernel. In: Matthews, J.N., Anderson, T.E. (eds.) Proceedings of the 22nd ACM Symposium on Operating Systems Principles 2009, SOSP 2009, Big Sky, Montana, USA, 11–14 October 2009, pp. 207–220. ACM (2009). https://doi.org/10.1145/1629575.1629596
11. Kuncak, V.: Developing verified software using Leon. In: Havelund, K., Holzmann, G., Joshi, R. (eds.) NFM 2015. LNCS, vol. 9058, pp. 12–15. Springer, Cham (2015). https://doi.org/10.1007/978-3-319-17524-9_2
12. Leroy, X.: Formal certification of a compiler back-end or: programming a compiler with a proof assistant. In: Morrisett, J.G., Jones, S.L.P. (eds.) Proceedings of the 33rd ACM SIGPLAN-SIGACT Symposium on Principles of Programming Languages, POPL 2006, Charleston, South Carolina, USA, 11–13 January 2006, pp. 42–54. ACM (2006). https://doi.org/10.1145/1111037.1111042
13. Letouzey, P.: A new extraction for Coq. In: Geuvers, H., Wiedijk, F. (eds.) TYPES 2002. LNCS, vol. 2646, pp. 200–219. Springer, Heidelberg (2003). https://doi.org/10.1007/3-540-39185-1_12
14. Letouzey, P.: Programmation fonctionnelle certifiée : L'extraction de programmes dans l'assistant Coq. (Certified functional programming : Program extraction within Coq proof assistant). Ph.D. thesis, University of Paris-Sud, Orsay, France (2004). https://tel.archives-ouvertes.fr/tel-00150912

15. Letouzey, P.: Extraction in Coq: an overview. In: Beckmann, A., Dimitracopoulos, C., Löwe, B. (eds.) CiE 2008. LNCS, vol. 5028, pp. 359–369. Springer, Heidelberg (2008). https://doi.org/10.1007/978-3-540-69407-6_39
16. The Coq development team: The Coq proof assistant reference manual. LogiCal Project (2004). http://coq.inria.fr, version 8.0
17. Milner, R.: A theory of type polymorphism in programming. J. Comput. Syst. Sci. **17**(3), 348–375 (1978). https://doi.org/10.1016/0022-0000(78)90014-4
18. Nipkow, T., Wenzel, M., Paulson, L.C. (eds.): Isabelle/HOL. LNCS, vol. 2283. Springer, Heidelberg (2002). https://doi.org/10.1007/3-540-45949-9
19. Odersky, M.: The scala language specification. Technical report, Programming Methods Laboratory, EPFL, Lausanne, Switzerland, June 2014
20. Odersky, M., Rompf, T.: Unifying functional and object-oriented programming with Scala. Commun. ACM **57**(4), 76–86 (2014). https://doi.org/10.1145/2591013
21. Odersky, M., Spoon, L., Venners, B.: Programming in Scala: A Comprehensive Step-by-Step Guide, 2nd edn. Artima Incorporation, USA (2011)

VDM at Large: Modelling the EMV® 2nd Generation Kernel

Leo Freitas(✉)

School of Computing, Newcastle University, Newcastle upon Tyne, UK
leo.freitas@newcastle.ac.uk

Abstract. The EMV® (EMV® is a registered trademark or trademark of EMVCo, LLC in the US and other countries.) organisation specify payment protocols to facilitate worldwide interoperability of secure electronic payments. This paper is about the application and scalability of formal methods to a current and complex industry application. We describe the use of VDM to model EMV® 2nd Generation Kernel (A preliminary version of this paper was presented at the 16th Overture Workshop, Oxford July 2018, where papers became a Newcastle Technical Report.). VDM is useful for both formal specification, as well as simulation, test coverage, and proof obligation generation for functional correctness.

1 Introduction

EMVCo is a technical body that publishes and manages the EMV® specifications to facilitate worldwide interoperability and acceptance of secure payment transactions. Their protocols have been around since the late nineties and are used by major payment services providers (*i.e.* American Express, Discover, JCB, MasterCard, UnionPay, and Visa). As of 2018, there are over 7 billion EMV® payment cards, up from 4.8 billion in 2016, representing 55% of all payment cards issued globally. Their cards cover 64% of all worldwide transactions, and 99% of transactions in Europe. They are responsible for major payment technologies, such as contact (Chip & Pin), contactless (Wave & Pay), 3D-Secure online payment validation, and so on. In practice, relevant attacks on EMV1 were discovered [2, 4–6], with financial fraud related to payment systems rising in the last few years both in volume and type: for example, in the UK, there has been a 80% increase in value between 2011–16, when the fraud losses were £M618 [10].

In this paper we describe our experience in using VDMSL as a tool for understanding a complex (1900 pages) requirements specification of the upcoming EMV® 2nd Generation Acceptance System Specifications (EMV2) [8]. They include the familiar Chip & Pin and contactless protocols, as well as a number of new operational modes and security verification types (including biometric). We assume the reader is familiar with VDM [15]. Unfortunately, due to NDA restrictions, detailed information about the model, the choice of VDM, what the model exercise achieved, and how its application might have an impact in

© Springer Nature Switzerland AG 2018
T. Massoni and M. R. Mousavi (Eds.): SBMF 2018, LNCS 11254, pp. 109–125, 2018.
https://doi.org/10.1007/978-3-030-03044-5_8

industry cannot be given. We hope to talk about this in future publications once EMV2 becomes public. Nevertheless, the underlying methodology we are following has recently been published [13].

We use VDMSL to formally specify the EMV 2nd Generation kernel to enable specific protocol runs. The results have been productive and substantial. To date, we have modelled about 80% of the EMV2 kernel, and hope to complete it before public release. It comprises 135 VDM-SL modules and about 50 KLOC in VDMSL, some (20%) of which is automatically generated from an XSD/XML data dictionary, which describe the data structures used by the kernel APIs.

Elegance, which academics have in high-regard and can be useful for clarity and maintainability, often needs to be compromised in order to ensure stakeholders notice/accept the formal results: they ought to see the formal model built as something they recognise, as their artefact, rather than a nicer (more elegant) abstraction. Moreover, the complexities involved are quite substantial. The system needs to run seamlessly for long periods of time in different countries, currencies, financial services, policies and banking institutions; quite a task.

The work unravelled many technical issues in VDM, the identification of VDM tool bugs, as well as the limits of Overture as a tool. We hope these issues are interesting and that the VDM community finds tool suggestions useful.

2   EMV Protocols and EMV2

The most common payment protocols are Chip & Pin and contactless, but a number of variations is technically possible. Analysis of EMV protocols is nontrivial due to the complexity of its requirements [7,9]. They have to incorporate competing (and conflicting) interests from multiple user needs, banks and financial regulators worldwide.

A key differentiating feature of EMV2 is the fact its many (14) modules are completely distributed and may run concurrently (see Fig. 1), as opposed to the monolithic sequential world of EMV1.

EMV protocols have many similarities. They constitute a series of steps encompassing a number of players, stages and features. The most common players are the so-called "point of interaction" (POI) terminals used by merchants (e.g. ATM machines, supermarket fuel pumps, card payment machines, etc.) and a card-profile used by customers (e.g. plastic cards, electronic tokens like smartphones/watches, etc.), as well as the issuer (e.g. banks and payment clearing systems). The main stages are:

1. **Application Selection** establishes the functionality of interest (e.g. credit card payment, or cash withdrawal from a specific account, etc.) with any additional extras (e.g. loyalty points, air miles, cash back, etc.), as well as the kind of transaction to engage with (e.g. acceptable challenge mechanisms, risk levels, information required by all parties, etc.);
2. **Transaction Processing** performs the necessary checks around agreed challenge mechanisms (e.g. pin-number, signature, biometric readers, etc.) and information required to make a decision about whether payment is to be approved, which may involve the issuer's approval;

3. **Other (kernel administrative)** stages exist for transaction restarting, rescuing, configuring, *etc.*

The core functionality comprises most kernel modules managing various protocol stages and features. The acceptance system comprises the POI and card communication layers. The former includes terminal management and card holder verification entry devices (*e.g.* pin pad, biometric scanners, *etc.*); whereas the latter implements a communication abstraction layer with the card-profile. This enables varying communication protocols to be instantiated outside the kernels core functionality.

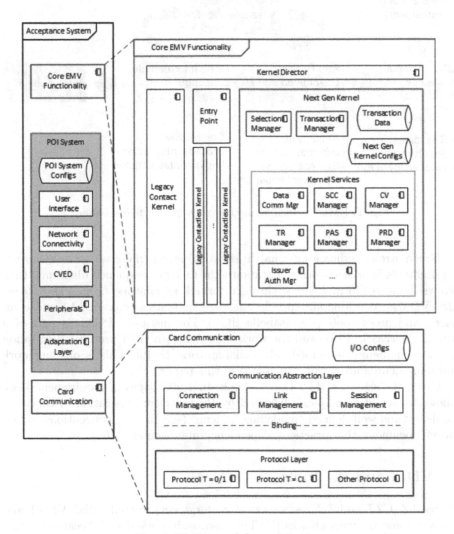

Fig. 1. EMV2 modules architecture

3   Socio-technical Challenges in Modelling EMV2

We have prior experience with formal verification of protocols in Mondex [14], and in discovering attacks in EMV1 [5]. We are developing a methodology for the modelling and analysis of payment protocols. It involves a number of specification languages and tools used to capture different aspects of the process (see Fig. 2). Crucially, these languages serve to shield payment-system engineers from formalism details, as well as to increase levels of automation as much as possible.

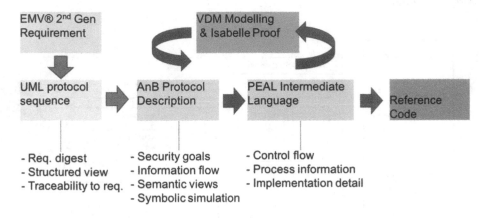

Fig. 2. EMV2 modelling methodology (Color figure online)

Green arrows indicate informal (if rigorous) steps where we encode/capture requirements in a semi-formal notation akin to UML sequence diagrams. Blue arrows indicate formal steps through formal simulators (*e.g.* VDM Overture/VDMJ), new domain specific language semantics (*e.g.* PEAL) and compilers, and proof tools (*e.g.* Isabelle/HOL). For instance, PEAL is part of a current Newcastle PhD, and the work with AnB, an IBM protocol description language, is being developed with collaborators [18,19]. This is ongoing work and more details are beyond the scope of this paper.

Given the size of EMV2 (*i.e.* 17 books in 1,900 pages of requirements), we followed a set of principles advocated by Praxis: clear separation of concerns, consistent and well-defined "modelling hygiene" (*e.g.* naming conventions, indentation/documentation practices, dependency management, *etc.*).

4   VDM and Its Tools

We used Z (CZT and Z/Eves, see czt.sourceforge.net) to analyse EMV1 [12] and uncover some relevant attacks [5]. This approach worked well because we had a combination of empirical knowledge of EMV1 through understanding of its specification in implemented simulators (thanks to our collaborator Dr. Martin

Emms). This meant our abstractions for how to represent the relevant parts of EMV1 were suitable to the practical realities of its protocols. Proof (or rather their failures) was used as the mechanism to identify and prevent theoretical threats, which we next tested for in practice with simulators using mobile-devices to perform attacks. This enabled us to practically demonstrate the severity, as well as the ease/difficulty, in enacting such attacks.

For EMV2, on the other hand, we believed a similar approach might not get us far. That is mostly because EMV2's considerably higher complexity and distinction in comparison to EMV1, in our view. We decided to use VDM and its formal simulation capabilities with Overture and VDMJ (see overturetool.org and github.com/nickbattle/vdmj) instead. This enabled a quicker prototyping of the kernel from its requirement specifications in order to provide us with the necessary knowledge about EMV2, and to start the discussion about its design decisions, as well as to enable the discovery of potential issues. We also envisaged the use of VDM's combinatorial testing [16] in order to exercise the number of protocol scenarios of most interest.

Moreover, we needed libraries for binary blobs and matrix manipulations. For the former, we used the nice VDM "DLL" style link with natively implemented libraries following the examples of IO and VDMUtil; whereas for the latter we used a combination of available and our own libraries from years of working with VDM's mathematical toolkit. For the most crucial libraries of binary blob transformers used for interfacing EMV1 legacy transactions within EMV2, and for matrix calculations used for transaction processing decision making, we used Isabelle/HOL (see isabelle.in.tum.de) to formally verify that proof obligations generated by the library definitions were correct. For example, in the binary library with varied word-size precision:

```
bv2nat: BitVector -> nat          nat2bv: nat -> BitVector

byte2bin: Byte -> BinByte         bin2byte: BinByte -> Byte
byte2bin(n) == binPad(nat2bv(n))  bin2byte(bv) == bv2nat(bv);
```

It transforms a bit vector into a nat and vice-versa, as well as their word-bounded variations with adequate padding. Beyond proving satisfiability of proof obligations in Isabelle/HOL, we also proved by induction interesting theorems like

$$bin2byte(byte2bin(bp-1), bp-1)$$

where $bp = 2^{wsize}$. This library also contains various operations over bit vectors like and, or, not, xor, etc.

4.1 VDM Language Issues

Our strategy to tackle design decisions led to interesting choices within the VDM language. In the process, a number of corner cases and interesting situations about language semantics arose. This led to a number of fruitful discussions with the VDM community, as well as tool extensions and corrections. Abstracting

away all involved details in order to get to a minimal example was often time
consuming and hard to tolerate. For example, lambda-expressions mistakenly
allowed access to mutable state, which when used as a function-parameter or
on-the-fly, led to unexpected behaviours.

```
op(x: nat) r: nat == is not yet specified ext wr c
post (lambda v: nat & v > c~)(c~+1);
```

Here Overture would not give an error, whereas VDMJ complains. In practice these lambda expressions were part of parameters to functions partici-
pating in the postcondition. The other example mistakenly allowed access to
explicit-operation definition's return values within the operation's body or its
precondition.

```
f(n: nat) r: nat == is not yet specified
pre some_condition_over(n, r);
```

Another interesting example had to do with type-invariant cascading/checks
that were not quite right, and despite being very common, have not been uncovered before. All three print statements ought to flag a type invariant violation.

```
types
Dot = nat inv d == d < 4;
Bag = set of Dot inv b == card b > 2;

functions
test: Bag -> Bag
test(b) == b;

> print inv_Dot(-1)    > print inv_Bag({2,3,4})
true                   true

>print test({2,3,4})
Error 4060: Type invariant violated for Bag
```

VDM does not seem to handle cross product type parameters uniformly.
For instance, it treats (T * T) -> T as a single tuple-input, whereas T * T
-> T as a two parameter input. In itself, this is okay. Yet when developing libraries that involved polymorphic parameters and high-level functions
(i.e. lambda-expressions as parameters) this distinction creates unnecessary confusion and difficult-to-debug/understand situations in the development of our
generic libraries for binary numbers and matrixes. It took a number of iterations
(and a lot of time) to get to the bottom of it with this minimal example of the
larger-scale scenario involving matrix calculations.

```
functions
f[@T]: @T -> @T * @T
f(a) == g[@T * @T](lambda x : @T * @T & x, mk_(a, a));

g[@T]: (@T -> @T) * @T -> @T
g(a, b) == a(b);

> p f[nat](1)
Error 4087: Cannot convert 1 (nat1) to (nat * nat) ...
6:        g(a, b) == a(b);
```

Calls to f fail with a cryptic error message, which did not help to figure out the underlying problem. It was about the same name of parameter @T was being used by f and g, but with @T referring to a different type in each case. When more than one polymorphic function is used in a call chain, the type parameter @T was not being uniformly passed. This, in combination with the function call non-uniformity, explained the reason why error messages were cryptic, and figuring out what was happening was difficult.

In Overture, export and import clauses are not treated properly. In imports, one can mix names of operation and functions without error or warnings, whereas VDMJ complaints. More seriously, **struct** export in Overture is not properly implemented at all, and works partially in what is quite confusing. Again VDMJ's stricter choices means if it is happy, so will Overture be. In a large specification where **exports all** is not adequate, the mishandling of (struct-)exports by Overture was a surprise with some cost as it was only discovered late. Finally, another quirk is VDM's "possible semantics", which in complex scenarios again led to a considerable amount of time to figure out what was going on. For example:

```
Type2 = bool | int;
Type3 = <A> | <B> |<C>;
Type4 = Type3 inv t4 == t4 in set {<A>, <B>};

functions
f1: Type2 -> bool                g1: Type4 -> bool
f1(y) == is not yet specified;   g1(y) == f1(y);

f2: [Type2] -> bool              g2: [Type4] -> bool
f2(y) == is not yet specified;   g2(y) == f2(y);
```

As expected, the definition of g1 gives an error about an inappropriate type for the argument. Nevertheless, g2 only gives a type-error at run time thanks to the possibility of a **nil** input. A nicer/stronger warning in such cases would be welcome.

```
> print g2(<A>)
Error 4087: Cannot convert <A> (<A>) to (bool | int) ...
35: g2(y) == f2(y)

> print g2(0)
Error 3061: Inappropriate type for argument 1 ...
Expect: [Type4] Actual: nat
```

In all, all these scenarios served to highlight relatively simple issues that have been fixed in recent versions of both Overture and VDMJ. This brings up some interesting question to ask. How much do we trust our own tools to do work in safety and reliability? What evidence do we have that the tools themselves are sound? Having two independent tools can be practically useful, yet theoretically also increase this soundness concern. Interesting examples of how this has been mitigated for some tools exist, such as the *Circus* model checker [11], the CakeML compiler (https://cakeml.org), and the seL4 verified system (https://sel4.systems).

4.2 VDM Language Patterns

We had to come up with a number of ingenious VDM constructs in order to capture specific design decisions. In some cases, an alternative (more elegant) solution would be possible in theory, but we could not afford to take it in practice. Yet, in other cases, we could not think of a nicer solution at all.

Payment protocols by nature involve a considerable amounts of data from both the kernel to the card and vice versa. For example, different cards/terminals might require different information in order to setup a transaction and enable variability. Effectively, they entail a sort of reflective request over internal kernel/card state. For example, if the kernel might need the card for its long number and its expiry date in some transactions, or its public signature keys in others.

One solution to this kind of query would be to have the kernel state defined as a map from a somewhat structured string into whatever the target type was. Unfortunately, there are hundreds of type (and invariant) definitions, some of which are grouped as records with invariants between constituent fields. That means a kernel module state map would require an extraordinarily complex (and pretty much unreadable) invariant. Thus, we kept (often simple) invariants very close to where they were defined, and the various composition needs imposed the overall compound invariant of interest.

Our solution to enable reflective access was to take the XSD-schemas used to define EMV's type dictionary in order to automatically generate (6,528 LOC over 52 VDMSL modules) various data types of interest, as well as map transformers needed for reflective access. Maps were defined from ID (structured strings) into the so-called VDM wildcard ("?") type[1]. This enabled both reflective access and update, where we transformed records into maps and vice-versa.

---

[1] An example of its use can be seen in the VDMUtil library definition.

```
types
  emv_[P]_[M]_map = map ID to ?
  inv map_ == dom map_ = { ''IDs of interest'' };

functions
  default_emv_[P]_[M]: () -> emv_[P]_[M]
  [P]_[M]2map: emv_[P]_[M] -> emv_[P]_[M]_map
  [P]_[M]_map2rec: emv_[P]_[M]_map -> emv_[P]_[M]
  [P]_[M]_map_update[@T]: emv_[P]_[M]_map * ID * @T ->
                          emv_[P]_[M]_map
```

For this we wrote a Java program (4,058 LOC) that processed XSD and XML files and transformed them into VDMSL based on a template VDMSL file of about 90 LOC. This is used to produce the actual VDMSL files populated with XML/XSD information, where XSD files has a corresponding VDMSL files representing data types and constraints. These VDMSL files varied from 80 to 500 LOC depending on the underlying record type size and complexity. The VDMSL template key functionality is defined by four exported functions.

The ''IDs of interest'', as well as the actual implementation of these functions, are populated through the data structures defined in the XSDs. The [P] stands for different packages, whereas [M] stand for different modules. Not all modules have packages and some packages have no modules API signatures for each kernel module and a few global configuration options are also defined by XSDs, which again we used to automatically generate top-level and internal operation signatures.

The use of "?" effectively enables a unbounded union type, something that arguably could have serious semantical consequences: that is why we do not struct export the map type. Even though this is arguably semantically dangerous, we are left with no alternative choice we could think of for specifying reflective (string based) access/update for records. The functions provide a default initialiser for the underlying record type (*i.e.* emv_[P]_[M]), conversion from the record to the corresponding map type (*i.e.* emv_[P]_[M]_map), conversion from the map type back to the record type, and finally a map update function for a given ID. The use of polymorphic type @T is important in order to ensure external users of the function satisfy the record type invariant not imposed within its corresponding map type. The update function has a precondition about the ID belonging to the domain of the map type as the invariant requires: this ensures only fields known within the record type can be "reflected" over the map type. With this setup, it is possible to write expressions like

```
x := x_map2rec(x_map_update[Type](x2map(x), id, value))
```

which projects a record (x) of corresponding record type (emv_[P]_[M]) into its map type (emv_[P]_[M]_map), updates it at the specific id name with a specific value of the right Type, and then transforms it back to the original record type. Thus, this provide reflective access/update to records represented as maps with type invariants implicitly guaranteed.

This way, we managed to have both strong type invariants across multiple fields and records, and yet still allow for reflective (string-based) access to kernel state via our automatically generated map transformers. In practice, this worked quite well: we anticipate changes to the kernel over time will most often come from data structure variations, rather than new API or protocol stages. When such changes happen, all we have to do is regenerate the mapping specification, and mostly all is automatically up to date with internal version updates prior to release. This process has proved invaluable for productivity: that is because considerable amount of (tedious and error prone) work is completely (and correctly/safely) automated.

Another pattern of interest was in the use of data structures for data exchange between the kernel and the external world (of the card and the POI). As with reflective state access, the data structures have to fetch kernel state data for a given list of IDs requested. That entails different (if often predictable under various conditions) data structures with invariants depending on the ids requested. In order to define such dynamic invariants, which are often only knowable once the specific request has been assembled, we defined records with structures like

```
types
  IDList = seq of ID
  ContainerData = seq of ?;
  Container ::
    dil    : IDList
    data   : ContainerData
    invariant : IDList * ContainerData +> bool
  inv mk_Container(list,data,invariant) ==
    --@doc all IDs have corresponding data
    len list = len data
    and
    ---@doc IDList within container must respect ID allowances
    respect_boundaries(list)
    and
    --@doc extra invariant to ensure specific needs
    invariant(list,data);
```

A concrete example of such dynamic invariants could be given by a mk_Container expression with a lambda-expression or invariant function with known conditions; or when in less unpredictable circumstances, an extended record where the actual known invariant per module can be checked:

```
KernelDirectorContainer = Container
inv mk_Container(list,data,invariant) ==
  invariant(list,data) <=> some_inv_function(<kd>,list,data);
```

4.3   Pushing Language Boundaries

Use of VDM Wildcard Type

In discussion with the VDM community about these issues, a number of language extensions were discussed. For instance, what roles (if any) should the wildcard ("?") type play? I first came across it within VDMUtil library, and when I looked at the VDMSL manual, it was not in the Lexer's token vocabulary! Yet, once I understood what it achieved, I started playing with its possibilities. Perhaps types involving "?" cannot ever be struct-exported. It was incredibly useful in a few places, yet it can also be incredibly dangerous to have around untamed. Without it, however, we would struggle to provide a sensible/scalable solution to state reflective-access and other problems. It can be quite dangerous to use, though: for the reflective maps above, our initial type was map ID to [?], given some values could be nil. The combination of wildcard that can be nil leads to a situation where both Overture and VDMJ get in quite some trouble without any sensible error message. The solution was to realise that nil was already part of "?", hence no need to define it twice!

Another interesting example was inspired by SPARK/Ada modules. We defined a Stack type as an abstract data type, which in SPARK terms means an opaque type with public APIs to manipulate it (*e.g.* push, pop, peek, *etc.*). In VDM, that would mean having a non-struct exported Stack type so that its internal implementation can never be exploited by its users, and only its public APIs are usable. This worked well in VDM with VDMJ checking for struct exports properly, but up to a point. Like with C++ template-class or Java Generics, what if we wanted a stack (however it is implemented), but of a specific type (*e.g.* Stack<nat>)? Because VDM does not allow polymorphic type declarations to participate in type definitions, this was quite hard/convoluted to impose/define. Again, we used the wildcard type for such module parametric types. Perhaps allowing polymorphic type variables in type definitions, or even have module type parameters might be an interesting language extension.

Framing Conditions

Coming from the Z world, I found the lack of linguistic support for complex state framing conditions an issue. VDM explicit-extended operation definitions allow the specifier to define framing conditions in terms of what can be read/written, which also define access conditions in pre/post specifications. This is quite useful, yet also quite limited. Assuming complex state, say with a number of fields, each as records with other fields, totalling 10 to 50 fields. What happens when an operation touches only one or two fields of one of these records? For example:

```
operations
  Some_API() ==
        (... x.a := y.b + 1;  ...)
  ext    rd y   wr x
  post   some_api_frame(x~,x) and ...;
```

It writes on one of the state fields (x), and uses information from another (y). The only state update involved is to change one field, and everything else remains constant. The VDM frame condition does not allow changes to y, but it does allow changes to any of the other fields in x that must remain constant. That entails the definition of a framing postcondition as:

```
functions
  some_api_frame: X_Type * X_Type -> bool
  some_api_frame(bx,ax) ==
    --bx.a == ax.a and
    bx.b == ax.b and bx.c == ax.c and ...;
```

These framing postconditions may also be conditional on possible paths taken within the API. The lack of a linguistic mechanism in VDM to tackle such complex-state simple framing-conditions became quite a drag within the many API implementations. In Z, this is easily done with a combination of schema calculus (*e.g.* Ξ and hiding) operators. An anecdotal summary was given by a collaborator within the VDM community: "you've touched on a couple of really interesting points: one about how the tools work, and one about the best way to write a specification!".

4.4 Overture and VDMJ

As a tool, Overture offers all the modern-day IDE "bells and whistles" most users expect, such as asynchronous specification checking (*i.e.* type check as you type), various useful dialogs and keyboard shortcuts for common tasks, integrated execution/building/debugging, and so on. VDMJ, on the other hand, works like a Linux command-line killer app, which includes all the functionalities Overture provides, as well as debugging and other facilities. So, users may wonder: why have both? Well, they are independent implementations from different sources. Yet, given their different interpretation of the language semantics, they effectively "speak" different VDM "dialects".

As far as I know, internally they are quite different in the sense that VDM ASTs were reengineered for various reasons [1]. In practice, the experience was that Overture cannot cope with the scale of a model of this size. From very early on, Overture started to lag considerably, and parsing/typechecking would take too long (5 to 20 s) to be productive. The debugger also stopped working without any warning/error: it simply freezes for reasons yet unknown. It was often more lax with language construct issues/errors, which entailed hours wasted chasing complicated red herrings of no interest.

VDMJ, on the other hand, has always been quite reliable. Most important, it is fast. All debugging and simulation since at least half way through the project has been done through it. Debugging in VDMJ is not as smooth as in the Overture Eclipse-like environment, but it works quite well and is more stable. Complex breakpoint conditions in Overture often led to connection errors and tool freezes, whereas in VDMJ they work reliably and were invaluable.

In practice, I work with a combination of both, where I use Overture for typesetting and project management chasing top-level (quick to parse and feedback) errors, and VDMJ for guaranteeing all is well, and for simulation, testing and debugging. It often happens that Overture will say a specification is okay, when VDMJ will throw you a number of residual errors; this is yet to happen the other way round. In early 2018, we experienced a quite severe lag in Overture, which led to some profiling with VisualVM (https://visualvm.github.io), and provided evidence there is a serious (deterministic) memory leak somewhere. In an industrial setting, this kind of complication, alongside the already alien nature of formal reasoning, can sadly become the excuse for non-adoption.

5 Evaluation and Discussion

Overall, the exercise has been quite worthwhile, and VDM and its tools have worked well. To give a clearer sense of scale, Table 1 gives a specification breakdown per module, where we point to the relative completion of each module, and its size in VDM lines[2]. Some modules have a large number of public APIs like the "Point of Interaction", but they are simple; whereas others like the "Cardholder Verification Manager" is small in API numbers but is way more complex. We are yet to work on the payment data and secure channel modules, as they are not crucial for the overall kernel functionality, but rather its additional services and secure communication features. The module data store comprises reflective access to state information via string-based named, data container types used for exchange between modules and external entities. We have an initial Java emulator implementation that is also development and is informed by our VDM model. At first, we considered using the Overture automatic code generator for Java with its translation of VDMSL into Java specifications in JML. Unfortunately, it quickly became clear the code generator's breath over VDMSL was not good enough for our needs. Simple constructs like constant value declarations could not be translated, even though constant functions with no input parameters (*i.e.* an alternative way to define constant values) did work. It would be a valuable exercise to extend the code generator for the future.

The lack of a mechanism for a VDM mathematical library/repository is a problem, and entails many people using VDM have to reinvent the wheel with respect to commonly used specification constructs. Perhaps something like the Maven-central (https://search.maven.org) repository in style, where all the necessary due diligence can be done by the repository manager would encourage more people to submit libraries themselves.

The distinction in error handling between Overture and VDMJ can be quite dangerous: it might completely knock of the confidence of users leaving them uncertain whether their choice for VDM was the right one. This, together with more targeted error messages to help developers fix the problems is quite

---

[2] Numbers were calculated with a mixture of string search, and Linux tools like `find` and `wc`.

Table 1. EMV2 VDM specification

Kernel module	Book	APIs	%	LOC
Kernel director	2	40	100	3,950
Selection manager	3	23	95	3,647
Transaction manager	4	20	95	3,423
Cardholder verification manager	5	18	100	3,613
Terminal risk manager	6	16	100	1,691
Additional services manager	7	9	10	1,081
Payment related data	8	?	0	0
Issuer authorisation manager	9	16	100	2,272
Data communication manager	10	31	95	2,633
Secure channel manager	11	?	0	0
Communication abstraction layer	12	11	20	1,006
Point of interaction terminal	13	35	90	1,944
Card profile and detection service	14	9	20	690
Data dictionary XSDS	15	0	100	9,537
Support				
Module data store	-	0	100	8,591
EMV database link	-	0	80	593
VDM support libraries	-	0	100	1,242
Total		228	80	137,739

important. The inability to debug/run EMV2 in Overture due to its freezing caused quite some concern at the time because it created a sense of time wasted and wrong choice of language made; this issue is still pending.

5.1   Tools Wish List

Throughout this work, there were a number of tool extension ideas. Some of them are EMV2-specific, yet a number can be of wider use, and we list them here as a suggestion to the VDM community in our perceived order of relevance.

1. **VDM profiler.** For larger modules, identifying where resources (time/memory) are being consumed is quite important in order to fine-tune modelling decisions. In CZT, users can instrument the tools to have counters for various specification constructs (*i.e.* number of names, or predicate parts, *etc.*), as well as detailed information about load times at what stages (*e.g.* parsing, typechecking).
2. **Direct separation between dialects.** In the current exercise, we had to cope with asynchronous API calls and a concurrent programming paradigm that we wanted to specify. VDM-RT already has **asynch** and thread concepts,

but it imposes on the user the extras of VDM++. That is, the VDM dialects (SL, ++, RT) are somewhat (unnecessarily) interwoven. In CZT, developers can pick and choose (sub-)dialects (*e.g.* Circus composes Z and CSP; TCOZ composes Object Z, CSP and Time; OhCircus comprises Z, CSP and an object oriented extension) and compose them according to need without having to have unwanted (sub-)dialects. It would be nice to have say SL with real time constructs and/or asynchronous calls and threads without VDM++ extensions.

3. **Dependencies-graph generator for imports xand operation call-graphs.** One way we found that minimised load time (from 57 s to 20 s in VDMJ) was to minimise dependencies, particularly circular dependencies. I presume Eclipse-based plugins already exists (in C and Java) for such dependency and call graph management.

4. **Heap images/serialisation to speed processing/execution.** For large specifications, reload time is costly. Once a specification stabilises and simulation time will be spent running/adjusting minor issues, avoiding total (lengthy) reloads would be useful. In CZT, that is viable through the use of ZML: an XML-encoding of ISO-Z that is lightening fast to process. Isabelle/HOL use Poly-ML heap images to store "compiled" proofs of larger libraries. Both these solutions serve to improve scalability and usability of tools and would greatly benefit users of larger VDM specifications.

5. **Test case generation from specification based on something like Eisenbach patterns.** Combinatorial testing in VDM is great, and enables productive specification validation. Yet, identifying what to test is sometimes difficult. A tool can create test cases of interest based on the shape of specifications involved and user instrumentation. For example, a disjunctive precondition A or B might need specific tests per disjunct; earlier work on VDM for this exist [3]. Predicate pattern-languages like Isabelle/HOL's Eisbach [17] could be used to determine what shapes tests should come from.

6. **Quickcheck/nitpick style test case generator for simulations.** QuickCheck is a test case generator written for Haskell programs[3], and now ported to a number of different situations. Nitpick identify counter examples to conjectures in Isabelle/HOL. A combination of these tools in Isabelle/HOL considerably improves proof effort. Something similar in VDM could help create test cases of interest and root out specification errors quickly.

7. **Record form filler for long record initialisers.** When modelling complex records, mk_ expressions can be quite awkward. Having an automatically generated GUI to construct such values from declared type information would be quite useful.

8. **XSD/XML/Swagger VDM integration.** XSD/XML and JSON-based languages like Swagger are used in industry to provide a semi-formal/rigorous type/API-signature definitions. A translator to/from VDM would be valuable: translating to VDM increases productivity, whereas translating from VDM keeps requirement specification documents accurate and up to date.

---

[3] See https://hackage.haskell.org/package/QuickCheck

9. **"Fix imports"** + **"quick-format" refactoring on imports and indentation.** Imports in VDM are a bit awkward. Explicit module imports (*i.e.* Module'Type) make it difficult to identify module dependencies, whereas complete import listing with renaming is quite tedious to do. Something like Eclipse's fix-imports and quick-formatting for indentation would be quite useful.

6   Conclusions

The work presented in this paper demonstrates it is possible to use VDM for a large scale (50 KLOC VDMSL) specification, despite various tool problems and practical challenges involved. The availability of a formal simulator for EMV2 and the careful documentation of its assumptions/commitments will hopefully pave the way for the influence of formal modelling within payment systems industry.

Acknowledgements. This work is associated with a long term collaboration with Dr. Martin Emms, an expert in EMV protocols, simulators, and hardware; and Dr. Paolo Modesti, an expert in security protocols design. We are part of a team developing the underlying methodology applied to EMV® 2nd Generation [13]. We are also grateful for EMV®'s support and technical discussions, specifically by Mike Ward and John Beric from the EMV® Security Working Group, and by Carlos Silvestre from the EMV® 2nd Generation Task Force. Finally, I am grateful for my department support, and Nick Battle and the VDM community for many interesting discussions, and patience in handling a number of issues.

References

1. Battle, N.: Analysis separation without visitors. In: 15th Overture Workshop, Newcastle University (2017)
2. Bond, M., Choudary, O., Murdoch, S.J., Skorobogatov, S., Anderson, R.: Chip and Skim: cloning EMV cards with the pre-play attack. In: S&P, pp. 49–64. IEEE (2014)
3. Dick, J., Faivre, A.: Automating the generation and sequencing of test cases from model-based specifications. In: Woodcock, J.C.P., Larsen, P.G. (eds.) FME 1993. LNCS, vol. 670, pp. 268–284. Springer, Heidelberg (1993). https://doi.org/10.1007/BFb0024651
4. Drimer, S., Murdoch, S.J., et al.: Keep your enemies close: distance bounding against smartcard relay attacks. In: USENIX Security Symposium, vol. 312 (2007)
5. Emms, M., Arief, B., Freitas, L., Hannon, J., van Moorsel, A.: Harvesting high value foreign currency transactions from EMV contactless credit cards without the pin. In: CCS, pp. 716–726. ACM (2014)
6. Emms, M., Arief, B., Little, N., van Moorsel, A.: Risks of offline verify PIN on contactless cards. In: Sadeghi, A.-R. (ed.) FC 2013. LNCS, vol. 7859, pp. 313–321. Springer, Heidelberg (2013). https://doi.org/10.1007/978-3-642-39884-1_26
7. EMVCo: EMV integrated circuit card specifications for payment systems [books 1 to 4], November 2011. https://www.emvco.com/emv-technologies/contact/

8. EMVCo: Next generation kernel system architecture overview. Technical report, EMVCo (2014)

9. EMVCo: EMV contactless specifications for payment systems [books a, b, c-1, c-2, c-3, c-4, c-5, c- 6, c-7 and d], February 2016. https://www.emvco.com/emv-technologies/contactless/

10. Financial Fraud Action: Fraud the fact. The definitive overview of payment industry fraud and measures to prevent it (2017). https://www.financialfraudaction.org.uk/fraudfacts17/

11. Freitas, L., Cavalcanti, A., Woodcock, J.: Taking our own medicine: applying the refinement calculus to state-rich refinement model checking. In: Liu, Z., He, J. (eds.) ICFEM 2006. LNCS, vol. 4260, pp. 697–716. Springer, Heidelberg (2006). https://doi.org/10.1007/11901433_38

12. Freitas, L., Emms, M.: Formal specification of EMV protocol. Technical report, Newcastle University (2014)

13. Freitas, L., Modesti, P., Emms, M.: A methodology for protocol verification applied to EMV(R) 1. In: Massoni, T., Mousavi, M.R. (eds.) SBMF 2018. LNCS, vol. 11254, pp. 180–197. Springer, Cham (2018)

14. Freitas, L., Woodcock, J.: Mechanising mondex with Z/Eves. Form. Asp. Comput. **20**(1), 117 (2008)

15. Jones, C.B.: Systematic Software Development Using VDM, vol. 2. Prentice Hall, Englewood Cliffs (1990)

16. Larsen, P.G., Lausdahl, K., Battle, N.: Combinatorial testing for VDM. In: SEFM, pp. 278–285. IEEE (2010)

17. Matichuck, D., Wenzel, M., Murray, T.: Eisbach User Manual. Technical University of Munich, October 2017

18. Modesti, P.: Efficient Java code generation of security protocols specified in *AnB/AnBx*. In: Mauw, S., Jensen, C.D. (eds.) STM 2014. LNCS, vol. 8743, pp. 204–208. Springer, Cham (2014). https://doi.org/10.1007/978-3-319-11851-2_17

19. Modesti, P.: *AnBx*: automatic generation and verification of security protocols implementations. In: Garcia-Alfaro, J., Kranakis, E., Bonfante, G. (eds.) FPS 2015. LNCS, vol. 9482, pp. 156–173. Springer, Cham (2016). https://doi.org/10.1007/978-3-319-30303-1_10

Constraint Reusing and k-Induction for Three-Valued Bounded Model Checking

Nils Timm$^{(\boxtimes)}$, Stefan Gruner, and Matthias Harvey

Department of Computer Science, University of Pretoria, Pretoria, South Africa
{ntimm,sgruner}@cs.up.ac.za

Abstract. Refinement-based model checking is an approach to software verification: Starting with an abstract software model, the model is iteratively refined until it is precise enough to prove or refute the property of interest. A downside is that it typically takes several iterations until the necessary precision is reached, and thus, resources are spent on repeating work that has already been performed in previous iterations. We tackle this by introducing a concept for reusing information between refinement iterations in order to reduce the computational overhead. Our approach extends our previous work on three-valued abstraction (3VA) and bounded model checking (BMC). 3VA allows to translate a verification problem into a SAT-encoded three-valued BMC problem that can be checked via a SAT solver. While there was formerly no information sharing between refinement iterations, we now show that logic constraints learned by the solver in the current iteration are also valid in future iterations. Reusing such constraints enables to prune the search space of SAT which leads to a speed-up of the iterative approach. Since we previously used standard BMC, the technique was incomplete and could be only used for detecting property violations but not for proving their absence. Here we combine three-valued BMC with k-induction, which makes the approach complete for model checking safety properties.

1 Introduction

Three-valued abstraction refinement (3VA) [15] is a technique for reducing the complexity of software verification. It proceeds by generating an abstract software model over predicates with the possible truth values *true*, *false* and *unknown*, where the latter is used to represent the loss of information due to abstraction. The model is iteratively refined by adding predicates until it is precise enough to prove or refute some temporal logic property. The evaluation of properties on such models is known as *three-valued model checking* (3MC) [3]. In 3VA both *true* and *false* results can be immediately transferred to the modelled system, whereas *unknown* indicates that the current abstract model is too coarse for a definite outcome. The advantage of 3VA is that it allows to gradually adjust the level of abstraction until the right balance between simplicity and precision is reached in order to verify the property. The downside is

T. Massoni and M. R. Mousavi (Eds.): SBMF 2018, LNCS 11254, pp. 126–143, 2018.
https://doi.org/10.1007/978-3-030-03044-5_9

that it typically takes several iterations until this happens, and thus, computational resources are spent on repeating work that has already been performed in earlier iterations. Here, we tackle this drawback by introducing a concept for sharing gathered information between refinement iterations in order to reduce the computational overhead.

Our approach extends previous work where we presented a verification technique for concurrent systems based on 3VA and *three-valued bounded model checking* (3BMC) [17,18]. Three-valued abstraction allows to translate verification problems into SAT-encoded 3BMC problems. Thus, verification is reduced to SAT solving. In each refinement iteration, a propositional formula that encodes the 3BMC problem for the current level of abstraction is generated and processed via a SAT solver. While there was formerly no information sharing between iterations, we now show that logic constraints learned by the solver in the current iteration are also valid in future iterations. SAT solvers employ *conflict-driven clause learning* [2] while processing a propositional formula, which generates constraint clauses that are used to prune the search space of the *current* SAT check. We prove that certain constraints that have been learned for our model checking encodings correspond to definite temporal logic properties of the encoded system. Since definite properties are preserved under three-valued abstraction refinement, it is permissible to *reuse* the associated constraints among iterations. Our inter-refinement iteration constraint reusing concept enables to considerably reduce the computational effort of 3VA-based verification.

In standard bounded model checking the bound $k \in \mathbb{N}$ restricts the length of execution paths of the modelled system, which makes the technique incomplete and only usable for detecting property violations but not for proving their absence. While our previous approach [17,18] has this limitation, we now establish completeness by integrating k-*induction* [16] into our approach. k-induction was originally introduced for verifying safety of hardware systems. It proceeds as follows: Given a state transition model of the system to be analysed and a state predicate $Safe$, it is checked whether all paths of length k that start in an initial state of the model are safe, i.e. whether $Safe$ holds in each state along the paths. This is the *base case* of k-induction, which is equivalent to standard bounded model checking. If the base case holds, then the *inductive step* is checked: Assuming k consecutive states where $Safe$ holds in each state, then $Safe$ also has to hold in every $(k+1)$-st successor state. The inductive step does not restrict the k consecutive states to start in an initial state. If the inductive step holds as well, then it can be concluded that *all* possible execution paths of the system are safe. Otherwise the procedure needs to be repeated with an incremented k.

Since hardware systems naturally correspond to state transition models, the application of k-induction is straightforward. In our software verification approach, we generate an *implicit* state transition model by applying abstraction and by encoding the state space of the abstract system in propositional logic. For the integration of k-induction, we define the base case and the inductive step of our verification tasks as 3BMC problems. Moreover, we combine our refinement procedure with a bound incrementation procedure. We use a top-level bound incrementation loop and therein two refinement loops, one for the base case and one for the step, that we independently abstract and refine. Each iteration is now characterised by a bound and a level of abstraction of the base case and the inductive step. Depending on the SAT-based verification outcome in an iteration, either the bound is incremented, refinement is applied, or the procedure terminates with a definite result that can be transferred to the input system. Learned constraints are reused between refinement iterations based on our novel clause reusing concept. Furthermore, we reuse constraints between bound iterations, which is permissible due to the *incremental bounded model checking principle* [11]. In experiments, we demonstrate that our approach enables the complete verification of concurrent systems within linear integer arithmetic and we show that our constraint reusing leads to significant performance improvements.

2   Concurrent Software Systems

Our approach focusses on linear integer concurrent systems. Almost all control structures of the C language, concurrency and the variable types *bool* and *int* are supported. There is currently no support for arrays and pointers. A system Sys consists of processes P_1 to P_n composed in parallel: $Sys = \|_{j=1}^{n} P_j$. It is defined over a set of variables $Var = Var_{Sys} \cup Var_{PC}$. Var_{Sys} is a set of arbitrary system variables and Var_{PC} is a special set that holds for each P_j a program counter pc_j ranging over the binary control locations $Loc_j = \{00, 01, ...\}$ of P_j. Locations of a process are labelled with guarded commands over system variables and with a reference to the next location. The form of a guarded command is $assume(e) : v_1 := e_1, ..., v_m := e_m$ where $v_1, ..., v_m \in Var_{Sys}$ and $e, e_1, ... e_m$ are expressions over Var_{Sys}. The state space over Var corresponds to the set S_{Var} of all variable valuations. Given a $s \in S_{Var}$ and an expression e over Var, $s(e)$ denotes the valuation of e in s. An example system for mutual exclusion is:

$$y : \texttt{semaphore where } y = 1;$$

$$P_1 :: \begin{bmatrix} \texttt{loop forever do} \\ \begin{bmatrix} \texttt{0: acquire } (y,1); \\ \texttt{1: CRITICAL} \\ \texttt{release } (y,1); \end{bmatrix} \end{bmatrix} \| P_2 :: \begin{bmatrix} \texttt{loop forever do} \\ \begin{bmatrix} \texttt{0: acquire } (y,1); \\ \texttt{1: CRITICAL} \\ \texttt{release } (y,1); \end{bmatrix} \end{bmatrix}$$

We have two processes operating on a counting semaphore y. The semantics of the operations are: $acquire(y, 1) = assume(y > 0) : y := y - 1$ and $release(y, 1) = assume(true) : y := y + 1$. We assume that for any Sys a deterministic initialisation of Var is given by a predicate $Init$, e.g. $Init = (y = 1) \wedge (pc_1 = 0) \wedge (pc_2 = 0)$. A computation of Sys corresponds to a sequence of commands where in each step one process is non-deterministically selected and the command at its current location is attempted to be executed. If the execution is not blocked by a guard, the variables are updated according to the assignment part and the process advances to the next location. A computation can be likewise considered as a state sequence $\pi = s_0 s_1 s_2 \ldots$ where the transition from s_i to s_{i+1} correctly characterises the execution of the associated command. A computation of our example system is: $\pi = \langle y = 1, pc_1 = 0, pc_2 = 0 \rangle \langle y = 0, pc_1 = 1, pc_2 = 0 \rangle \langle y = 1, pc_1 = 0, pc_2 = 0 \rangle \ldots$ Explicit-state verification constructs transition models that represent all possible computations of the analysed system. In our approach, we construct a propositional encoding that represents the computations *implicitly*. Before we introduce our encoding, we look at the temporal properties that we want to verify.

3   Checking Safety via k-Induction

Verification involves checking all possible computations of a system with regard to correctness requirements. Of particular interest are safety properties, which require that all states reached in a computation satisfy some predicate $Safe$. For our example system *mutual exclusion* is a safety property that corresponds to $Safe = \neg(pc_1 = 1) \vee \neg(pc_2 = 1)$. It requires that not both processes are at their critical location 1 at the same time. Verification means to prove or refute that for all computations starting in an initial state $Safe$ always holds, or formally:

$$[Sys, Init \models_\forall \text{ always } Safe] \quad := \quad \forall \pi = (s_0 s_1 s_2 \ldots) : s_0(Init) \rightarrow \bigwedge_{i=0}^{\infty} s_i(Safe)$$

A method to address such verification problems is *k-induction* [16]: Let Sys be a system with computations in terms of state sequences and let $k \in \mathbb{N}$. In the *base case* it is checked if for all computations starting in an initial state the first k states are $Safe$. In the *induction step* it is checked if, assuming a computation consisting of a sequence of k $Safe$ states, also any successor state is $Safe$. In contrast to the base case, the step does not contain a constraint on the initial state. This is necessary for the soundness of k-induction. These universal problems, referring to the safety of all computations, can be transformed into complementary existential problems referring to the existence of unsafe computations; as we can see, only the base case contains the initial state constraint $s_0(Init)$:

$$[Sys, Init \models_\exists Base]_k \quad := \quad \exists \pi = (s_0 \ldots s_k) : s_0(Init) \wedge \bigvee_{i=0}^{k} s_i(\neg Safe)$$
$$[Sys, true \models_\exists Step]_{k+1} \quad := \quad \exists \pi = (s_0 \ldots s_{k+1}) : \bigwedge_{i=0}^{k} s_i(Safe) \wedge s_{k+1}(\neg Safe)$$

Hence, proving the universal problems is equivalent to disproving the existential ones. The latter can be efficiently done via SAT or SMT solving. k-induction is typically performed incrementally with regard to k. Thus, when checking the base case for some k we can assume that all shorter base cases have already been proven to be safe, and we can add these facts as constraints to the problem to be solved. Furthermore, in order to make k-induction complete, i.e. terminating for finite-state systems, it is necessary to restrict the inductive step to *loop-free* computations [16]. This gives us a slightly revised base case and step, for simplicity we abbreviate the verification problems by just $[Base]_k$ and $[Step]_{k+1}$:

$$[Base]_k \quad := \quad \exists \pi = (s_0 \ldots s_k) : s_0(Init) \wedge \bigwedge_{i=0}^{k-1} s_i(Safe) \wedge s_k(\neg Safe)$$
$$[Step]_{k+1} \quad := \quad \exists \pi = (s_0 \ldots s_{k+1}) : \pi(LoopFree) \wedge \bigwedge_{i=0}^{k} s_i(Safe) \wedge s_{k+1}(\neg Safe)$$

where $\pi(LoopFree) = \bigwedge_{0 \leq i < j \leq k+1}(s_i \neq s_j)$ assuming that $\pi = (s_0, \ldots, s_{k+1})$. k-induction is still applicable to systems with loop computations in terms of recurring states, but for checking safety it is sufficient to only consider loop-free ones. The procedure below illustrates the principle of incremental k-induction:

---

1 **for** $k = 0$ **to** ∞ **do**
2   **if** $([Base]_k$ holds) **then**
3 | **return** "safety property fails"
4   **if** $([Step]_{k+1}$ does not hold) **then**
5 | **return** "safety property holds"

---

k-induction allows to reduce an unbounded verification problem to two bounded ones: the base case and the inductive step. Base case and step can be formulated as bounded model checking problems. Bounded model checking requires a state transition model of the system to be analysed. For hardware, such models can be straightly encoded in propositional logic and verification can be done via SAT solving. k-induction-based hardware verification has been applied in [7,16]. For software it is significantly harder to capture its complex features in propositional logic. Therefore, most k-induction approaches to software verification use an SMT solver [6,10]: The input system is transformed into a k-bounded one, where k typically refers to the number of unrollings of loops. The bounded system is then fed into an SMT solver to check the base case and the step of the verification problem. In our new approach, we use a combination of SMT and SAT: Via SMT solving we generate a three-valued abstraction of the system. Due to the reduced complexity the abstract system can be straightforwardly encoded in propositional logic and verification can be efficiently done via SAT solving. Next, we give a brief introduction to three-valued abstraction.

4   Three-Valued Predicate Abstraction and Refinement

To make SAT-based k-induction applicable to software verification, we follow the abstraction refinement paradigm: We employ SMT-based *three-valued predicate abstraction* [15] to our concrete systems, which yields abstract systems over predicates that can take the values *true*, *false* and *unknown*. *Unknown* represents loss of details due to abstraction. Three-valued abstraction generates an approximation in the sense that all definite verification results (*true*, *false*) obtained for an abstract system can be transferred to the concrete system. Only *unknown* results necessitate refinement for which we developed an automatic procedure [17]. Later we show that for an abstract system and a safety property any base case or step of k-induction can be reduced to two Boolean SAT problems. We now briefly outline three-valued abstraction. Details can be found in [15]. Our approach is based on the Kleene logic $\mathcal{K}_3$ [8] where *unknown*, abbreviated by u, is a used as a third truth value. In abstract systems guarded commands do not refer to concrete variables but to abstract predicates A_{Sys} over Var_{Sys}. Predicates in A_{Sys} may be set to u due to the execution of an abstract command. While our three-valued abstraction reduces the complexity induced by system variables, it preserves the original control flow. For this, we use the set of two-valued predicates $A_{PC} = \{(pc_j = b_m \ldots b_0) \mid pc_j \in Var_{PC},\, b_m \ldots b_0 \in Loc_j\}$ that covers all possible locations of the system. The overall predicate set is $A = A_{Sys} \cup A_{PC}$. Given a concrete system Sys over Var, an initialisation $Init$ and a property ψ, we refer to the corresponding concrete verification task by $_{Var}[Sys, Init \models_Q \psi]$ with $Q \in \{\forall, \exists\}$. Additionally given a predicate set A over Var we refer to the abstract verification task by $_A[Sys, Init \models_Q \psi]$. From [15] we get the theorem:

Theorem 1 (Property Preservation under Three-Valued Abstraction).
Let Sys, Var, $Init$, A and Q as above. Moreover, let ψ be a property that is expressible in linear temporal logic (LTL) and let $z \in \{true, false\}$. Then:

$$_A[Sys, Init \models_Q \psi] = z \;\Rightarrow\; {}_{Var}[Sys, Init \models_Q \psi] = z$$

Since the properties in our k-induction approach are expressible in LTL, we can make use of Theorem 1. Definite results under abstraction can be transferred to the concrete system. For *unknown* results we have our refinement technique [17] that yields an extended predicate set $A^{r+1} = A^r \cup \{p \mid p \text{ predicate over } Var, p \notin A^r\}$ where $r = 0, 1, \ldots$ denotes the current refinement iteration. We get:

Corollary 1. *Let Sys, $Init$, ψ, A^r, A^{r+1}, Q and z as above. Then:*

$$_{A^r}[Sys, Init \models_Q \psi] = z \;\Rightarrow\; {}_{A^{r+1}}[Sys, Init \models_Q \psi] = z$$

Thus, definite properties are also preserved under abstraction refinement.

5 Three-Valued Bounded Model Checking

So far, we have defined verification tasks and corresponding abstractions. To practically perform verification, we need a computational model. Abstract state spaces can be defined as three-valued Kripke structures and safety properties can be formalised in temporal logic. On this basis, verification tasks can be expressed as three-valued bounded model checking (3BMC) problems.

Definition 1 (Three-Valued Kripke Structure). *A* three-valued Kripke structure *over a set of atomic predicates A is a tuple $M = (S, S_0, R, L)$ where S is a set of states, $S_0 \subseteq S$ is a set of initial states, $R : S \times S \to \{true, u, false\}$ is a transition function, and $L : S \times A \to \{true, u, false\}$ is a labelling function.*

We assume that Kripke structures are *complementary-closed*, i.e. for each $p \in A$ there is a complementary $\bar{p} \in A$ such that $\forall s \in S : L(s, p) = \neg L(s, \bar{p})$. A path π is a sequence of states $s_0 s_1 s_2 \ldots$ with $\forall i : R(s_i, s_{i+1}) \in \{true, u\}$. $\pi(i)$ denotes the i-th state of π. By Π_M we denote the set of all paths of M starting in an initial state. Paths are considered for the evaluation of temporal properties. Here we use the bounded temporal logic (BTL) which is a fragment of LTL.

Definition 2 (Syntax of Bounded Temporal Logic (BTL)). *Let A be a predicate set and $k \in \mathbb{N}$ a bound. The set of BTL formulas BTL over A and k is*

- *if $p \in A$ and $i \in [0, k]$ then $p_i \in BTL$ and $\neg p_i \in BTL$,*
- *if $\psi \in BTL$ then $\neg\psi \in BTL$,*
- *if $\psi \in BTL$ and $\psi' \in BTL$ then $\psi \vee \psi' \in BTL$ and $\psi \wedge \psi' \in BTL$.*

Definition 3 (Three-Valued Evaluation of BTL). *Let $M = (S, S_0, R, L)$ be over A and let π be a path of M. Let $k \in \mathbb{N}$ and $i \in [0, k]$. Then the evaluation of a k-bounded BTL formula ψ on π, written $[\pi \models \psi]_k$, is inductively defined as:*

$$[\pi \models p_i]_k \quad = \quad L(\pi(i), p) \wedge \bigwedge_{j=0}^{i-1} R(\pi(j), \pi(j+1))$$
$$[\pi \models \neg p_i]_k \quad = \quad L(\pi(i), \overline{p}) \wedge \bigwedge_{j=0}^{i-1} R(\pi(j), \pi(j+1))$$
$$[\pi \models \psi \circ \psi']_k \quad = \quad [\pi \models \psi]_k \circ [\pi \models \psi']_k \qquad with \circ \in \{\wedge, \vee\}$$
$$[\pi \models \neg(\psi \circ \psi')]_k \quad = \quad [\pi \models \neg\psi]_k \overline{\circ} [\pi \models \neg\psi']_k \qquad with \overline{\wedge} = \vee \ and \ \overline{\vee} = \wedge$$

The universal evaluation of a BTL formula ψ on M over A is $_A[M, S_0 \models_\forall \psi]_k = \bigwedge_{\pi \in \Pi_M} [\pi \models \psi]_k$. The existential one is $_A[M, S_0 \models_\exists \psi]_k = \bigvee_{\pi \in \Pi_M} [\pi \models \psi]_k$.

Checking BTL properties of three-valued Kripke structures is *three-valued bounded model checking* [18] with the possible outcomes *true, false, u*. The state space of an abstracted system *Sys* can be modelled as a Kripke structure M such that there is a one-to-one correspondence between the states of *Sys* and M, and the transitions of M correspond to the execution of guarded commands of *Sys*. Hence, paths of M represent computations of *Sys*. From [15] we get the theorem:

Theorem 2. *Let Sys be abstracted over A and let M be the three-valued Kripke structure representing the abstract state space of Sys. Moreover, let $Q \in \{\forall, \exists\}$. Then for all linear temporal logic properties ψ the following holds:*

$$_A[Sys, Init \models_Q \psi]_k \quad \equiv \quad _A[M, S_0 \models_Q \psi]_k$$

Thus, verification is equivalent to solving the corresponding 3BMC problem. This is an important fact since 3BMC can be reduced to propositional satisfiability and thus effectively performed via SAT solving. We now define the base case and the step of k-induction-based verification as 3BMC problems. For our example with $Safe_i = \neg(pc_1 = 1)_i \vee \neg(pc_2 = 1)_i$ and $(pc_1 = 1), (pc_2 = 1) \in A$ we get

$$_A[Base]_k \quad \equiv \quad _A[M, S_0 \models_\exists \bigwedge_{i=0}^{k-1} Safe_i \wedge \neg Safe_k]_k$$
$$_A[Step]_{k+1} \quad \equiv \quad _A[M, S \models_\exists \bigwedge_{i=0}^{k} Safe_i \wedge \neg Safe_{k+1} \wedge LoopFree(0..k+1)]_{k+1}$$

with $LoopFree(0..k+1) = \bigwedge_{0 \le i < j \le k+1} \left(\bigvee_{p \in A} ((p_i \wedge \neg p_j) \vee (\neg p_i \wedge p_j)) \right)$. The *loop-free* property expresses that all states along a prefix are pairwise different. Note that in the 3BMC problem representing the inductive step the set of initial states is simply S, i.e. an arbitrary state can be the initial state. Next, we take a look on how these 3BMC problems can be encoded in propositional logic.

6   Propositional Logic Encoding

In [18] we showed how a 3BMC problem $_A[M, S_0 \models_\exists \psi]_k$ corresponding to a system Sys abstracted over A and a property ψ can be encoded as a propositional formula $_A[\![M, \psi]\!]_k$. The encoding can be directly constructed based on the abstract system. It corresponds to an implicit representation of the model checking problem such that the construction and exploration of an explicit state transition model is avoided. $_A[\![M, \psi]\!]_k$ is defined over a set of Boolean atoms $Atoms$, the constants $true$, $false$, and a special atom $\bot$ that we use to represent the $unknowns$ due to abstraction. $\bot$ occurs solely non-negated in $_A[\![M, \psi]\!]_k$. 3BMC can now be performed via two SAT checks. One check considers an $over$-$approximating\ completion$, marked with '+', where all $\bot$'s are assumed to be $true$:

$$_A[\![M, \psi]\!]_k^+ := {}_A[\![M, \psi]\!]_k[\bot \mapsto true]$$

and the second check considers an $under$-$approximating\ completion$, marked with a '−', where all $\bot$'s are assumed to be $false$:

$$_A[\![M, \psi]\!]_k^- := {}_A[\![M, \psi]\!]_k[\bot \mapsto false].$$

Here $[\bot \mapsto z]$, $z \in \{true, false\}$ denotes the assumption that the special atom $\bot$ is assigned to z. This gives us the notion of three-valued satisfiability sat_3:

Definition 4 (sat_3). Let $_A[\![M, \psi]\!]_k$ over $Atoms$ be the propositional encoding of $_A[M, S_0 \models_\exists \psi]_k$, let $\{\mathcal{A}|\mathcal{A} : Atoms \rightarrow \{true, false\}\}$ be the set of all possible truth assignments to the atoms in $Atoms$. Then sat_3 is defined as:

$$sat_3(_A[\![M, \psi]\!]_k) = \begin{cases} false & \text{if } \forall \mathcal{A} : \mathcal{A}(_A[\![M, \psi]\!]_k^+) = false \\ true & \text{if } \exists \mathcal{A} : \mathcal{A}(_A[\![M, \psi]\!]_k^-) = true \\ unknown & \text{else} \end{cases}$$

In [18] the following theorem has been proven:

Theorem 3. Let $_A[\![M, \psi]\!]_k$ and $_A[M, S_0 \models_\exists \psi]_k$ be as above. Then:

$$sat_3(_A[\![M, \psi]\!]_k) = {}_A[M, S_0 \models_\exists \psi]_k$$

Hence, the sat_3 result obtained for the encoding corresponds to the model checking result. We now briefly explain how the translation into Boolean satisfiability works. The details can be found in [18]. Remember that paths of Kripke structures as well as BTL properties correspond to expressions over $A = A_{Sys} \cup A_{PC}$ indexed with $i \in [0, k]$ where i denotes a position along a k-prefix. Thus, our encoding is inductively defined over indexed expressions. Predicates in A_{Sys} have a $three$-$valued$ domain, whereas the encoding is two-$valued$ and we use the special atom $\bot$ to represent the '$unknown$'. In order to reduce a three-valued problem to a two-valued one, we use two Boolean atoms for each $p \in A_{Sys}$ and $i \in [0, k]$:

$$Atoms_{Sys} := \{p[u]_i, p[b]_i \mid p \in A_{Sys},\ i \in [0, k]\}$$

Atom $p[u]_i$ will let us indicate whether p evaluates to *unknown* or to a definite value at position i, and $p[b]_i$ will let us indicate whether p evaluates to *true* or *false*. For encoding counter predicates $(pc_j = l_m \ldots l_0) \in A_{PC}$ we use the set

$$Atoms_{PC} := \{l_j[m]_i, \ldots, l_j[0]_i \mid (pc_j = l_m \ldots l_0) \in A_{PC}, \, i \in [0, k]\}$$

Since a program counter location $l_m \ldots l_0$ is a binary number, it can be straight-forwardly encoded as a conjunction of literals over $l_j[m]_i, \ldots, l_j[0]_i$. The overall set of atoms of our encoding is $Atoms = Atoms_{Sys} \cup Atoms_{PC}$. Now we can define the Boolean encoding of arbitrary indexed expressions over A and $[0, k]$:

Definition 5 (Encoding of Logical Expressions). *Let $A = A_{Sys} \cup A_{PC}$ be a predicate set with $p \in A_{Sys}$ and $(pc_j = l_m \ldots l_0) \in A_{PC}$. Let $k \in \mathbb{N}$. The encoding of expressions e over A indexed over $[0, k]$, written $[\![e]\!]_k$, is defined as:*

$$
\begin{aligned}
[\![p_i = unknown]\!]_k &:= p[u]_i \\
[\![p_i = true]\!]_k &:= \neg p[u]_i \wedge p[b]_i \\
[\![p_i = false]\!]_k &:= \neg p[u]_i \wedge \neg p[b]_i \\
[\![p_i]\!]_k &:= [\![p_i = true]\!]_k \vee ([\![p_i = unknown]\!]_k \wedge \bot) \\
[\![\neg p_i]\!]_k &:= [\![p_i = false]\!]_k \vee ([\![p_i = unknown]\!]_k \wedge \bot) \\
[\![(pc_j = l_m \ldots l_0)_i]\!]_k &:= \bigwedge_{d=0}^{m} (\text{if } l_d = 1 \text{ then } l_j[d]_i \text{ else } \neg l_j[d]_i) \\
[\![\neg (pc_j = l_m \ldots l_0)_i]\!]_k &:= \neg [\![(pc_j = l_m \ldots l_0)_i]\!]_k
\end{aligned}
$$

The encoding of $e \vee e'$, $e \wedge e'$, $\neg(e \vee e')$ and $\neg(e \wedge e')$ is trivial and thus omitted.

We can build the formula $_A[\![M, \psi]\!]_k = {}_A[\![M]\!]_k \wedge {}_A[\![\psi]\!]_k$ over *Atoms* where $_A[\![M]\!]_k$ encodes all k-bounded paths of M and $_A[\![\psi]\!]_k$ constrains paths to those satisfying ψ. E.g., the property $\bigwedge_{i=0}^{k} Safe_i$ with $Safe_i = \neg(pc_1 = 1)_i \vee \neg(pc_2 = 1)_i$ gets encoded to $\bigwedge_{i=0}^{k}(\neg l_1[0]_i \vee \neg l_2[0]_i)$. Each assignment $\mathcal{A}$ that satisfies $_A[\![M, \psi]\!]_k^-$ characterises a path π in M with $[\pi \models \psi] = true$. If there is no such assignment for $_A[\![M, \psi]\!]_k^+$ then $\forall \pi$ we have $[\pi \models \psi] = false$. This reduces 3BMC to SAT.

7 Iterative Refinement with Constraint Reusing

Our SAT-based verification technique combines three-valued abstraction with *iterative refinement*. Given a system Sys over Var, a k-bounded property ψ and a predicate set A^r, we construct the encoding $_{A^r}[\![M, \psi]\!]_k$ of the corresponding three-valued bounded model checking problem $_{A^r}[M \models_E \psi]_k$, where $r = 0, 1, \ldots$ denotes the current refinement iteration. In this section, we introduce the concept of *constraint reusing* between refinement iterations. Algorithm *SATBMC* illustrates our refinement approach and gives a first idea of constraint reusing: *SATBMC* gets a model checking problem and a predicate set A^h as an input, where $h \in \mathbb{N}$ denotes the refinement level to start with. h is typically 0 but may be also greater when we combine iterative refinement with *bound incrementation* (Sect. 8). Unsatisfiability of the over-approximating completion and satisfiability of the under-approximating one let us immediately derive a corresponding definite model checking result. If this is not possible in iteration r, we apply

---

Algorithm 1. $SATBMC([M, S_0 \models_E \psi]_k, A^h)$

---

1 *definite constraint set* $\mathbb{C} := \varnothing$
2 **for** $r = h$ **to** ∞ **do**
3   **if** $_{A^r}[M, \psi]_k^+ \wedge \mathbb{C}$ *unsatisfiable* **then**
4 | **return** $_{A^r}[M, S_0 \models_E \psi]_k = false$
5   **if** $_{A^r}[M, \psi]_k^- \wedge \mathbb{C}$ *satisfiable* **then**
6 | **return** $_{A^r}[M, S_0 \models_E \psi]_k = true$
7   **else**
8 | $A^{r+1} := A^r \cup \{p \mid p \notin A^r\}$
9 | *add definite constraints learned in current iteration to* $\mathbb{C}$

---

our counterexample-guided refinement [17] which yields an extended predicate set $A^{r+1} := A^r \cup \{p \mid p \text{ predicate over } Var, p \notin A^r\}$ and a corresponding refined encoding $_{A^{r+1}}[M, \psi]_k$. We then run the necessary SAT tests and repeat these steps until a definite result is obtained. As we can see, the encodings in our algorithm are conjuncted with a constraint set $\mathbb{C}$. A constraint is a clause over the atoms of the encoding that has been inferred by the solver via clause learning [2]. $\mathbb{C}$ is extended with newly learned constraints in each iteration. Thus, constraints learned in the past are reused in future iterations. The motivation for constraint reusing is that adding (valid) constraints to a formula reduces the search space of the corresponding SAT problem, which can improve the solving time.

However, reusing constraints between refinement iterations is not straightforward. A clause learned in iteration r is not necessarily a valid constraint in $r + 1$. The formulas $_{A^r}[M, \psi]_k$ and $_{A^{r+1}}[M, \psi]_k$ evidently share a common set of atoms over which they are defined, but their structure is typically completely different: The addition of new predicates by refinement can involve extensive changes of the abstract state space and its encoding. Thus, $_{A^{r+1}}[M, \psi]_k$ cannot be obtained from $_{A^r}[M, \psi]_k$ by simply adding more clauses. This makes our refinement generally incompatible with standard *incremental* SAT solving [13] where learned constraints can be reused between consecutive SAT instances without any restriction. Our novel constraint reusing concept for iterative refinement is based on a check of whether a learned constraint is *definite* in terms of the encoded three-valued model checking problem. A definite constraint characterises a temporal property that definitely holds at the current refinement level. Since definite properties are preserved under refinement (Corollary 1), we can prove that definite constraints are also valid at any higher refinement level.

We start with a few basics. A learned constraint is a clause C that is syntactically inferred from a formula F by the solver: $F \vdash C$. The following holds: $(F \vdash C) \Rightarrow (F \models C)$, i.e. a syntactic consequence is also a semantic one. If $F \models C$ holds, we say C is a *valid constraint* of F. We implemented over- and under-approximating completions of $F = {_{A^r}[M, \psi]_k}$ as assumptions over $\bot$. This has the effect that all learned constraints are *assumption-independent* [7], i.e. they are logical consequences irrespective of the value assigned to $\bot$. Hence, we say C has been learned for F if it has been learned for F^+ or for F^-. Since

F^+ and F^- only differ in the assumption over $\bot$, we get $(F^+ \vdash C) \Rightarrow (F^- \models C)$. Thus, all C learned for F^+ can be reused when solving F^- in the *same* iteration.

We now describe how constraints can be reused *between* refinement iterations $r < r'$. This is feasible for constraints that characterise temporal properties that definitely hold in iteration r. In order to identify such *definite constraints* we use an enhancement of the encoding $_{A^r}[\![M, \psi]\!]_k$ based on the *Tseytin transformation* (TT) [19] where sub-formulas are represented by auxiliary atoms:

$$Atoms_{Aux} \;=\; \{p[t]_i, p[f]_i \mid p \in A^r_{Sys}, \; i \in [0,k]\}$$

The enhanced encoding revises Definition 5 in two cases only:

Definition 6 (Enhanced Encoding). *Let $p \in A^r_{Sys}$ and $i \in [0,k]$. Then:*

$$[\![p_i = true]\!]_k \; := \; p[t]_i \qquad\qquad [\![p_i = false]\!]_k \; := \; p[f]_i$$

Hence, definite information with regard to a predicate p at position i can now be derived from a *single literal* (e.g. $p[t]_i$), rather than from a *conjunction of literals* (e.g. $\neg p[u]_i \wedge p[b]_i$) as in the original encoding. Note that a constraint is always a *disjunction* of single literals. Thus, only with our enhanced encoding a learned constraint may tell us something definite about a predicate p. We still need to put $p[t]_i$, $p[f]_i$ and $p[u]_i$ into a relation to correctly encode that a three-valued predicate can only hold one truth value at a time. According to TT, we conjunct the overall encoding with the following equivalences:

$$\bigwedge\nolimits_{p \in A^r_{Sys}} \bigwedge\nolimits_{i=0}^{k} \left((p[t]_i \leftrightarrow \neg p[u]_i \wedge p[b]_i) \wedge (p[f]_i \leftrightarrow \neg p[u]_i \wedge \neg p[b]_i) \right)$$

Thus, the single auxiliary atoms represent sub-formulas that indicate definite information with regard to predicates. Let $_{A^r}[\![M, \psi]\!]_k$ over *Atoms* be the resulting enhanced encoding. We now define the set of *definite literals* DL over *Atoms* as:

$$
\begin{aligned}
DL \;=\; & \{p[t]_i, p[f]_i \mid p \in A^r_{Sys}, \; i \in [0,k]\} \\
& \cup \{l_j[d]_i, \neg l_j[d]_i \mid (pc_j = l_m \dots l_0) \in A^r_{PC}, \; i \in [0,k], \; d \in [0,m]\}
\end{aligned}
$$

DL contains all auxiliary atoms, and all program counter atoms and their negations. We denote constraints that are purely composed of literals from DL as *definite constraints*. BTL formulas corresponding to definite constraints are:

Definition 7 (BTL Formulas Corresponding to Definite Constraints). *Let $_{A^r}[\![M, \psi]\!]_k$ be the enhanced encoding of $_{A^r}[\![M, S_0 \models_\exists \psi]\!]_k$. Moreover, let $C = c_1 \vee \dots \vee c_n$ over DL be a definite constraint learned for $_{A^r}[\![M, \psi]\!]_k$. Then the BTL formula corresponding to C, written $btl(C)$, is inductively defined as:*

$$
\begin{aligned}
btl(p[t]_i) \qquad &:= \; p_i \\
btl(p[f]_i) \qquad &:= \; \neg p_i \\
btl(l_j[d]_i) \qquad &:= \; \bigvee\nolimits_{(l_m \dots l_0) \in Loc_j, l_d = 1} (pc_j = l_m \dots l_0)_i \\
btl(\neg l_j[d]_i) \qquad &:= \; \bigvee\nolimits_{(l_m \dots l_0) \in Loc_j, l_d = 0} (pc_j = l_m \dots l_0)_i \\
btl(c_1 \vee \dots \vee c_n) \; &:= \; btl(c_1) \vee \dots \vee btl(c_n)
\end{aligned}
$$

We get the following lemma wrt. constraints and corresponding BTL formulas:

Lemma 1. *Let $_{A^r}[\![M, \psi]\!]_k$ be the enhanced encoding of $_{A^r}[M, S_0 \models_\exists \psi]_k$. Moreover, let C over DL be a definite constraint. Then*

$$_{A^r}[\![M, \psi]\!]_k \vdash C \;\Rightarrow\; _{A^r}[M, S_0 \models_\forall (\psi \to btl(C))]_k = true$$

Proof. See http://github.com/ssfm-up/TVMC/raw/unbounded/proofs.pdf.

Hence, even if the current refinement level is too coarse to prove the actual property of interest ψ, a learned definite constraint C tells us that all paths satisfying ψ must also satisfy $btl(C)$. This is a definite result of a three-valued model checking problem with refinement level r. Corollary 1 allows us to transfer this result to all refinement levels $r' > r$: $_{A^r}[M, S_0 \models_\forall (\psi \to btl(C))]_k = true \;\Rightarrow\; _{A^{r'}}[M, S_0 \models_\forall (\psi \to btl(C))]_k = true$. Next, we show that a constraint C associated with a definite property $\psi \to btl(C)$ is also valid at higher levels.

Lemma 2. *Let $_{A^r}[\![M, \psi]\!]_k$ be the encoding of $_{A^r}[M, S_0 \models_\exists \psi]_k$ and let C be a definite constraint. Then*

$$_{A^r}[M, S_0 \models_\forall (\psi \to btl(C))]_k = true \;\Rightarrow\; _{A^r}[\![M, \psi]\!]_k \models C$$

Proof. See http://github.com/ssfm-up/TVMC/raw/unbounded/proofs.pdf.

We get the following Corollary that establishes the reusability of definite constraints between refinement iterations.

Corollary 2 (Reusability of Definite Constraints). *Let $_{A^r}[\![M, \psi]\!]_k$ be the encoding of $_{A^r}[M, S_0 \models_\exists \psi]_k$. Let C be a definite constraint and $r' > r$. Then*

$$
\begin{array}{ccc}
_{A^r}[\![M, \psi]\!]_k \vdash C & & _{A^{r'}}[\![M, \psi]\!]_k \models C \\[2pt]
\Big\Downarrow \text{\scriptsize Lemma 1} & & \Big\Uparrow \text{\scriptsize Lemma 2} \\[2pt]
_{A^r}[M, S_0 \models_\forall (\psi \to btl(C))]_k = true & \overset{\text{Cor. 1}}{\underset{\text{Thm. 2}}{\Longrightarrow}} & _{A^{r'}}[M, S_0 \models_\forall (\psi \to btl(C))]_k = true
\end{array}
$$

Hence, a definite constraint C learned in iteration r implies that $\psi \to btl(C)$ universally holds at r and any higher refinement level r' as well. Consequently, C must be also a valid constraint of the encoding in all iterations $r' > r$. We utilise this by determining definite constraints in each iteration and adding them to the set $\mathbb{C}$ that we use as a constraint set of the SAT problems to be solved in $SATBMC$. Our concept is based on TT. Thus, it does not lead to an increased complexity of the SAT problem. In fact, we also use TT to transform the overall encoding into conjunctive normal form, which introduces further auxiliary atoms. This does not affect our constraint reusing since we use the same auxiliary atoms for representing sub-formulas recurring in multiple refinement iterations. After TT, all clauses purely containing definite literals and auxiliary atoms referring to definite constraints can be reused between refinement iterations.

We illustrate our constraint reusing concept based on our running example. Let $_{A^0}[\![M, Safe_0 \wedge Safe_1]\!]_1$ with $A^0 = \{(pc_1 = 0), (pc_1 = 1), (pc_2 = 0), (pc_2 = 1)\}$ and $Safe_i = \neg(pc_1 = 1)_i \vee (pc_2 = 1)_i$ be the encoding of the base case of checking safety of the mutual exclusion system. The atom set used for the encoding is $Atoms = \{l_1[0]_0, l_2[0]_0, l_1[0]_1, l_2[0]_1, \}$. SAT solving yields *unknown*, since no information about the semaphore is considered at the current abstraction level. However, the solver infers the following constraint clauses $(\neg l_1[0]_1 \vee \neg l_2[0]_1)$ and $(l_1[0]_1 \vee l_2[0]_1)$ with the corresponding temporal logic formulas:

$$((pc_1 = 0)_1 \vee (pc_2 = 0)_1) \text{ and } ((pc_1 = 1)_1 \vee (pc_2 = 1)_1)$$

Hence, at position 1 of any execution path either only process 1 or only process 2 is at its critical location. According to our corollary, the constraint clauses that characterise this property can be reused in all future refinement iterations for pruning the search space of SAT. In the next iteration, we add the predicate $p := (y = 1)$ and SAT solving infers another reusable constraint clause $(p[f]_1)$. It tells us that at position 1 of any path the semaphore will be occupied. Next, we show how we integrated $SATBMC$ into an incremental k-induction procedure.

8 Implementation

We implemented an automatic verification tool for concurrent software systems[1]. Our tool extends our existing SAT-based bounded model checking framework [17] by integrating the k-induction principle with base case and inductive step, which makes our formerly incomplete approach complete. It employs three-valued abstraction in order to reduce the complexity of the state space encodings. Abstraction is combined with iterative refinement. As an input we take a system Sys in a C-like syntax with *int, bool* and *semaphore* as data types, an initial state predicate $Init$ and a safety predicate $Safe$. To verify whether $[Sys, Init \models_\forall \text{ always } Safe]$ holds, we determine the abstract model checking problems corresponding to the base case and step of k-induction

$$[Base]_k = [M, S_0 \models_\exists \bigwedge_{i=0}^{k-1} Safe_i \wedge \neg Safe_k]_k \text{ over } A^{r_B}$$
$$[Step]_{k+1} = [M, S \models_\exists \bigwedge_{i=0}^{k} Safe_i \wedge \neg Safe_{k+1} \wedge LoopFree(0..k+1)]_{k+1} \text{ over } A^{r_S}$$

where A^{r_B} denotes the predicate set used for the three-valued abstraction of the base case and A^{r_S} the set used for the inductive step. The bound k and the predicate sets are so far only uninitialised parameters and instead of explicitly constructing the Kripke structure M and exploring its state space, we take the bounded model checking problems as the input of our k-induction algorithm:

The variables r_B and r_S indicate the current refinement iteration of the base case and of the inductive step. Both are initialised with 0. The corresponding sets of abstraction predicates A^{r_B} and A^{r_S} are also initialised by the k-induction

---

[1] Available at www.github.com/ssfm-up/TVMC/tree/unbounded.

Algorithm 2. k-$induction([Base]_k, [Step]_{k+1})$

---

1 $r_B := 0, \; A^{r_B} := initialiseA^{r_B}()$
2 $r_S := 0, \; A^{r_S} := initialiseA^{r_S}()$
3 **for** $k = 0$ **to** ∞ **do**
4   **if** $(SATBMC([Base]_k, A^{r_B}) = true)$ **then**
5 | **return** "safety property fails"
6   **if** $(SATBMC([Step]_{k+1}, A^{r_S}) = false)$ **then**
7 | **return** "safety property holds"

---

algorithm. Initially, they contain all control flow predicates and potentially further predicates over system variables that are referenced in the property to be checked. After the initialisation, k-induction iterates over the bound. In each k-iteration $SATBMC$ is called for the bounded model checking problems associated with the base case and with the step. Within $SATBMC$ we have a further iteration: The set of abstraction predicates is iteratively extended via refinement. Each refinement iteration consists of the propositional encoding of the three-valued model checking problem for the current predicate set and the execution of the corresponding SAT checks. $SATBMC$ terminates once a refinement level is reached where a definite model checking result can be obtained. k-induction terminates when it can be either proven or refuted that safety holds for the system. Termination is guaranteed for finite-state systems.

As another new feature, our tool supports constraint reusing on three levels. (I): Constraints are reused between bound iterations $k < k'$ based on incremental SAT with assumption literals [13]. (II): Similarly, we reuse assumption-independent constraints between the over- and the under-approximating completion in each refinement iteration r. (III): Finally, we reuse definite constraints between refinement iterations $r < r'$ based on the results from Sect. 7. The diagram below illustrates the directions of constraint reusing for the base case:

9 Experimental Results

We experimentally investigated the impact of our novel clause reusing concepts (II) and (III) on the verification time. While detecting safety violations in faulty systems was generally very fast, we focused in our case study on proving safety of *correct* systems: We verified deadlock-freedom of a semaphore-based dining philosophers algorithm and we proved mutual exclusion of Dijkstra's mutex algorithm [5]. In each benchmark we considered systems with increasing numbers of processes. A general optimisation that we used was checking the over-approximation of the base case always first and in case of a *false* result skipping the then redundant under-approximation check (see Definition 4 and Theorem 3). Analogously, we always checked the under-approximation of the step first and in case of a *true* result skipped the over-approximation check. The intuition behind this is that for safe systems we can always expect a sequence of iterations where the base case fails and the step holds until in the final iteration the step fails, which corresponds to a correctness result. The experimental results are depicted below.

Benchmark	Processes	Final bound	Refinements (base/step)	Time with (I) only	Time with (I), (II) and (III)
PHILOSOPHERS	2	3	1/2	0.45 s	0.44 s
	3	6	2/3	0.75 s	0.66 s
	4	12	3/4	4.67 s	3.85 s
	5	24	4/5	91.1 s	68.5 s
DIJKSTRA	2	12	1/6	4.80 s	3.32 s
	3	16	1/9	31.87 s	22.21 s
	4	21	2/12	73 min	52 min
	5	25	2/15	244 min	158 min

The experiments were conducted on a 3.4 GHz Core i7 with 8 GB memory. As we can see, our two novel constraint reusing concepts (II) and (III) together could lead to noticeable performance improvements in comparison to only using the established inter-bound constraint reusing (I). The computational savings were more evident for Dijkstra's algorithm where the number of refinement iterations was generally higher, i.e. where there were more capabilities for inter-refinement clause reusing. When we investigated the individual speed-up effect of (II) and of (III), we observed that (II) had a stronger impact when the number of refinements was small, whereas for cases with many refinements the performance impact of the two concepts was nearly equally strong, e.g. for Dijkstra 4: savings of 12 min with (II) only, savings of 14 min with (III) only, and of 21 min both together. This also shows that there is an overlap of savings due to (II) and due to (III). The experiments also revealed that it is beneficial to abstract and refine the base case and the step *individually*. The base case could be always accomplished based on fewer refinements, i.e. a less complex encoding. This advantage would not come into effect with a joint abstraction refinement of base case and step.

10   Related Work

k-induction was first introduced in [16] as a technique for verifying hardware systems that correspond to finite-state transition models. It extends classical bounded model checking from falsification to verification. It has been combined with incremental SAT, which allows to reuse learned constraints between bound iterations [7]. In comparison to our approach, the *bound* is the only dimension of incrementation. Since hardware is generally simpler than software, there is no concept for abstraction refinement used in the above-mentioned papers. Our software verification technique adds the *level of abstraction* as a second dimension of incrementation and we show that constraint reusing is also feasible between refinement iterations. Our major focus is the verification of safety properties of *concurrent systems*, e.g. mutual exclusion and deadlock-freedom. In the context of software verification, k-induction has been used for checking safety of *loop programs* [1,6,9,10,14]. In these papers, the bound k determines the number of loop unwindings. The unwound program is encoded into a formula that can be processed by an SMT solver. SMT generally allows for more compact encodings than SAT. While [1,6,9,10,14] directly operate on the *concrete program*, we follow the *abstraction refinement paradigm* [4]. SMT-based predicate abstraction [12] allows us to generate a propositional state transition encoding that is compact enough to be efficiently processed by a SAT solver. In particular, our abstraction approach enables to omit details along the explored paths that are not relevant for solving the verification problem. Missing but necessary details are iteratively added by refinement, where our constraint reusing concept alleviates the computational overhead of the iterative approach. In [1,6,9,10,14] the performance of verification is improved by inferring loop invariants that are added as assumptions to the program, which is a particular form of constraint using in the context of loop programs. While earlier works are based on manually specified invariants [6], recent approaches use automatic invariant generation [14] or refine invariants in each bound iteration [1]. Regarding background theories, k-induction approaches to the verification of loop programs range from integer arithmetic [9], real arithmetic and uninterpreted functions [1] to pointers [10].

11   Conclusion

We introduced a safety verification technique for concurrent software systems based on a combination of three-valued abstraction refinement and SAT-based k-induction. The approach extends our prior work on (incomplete) three-valued bounded model checking [17,18]. The main contributions of this paper are as follows: We showed that, after the application of abstraction, base case and inductive step of the k-induction technique can be formulated as bounded model checking problems and encoded in propositional logic, which facilitates *complete* verification. We integrated the k-induction approach into a twofold-iterative verification procedure that enables to reach the necessary bound and the right level of abstraction in order to prove or refute safety properties. We enhanced this iterative approach by adopting k-incremental SAT solving and by extending the idea of reusing logical constraints to two new levels: In our three-valued setting, constraints can be reused between over- and under-approximations and also between refinement iterations. The latter is a non-straightforward concept that we proved to be sound. In experiments we demonstrated the effectiveness of our approach as formal method for software model checking and we showed that our novel constraint reusing concepts can lead to significant computational savings.

References

1. Beyer, D., Dangl, M., Wendler, P.: Boosting k-induction with continuously-refined invariants. In: Kroening, D., Păsăreanu, C.S. (eds.) CAV 2015. LNCS, vol. 9206, pp. 622–640. Springer, Cham (2015). https://doi.org/10.1007/978-3-319-21690-4_42
2. Biere, A., Heule, M., van Maaren, H., Walsh, T.: Conflict-driven clause learning sat solvers. In: Biere, A., Heule, M., van Maaren, H., Walsh, T. (eds.) Handbook of Satisfiability, pp. 131–153. IOS Press, Amsterdam (2009)
3. Bruns, G., Godefroid, P.: Model checking partial state spaces with 3-valued temporal logics. In: Halbwachs, N., Peled, D. (eds.) CAV 1999. LNCS, vol. 1633, pp. 274–287. Springer, Heidelberg (1999). https://doi.org/10.1007/3-540-48683-6_25
4. Clarke, E., Grumberg, O., Jha, S., Lu, Y., Veith, H.: Counterexample-guided abstraction refinement. In: Emerson, E.A., Sistla, A.P. (eds.) CAV 2000. LNCS, vol. 1855, pp. 154–169. Springer, Heidelberg (2000). https://doi.org/10.1007/10722167_15
5. Dijkstra, E.W.: Solution of a problem in concurrent programming control. In: Broy, M., Denert, E. (eds.) Software Pioneers, pp. 347–350. Springer, Heidelberg (2002). https://doi.org/10.1007/978-3-642-59412-0_20
6. Donaldson, A.F., Haller, L., Kroening, D., Rümmer, P.: Software verification using k-induction. In: Yahav, E. (ed.) SAS 2011. LNCS, vol. 6887, pp. 351–368. Springer, Heidelberg (2011). https://doi.org/10.1007/978-3-642-23702-7_26
7. Een, N., Sörensson, N.: Temporal induction by incremental sat solving. Electron. Notes Theor. Comput. Sci. **89**(4), 543–560 (2003). BMC 2003
8. Fitting, M.: Kleene's 3-valued logics. Fund. Inf. **20**(1–3), 113–131 (1994)
9. Franzén, A.: Using satisfiability modulo theories for inductive verification of lustre programs. ENTCS **144**(1), 19–33 (2006)
10. Gadelha, M., Ismail, H., Cordeiro, L.: Handling loops in bounded model checking of C programs via k-induction. STTT **19**(1), 97–114 (2017)
11. Günther, H., Weissenbacher, G.: Incremental bounded software model checking. In: SPIN 2014, pp. 40–47. ACM (2014)
12. Lahiri, S.K., Nieuwenhuis, R., Oliveras, A.: SMT techniques for fast predicate abstraction. In: Ball, T., Jones, R.B. (eds.) CAV 2006. LNCS, vol. 4144, pp. 424–437. Springer, Heidelberg (2006). https://doi.org/10.1007/11817963_39
13. Nadel, A., Ryvchin, V., Strichman, O.: Ultimately incremental SAT. In: Sinz, C., Egly, U. (eds.) SAT 2014. LNCS, vol. 8561, pp. 206–218. Springer, Cham (2014). https://doi.org/10.1007/978-3-319-09284-3_16
14. Rocha, W., Rocha, H., Ismail, H., Cordeiro, L., Fischer, B.: DepthK: a k-induction verifier based on invariant inference for C programs. In: Legay, A., Margaria, T. (eds.) TACAS 2017. LNCS, vol. 10206, pp. 360–364. Springer, Heidelberg (2017). https://doi.org/10.1007/978-3-662-54580-5_23
15. Schrieb, J., Wehrheim, H., Wonisch, D.: Three-valued spotlight abstractions. In: Cavalcanti, A., Dams, D.R. (eds.) FM 2009. LNCS, vol. 5850, pp. 106–122. Springer, Heidelberg (2009). https://doi.org/10.1007/978-3-642-05089-3_8

16. Sheeran, M., Singh, S., Stålmarck, G.: Checking safety properties using induction and a SAT-solver. In: Hunt, W.A., Johnson, S.D. (eds.) FMCAD 2000. LNCS, vol. 1954, pp. 127–144. Springer, Heidelberg (2000). https://doi.org/10.1007/3-540-40922-X_8

17. Timm, N., Gruner, S.: Three-valued bounded model checking with cause-guided abstraction refinement (2018, manuscript submitted for publication)

18. Timm, N., Gruner, S., Harvey, M.: A bounded model checker for three-valued abstractions of concurrent software systems. In: Ribeiro, L., Lecomte, T. (eds.) SBMF 2016. LNCS, vol. 10090, pp. 199–216. Springer, Cham (2016). https://doi.org/10.1007/978-3-319-49815-7_12

19. Tseitin, G.S.: On the complexity of derivation in propositional calculus. In: Siekmann, J.H., Wrightson, G. (eds.) Automation of Reasoning, pp. 466–483. Springer, Heidelberg (1983). https://doi.org/10.1007/978-3-642-81955-1_28

TeSSLa: Temporal Stream-Based Specification Language

Lukas Convent[✉], Sebastian Hungerecker[✉], Martin Leucker[✉],
Torben Scheffel[✉], Malte Schmitz[✉], and Daniel Thoma[✉]

Institute for Software Engineering and Programming Languages,
University of Lübeck, Lübeck, Germany
{convent,hungerecker,leucker,scheffel,schmitz,
thoma}@isp.uni-luebeck.de

Abstract. Runtime verification is concerned with monitoring program
traces. In particular, stream runtime verification (SRV) takes the program trace as input streams and incrementally derives output streams.
SRV can check logical properties and compute temporal metrics and
statistics from the trace. We present TeSSLa, a temporal stream-based
specification language for SRV. TeSSLa supports timestamped events
natively and is hence suitable for streams that are both sparse and fine-
grained, which often occur in practice. We prove results on TeSSLa's
expressiveness and compare different TeSSLa fragments to (timed)
automata, thereby inheriting various decidability results. Finally, we
present a monitor implementation and prove its correctness.

1 Introduction

The essence of software verification is to check whether a program meets its specification. Runtime verification (RV) is an applied formal technique that has been
established as a complement to traditional verification techniques such as model
checking [19,22]. Compared to static verification, RV considers only a single run
of a system and checks whether it satisfies a property. Thus, RV can be seen as
a lightweight, but formal extension to testing and debugging. RV can be applied
offline to previously recorded traces or online to evaluate correctness properties
at the runtime of the system under scrutiny. Typically, a property to be checked
is specified as a logical formula, e.g. in (past time) LTL, and then synthesized to
a monitor which can evaluate a run [5,20]. Stream runtime verification (SRV) [7],
as pioneered by the language LOLA [10,15], takes a different approach by incrementally relating a set of input streams to a set of output streams. This allows
not only the monitoring of correctness properties but also of quantitative measures. In this paper we introduce the novel temporal stream-based specification

This work is supported in part by the European COST Action ARVI, the BMBF
project ARAMiS II with funding ID 01 IS 16025, and the European Horizon 2020
project COEMS under number 732016.

T. Massoni and M. R. Mousavi (Eds.): SBMF 2018, LNCS 11254, pp. 144–162, 2018.
https://doi.org/10.1007/978-3-030-03044-5_10

language TeSSLa which is tailored for SRV of cyber-physical systems, where timing is a critical issue. While traditional SRV approaches process event streams without considering timing information, TeSSLa supports timestamped events natively, which allows efficient processing of streams with sparse and fine-grained event sequences. Preliminary versions of TeSSLa have already been studied with regard to their usability to monitor trace data generated by embedded tracing units of processors [11]; how to implement stream-based monitors on hardware has been studied in theory [23] and practice [12]. These versions share the basic idea of transforming timed event streams but they did not allow for recursive equations and comprised only a set of ad-hoc operators. In this paper we define a minimal language with support for recursive definitions that allows us to obtain strong guarantees for evaluation algorithms, expressiveness results and meaningful fragments. While the practical applicability of such a language has been demonstrated by the previous papers, these papers lack a concise and clear theoretical basis and investigation. As an example for SRV, consider the following specification which checks whether a measured temperature stays within given boundaries. For every new event (measurement) on the temperature stream, new events on the derived streams *low*, *high* and *unsafe* are computed:

$$low := temperature < 3$$
$$high := temperature > 8$$
$$unsafe := low \lor high$$

SRV is a combination of complex event processing (CEP) and traditional RV approaches: Streams are transformed into streams and there is not only one final verdict but the output is a stream of the property being evaluated at every temperature change. Furthermore, the user gets more detailed information about why an error occurred by being able to distinguish between the two separate causes *low* and *high*.

In the rest of this section we introduce the main features of TeSSLa and contrast them with related specification languages. The next section presents the language and its semantics formally, in Sect. 3 we present several results regarding the expressiveness of TeSSLa and in Sect. 4 we focus on comparing (fragments of) the language to variants of (timed) automata. Finally in Sect. 5 we discuss different approaches to implement TeSSLa monitors and present our TeSSLa tool suite. An extended preprint version of this paper is available as [9].

Asynchronous Streams. In the previous example of traditional SRV, every stream has an event for every step of the system. TeSSLa requires the events of all streams to be in a global order, but doesn't require all streams to have simultaneous events. As a consequence, both sparse and high-frequency streams can be modeled. As cyber-physical systems often give rise to streams at unstable frequencies or continuous signals, this asynchronous setting is especially suitable. Consider as an example a ring buffer where the number of write accesses should not exceed the number of read accesses too much:

$$numReads := \mathbf{count}(read)$$
$$numWrites := \mathbf{count}(write)$$
$$safe := numWrites - numReads \leq 2$$

Read and write events occur independently at different frequencies. The derived stream $numReads$ ($numWrites$) counts the number of events of the input stream $read$ ($write$). While the $read$ and $write$ streams contain only discrete events, the number of events can be seen as a piece-wise constant signal with the initial value of 0. The difference between the two signals is evaluated every time one of the two signals changes its value using the *last known value* of both signals. We call this concept *signal semantics*: TeSSLa handles internally only streams of discrete events, but one can express operators following signal semantics in TeSSLa and hence these discrete events can be seen as those points in time where the signal changes its value. In these introductory examples operators are automatically lifted to signal semantics, which is formally introduced as the **slift** operator later.

Recursive Equations. Like existing SRV approaches, TeSSLa relates a set of input streams to a set of output streams via mutually recursive equations, which allows self-references to the past, e.g. counting events of a stream x as in the previous example is expressed in TeSSLa as follows:

$$count := \mathbf{merge}(\mathbf{last}(count, x) + 1, 0)$$

The **last** operator outputs the last known value of the *count* stream, on every event of the stream x. The base of the recursion is provided by merging with 0, which is a stream with one initial event of value 0. Since **last** only refers to events strictly lying in the past, the unique solution of such recursive equations can be computed incrementally (see Sect. 2).

Time as First-Class Citizen. In TeSSLa, every event has a timestamp which can be accessed via the **time** operator. Since every event has a timestamp which is referring to a global clock and is unique for its stream, accessing the timestamps of events serves two purposes: Accessing the global order of events by comparing timestamps and performing calculations with the timestamps. Consider e.g. the following specification which checks whether the lapse of time between two write events exceeds 5 time units and outputs the overtime if it does:

$$diff := \mathbf{time}(write) - \mathbf{last}(\mathbf{time}(write), write)$$
$$error := \mathbf{filter}(diff > 5, diff - 5)$$

In the example, the stream $diff - 5$ is filtered by the condition $diff > 5$. Note that the property violation is only reported when the delayed event happens. To report such errors as soon as possible, TeSSLa has the ability to create events at certain points in time via the **delay** operator. The following specification checks the same property but raises a unit event on the *error* stream as soon as we know that there was no *write* event in time:

$$timeout := \mathbf{const}(5)(write)$$

$$error := \mathbf{delay}(timeout, write)$$

The **delay** function works as a timer, which is set to a timeout value with the first argument and reset with any event on the second argument. In the example, the function $\mathbf{const}(5)(write)$ maps the values of events to the constant value of 5, which is then used as timeout value. While in all the other examples the derived streams only contain events with timestamps taken from the input streams, in this example events with additional timestamps are generated. Like **last**, the **delay** operator can be used in recursive equations, for example the equation

$$period := \mathbf{merge}(\mathbf{const}(5)(\mathbf{delay}(period, \mathbf{unit})), 5)$$

produces an infinite stream with an event every 5 time units. The **merge** is used to provide a base case for the recursion and **const** is used to map the value of the generated events to 5 so that they can be used as the new timeout value.

Efficient Parallel Evaluation. TeSSLa's design follows two principles to allow efficient evaluation on parallel hardware: *Explicit memory usage* and *local operator composition*. If TeSSLa operates only on streams with bounded data-types of constant size, then the operators only need finite memory because every operator only needs to store at most one data value. This allows implementations on systems without random access memory, e.g. FPGAs or embedded systems. TeSSLa consists of a small set of primitive operators which can be flexibly combined. The TeSSLa semantics is defined in a way that allows a local composition of the individual operators, which can be realized via message passing without the need for global synchronization. Because of an explicit notion of progress for every stream describing how far the stream is known, local message passing is also sufficient to compute solutions for the recursive TeSSLa equations. Implementing an efficient evaluation on FPGAs is part of our EU research project COEMS[1].

Related Work and Comparison. LOLA [10,15] is a synchronous stream specification language in the following sense: Events arrive in discrete steps and for every step, all input streams provide an event and all output streams produce an event, which means that it is not suitable for handling events with arbitrary real-time timestamps arriving at variable frequencies. The not yet formally published RTLola [16] is an extension of LOLA which introduces asynchronous streams to perform aggregations over real-time intervals. A major difference between RTLola and TeSSLa is that RTLola focuses on splitting input streams and aggregating over them, whereas TeSSLa provides a more general framework that in particular allows the (recursive) definition of aggregation operators while giving strict memory guarantees at the same time. Focus [8] is a formalism for the specification of stream-based systems. Their timed streams progress by discrete

---

[1] https://www.coems.eu.

ticks that separate events inbetween, thereby allowing multiple events at the same timestamp. The synchronous stream programming languages Lustre [18], Esterel [6] and Signal [17], the stream specification language Copilot [25] as well as the class of functional reactive programming (FRP) languages [14] allow the description of the transformation in a linear style, i.e. an input stream is read chronologically and is thereby evaluated. TeSSLa also supports linear evaluation because there are no future-references and the number of past-references is limited by the specification size. The only complement to linear evaluation is the creation of additional events via the **delay** operator. Quantitative regular expressions (QREs) [2] and logics like Signal Temporal Logic (STL) [24] and Time-Frequency Logic (TFL) [13] allow the mapping from complete streams to one final verdict/quantity. They cannot generally be evaluated in a linear way. The idea used in TeSSLa of supporting signals and event streams has also been used for Timed Regular Expressions [4], but those have two explicitly different stream types, where TeSSLa internally represents signals as event streams. Recently, synthesis of hardware-based monitors from stream specifications has become an important field: For LOLA [10] constant memory bounds for an algorithm that evaluates well-formed specifications exist and for LOLA 2.0 [15] future references must be eliminated to gain constant memory bounds. There has been work on synthesis of STL to FPGAs in different ways as well [21,26].

2   Formal Definition of the TeSSLa Core Language

In this section we introduce syntax and semantics of the minimal core of TeSSLa. In examples we use parametrized definitions, e.g. **merge**$(x, y) := \ldots$ on top, which are expanded to their definitions until only core operators remain.

Preliminaries. Given a partial order $(A, \leq)$, a set $D \subseteq A$ is called *directed* if $\forall a, b \in D : a \leq b \vee b \leq a$. $(A, \leq)$ is called *directed-complete partial order (dcpo)* if there exists a supremum $\bigvee D$ for every directed subset $D \subseteq A$. Let $f \in A \to B$ be a function and $(A, \leq)$, $(B, \leq')$ partial orders. f is called *monotonic* if it preserves the order, i.e. $\forall a_1, a_2 \in A : a_1 \leq a_2 \Rightarrow f(a_1) \leq' f(a_2)$. f is called *continuous* if it preserves the supremum, i.e. $\bigvee f(D) = f(\bigvee' D)$ for all directed subsets $D \subseteq A$. By the Kleene fixed-point theorem, every monotonic and continuous function $f : A \to A$ has a least fixed point μf if $(A, \leq)$ is a dcpo with a least element $\bot$. μf is the least upper bound of the chain iterating f starting with the bottom element: $\mu f = \bigvee \{f^n(\bot) \mid n \in \mathbb{N}\}$.

Syntax. A TeSSLa specification φ consists of a set of possibly mutually recursive stream definitions defined over a finite set of variables $\mathbb{V}$ where an equation has the form $x := e$ with $x \in \mathbb{V}$ and

$$e ::= \mathbf{nil} \mid \mathbf{unit} \mid x \mid \mathbf{lift}(f)(e, \ldots, e) \mid \mathbf{time}(e) \mid \mathbf{last}(e, e) \mid \mathbf{delay}(e, e).$$

All variables not occuring on the left-hand side of equations are *input variables*. All variables on the left-hand side are *output variables*. We call a TeSSLa specification *flat* if it does not contain any nested expressions. Every specification can be represented as a flat specification by using additional variables and equations.

Semantics. We define the semantics of TeSSLa in terms of an abstract time domain which only requires a total order and corresponding arithmetic operators:

Definition 1. *A* time domain *is a totally ordered semi-ring* $(\mathbb{T}, 0, 1, +, \cdot, \leq)$ *that is not negative, i.e.* $\forall_{t \in \mathbb{T}}\ 0 \leq t$.

We extend the order on time domains to the set $\mathbb{T}_\infty = \mathbb{T} \cup \{\infty\}$ with $\forall_{t \in \mathbb{T}}\ t < \infty$.

Conceptually, streams are timed words that are known inclusively or exclusively up to a certain timestamp, its progress, that might be infinite. A stream might contain an infinite number of events even if its progress is finite.

Definition 2. *An* event stream *over a time domain* $\mathbb{T}$ *and a data domain* $\mathbb{D}$ *is a finite or infinite sequence* $s = a_0 a_1 \cdots \in \mathcal{S}_\mathbb{D} = (\mathbb{T} \cdot \mathbb{D})^\omega \cup (\mathbb{T} \cdot \mathbb{D})^+ \cup (\mathbb{T} \cdot \mathbb{D})^* \cdot (\mathbb{T}_\infty \mathbb{T} \cdot \{\bot\})$ *where* $a_{2i} < a_{2(i+1)}$ *for all* i *with* $0 < 2(i+1) < |s|$ *(*$|s|$ *is* ∞ *for infinite streams). The* prefix relation *over* $\mathcal{S}_\mathbb{D}$ *is the least relation that satisfies* $s \sqsubseteq s$, $u \sqsubseteq s$ *if* $uv \sqsubseteq s$ *and* $ut'\bot \sqsubseteq s$ *if* $ut \sqsubseteq s$, $t' < t, t \in \mathbb{T}_\infty$ *and* $t' \in \mathbb{T}$.

We say a stream has an event with value d at time t if in its sequence d directly follows t. We say a stream is known at time t if it contains a strictly larger timestamp or a non-strictly larger timestamp followed by a data value or $\bot$. Where convenient, we also see streams as functions $s \in \mathbb{T} \to \mathbb{D} \cup \{\bot, ?\}$ such that $s(t) = d$ if the stream has value d at time t, $s(t) = \bot$ if it is known to have no value, and $s(t) = ?$ otherwise. We refer to the supremum of all known timestamps of a stream as inclusive or exclusive progress, depending on whether it is itself a known timestamp. The prefix relation realises the intuition of cutting a stream at a certain point in time while keeping or removing the cutting point.

In the following, we present the denotation of a specification φ as a function between input streams and output streams.

Definition 3 (TeSSLa semantics). *Given a specification* φ *of equations* $y_i := e_i$, *every* e_i *can be interpreted as a function of input streams* $s_1, \ldots, s_k$ *and output streams* $s'_1, \ldots, s'_n$, *that is composed of the primitive functions whose denotation is given in the rest of this section. Input variables are mapped to input streams,* $[\![x_i]\!]_{s_1, \ldots, s_k, s'_1, \ldots, s'_n} = s_i$ *and output variables to output streams,* $[\![y_i]\!]_{s_1, \ldots, s_k, s'_1, \ldots, s'_n} = s'_i$. *Thus for fixed input streams* $s_1, \ldots, s_k$ *and every* e_i, *we obtain a function* $[\![e_i]\!]_{s_1, \ldots, s_k} \in \mathcal{S}_{\mathbb{D}'_1} \times \ldots \times \mathcal{S}_{\mathbb{D}'_n} \to \mathcal{S}_{\mathbb{D}'_i}$ *and in combination a function* $[\![e_1, \ldots, c_n]\!]_{s_1, \ldots, s_k} \in \mathcal{S}_{\mathbb{D}'_1} \times \ldots \times \mathcal{S}_{\mathbb{D}'_n} \to \mathcal{S}_{\mathbb{D}'_1} \times \ldots \times \mathcal{S}_{\mathbb{D}'_n}$. *We now define the denotation of a specification* φ *as the least fixed-point of this function.*

$$[\![\varphi]\!] \in \mathcal{S}_{\mathbb{D}_1} \times \ldots \times \mathcal{S}_{\mathbb{D}_k} \to \mathcal{S}_{\mathbb{D}'_1} \times \ldots \times \mathcal{S}_{\mathbb{D}'_n}$$

$$[\![\varphi]\!](s_1, \ldots, s_k) = \mu\left([\![e_1, \ldots, e_n]\!]_{s_1, \ldots, s_k}\right)$$

The function $[\![e_1, \ldots, e_n]\!]_{s_1, \ldots, s_k}$ is monotonic and continuous because all primitive TeSSLa functions defined later in this section are monotonic and continuous and both properties are closed under function composition and cartesian products. $(\mathcal{S}_\mathbb{D}, \sqsubseteq)$ and by extension $(\mathcal{S}_{\mathbb{D}_1} \times \ldots \times \mathcal{S}_{\mathbb{D}_n}, \sqsubseteq \times \ldots \sqsubseteq)$ are dcpos.

By the Kleene fixed-point theorem $[\![e_1, \ldots, e_n]\!]_{s_1,\ldots,s_k}$ has a least fixed point, which is the least upper bound of its Kleene chain.

Next we give the semantics of the primitive TeSSLa functions. The dependency of the input and output streams $s_1, \ldots, s_k, s_1', \ldots, s_n'$ is assumed implicitly.

Definition 4. Nil *is a constant for the completely known stream without any events:* $[\![\mathbf{unit}]\!] = \infty \in \mathcal{S}_\mathbb{D}.$

We use the unit type $\mathbb{U} = \{\square\}$ for streams that can carry only the single value $\square$.

Definition 5. Unit *is a constant for the completely known stream with a single unit event at timestamp zero:* $[\![\mathbf{unit}]\!] = 0 \,\square\, \infty \in \mathcal{S}_\mathbb{U}$

The following functions are given by specifying two conditions: the first for positions where an output event occurs, and the second where no output event occurs. Thereby the progress of the stream is defined indirectly as the position where the output can no longer be inferred from these conditions.

Definition 6. *The* time *operator returns the stream of the timestamps of another stream* $[\![\mathbf{time}(e)]\!] = \mathsf{time}([\![e]\!])$ *where* $\mathsf{time} \in \mathcal{S}_\mathbb{D} \to \mathcal{S}_\mathbb{T}$ *is defined as* $\mathsf{time}(s) = s'$ *such that*

$$\forall_t s'(t) = t \Leftrightarrow s(t) \in \mathbb{D} \qquad \forall_t s'(t) = \bot \Leftrightarrow s(t) = \bot.$$

The lift operator lifts an n-ary function f from values to streams. The notation $A_1 \times \ldots \times A_n \rightarrowtail B$ denotes the set of functions where all A_i and B have been extended by the value $\bot$.

Definition 7. *Unary* lift *is defined as* $[\![\mathbf{lift}(f)(e)]\!] = \mathsf{lift}_1(f)([\![e]\!])$ *where* $\mathsf{lift}_1 \in (\mathbb{D} \rightarrowtail \mathbb{D}') \to (\mathcal{S}_\mathbb{D} \to \mathcal{S}_{\mathbb{D}'})$ *is given by* $\mathsf{lift}_1(f)(s) = s'$ *such that*

$$\forall_{t,d\in\mathbb{D}'} s'(t) = d \Leftrightarrow s(t) \in \mathbb{D} \wedge f(s(t)) = d$$
$$\forall_t s'(t) = \bot \Leftrightarrow s(t) = \bot \vee s(t) \in f(s(t)) = \bot.$$

Definition 8. *Binary* lift *is given as* $[\![\mathbf{lift}(f)(e_1, e_2)]\!] = \mathsf{lift}_2(f)([\![e_1]\!], [\![e_2]\!])$ *where* $\mathsf{lift}_2 \in (\mathbb{D}_1 \times \mathbb{D}_2 \rightarrowtail \mathbb{D}') \to (\mathcal{S}_{\mathbb{D}_1} \times \mathcal{S}_{\mathbb{D}_2} \to \mathcal{S}_{\mathbb{D}'})$ *is given by* $\mathsf{lift}_2(f)(s, s') = s''$ *s.t.*

$$\forall_{t,d\in\mathbb{D}'} s''(t) = d \Leftrightarrow (s(t) \in \mathbb{D}_1 \vee s'(t) \in \mathbb{D}_2) \wedge \mathsf{known}(t) \wedge f(s(t), s'(t)) = d$$
$$\forall_t s''(t) = \bot \Leftrightarrow (s(t) = \bot \wedge s'(t) = \bot) \vee \mathsf{known}(t) \wedge f(s(t), s'(t)) = \bot$$

where $\mathsf{known}(t) := s(t) \neq ? \wedge s'(t) \neq ?.$

The binary lift can naturally be extended to an n-ary lift by recursively combining two streams into a stream of tuples or partially applied functions until the final result is obtained. Alternatively, the scheme of the binary lift can be easily extended to higher arities.

Example 1. *Merge* combines events of two streams, prioritising the first one.

$$\mathbf{merge}(x,y) := \mathbf{lift}(\mathsf{mergeaux})(x,y)$$
$$\mathsf{mergeaux}(a \neq \bot, b) := a$$
$$\mathsf{mergeaux}(\bot, b) := b$$

Example 2. *Const* maps the values of all events of the input stream to a constant value: $\mathbf{const}(c)(a) := \mathbf{lift}(\mathsf{constaux}(c))(a)$ with $\mathsf{constaux}(c)(a) := c$. Using $\mathbf{const}$ we can lift constants into streams representing a constant signal with this value, e.g. $\mathbf{true} := \mathbf{const}(\mathrm{true})(\mathbf{unit})$ or $\mathbf{zero} := \mathbf{const}(0)(\mathbf{unit})$.

Definition 9. *The* last *operator takes two streams and returns the previous value of the first stream at the timestamps of the second. It is defined as $[\![\mathbf{last}(e_1, e_2)]\!] = \mathsf{last}([\![e_1]\!], [\![e_2]\!])$ where $\mathsf{last}_{\mathbb{D}, \mathbb{D}'} \in \mathcal{S}_{\mathbb{D}} \times \mathcal{S}_{\mathbb{D}'} \to \mathcal{S}_{\mathbb{D}}$ is given as $\mathsf{last}(s, s') = s''$ such that*

$$\forall_{t, d \in \mathbb{D}}\, s''(t) = d \Leftrightarrow s'(t) \in \mathbb{D}' \wedge \exists_{t' < t}\, s(t') = d \wedge \mathsf{noData}(t', t)$$
$$\forall_t\, s''(t) = \bot \Leftrightarrow s'(t) = \bot \wedge \mathsf{defined}(t) \vee \forall_{t' < t}\, s(t') = \bot$$

where $\mathsf{noData}(t, t') := \forall_{t'' \mid t < t'' < t'}\, s(t'') = \bot$ *and* $\mathsf{defined}(t) := \forall_{t' < t}\, s''(t') \neq ?$.

Note that while TeSSLa is defined on event streams, **last** realizes some essential aspects of the signal semantics: With this operator one can query the last known value of an event stream at a specific time and hence interpret the events on this stream as points where a piece-wise constant signal changes its value.

Example 3. By combining the **last** and the **lift** operators, we can now realize the *signal lift* semantics implicitly used in the introduction:
$\mathbf{slift}(f)(x,y) := \mathbf{lift}(\mathsf{sliftaux}(f))(x', y')$ with

$$x' := \mathbf{merge}(x, \mathbf{last}(x, y)) \text{ and}$$
$$y' := \mathbf{merge}(y, \mathbf{last}(y, x)).$$
$$\mathsf{sliftaux}(f)(a \neq \bot, b \neq \bot) := f(a, b)$$
$$\mathsf{sliftaux}(f)(\bot, b) := \bot$$
$$\mathsf{sliftaux}(f)(a, \bot) := \bot$$

Example 4. In order to *filter* an event stream with a dynamic condition, we apply the last known filter condition to the current event:
$\mathbf{filter}(z, x) := \mathbf{lift}(\mathsf{filteraux})(\mathbf{merge}(z, \mathbf{last}(z, x)), x)$

$$\mathsf{filteraux} : \mathbb{B} \times A \rightharpoonup A$$
$$\mathsf{filteraux}(c \neq \mathrm{true}, a) = \bot$$
$$\mathsf{filteraux}(\mathrm{true}, a) = a$$

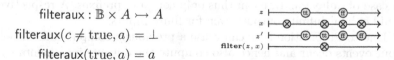

Definition 10. *The* delay *operator takes delays as its first argument. After a delay has passed, a unit event is emitted. A delay can only be set if a reset event is received via the second argument, or if an event is emitted on the output.*

Formally, $\llbracket \mathbf{delay}(e_1, e_2) \rrbracket = \mathsf{delay}(\llbracket e_1 \rrbracket, \llbracket e_2 \rrbracket)$ *where* $\mathsf{delay}_\mathbb{D} \in \mathcal{S}_{\mathbb{T} \setminus \{0\}} \times \mathcal{S}_\mathbb{D} \to \mathcal{S}_\mathbb{U}$
is given as $\mathsf{delay}(s, s') = s''$ *such that*

$$\forall_t s''(t) = \square \Leftrightarrow \exists_{t' < t} s(t') = t - t' \wedge \mathsf{setable}(t') \wedge \mathsf{noreset}(t', t)$$
$$\forall_t s''(t) = \bot \Leftrightarrow$$
$$\mathsf{defined}(t) \wedge \forall_{t' < t} s(t') \neq ? \wedge s(t') \neq t - t' \vee \mathsf{unsetable}(t') \vee \mathsf{reset}(t', t)$$

where $\mathsf{setable}(t) := s''(t) = \square \vee s'(t) \in \mathbb{D}$, $\mathsf{unsetable}(t) := s''(t) = \bot \wedge s'(t) = \bot$,
$\mathsf{noreset}(t, t') := \forall_{t'' | t < t'' < t'} s'(t'') = \bot$ *and* $\mathsf{reset}(t, t') := \exists_{t'' | t < t'' < t'} s'(t'') \in \mathbb{D}$.

In many applications the delay operator is used in simplified versions: In the first example of the introduction that uses the delay operator, the delay and the reset argument can be the same because the delay is used only in non-recursive equations and every new delay is a reset, too. If a periodical event pattern is generated independently from input events then the second argument can be set to unit because only an initial reset event is needed. The full complexity of the delay operator is only needed if the delay is used in recursive equations with input dependencies and ensures that the fixed-point is unique.

We can observe that all basic functions are monotonic and continuous. From the fact, that these properties are closed under composition and the smallest fixed-point is determined by the Kleene chain, we can therefore conclude:

Proposition 1. *The semantics of a TeSSLa specification is monotonic and continuous in the input streams.*

In other words, the semantics will provide an extended result for an extended input and is therefore suited for online monitoring.

We can further observe that the pre-fixed-points on the Kleene chain have the following property: the progress only increases a finite number of times until a further event has to be appended. This is due to the basic functions that do handle progress in this way. We therefore obtain:

Theorem 1. *For a specification* φ *every finite prefix of* $\llbracket \varphi \rrbracket(s_1, \ldots, s_k)$ *can be computed assuming all lifted functions are computable. Assuming they are computable in* $O(1)$ *steps, the prefix can be computed in* $O(k \cdot |\varphi|)$ *steps where* k *is the number of events over all involved streams.*

Note that in case the specification contains no **delay** output streams cannot contain any such timestamps that did not occur already in the inputs. Further note, that fixed-points might contain infinitely many positions with data values (in case of **delay**) and we can thus only compute prefixes. A respective monitor would exhibit infinite outputs even for finite inputs.

Due to Proposition 1 we can reuse a previously computed fixed-point if new input events occur and hence also compute the outputs incrementally.

Well-Formedness. While the least fixed-point is unique it does not have to be the only fixed-point. In that case, the least fixed-point is often the stream with progress 0 or some other stream with too little progress and one would be interested in (one of) the maximal fixed-points. Since the largest fixed-points would be more difficult to compute, especially in the setting of online monitoring, we define a fragment for which a unique fixed-point exists.

Definition 11. *We call a TeSSLa specification φ well-formed if every cycle of the dependency graph (of the flattened specification) contains at least one delayed-labelled edge. The dependency graph of a flat TeSSLa specification φ of equations $y_i := e_i$ is the directed multi-graph $G = (V, E)$ of nodes $V = \{y_1, \ldots, y_n\}$. For every $y_i := e_i$ the graph contains the edge (y_i, y_j) iff y_j is used in e_i. We label edges corresponding to the first argument of **last** or **delay** with delayed.*

Theorem 2. *Given a well-formed specification φ of equations $y_i := e_i$ and input streams $s_1, \ldots, s_k$ then $\mu(\llbracket e_1, \ldots, e_n \rrbracket_{s_1, \ldots, s_k})$ is the only fixed-point.*

Proof. From the Kleene fixed-point theorem we know $\mu(\llbracket e_1, \ldots, e_n \rrbracket_{s_1, \ldots, s_k}) = \bigsqcup \{\llbracket e_1, \ldots, e_n \rrbracket^n_{s_1, \ldots, s_k}(\bot) \mid n \in \mathbb{N}\}$. Because φ is well-formed, every $\llbracket e_i \rrbracket_{s_1, \ldots, s_k}$ is either constant or contains at least one **last** or **delay**. The input streams $s_1, \ldots, s_k$ limit progress, i.e. the maximal timestamp produced, of $\llbracket e_i \rrbracket_{s_1, \ldots, s_k}$. The progress strictly increases with every step of the iteration of $\llbracket e_1, \ldots, e_n \rrbracket_{s_1, \ldots, s_k}$ in the Kleene chain until the limit given by the input streams is reached. Every other fixed-point of $\llbracket e_1, \ldots, e_n \rrbracket_{s_1, \ldots, s_k}$ must be an extension of the least fixed-point, but the least fixed-point has already the maximal progress permitted by the input streams. $\square$

3   Expressiveness of TeSSLa

We discuss the expressiveness of four different TeSSLa fragments: TeSSLa specifications without the delay operator can only produce events with timestamps which are already included in the input streams and TeSSLa specifications with the delay operator can produce arbitrary event patterns even without any input event. On the other hand we distinguish between TeSSLa specifications which use only bounded data structures, which can only consider finitely many past events, and those with unbounded data structures which can consider infinitely many past events in the computation of new events. For an overview of the different TeSSLa fragments see Fig. 1 at the end of the next section.

To characterize functions which can be expressed in TeSSLa we define *timestamp conservatism* and *future independence* in addition to monotonicity and continuity. For a stream $a \in \mathcal{S}_{\mathbb{D}}$ we denote with $T(a)$ the set of timestamps present in the stream a and for multiple streams $T(a_1, \ldots, a_n) := \bigcup_{1 \leq i \leq n} T(a_i)$.

Definition 12 (Timestamp Conservatism). *We call a function $f \in \mathcal{S}_{\mathbb{D}_1} \times \ldots \times \mathcal{S}_{\mathbb{D}_k} \to \mathcal{S}_{\mathbb{D}'_1} \times \ldots \times \mathcal{S}_{\mathbb{D}'_n}$ on streams timestamp conservative iff it does not introduce new timestamps, i.e. for input streams $a \in \mathcal{S}_{\mathbb{D}_1} \times \ldots \times \mathcal{S}_{\mathbb{D}_k}$ and output streams $b \in \mathcal{S}_{\mathbb{D}'_1} \times \ldots \times \mathcal{S}_{\mathbb{D}'_n}$ we have $f(a) = b$ implies $T(a) \supseteq T(b)$.*

Note that TeSSLa specifications without delay are timestamp conservative because only delay can introduce new timestamps.

For a stream $a \in \mathcal{S}_\mathbb{D}$ we denote with $a|_t$ the prefix of a with progress t.

Definition 13 (Future Independence). *We call a function* $f \in \mathcal{S}_{\mathbb{D}_1} \times \ldots \times \mathcal{S}_{\mathbb{D}_k} \to \mathcal{S}_{\mathbb{D}'_1} \times \ldots \times \mathcal{S}_{\mathbb{D}'_n}$ *on streams* future independent *iff output events only depend on current or previous events, i.e. for input streams* $a \in \mathcal{S}_{\mathbb{D}_1} \times \ldots \times \mathcal{S}_{\mathbb{D}_k}$ *and output streams* $b \in \mathcal{S}_{\mathbb{D}'_1} \times \ldots \times \mathcal{S}_{\mathbb{D}'_n}$ *we have* $f(a) = b$ *implies* $\forall_{t \in \mathbb{T}} \ f(a_1|_t, \ldots, a_k|_t) = (b_1|_t, \ldots, b_n|_t)$.

Note that every TeSSLa specification is future independent because the operators **last** and **delay** are the only operators referring to events with different timestamps and they refer only to previous events.

Theorem 3 (Expressiveness of TeSSLa Without Delay). *Every function* $f \in \mathcal{S}_{\mathbb{D}_1} \times \ldots \times \mathcal{S}_{\mathbb{D}_k} \to \mathcal{S}_{\mathbb{D}'_1} \times \ldots \times \mathcal{S}_{\mathbb{D}'_n}$ *on streams can be represented as a TeSSLa specification without delay iff it is (a) monotonic and continuous, (b) timestamp conservative and (c) future independent.*

Proof Sketch. Represent the function f as the iterative function $\tilde{f}(m, d, t) = m'$ taking a memory state m, the current input values d, and the corresponding current timestamp t and returning the new memory state m'. Output events for all output streams can be derived from m'. Because f is monotonic it is sufficient to compute the output events step by step; because f is future independent it is sufficient to allow $\tilde{f}$ to store arbitrary information about the past events; and because f is timestamp conservative it is sufficient to execute $\tilde{f}$ for every timestamp in the input events. Translate $f(x_1, \ldots, x_k) = y_1, \ldots, y_n$ into an equivalent TeSSLa specification: $t := \textbf{time}(\textbf{merge}(x_1, \ldots, x_k))$, $m := \textbf{lift}(\tilde{f})(\textbf{last}(m, t), x_1, \ldots, x_k, t)$ and $\forall_{i \leq n} \ y_i := \textbf{lift}(\tilde{o}_i)(m)$.

If all data types in the TeSSLa specification φ are bounded, $\tilde{f}$ uses a finite memory cell m, which can only store a constant number of current and previous events. Monotonicity guarantees that we can compute output events incrementally and by future independence we know that knowledge about the previous events is sufficient to derive new events. From the combination of both properties we know that it is not necessary to queue (arbitrarily large) event sequences to compute the output events. Instead one memory cell (capable of storing one element of the data domain) per delay and per last operator in the specification is sufficient. Restricting TeSSLa to bounded data types allows TeSSLa implementations on embedded systems without addressable memory because then finite memory is sufficient. Such a restricted TeSSLa specification can compute new events only based on a finite number of current and previous events.

Theorem 4 (Expressiveness of TeSSLa With Delay). *Every function* $f \in \mathcal{S}_{\mathbb{D}_1} \times \ldots \times \mathcal{S}_{\mathbb{D}_k} \to \mathcal{S}_{\mathbb{D}'_1} \times \ldots \times \mathcal{S}_{\mathbb{D}'_n}$ *can be represented as a TeSSLa specification with delay iff it is (a) monotonic and continuous and (b) future independent.*

The proof accompanies the step-function $\tilde{f}$ with a timeout function $\tilde{u}$ which is evaluated on every new memory state. $\tilde{u}$ returns the timestamp of the next evaluation of $\tilde{f}$, which allows arbitrary event generation. The effect of $\tilde{u}$ can be realized using the **delay** operator.

We call a stream *Zeno* if it contains two timestamps t_1 and t_2 with infinitely many events between t_1 and t_2. With the delay operator it is possible to construct such Zeno streams because the timeout function is not restricted in any way. By Rice's theorem it is impossible to check for an arbitrary timeout function whether it only generates non-Zeno timestamp sequences. Hence, one would need to restrict allowed timeout functions more drastically, which would restrict the possible event sequences generated by a TeSSLa specification further than necessary. For that reason we decided to include the capability to generate Zeno streams with TeSSLa.

As a consequence of Theorem 4 we obtain:

Corollary 1. *A TeSSLa specification with multiple delays can be translated into an equivalent specification with only one delay.*

TeSSLa with and without delay are closely related because TeSSLa without delay can verify the relation of given input/output streams with respect to a TeSSLa specification that uses delay. The delay is only needed to actively generate the events at specified times. In the following we denote with $[\![\varphi|_y]\!](x_1,\ldots,x_k) \in \mathbb{B}$ the boolean function indicating whether the boolean output stream $y \in \mathcal{S}_\mathbb{B}$ of the TeSSLa specification φ contains only events with value true for the input streams $x_1,\ldots,x_k \in \mathcal{S}_{\mathbb{D}_1} \times \ldots \times \mathcal{S}_{\mathbb{D}_k}$.

Theorem 5 (Delay Elimination). *For every TeSSLa specification φ with $[\![\varphi]\!] \in \mathcal{S}_{\mathbb{D}_1} \times \ldots \times \mathcal{S}_{\mathbb{D}_k} \to \mathcal{S}_{\mathbb{D}'_1} \times \ldots \times \mathcal{S}_{\mathbb{D}'_n}$ with delay operators there exists a TeSSLa specification φ' without delay operators, which derives a boolean stream $z \in \mathcal{S}_\mathbb{B}$, s.t. for any input streams $x_1,\ldots,x_k$ and output streams $y_1,\ldots,y_n$ we have $[\![\varphi]\!](x_1,\ldots,x_k) = y_1,\ldots,y_n$ iff $[\![\varphi'|_z]\!](x_1,\ldots,x_k,y_1,\ldots,y_n)$.*

The above theorem follows from Theorem 3 and the fact that $[\![\varphi'|_z]\!]$ is timestamp conservative, because the output stream z only contain events when any input stream contains an event.

4   TeSSLa Fragments and Transducers

In this section we investigate two TeSSLa fragments related to deterministic Büchi automata and timed automata, resp. We translate TeSSLa specifications to transducers, which can be seen as automata taking the in- and output of the corresponding transducer as input word. Thus by relating TeSSLa fragments to certain transducer classes, we inherit complexity and expressiveness results from the well-known automata models.

Boolean Fragment. The fragment TeSSLa$_{bool}$ restricts TeSSLa to boolean streams and the operators **last**, **lift** and **slift** with $\geq$ on timestamps. In the syntax expressions are restricted as follows, where f is a function $f : \mathbb{B}^n \rightarrowtail \mathbb{B}$:

$$e := \mathbf{nil} \mid \mathbf{unit} \mid x \mid \mathbf{lift}(f)(e,\dots,e) \mid \mathbf{slift}(\geq)(\mathbf{time}(e),\mathbf{time}(e)) \mid \mathbf{last}(e,e)$$

Note that since one can only compare timestamps, for a TeSSLa$_{bool}$-formula φ and two tuples of input streams $S, S' \in \mathcal{S}_{\mathbb{D}_1} \times \dots \mathcal{S}_{\mathbb{D}_n}$ we have $[\![\varphi]\!](S) = [\![\varphi]\!](S')$ iff all events in S' carry the same values in the same order as those in S, independent from the exact timestamps of the events.

A *deterministic finite state transducer (DFST)* is a 5-tuple $R = (\Sigma, \Gamma, Q, q_0, \delta)$ with input alphabet Σ, output alphabet Γ, state set Q, initial state $q_0 \in Q$ and transition function $\delta : Q \times \Sigma \to Q \times \Gamma$. For an input word $w = w_0 w_1 w_2 \dots$ we call a sequence $s_0 \xrightarrow{w_0/o_0} s_1 \xrightarrow{w_1/o_1} s_2 \xrightarrow{w_2/o_2} \dots$ a run of a DFST R with output $[\![R]\!](w) = o_0 o_1 o_2 \dots \in \Gamma^\infty$ iff $s_0 = q_0$ and $\delta(s_i, w_i) = (s_{i+1}, o_i)$ for all $i \geq 0$. To show that TeSSLa$_{bool}$ and DFSTs have the same expressiveness, we encode DFST words as TeSSLa$_{bool}$ streams and vice versa. The function $\alpha_\Sigma(w) = S$ encodes a DFST word $w = w_0 w_1 \dots \in \Sigma^\infty$ as a corresponding set of TeSSLa$_{bool}$ streams: For every $p \in \Sigma$ a stream $s_p \in S$ exists with $s_p = 0 d_0 1 d_1 \dots \infty \Leftrightarrow \forall i : (d_i \Leftrightarrow w_i = p)$. The function $\beta_\Sigma(s_1, \dots, s_k) = w = w_0 w_1 \dots \in \Sigma^\infty$ encodes TeSSLa$_{bool}$ streams as a synchronized DFST word w over the alphabet $\Sigma = \{z_1, \dots, z_k\} \to$ Val with Val $= \{\bot, d, <', \bot', d' \mid d \in \{\mathtt{tt}, \mathtt{ff}\}\}$ which maps stream names to their current values: Let $T = \{t_0 = 0, t_1, t_2, \dots\}$ be the set of all timestamps present in the streams including 0 with $t_i < t_{i+1}$. Then $w_i(s) = <'$ if s has exclusive progress of t_i, $w_i(s) = s(t_i)'$ if s has inclusive progress of t_i or $w_i(s) = s(t_i)$ otherwise.

Theorem 6. *For a DFST $R = (\Sigma, \Gamma, Q, q_0, \delta)$ there is a TeSSLa$_{bool}$ formula φ_R and for a TeSSLa$_{bool}$ formula φ there is a DFST $R_\varphi = (\Sigma, \Gamma, Q, q_0, \delta)$ s.t.*

$$\alpha_\Gamma \circ [\![R]\!] = [\![\varphi_R]\!] \circ \alpha_\Sigma \quad and \quad \beta_\Gamma \circ [\![\varphi]\!] = [\![R_\varphi]\!] \circ \beta_\Sigma.$$

Note that since the boolean transducers produce one output symbol per input symbol one could reattach the timestamps of the input streams to the output streams to preserve the exact timestamps, too.

Translating DFST to TeSSLa$_{bool}$. We represent the states $q \in Q \backslash \{q_0\}$ as stream which is true iff the transducer is in it: $a_q := \mathbf{merge}(x_q, \mathbf{false})$ and the initial state $a_{q_0} := \mathbf{merge}(x_{q_0}, \mathbf{true})$, where $x_{q'} := \bigvee_{(a_q, \sigma, a_{q'}, \gamma) \in \delta} d_{a_q, \sigma}$. For every transition $\eta_i = (q, \sigma, q', \gamma)$ we add $d_{q,\sigma} := \mathbf{last}(a_q, \mathbf{merge}\{s_p \mid p \in \Sigma\}) \wedge s_\sigma$ and $o_i := \mathbf{filter}(d_{q,\sigma}, \mathbf{const}(\gamma)(d_{q,\sigma}))$. The merge of all the output streams is the output: $output := \mathbf{merge}\{o_i \mid \eta_i \in \delta\}$.

Translating TeSSLa$_{bool}$ to DFST. We translate every equation of the flattened specification φ into individual DFSTs, which are then composed into one DFST R_φ. For every DFST the input symbols are functions from the names of the input streams to Val and the output symbols are functions from the name of the equation to Val. As discussed in the previous section, for this finite data domain we only need to consider finitely many different internal states for every equation. The transition function realizes the state changes the current output based on the current state.

For the composition of the individual DFSTs every two $R = (I \rightarrow \text{Val}, O \rightarrow \text{Val}, Q, q_0, \delta)$ and $R' = (I' \rightarrow \text{Val}, O' \rightarrow \text{Val}, Q', q_0', \delta')$ are then composed parallel into $R'' = (I \cup I' \rightarrow \text{Val}, O \cup O' \rightarrow \text{Val}, Q \times Q', (q_0, q_0'), \delta'')$ with $\delta''((s_1, s_2), g'') = ((s_1', s_2'), h'') \iff \delta(s_1, g) = (s_1', h) \wedge \delta'(s_2, g') = (s_2', h') \wedge g'' = g \cup g' \wedge \forall \sigma \in I \cap I' : g(\sigma) = g'(\sigma) \wedge h'' = h \cup h'$ until one transducer $R_A = (I_A \rightarrow \text{Val}, O_A \rightarrow \text{Val}, Q_A, q_{0A}, \delta_A)$ represents all equations. R_A contains transitions with the same in- and output values for certain propositions which represents dependencies between the original equations. We now build the closure of this transducer which roughly resembles substituting the variables and computing the fixed-point of the equations: $R_\varphi = (I_A \backslash O_A \rightarrow \text{Val}, O_A \rightarrow \text{Val}, Q_A, q_{0A}, \delta_\varphi)$, where $\delta_\varphi(s, g) = (s', h) \iff \delta_A(s, g') = (s', h) \wedge g = g'|_{I_A \backslash O_A} \wedge (\forall a \in I_A \cap O_A : g'(a) = h(a))$ for $g|_I := g \cap (I \times \text{Val})$.

Equivalence of deterministic Büchi automata is in P and because the constructed DFSTs can be represented as those we can conclude:

Theorem 7. *Equivalence of TeSSLa$_{bool}$-formulas is in P.*

Timed Fragment. TeSSLa$_{bool+c}$ extends TeSSLa$_{bool}$ with the comparison of a timestamp with another, previous timestamp and a constant. In the syntax, expressions are restricted as follows, where $f \in \mathbb{B}^n \rightarrowtail \mathbb{B}$:

$$e := \textbf{nil} \mid \textbf{unit} \mid x \mid \textbf{lift}(f)(e, \ldots, e) \mid$$
$$\textbf{lift}(g_v)(\textbf{time}(e), \textbf{last}(\textbf{time}(e), e)) \mid \textbf{last}(e, e)$$

Time comparison is restricted to expressions $\textbf{lift}(g_v)(\textbf{time}(a), \textbf{last}(\textbf{time}(b), a))$ for streams $a, b \in \mathcal{S}_\mathbb{B}$ and a constant $v \in \mathbb{T}$, where g_v is a function $g_v : \mathbb{T} \times \mathbb{T} \rightarrow \mathbb{B}$ of the form $g_v(t_1, t_2) = t_1 \lesseqgtr t_2 + v$ with $\lesseqgtr \in \{<, >\}$, which allows checking the temporal distance of the current events of two streams. This is directly related to how clock constraints in timed automata [1,3] work.

A *timed finite state transducer (TFST)* is a DFSTs with an additional set of clocks C and $\delta : Q \times \Sigma \times \Theta(C) \rightarrow Q \times 2^C \times \Gamma$ where $\Theta(C)$ is the set of clock constraints. A clock constraint $\vartheta \in \Theta(C)$ is defined over the grammar $\vartheta ::= true \mid T \leq x + c \mid T \geq x + c \mid \neg \vartheta \mid \vartheta \wedge \vartheta$, where $x \in C$, and $c \in \mathbb{T}$ is a constant and T refers to the current time. δ now also takes a clock constraint and provides a set of clocks that have to be reset to T when taking this transition. A run of a TFST extends a run of a DFST with timestamps in the input and output word. An additional clock constraint has to be fulfilled to take a transitions and when taking a transitions, some clocks are set to the current time T.

TFSTs resemble timed automata using the notion of clock constraints from [3]. A TFST is called *deterministic*, or DTFST, iff for any two different transitions $\eta_1, \eta_2 \in \delta$ their conjuncted clock constraints $\vartheta_{\eta_1} \wedge \vartheta_{\eta_2}$ are unsatisfiable.

To show that TeSSLa$_{bool+c}$ and DTFSTs have the same expressiveness, we again encode words as streams and vice versa, but this time α_Σ and β_Σ preserve the timestamps. Hence both representations are now isomorphic and we can use the inverse encoding functions for decoding:

Theorem 8. *For a DTFST $R = (\Sigma, \Gamma, Q, q_0, C, \delta)$ a TeSSLa$_{bool+c}$ formula φ_R exists and for a TeSSLa$_{bool+c}$ formula φ a DTFST $R_\varphi = (\Sigma, \Gamma, Q, q_0, C, \delta)$ exists:*

$$[\![R]\!] = \alpha_\Gamma^{-1} \circ [\![\varphi_R]\!] \circ \alpha_\Sigma \quad and \quad [\![\varphi]\!] = \beta_\Gamma^{-1} \circ R_\varphi \circ \beta_\Sigma.$$

Translating DTFST to TeSSLa$_{bool+c}$. We reuse the translation for DFSTs with the following adjustments: We extend the stream $d_{q,\sigma}$ to $d_{q,\sigma,\vartheta}$ by adding the timing constraint ϑ, which is translated by lifting the boolean combination to signal semantics and translating the constraint $T \lesseqgtr x + c$ to $\mathbf{time}(\mathbf{merge}\{s_p \mid p \in \Sigma\}) \lesseqgtr \mathbf{last}(\mathbf{time}(\mathbf{merge}(b_x, \mathbf{unit})), \mathbf{merge}\{s_p \mid p \in \Sigma\}) + c$. Also for every clock $x \in C$ we add $b_x := \mathbf{merge}\{\mathbf{filter}(d_{q,\sigma,\vartheta}, d_{q,\sigma,\vartheta}) \mid (q, \sigma, \vartheta, q', r, \gamma) \in \delta \wedge x \in r\}$.

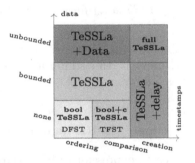

Fig. 1. TeSSLa fragments are restricted regarding (a) event values and available *data* structures and (b) event *timestamps* and how events sequences are recognized and generated: TeSSLa$_{bool}$ only checks event *ordering* like deterministic Büchi automata and BSRV [7] (LOLA restricted to boolean streams). TeSSLa$_{bool+c}$ additionally has timestamp *comparison* with constants like deterministic timed automata. TeSSLa has arbitrary *bounded* data structures and arbitrary computations on the timestamps. Full TeSSLa allows *unbounded* data structures and the creation of new timestamps via **delay**.

Translating TeSSLa$_{bool+c}$ to DTFST. The transducers from the equations in φ are build as before, but instead of translating equations that compare timestamps, we now translate equations of the form $\mathbf{lift}(g_v)(\mathbf{time}(a), \mathbf{last}(\mathbf{time}(b), a))$. Besides the **lift** and **last** operators, it also contains a comparison on timestamps, which is translated using the clocks and clock constraints of the DTFSTs to remember and compare timestamps. The parallel composition algorithm for DFSTs is extended by conjuncting the timing constraints of the composed transducers. Afterwards the same closure algorithm is applied. Equivalence of deterministic timed automata is PSPACE-complete [1] and because the constructed DTFSTs can be represented as those we can conclude:

Theorem 9. *Equivalence of TeSSLa$_{bool+c}$-formulas is PSPACE-complete.*

Figure 1 shows the modularity of the different TeSSLa fragments.

5   TeSSLa Implementations and Tool Support

The TeSSLa semantics presented in this paper allows multiple implementation styles: Centralized implementations using global memory which take one synchronized input word, as well as distributed implementations using message passing which take individual asynchronous input streams.

Centralized implementations are based on the same idea as the transducers: A global step function triggers the reevaluation of all TeSSLa operators involved in the specification for one timestamp, i.e. until a delayed-labelled edge in the dependency graph is reached. This step function is either triggered by new input events or a timeout of a delay if that has a smaller timestamp. Therefore every delay can register its timeouts globally s.t. the programs main loop can check with every incoming new events if the step function must be triggered for earlier delays before handling the external input. This implementation form is well-suited for software implementations running on traditional CPUs because it minimizes the internal communication overhead. Because software implementations can use dynamic memory management, the integration of unbounded data structures is straightforward.

As motivated in the introduction, one goal of TeSSLa's design is to allow distributed, parallel implementations with finite memory, e.g. on embedded systems or FPGAs. In this scenario we neither have dynamic memory management nor can we implement a global step function. Instead, every operator in the dependency graph is translated into a computation node with a fixed-size memory cell and finite input queues storing incoming events for every dependency. This setup has already been discussed for a preliminary non-recursive version of TeSSLa in [23]. The streams used in the TeSSLa semantics presented in this paper have an explicit notion of progress, which allows the local composition of TeSSLa operators without a global synchronization. Hence every computation node can produce a new output value if at least one input queue contains a new event and all other input queues contain at least progress until the timestamp of this event. The output value is sent to the input queues of all nodes depending on this node. While recursive equations in the transducers are solved by building the closure of the transducer created by applying the parallel composition to all computation nodes, in this message passing scenario we actually implement the Kleene chain of the fixed-point defined in the TeSSLa semantics in Definition 3: Progress and values are circulated in the cyclic graph of computation nodes until the progress increases no longer, which is exactly when the fixed point is reached. Since every computation node only produces new output events if there is enough progress on every input queue, we can guarantee that the fixed point is computed before new external events are processed.

For practical evaluations of TeSSLa we implemented a TeSSLa compiler in Scala which parses the TeSSLa specification, performs static type checking and converts the specification to flat TeSSLa. Additionally we added a macro system to be able to specify more complex functions based on the basic TeSSLa operators. The macro system allows to build application-domain-specific standard libraries, which makes TeSSLa a very flexible and powerful but still convenient and easy-to-learn specification language.

Furthermore, the types of the input streams are declared explicitly and the user can specify which streams should be contained in the output. Using the macro system, implicit application of **slift** to functions and implicit conversion from constants to constant signals, we can write the event counting example from the introduction as follows:

```
def count[A](a: Events[A]) := {            in x: Events[Unit]
    def c: Events[Int] := merge(last(c, a) + 1, 0)    def y := count(x)
    c }                                    out y
```

We combined the compiler with an interpreter written in Scala, which allows the usage of Java data structures. In order to apply TeSSLa for runtime verification we instrument the LLVM byte code of C programs and analyse this trace online with TeSSLa. This tool chain is available as a Docker container and a web IDE[2].

6 Conclusion

In this paper we presented the real-time specification language TeSSLa which operates on independent, timed streams and proved that it is suitable for online monitoring. We characterized the expressiveness of TeSSLa in terms of certain classes of stream-transforming functions. We also proved the equivalence of a boolean and a timed fragment of TeSSLa to respective classes of transducers and thereby obtained that equivalence for those fragments is in P and PSPACE, resp. These results facilitate advanced optimizations and static analyses of specifications, e.g. whether such a specification can generate certain outputs. We presented an implementation based on infinite-state transducers and sketched how TeSSLa is also suitable for parallelized implementations.

References

1. Alur, R., Dill, D.L.: A theory of timed automata. TCS **126**(2), 183–235 (1994)
2. Alur, R., Fisman, D., Raghothaman, M.: Regular programming for quantitative properties of data streams. In: Thiemann, P. (ed.) ESOP 2016. LNCS, vol. 9632, pp. 15–40. Springer, Heidelberg (2016). https://doi.org/10.1007/978-3-662-49498-1_2
3. Alur, R., Henzinger, T.A.: Back to the future: towards a theory of timed regular languages. In: IEEE FOCS, pp. 177–186 (1992)
4. Asarin, E., Caspi, P., Maler, O.: Timed regular expressions. J. ACM **49**(2), 172–206 (2002)

---

[2] http://www.tessla.io.

5. Bauer, A., Leucker, M., Schallhart, C.: Runtime verification for LTL and TLTL. ACM TOSEM **20**(4), 14 (2011)
6. Berry, G.: The foundations of Esterel. In: Plotkin, G., Stirling, C., Tofte, M. (eds.) Proof, Language, and Interaction: Essays in Honour of Robin Milner, pp. 425–454. MIT Press, Cambridge (2000)
7. Bozzelli, L., Sánchez, C.: Foundations of boolean stream runtime verification. In: Bonakdarpour, B., Smolka, S.A. (eds.) RV 2014. LNCS, vol. 8734, pp. 64–79. Springer, Cham (2014). https://doi.org/10.1007/978-3-319-11164-3_6
8. Broy, M., Stølen, K.: Specification and Development of Interactive Systems - Focus on Streams, Interfaces, and Refinement. Springer, New York (2001). https://doi.org/10.1007/978-1-4613-0091-5
9. Convent, L., Hungerecker, S., Leucker, M., Scheffel, T., Schmitz, M., Thoma, D.: TeSSLa: temporal stream-based specification language. arXiv:1808.10717, August 2018
10. D'Angelo, B., et al.: LOLA: runtime monitoring of synchronous systems. In: TIME, pp. 166–174. IEEE (2005)
11. Decker, N., et al.: Online analysis of debug trace data for embedded systems. In: DATE. IEEE (2018)
12. Decker, N., et al.: Rapidly adjustable non-intrusive online monitoring for multi-core systems. In: Cavalheiro, S., Fiadeiro, J. (eds.) SBMF 2017. LNCS, vol. 10623, pp. 179–196. Springer, Cham (2017). https://doi.org/10.1007/978-3-319-70848-5_12
13. Donzé, A., Maler, O., Bartocci, E., Nickovic, D., Grosu, R., Smolka, S.A.: On temporal logic and signal processing. ATVA **7561**, 92–106 (2012)
14. Eliot, C., Hudak, P.: Functional reactive animation. In: ICFP, pp. 163–173 (1997)
15. Faymonville, P., Finkbeiner, B., Schirmer, S., Torfah, H.: A stream-based specification language for network monitoring. In: Falcone, Y., Sánchez, C. (eds.) RV 2016. LNCS, vol. 10012, pp. 152–168. Springer, Cham (2016). https://doi.org/10.1007/978-3-319-46982-9_10
16. Faymonville, P., Finkbeiner, B., Schwenger, M., Torfah, H.: Real-time stream-based monitoring. arXiv:1711.03829, November 2017
17. Gautier, T., Le Guernic, P., Besnard, L.: SIGNAL: a declarative language for synchronous programming of real-time systems. In: Kahn, G. (ed.) FPCA 1987. LNCS, vol. 274, pp. 257–277. Springer, Heidelberg (1987). https://doi.org/10.1007/3-540-18317-5_15
18. Halbwachs, N., Caspi, P., Pilaud, D., Plaice, J.: LUSTRE: a declarative language for programming synchronous systems. In: POPL, pp. 178–188. ACM Press (1987)
19. Havelund, K., Goldberg, A.: Verify your runs. In: Meyer, B., Woodcock, J. (eds.) VSTTE 2005. LNCS, vol. 4171, pp. 374–383. Springer, Heidelberg (2008). https://doi.org/10.1007/978-3-540-69149-5_40
20. Havelund, K., Roşu, G.: Synthesizing monitors for safety properties. In: Katoen, J.-P., Stevens, P. (eds.) TACAS 2002. LNCS, vol. 2280, pp. 342–356. Springer, Heidelberg (2002). https://doi.org/10.1007/3-540-46002-0_24
21. Jaksic, S., Bartocci, E., Grosu, R., Kloibhofer, R., Nguyen, T., Nickovic, D.: From signal temporal logic to FPGA monitors. In: MEMOCODE, pp. 218–227 (2015)
22. Leucker, M., Schallhart, C.: A brief account of runtime verification. J. Logic Algebr. Progr. **78**(5), 293–303 (2009)
23. Leucker, M., Sánchez, C., Scheffel, T., Schmitz, M., Schramm, A.: TeSSLa: runtime verification of non-synchronized real-time streams. In: SAC. ACM (2018)

24. Maler, O., Nickovic, D.: Monitoring temporal properties of continuous signals. In: Lakhnech, Y., Yovine, S. (eds.) FORMATS/FTRTFT -2004. LNCS, vol. 3253, pp. 152–166. Springer, Heidelberg (2004). https://doi.org/10.1007/978-3-540-30206-3_12
25. Pike, L., Goodloe, A., Morisset, R., Niller, S.: Copilot: a hard real-time runtime monitor. In: Barringer, H., et al. (eds.) RV 2010. LNCS, vol. 6418, pp. 345–359. Springer, Heidelberg (2010). https://doi.org/10.1007/978-3-642-16612-9_26
26. Selyunin, K., et al.: Runtime monitoring with recovery of the SENT communication protocol. In: Majumdar, R., Kunčak, V. (eds.) CAV 2017. LNCS, vol. 10426, pp. 336–355. Springer, Cham (2017). https://doi.org/10.1007/978-3-319-63387-9_17

Automatic Test Case Generation for Concurrent Features from Natural Language Descriptions

Rafaela Almeida[1]([✉]), Sidney Nogueira[1]([✉]), and Augusto Sampaio[2]

[1] Universidade Federal Rural de Pernambuco, Recife, PE, Brazil
{rafaela.almeida,sidney.nogueira}@ufrpe.br
[2] Universidade Federal de Pernambuco, Recife, PE, Brazil

Abstract. Contemporary computing applications have an increasing level of concurrency; new techniques are demanded to tackle the challenge of testing the plentiful interactions that arise from concurrent behaviour. Current approaches for automatic test generation from natural language models do not allow the explicit specification of concurrent behaviour. This paper extends our previous test case generation approach to support concurrent mobile device features. A natural language notation is proposed to express the composition of sequential and concurrent behaviour. The notation can be automatically translated to a CSP model, from which tests are automatically produced using the FDR refinement checker. The approach is illustrated with a mobile application that includes concurrent features.

Keywords: Concurrent feature · Software testing · CSP

1 Introduction

Testing is an expensive activity that can be even more costly when the implementation under test is concurrent. Verifying the behaviour of concurrent software is challenging because of the possible interleaving among a variety of execution flows [4]. New technologies like multi-core and distributed architectures have stimulated the significant increase of concurrency in computational systems [6]. For instance, in the most recent versions of Android [1], the user has the possibility to interact within a multi-window perspective, where various applications may be exhibited at the same time. Therefore, concurrent systems demand fast and efficient testing approaches.

Model-based testing (MBT) enables the automatic generation and execution of tests of sequential and concurrent systems [7]. One of the barriers to the adoption of MBT is that the main input for test generation is formal models. Formal notations contrast with the ones adopted by traditional software engineering approaches, such as use case models. To facilitate its adoption, MBT approaches that use (structured) natural language notations to specify input models have

© Springer Nature Switzerland AG 2018
T. Massoni and M. R. Mousavi (Eds.): SBMF 2018, LNCS 11254, pp. 163–179, 2018.
https://doi.org/10.1007/978-3-030-03044-5_11

been proposed [8,10]. Such approaches automatically generate test cases from formal models that are automatically and transparently obtained from natural language input models. As an example, in previous work [15] we present an approach that is implemented by an automatic test case generation tool, TaRGeT, which is used in a partnership with Motorola Mobility (a Lenovo company) to generate black-box tests for mobile applications. The input model for TaRGeT is a use case template that is authored using a structured natural language notation. These templates are automatically translated into CSP [16,17] models, from which test cases are automatically generated and translated back into natural language, for manual execution or to serve as a basis for automation. A limitation of this approach is that it cannot handle concurrency.

Concurrency in the context of black-box testing of mobile applications can arise from multiple sources. We consider two sources of concurrency that are often found in this context. One is the concurrency in the scope of a single application. For instance, the user of an email application can list emails while new emails can be received and handled by another part of the application, which updates the email list. Another possibility is the concurrency that arises from distinct applications that run simultaneously. For instance, an email application running concurrently with a video player application in different parts of the screen.

This paper extends our previous approach to support automatic test case generation for concurrent features. An extension of the use case template is proposed to allow modelling of concurrent features. This extension allows the specification of the two levels of concurrency discussed above: intra-feature concurrency is used to specify active use cases, whose execution flow interleaves with other use cases that are part of the same feature; and inter-feature concurrency that is used to model the interleaving of different features. The extended template can be automatically translated to a CSP model, from which test cases are automatically produced using the FDR refinement checker. The approach is illustrated with a mobile device application that includes concurrent features.

The next section gives an overview of the notation and semantics of CSP. Section 3 introduces the extension of the use case template to allow the specification of concurrent behaviour. Section 4 presents the CSP model that defines a formal semantics to the use case template with concurrent behaviour. Then, Sect. 5 shows how test cases are automatically generated from the CSP models using the FDR model checker. Finally, Sect. 6 summarises our results and discuss related and future work.

2   CSP

This section introduces the notation and the traces semantic model of CSP used in this paper. Notably, we use the notation of CSP_M [19], a machine-readable version of CSP and input format for the FDR tool [11].

The core element of the CSP notation is a process: it is an entity that can specify sequential and concurrent behaviour. The set of events communicated by a process forms its alphabet. The simplest CSP process is STOP. Such a process specifies deadlock behaviour; it does communicate events and does not progress. Another primitive process is SKIP, which represents successful termination. After communicating the special event ✓ this process deadlocks.

Basic CSP operators are used to model the sequential behaviour of use cases. The prefix operator -> is used to specify sequential events. The notation a -> P specifies a process that offers the event a and waits until the environment is ready to communicate. Once a is communicated, it behaves as the process P. A channel in CSP is an abstraction for a set of events with a common prefix. The notation channel c : T stands for a channel c that communicates events in $\{c.t \mid t \in T\}$. For instance, consider the channel channel c : 0,1,2, the process c!0 -> STOP communicates the event c.0 and deadlocks. Additionally, the syntax c?t denotes the environment binds a value v in T to the variable t and communicates the event c.v. Sequential composition is another suitable operator to model sequential behaviour. The expression P;Q behaves like P until it terminates successfully (behave as SKIP), then the control is taken by Q. For instance, the behaviour of the process a -> SKIP; b -> STOP is equivalent to a -> b -> STOP.

CSP allows the specification of choice between processes. For instance, the external choice between the processes P and Q, namely P [] Q, can behave as the process P or Q. The choice is made by the environment. The concurrent behaviour between features is specified using the parallel composition operator of CSP. The expression P [|X|] Q denotes the parallel composition of the processes P and Q. In this composition, the events in the set X happen synchronously (simultaneously in both sides); other events communicate independently. The expression P ||| Q denotes the interleave of the processes P and Q, a special case of the parallel composition where there is no synchronisation (empty synchronisation set). For instance, the process a -> b -> STOP [|{a}|] a -> b -> STOP behaves as the process a -> (b -> STOP ||| c -> STOP), which communicates the event a and then behaves as b -> STOP ||| c -> STOP. The latter interleaves the communication of the events b and c. A parallel composition only terminates if both process in the composition terminate (distributed termination).

The CSP operator \ is used to hide process communications. Therefore, the process P\X communicates the events of P, except the events in the set X. Finally, we introduce the notation P /\ Q, where /\ stands for the interruption operator. This notation indicates the process Q can interrupt the behaviour of P if an event of Q is communicated. The simplest semantic model of CSP is the traces model, where a process is identified with the set of all the traces it can perform. Our approach performs traces refinement verifications using the FDR tool [20] to generate test scenarios. A trace is a sequence of visible actions performed by a process. For instance, the traces model of the process x -> y -> STOP is the set {<>, <x>, <x,y>}. A process Q refines a process P, namely P [T= Q, if the traces Q is a subset of the traces of P. If a refinement does not hold, FDR yields a (counter-example) trace of Q that is not in P. For instance, the process P1 = a

`-> SKIP; accept -> STOP` is refined, in the traces model, by the process `STOP`, namely `P1 [T= STOP`. The traces of the former process is $\{<>,<a>,<a,\checkmark>\}$ and those for the latter is $\{<>\}$. Let the CSP process `Q1` be defined by the expression `Q1 = a -> SKIP`. The refinement `Q1 [T= P1` does not hold because `<a,accept>` belongs to the traces of `P1` and does not belong to the traces of `Q1`, which is the set $\{<>,<a>,<a,\checkmark>\}$. Thus, `<a,accept>` is a counter-example for `Q1 [T= P1`. More details about the traces (and other semantic models of CSP) can be found in [16].

3   Modelling Concurrency

Figure 1 gives an overview of the approach we proposed in previous work [15] and adapt to handle concurrent features in the current paper. The approach inputs document templates written in natural language and generates black-box test cases for manual testing of mobile application. Feature descriptions are automatically translated into CSP models, from which test cases are automatically generated using FDR. Finally, test cases are translated from CSP to a Controlled Natural Language (CNL) notation. A limitation of this approach is that it can only generate tests for sequential behaviour. It is not possible to model and generate test cases for concurrent features.

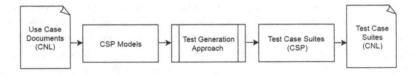

Fig. 1. TaRGeT test generation approach.

A relevant adaptation of the previous approach is the extension of the use case template to allow the specification of concurrency. The remainder of this section introduces an extension of the TaRGeT use case template to model concurrent features. Such an extension is conservative since it adds new elements and preserves all the previous template elements. Thus, the extension allows modelling and generating test cases for both sequential and concurrent features.

The main contribution of this work is to introduce two forms of concurrency:

1. Intra-feature: models the concurrent execution of use cases that belong to the same feature. This abstracts concurrent behaviour that arises from different parts of the same application. Use cases can perform concurrent access of data shared in the scope of the feature.
3. Inter-feature: models the concurrent execution of features, abstracting concurrent behaviour that arises from the interaction of applications of different features.

The next subsections detail each of these forms of concurrency using as running example features that run on mobile devices.

3.1 Modelling Active Use Cases

The previous use case template [15] for automatic test case generation is formed of features, and each feature can have multiple use cases. Each use case has one or more execution flows that can be interconnected. In the previous template, in a feature a unique execution flow is performed at a time; one flow is resumed before the next starts; the use cases are performed sequentially. We extend the template with *active* use cases, which can be performed concurrently with the flow of other use cases of a feature.

For illustrating intra-feature concurrency, our running example is the partial model of an email application that is composed of two use cases. This application is modelled as the Feature F1 whose model includes some data definition (Fig. 2) and two uses cases (Figs. 3 and 4). Figure 2 exhibits data within the scope of the email feature. Types, constants and variables are defined. For test generation, the range of values is limited to avoid the explosion of the number of test cases. The type Natural specifies the range of integer values to the set $\{0, 1, 2, 3, 4, 5\}$, which is abbreviated by the notation [0,5]. The constant MAX_EMAILS is the maximum number of emails that the inbox folder can reach. The variable read represents the number of read emails, and has two as the initial value. The variable unread stands for the number of unread emails; its initial value is one.

F1: EMAIL

Data Definition

Type	Description	Elements
Natural	Numeric range	[0,5]

Constant	Description	Value
MAX_EMAILS	The maximum number of emails	4

Variable	Description	VarType	Value
read	Number of read emails	Natural	2
unread	Number of unread emails	Natural	1

Fig. 2. Data definition for Feature F1.

The first use case of Feature F1, namely UC01, describes the behaviour of checking unread emails (Fig. 3). This use case has main and alternative flows. Each flow has a sequence of identified steps that are composed of three fields: the user input action, a system condition (the precondition for performing the step) and the respective system response. The first step of UC01 main flow (1M) verifies the existence of new emails. In this feature, an unread email is equivalent to a

UC01 - Verify unread emails

Main Flow
From Step: START
To Step: END

Step ID	User Action	System State	System Response
1M	Verify the existence of newly received email.	There is unread email. %unread> 0%	The unread emails are highlighted.
2M	Open unread emails. %Input x: Natural from {1..unread}%		Unread emails are marked as read. %unread := unread – x, read := read + x%

Alternative Flow
From Step: START
To Step: END

Step ID	User Action	System State	System Response
1A	Verify the existence of newly received email.	%unread = 0%	There are no unread emails.

Fig. 3. Use case 1 (Email).

new email. Thus, the condition for this step is that there is at least one unread email. The use case template defines a CNL notation to specify user input values (in the user action), conditional expressions (in the system state) and system outputs/updates (in the system response). These appear enclosed between two occurrences of the % symbol. For instance, the expression %unread > 0% in the Step 1M is a guard that is true if the value assigned to unread is greater than 0 (zero). In the sequel, the second step (2M) captures opening unread emails. The expression in the user action %Input x: Natural from {1..unread}% specifies an input value x that is defined by the user. Such a value is between one and the current number of unread messages. The system response is to mark messages as read, decrement (increment) the number of unread (read) messages by the number of read messages (%unread := unread x, read : = read + x%). For more details about the CNL notation refer to [15].

Use case flows are preceded by the fields From Step and To Step, which are used to indicate the origin and continuation of the flow, respectively. In UC01, the origin of the main flow is START which indicates this flow can be performed in the initial state of the feature. The continuation of this use case is END, which indicates this flow resumes after completing its last step. If the origin (continuation) is a step id, then the flow starts (continues) in the step of another flow.

The bottom part of Fig. 3 shows the alternative flow of UC01, which continues after the initial state of the main flow. The condition of the Step 1A is that there are no unread emails (%unread = 0%). This condition is only satisfied if the condition of the Step 1M is not. In this case, the alternative flow is performed instead of the main flow. The action of the Step 1A is to verify the existence of new emails and the system response is that no emails are found at all.

Figure 4 presents an active use case, namely Use Case UC02, which specifies the handling of new emails that can be performed concurrently with email reading. Active use cases are identified by the label <<active>> that is placed as a suffix of the use case name. The structure of an active use case is the same as that for non-active use cases; however, it has an independent execution flow. As a consequence, an active use case can interleave with the execution of other use cases. The active use case of our example takes as input a number of messages that are received from the network. This is specified in Step 1M by the input x whose value must not exceed the maximum capacity of the messages, considering the already existent messages in the application (%Input x: Natural from {1..MAX_EMAILS - (read+unread)} %). The enabling condition for this step is that the number of existent messages must be less than the maximum allowed (%read + unread < MAX_EMAILS%). If the condition holds, the amount of unread messages is updated (%unread := unread + x%). This use case mimics a component of the email application that is responsible for receiving new emails and runs simultaneously with Use Case UC01.

UC02: Handle new Email <<active >>

Main Flow
From Step: START
To Step: END

Step ID	External Action	System State	System Response
1M	Handle x email(s). %Input x: Natural from {1..MAX_EMAILS - (read+unread)} %	%read + unread < MAX_EMAILS%	Inbox folder updated. %unread := unread + x%

Fig. 4. Active use case.

3.2 Modelling Concurrent Features

This section proposes an extension of the template to deal with concurrent features.

We use an Android functionality as illustration. The android split screen is introduced in Android N [2] and allows the screen to be split into two separate views; each view runs a distinct application. At the uppermost part of the screen is a main (fixed) application, and at the bottom part of the screen is a second application that is executed concurrently with the main one. We show how to model the Email Application (specified as the Feature F1 in the previous section) running in the uppermost view, and a Video Player application executing in the bottom view, simultaneously.

Figure 5 depicts Feature F2 that specifies the Video Player Application. This feature has a single use case with a main flow, whose steps consist on selecting a video (Step 1M) and verifying whether the selected video starts playing after clicking play (Step 2M).

F2: VIDEO

UC01: Video Playing

Main Flow
From Step: START
To Step: END

Step ID	External Action	System State	System Response
1M	Select a video		The video is highlighted
2M	Click on "Play" button		The selected video starts to play

Fig. 5. Use case 1 (Video).

The extension proposed to model concurrency between features consists on specifying how the features of a document are composed. The internal structure of features is not changed. The features can be configured to execute sequentially, concurrently, or the combination of these two possibilities. We introduce a notation for the specification of such composition in what follows.

$$\text{Composition} := \text{fid}$$
$$| \quad (\text{Composition OR Composition})$$
$$| \quad (\text{Composition AND Composition})$$

According to the notation above, a composition has one or more feature identifiers that can be combined with the constructors OR and AND. The constructor OR specifies that the arguments of the composition are executed as a choice, so only one of the features is executed at a time; in the case of iterated executions, they happen sequentially. The constructor AND specifies that the composed features are performed simultaneously, so their behaviours are interleaved. For instance, the composition (F1 AND F2) defines that the features F1 and F2 are executed concurrently, so it models the behaviour of the aforementioned Android functionality while executing Email and Video Player applications in the same screen. As another example, the composition (F1 OR F2) defines that F1 and F2 are executed one at a time.

4   CSP Semantics for Concurrent Features

This section presents the CSP semantics for the extended use case template introduced in the previous section. The presentation follows the order of the elements in the use case template.

Types and constants are translated into types and constants in the CSP model. Table 1 shows the CSP representation for the data elements defined in the scope of Feature F1 (Fig. 2). The type Natural becomes a nametype in CSP (line 01), and the constant MAX_EMAILS a constant with the same name in the CSP model (line 03). Variables become elements of the set Vars that is defined in CSP_M as a datatype (line 05).

Table 1. CSP model for data elements of Feature F1.

```
01 nametype F1_Natural = {0..5}
02
03 MAX_EMAILS = 4
04
05 datatype Vars = F1_read | F1_unread
06
07 channel get,set : Var.F1_Natural
08
09 channel startStep, endStep : IDS_F.IDS_UC.IDS_S
```

CSP processes are stateless and, therefore, there are no variables. We adopt the usual approach to modelling state as a memory process. The channels get and set declared in Table 1 (line 07) are used in the CSP model of a use case to read the value of a variable in the memory and to update the value of a variable, respectively. Later, we show that the memory process is composed in parallel with the feature use cases, so the use cases can communicate with the memory through these channels. We exemplify the usage of such channels in the semantics of Use Case UC01 depicted in Table 2. In line 08 of Table 2, the communication get!F1_unread?unread reads the value of the variable F1_unread from the memory and binds this value to unread. As another example, in line 16 of the same table, the event set!F1_read!(read + x) is a message to the memory to update the variable F1_read to the value of the expression (read + x). The complete CSP model for this use case is presented in what follows. More details about the memory process can be found in [13].

The next part of Feature F1 is the Use Case UC01 whose CSP model is presented in Table 2. In this table, UC01 is specified by the process F1_UC01 that behaves as F1_UC01_START. Remember from Sect. 3.1 that START represents the initial state of a use case, consequently START is represented as a process in the CSP model. Since main and alternative flows initiate from START, the behaviour of F1_UC01_START is the choice between the processes F1_UC01_1M (first step of the main flow) and F1_UC01_1A (first step of the alternative flow). The process F1_UC01_1M represents the step 1M of UC01. Initially, this process communicates the control event startStep.1.1.1 and reads the current value of the variable unread by communicating the event get!F1_unread?unread (line 08). The guarded process g & P, where g is a guard and P is a process, is equivalent to if g then P else STOP. After reading the variable value, the CSP model verifies the system condition, modelled as a guard (line 08). If the guard holds (**unread > 0**) the process flow continues, otherwise it deadlocks. If the flow continues, the event **verify_newly_received** that represents the step action is performed, followed by the event that represents the system response (**unread_highlithed**), the control event **endStep.1.1.1** and successful termination. After terminating, the control is taken by the process that represents Step 2M (**F1_UC01_2M**).

Table 2. CSP model for Use Case UC01 of Feature F1.

```
01 channel in_1_UC01_2M_x : Naturals
02
03 F1_UC01 = F1_UC01_START
04
05 F1_UC01_START = (F1_UC01_1M [] F1_UC01_1A)
06
07 F1_UC01_1M = startStep.1.1.1 ->
08    get!F1_unread?unread -> unread > 0 &
09    verify_newly_received -> unread_highlithed ->
10    endStep.1.1.1 -> SKIP ; (F1_UC01_2M)
11
12 F1_UC01_2M = startStep.1.1.2 ->
13    get!F1_unread?unread -> get!F1_read?read ->
14    in_1_UC01_2M_x?x:{1..unread} ->
15    open_unread -> unread_marked_read ->
16    set!F1_unread!(unread - x) -> set!F1_read!(read + x) ->
17    endStep.1.1.2 -> SKIP
18
19 F1_UC01_1A = startStep.1.1.3 ->
20    get!F1_unread?unread -> unread == 0 &
21    verify_newly_receive_A -> no_unread_A ->
22    endStep.1.1.3 -> SKIP
```

In the testing theory originally developed in [14], and adopted here, traces of the CSP model must not mix events of different steps, as it requires that an user action (categorised as an input event) must be followed by the respective system response (an output event). However, mixing steps of use cases performed concurrently does not violate any aspect of the theory. To ensure the atomicity of a step, a standard mechanism of critical region is used. The control events **startStep.1.1.1** and **endStep.1.1.1** are used to define the start and end of a critical region. Table 1 declare the channels **startStep** and **endStep** (line 09). The sets **IDS_F**, **IDS_UC** and **IDS_S** are indices for the features, use cases and steps. In our example, these sets are {1..2}, {1..2} and {1..3}, respectively.

The process **F1_UC01_2M** (line 12) is the CSP model for Step 2M of Use Case **UC01**. This process initially reads, from the memory, the variable values using **get**, then inputs a value x (line 14) that represents the number of emails to be opened. The input is communicated by the channel **in_1_UC01_2M_x** (line 01). Subsequently, the process communicates the events that represent the action of opening emails (**open_unread**) and the system response that shows the opened messages marked as read (unread_marked_read). Next, the events set!F1_unread!(unread - x) and set!F1_read!(read + x) represent the updates specified in Step 2M. Finally, the process terminates successfully.

The process F1_UC01_1A (line 19) is the CSP model for Step 1A. Initially, it gets the number of unread messages from the memory (variable unread) using a get event and verifies the system condition (unread == 0). If the condition fails, the process deadlocks; otherwise, the process communicates the events for verifying the existence of new received email and the system response that there are no unread email. Afterwards, the process terminates.

The processes F1_UC01_1M and F1_UC01_1A are in choice in the process F1_UC01_START (line 05) and their guards are disjoint. The first process progresses if there are unread messages, otherwise the second one progresses. Hence the main and the alternative flow are excluding.

Table 3 shows the CSP semantics for the active use case UC2 defined in Feature F1. As commented in Sect. 3.2, the structure of an active use case has no particularities. The difference is that it interleaves with the non active use cases of the feature, as will be explicit in the CSP model for the feature. The process F1_UC02 (line 03) specifies the behaviour of this use case. The CSP semantics for this process uses the same strategy used to obtain the semantics of Use Case UC01, so we abbreviate the explanation. Initially, this process reads the values for the variables using get events (line 08) and evaluates the system condition (line 09). If the condition holds, it inputs a value x defined by the environment (line 10), communicates the events that represent the action to handle new emails and the respective system response (line 11). Next, it uses a set event to update the value for the unread variable (line 12) and terminates.

Table 3. CSP model for Use Case UC02 from Feature F1.

```
01 channel in_1_UC02_1M_x : Naturals
02
03 F1_UC02 = F1_UC02_START
04
05 F1_UC02_START = F1_UC02_1M
06
07 F1_UC02_1M = startStep.1.2.1 ->
08    get!F1_unread?unread -> get!F1_read?read ->
09    read + unread < MAX_EMAILS &
10    in_1_UC02_1M_x?x:{1..(MAX_EMAILS - (read+unread))} ->
11    handle_emails -> inbox_updated ->
12    set!F1_unread!(unread + x) ->
13    endStep.1.2.1 -> SKIP
```

The CSP model for a feature F that does not have variables behaves as F_UCs, where F_UCs is the process that specifies the composition of the use cases. The composition of the use cases is defined as the external choice between the use case processes (F_UC1 [] ... [] F_UCi) interleaving with the combination of the active use cases (F_UCa_1 ||| ... ||| F_UCa_j), where i is the number of non active use cases and j is the number of active use cases. Moreover, F_UCa_k is defined as the choice (F_UCak [] SKIP), where F_UCak is the process that represents an active use case for $1 \leq k \leq j$. The choice in (F_UCak [] SKIP) states that this process behaves as F_UCak or as SKIP, as a consequence, the use case combination considers execution flows that interleave with the active use case and flows that do not (when the process behaves as SKIP). In other words, it considers all the combinations of behaviour.

The CSP model for a feature F that has variables is defined as the composition F_UCs [|aMEM|] (F_MEMORY /\ SKIP), where F_MEMORY is the memory process and aMEM the memory alphabet. In the right-hand side of the parallel composition, the process F_MEMORY is interrupted by SKIP to allow the successful termination of the feature process.

The process F1 presented in Table 4 is the CSP model for Feature F1. In this process, the combination of the use cases is F1_UC01 and the combination of active use case is (F1_UC02 [] SKIP).

Table 4. CSP model for Feature F1.

```
01 F1 = (F1_UC01 ||| (F1_UC02 [] SKIP))
02         [|aF1_MEM|]
03         (F1_MEMORY /\ SKIP)
```

For conciseness, we omit the CSP model for the Feature F2.

The model for the system to be tested combines all the features and uses the process stepCR in its definition. Such a process when composed in parallel with the features ensures the use case steps are executed atomically. Table 5 shows the specification for this process. The process stepCR is a recursive process that waits for the environment to communicate an event from the channel startStep and then an event from the channel endStep. Consider CONTROL is the set that includes all the events of the channels startStep and endStep. The parallel composition of stepCR with the features with synchronisation set equals CONTROL ensures only a step is performed at time.

Table 5. CSP process that ensures critical region.

```
01 stepCR = startStep?f?uc?s -> endStep!f!uc!s -> stepCR
```

Finally, the CSP process that models the system to be tested, namely SYS, behaves as (Fs [|CONTROL|] (stepCR /\ SKIP)) \ CONTROL, where the process Fs stands for the composition of features. For our example, we have:

```
SYS0 = ((F1 [] F2) [|CONTROL|] (stepCR /\  SKIP)) \ CONTROL

SYS1 = ((F1 ||| F2) [|CONTROL|] (stepCR /\ SKIP)) \ CONTROL
```

The process stepCR is interrupted by SKIP to allow the parallel composition in SYS to terminate successfully. Recall from Sect. 3.2 that features can be combined using the constructors OR and AND. The CSP model for a composition of features Fs is obtained replacing the feature id by the respective feature process, the constructor OR by the CSP external choice operator, and the construct AND by the CSP interleaving operator. For instance, the system models for the compositions F1 OR F2 and F1 AND F2 are the processes SYS0 and SYS1. One can find the complete semantics of sequential features in our previous work [14]. We intend to further detail the semantics for concurrent features in future work.

5   Test Generation for Concurrent Features

This section illustrates the use of FDR for automatic generation of test cases for concurrent features, following the approach introduced in [15].

To generate test scenarios using FDR, our approach uses a special event (accept) to mark the scenarios we want to produce from the specification process, say S. Consider S' is the specification process modified by including an accept event at the end of the scenarios. Since the mark event is not in the alphabet of S, the refinement S [T= S' does not hold, and counter-examples yielded by FDR for this refinement verification are test scenarios. We exemplify test generation using the system specification model SYS0 introduced in the previous section. The modified process for SYS0 that includes the event accept after the traces that lead to successful termination is the process SYS0; accept -> STOP. The assert command of FDR runs a refinement verification and yields the shortest counter-example trace if the refinement does not hold. Thus, the FDR assertion

```
assert SYS0 [T= SYS0;  accept -> STOP
```

does not hold and yields the following counter-example trace.

```
t1 = <get.F1_unread.1, verify_newly_received, unread_highlithed,
get.F1_unread.1, get.F1_read.2, in_1_UC01_2M_x.1, open_unread,
unread_marked_read, set.F1_unread.0, set.F1_read.3, accept>
```

Excluding get and accept events, the trace above represents the behaviour of the alternative flow of the Use Case UC01 of Feature F1. To generate other test scenarios from SYS0 we use the CSP function Proc that is introduced in [14]. Such a function receives as input a sequence of events and generates a process whose maximum trace corresponds to the input sequence. For instance, to generate a second test scenario we use the process SYS0 [] Proc(t1) as the specification process. Such a process contains the trace t1, hence t1 is not a counter-example for the refinement assertion below,

```
assert SYS0 [] Proc(t1) [T= SYS0; accept -> STOP
```

which yields the following test scenario as a counter-example for the above refinement.

```
t2 =  <get.F1_unread.1, get.F1_read.2, in_1_UC_02_1M_x.1,
handle_emails,inbox_updated, set.F1_unread.2, get.F1_unread.2,
verify_newly_received, unread_highlithed, get.F1_unread.2,
get.F1_read.2, in_1_UC01_2M_x.1, open_unread, unread_marked_read,
set.F1_unread.1, set.F1_read.3, accept>
```

In general, for obtaining the $(n+1)^{th}$ test scenario (counter-example) from a specification, we need to augment the left-hand side of the refinement expression with the test scenarios already generated, and verify the expression using FDR. Formally, the refinement expression for obtaining the $(n+1)^{th}$ test scenario is

```
S [] Proc(ts_1) [] ... [] Proc(ts_n) [T= S'
```

There is a total of six test scenarios that can be obtained from the process SYS0 using the expression above. A future work is to integrate the proposed model for concurrent features in the TaRGeT tool. Such a tool automatizes the process of generating test scenarios for sequential features by running FDR refinements in background until some stop criteria is reached [15]. The simplest criteria is to generate test scenarios until the number of test scenarios reaches a threshold. Natural language test purposes can also be used to describe scenarios that match particular steps and states of the use case specification. Recently, TaRGeT has been improved to consider structural coverage [12]. Using FDR, it is possible to have access to the underlying LTS models (operational semantics) for the CSP specification and to measure the coverage of events or transitions for a set of test scenarios. Since there is a mapping between the underlying LTS models and the CSP specification, TaRGeT considers three structural criteria to stop the generation of test scenarios: (1) coverage of use case steps (at least once), (2) coverage of use case steps and all possible combinations of inputs values, and (3) coverage of use case steps and all possible combinations of input values that match a given test purpose.

The trace t2 represents a test scenario for intra-feature concurrency in Feature F1. In this scenario, the main flow of the the Use Case UC01 is preceded by the active use case (Use Case UC02), which is performed concurrently. Figure 6 depicts a test case that can be obtained from this test scenario.

The format of the generated test cases is suitable for manual execution (see Fig. 6). In related work [5,18], we introduce tools for automating the execution of test cases written in natural language. Such tools can support the automation of concurrent test cases in the style generated by the approach proposed here. However, currently, there is no integration between our test generation approach and existing test automation tools. This will be addressed as future work.

Test Case ID: 002
Initial Conditions: read = 2, unread = 1

Id	Steps	Expected Results
1	Handle 1 email(s)	Inbox folder updated
2	Verify the existence of newly received email	The unread emails are highlighted
3	Open unread emails	Unread emails are marked as read

Final Conditions: read = 3, unread = 1

Fig. 6. Test case from t2.

6   Conclusion

This work adapts and extends our previous test case generation approach to allow the automatic generation of tests cases for concurrent features as well as concurrent use cases of the same feature. We have proposed an extension of the use case template to allow modelling these two forms of concurrency: intra-feature and inter-feature concurrency. The first one introduces the concept of active use cases, whose flow interleaves with the flow of other use cases that are part of the same feature. The second one proposes a notation for specifying the composition of features. Such a notation allows combining features sequentially as well as concurrently. Furthermore, the templates in natural language are given a formal semantics via a mapping into the CSP process algebra. Finally, traces refinement checking is used to extract test cases automatically from the CSP model using the FDR refinement checker. The contribution is illustrated using a mobile device application that has concurrent behaviour.

The proposed extension is conservative, so the previous template capabilities are preserved, and the same template can be used for the specification of sequential or concurrent behaviour. Additionally, to our knowledge, the approach we propose is the only automatic test case generation approach that input documents authored using natural language to model the two considered forms of concurrency, allowing data sharing between concurrent use cases.

The test generation strategy proposed in [3] is close to ours. It inputs test models authored in natural language (use case templates) and is designed for modelling interruptions in mobile device applications; these interruptions are urgent events like an incoming call that pause the execution of the current state of the application until the interruption event is concluded. An interruption may be seen as a particular type of concurrent behaviour since it allows the main flow to be interrupted at any time during its execution. The approach we propose in this paper does not model interruption because current mobile device applications are not interrupted by calls or by other events; all applications must run concurrently. Another difference to our work is that we consider two forms of concurrency, and data sharing between concurrent use cases.

Another related approach is introduced in [9]. This work proposes a strategy (NAT2TEST) that automatically extracts DFRS (Data-Flow Reactive Systems) formal models from requirements written in natural language, aiming at generating sound test cases for reactive systems. The structure of the input specification and domain of application in [9] are very different from ours. We focus on mobile applications describe as interactions via a user interface, whereas their application domain is reactive applications like avionics and automobile control systems. Similarly to our approach, their work represents data information as inputs/output values and can model interleaving between different system flows. On the other hand, in their work concurrent behaviour arises only when the precondition guards of different system functionalities become enabled at the same time. Hence, concurrency is not expressed explicitly, as it is specified by our approach. On the other hand, they deal with time aspects and we do not.

As future work, we intend to automate our test case generation approach, extending TaRGeT to implement the proposed approach. This will allow the tool to generate both sequential and concurrent test case scenarios. Additionally, we plan to integrate the proposed approach with existent tools that generate scripts for the automatic execution of concurrent test cases. Another future work is to perform a controlled experiment to compare the quality of the test cases generated using our approach with that of the tests produced manually in the context of the partnership with Motorola.

Acknowledgements. We thank CAPES and the partnership CIn/UFPE-Motorola Mobility (a Lenovo company) for partially supporting the authors. Particularly, we thank Motorola's Modem Testing Team for providing feedback about this work and opportunity to carry out a case study.

References

1. Android Developers – www.android.com, July 2018. https://developer.android.com
2. Android N – www.android.com, July 2018. https://www.android.com/versions/nougat-7-0/
3. Andrade, W.L., Machado, P.D.: Testing interruptions in reactive systems. Form. Asp. Comput. **24**(3), 331–353 (2012)
4. Andrews, G.R., Schneider, F.B.: Concepts and notations for concurrent programming. ACM Comput. Surv. (CSUR) **15**(1), 3–43 (1983)
5. Arruda, F., Sampaio, A., Barros, F.A.: Capture & replay with text-based reuse and framework agnosticism. In: SEKE, pp. 420–425 (2016)
6. Bianchi, F., Margara, A., Pezze, M.: A survey of recent trends in testing concurrent software systems. IEEE Trans. Softw. Eng. **1**, 1–1 (2017)
7. Broy, M., Jonsson, B., Katoen, J.-P., Leucker, M., Pretschner, A. (eds.): Model-Based Testing of Reactive Systems. LNCS, vol. 3472. Springer, Heidelberg (2005). https://doi.org/10.1007/b137241
8. Carvalho, G.: NAT2TEST: Generating Test Cases from Natural Language Requirements based on CSP. Ph.D. thesis, Federal University of Pernambuco (2016)
9. Carvalho, G., Barros, F., Carvalho, A., Cavalcanti, A., Mota, A., Sampaio, A.: NAT2TEST tool: from natural language requirements to test cases based on CSP. In: Calinescu, R., Rumpe, B. (eds.) SEFM 2015. LNCS, vol. 9276, pp. 283–290. Springer, Cham (2015). https://doi.org/10.1007/978-3-319-22969-0_20
10. Ferreira, F., Neves, L., Silva, M., Borba, P.: TaRGeT: a model based product line testing tool. In: Proceedings of CBSoft 2010 – Tools Panel (2010)

11. Gibson-Robinson, T., Armstrong, P., Boulgakov, A., Roscoe, A.W.: FDR3 — a modern refinement checker for CSP. In: Ábrahám, E., Havelund, K. (eds.) TACAS 2014. LNCS, vol. 8413, pp. 187–201. Springer, Heidelberg (2014). https://doi.org/10.1007/978-3-642-54862-8_13

12. Nogueira, S., Araujo, H., Araujo, R., Iyoda, J., Sampaio, A.: Test case generation, selection and coverage from natural language. Science of Computer Programming (2018, under revision)

13. Nogueira, S., Sampaio, A., Mota, A.: Test Generation from State Based Use Case Models. Technical report, Cin-UFPE (2010). http://www.cin.ufpe.br/~scn/reports/jss10Extended.pdf

14. Nogueira, S., Sampaio, A., Mota, A.: Test generation from state based use case models. Form. Asp. Comput. **26**(3), 441–490 (2014)

15. Cornélio, M., Roscoe, B. (eds.): SBMF 2015. LNCS, vol. 9526, pp. 145–161. Springer, Cham (2016). https://doi.org/10.1007/978-3-319-29473-5. chap. Automatic Generation of Test Cases and Test Purposes from Natural Language

16. Roscoe, A.W.: The Theory and Practice of Concurrency. Prentice Hall PTR, Upper Saddle River (1998)

17. Roscoe, A.W.: Understanding Concurrent System. Springer, London (2011). https://doi.org/10.1007/978-1-84882-258-0

18. Sampaio, A., Arruda, F.: Formal testing from natural language in an industrial context. In: Ribeiro, L., Lecomte, T. (eds.) SBMF 2016. LNCS, vol. 10090, pp. 21–38. Springer, Cham (2016). https://doi.org/10.1007/978-3-319-49815-7_2

19. Scattergood, J.: The Semantics and Implementation of Machine-Readable CSP. Ph.D. thesis, Oxford University Computing Laboratory (1998)

20. University of Oxford: FDR3 Web Site, May 2015

A Methodology for Protocol Verification Applied to EMV® 1

Leo Freitas[1(✉)], Paolo Modesti[2], and Martin Emms[1]

[1] School of Computing, Newcastle University, Newcastle upon Tyne, UK
leo.freitas@newcastle.ac.uk
[2] School of Computer Science, University of Sunderland, Sunderland, UK

Abstract. The EMVCo (EMV® is a registered trademark or trademark of EMVCo, LLC in the US and other countries.) organisation (*i.e.* MasterCard, Visa, *etc.*) protocols facilitate worldwide interoperability of secure electronic payments. Despite recent advances, it has proved difficult for academia to provide an acceptable solution to construction of secure applications within industry's constraints. In this paper, we describe a methodology we have applied to EMV1. It involves domain specific languages and verification tools targeting different analysis of interest. We are currently collaborating with EMVCo on their upcoming EMV® 2nd Generation (EMV2) specifications.

1 Introduction

In principle, payment protocols are designed to be secure, with adequate and effective cryptographic methods employed to ensure confidentiality, integrity, authentication, identification, *etc.* In practice, relevant attacks [9,17–19] still occur in the industry, with financial fraud related to payment systems rising in the last few years: for example, in the UK, there has been a 80% increase in value of losses between 2011 and 2016, when the fraud losses were £618 million [24].

EMV, commonly termed *Chip & PIN*, is the dominant card based payment technology and is managed by EMVCo (www.emvco.com). In 2015, their protocols generated US433 billion in payments worldwide, protecting users from fraud and identity theft. Their protocols were designed to operate with cards being physically inserted into POS-terminal/ATM and used a wired connection to communicate. The introduction of EMV contactless made payments more convenient but created new security challenges as a wireless interface has been added to EMV cards and PIN entry has been waived.

More in general, with the recent publication of *PSD2* [13] and *Open Banking* APIs (openbanking.org.uk), regulation is pushing innovation. The payment/banking industry is being driven towards novel complex (cloud-based) protocols. Potential threats from systematic fraud are real. Thus, current development strategies would benefit from early safety-critical mindset.

Despite recent advances [14,15], adequate solutions suitable for industry's problems, within its constraints, are still lacking. Solutions developed in

© Springer Nature Switzerland AG 2018
T. Massoni and M. R. Mousavi (Eds.): SBMF 2018, LNCS 11254, pp. 180–197, 2018.
https://doi.org/10.1007/978-3-030-03044-5_12

academia are too complex to be used effectively by practitioners, who generally prefer to describe requirements in a way that is understandable by a wide range of IT professionals. Therefore, it is common to find in software requirement specification documents, even for large application such as EMV, an informal/semi-formal description based on natural language sentences and diagrams.

Analysis of EMV protocols is non-trivial due to the complexity of its requirements [22,23]. They have to incorporate competing (and conflicting) interests from multiple issuers and from financial regulators worldwide. The introduction of contactless payments has significantly increased its complexity. While EMV contact (Chip & PIN) specification describes a unified payment protocol sequence (kernel) for all card types, the specification for contactless payments contains seven protocol sequences, one per card issuer. Complexity is reflected in expansion from four books (765 pages) for contact transactions [22], to additional ten books (1627 pages) for contactless [23].

This paper presents a new methodology used for the analysis of the safety and security of EMV's contactless protocols. It is illustrated by considering the security of contactless transaction protocols as stand-alone processes and the wider impact of contactless technology. Our key contribution is a structured analysis methodology involving various languages and tools that is tailored to EMV audiences/developers (*i.e.* acceptable to the industry partners we have been working with). Such methodology has identified and demonstrated the impact of vulnerabilities in the EMV1 protocols.

Related Work. Several works have investigated on various aspects of the EMV protocol suite. Some researchers focused on attacks on existing implementations. The discovery in [39] allows attackers to buy goods from retailers, whereas the discovery in [9] allows attackers to extract money from the victim's account. Relay attacks [17,18] allow fraudulent transactions to be collected from contactless cards without the knowledge of the cardholder. In the area of formal methods, the first comprehensive formal description of EMV [15] used an F# model translated to Applied-pi [6], in order to make it amenable for analysis with the *ProVerif* verifier [7]. This analysis confirmed all known weaknesses without revealing any new vulnerabilities. [14] proposes an open specification of an EMV-compliant protocol that can be securely used on mobile devices, even if infected by malicious applications. The model is validated with Tamarin [40]. Other works [10,30] have analysed cryptographic aspects, focusing on protocols for secure key agreement and channel establishment. Finally, we worked on a Z encoding of Kernel 3 [25] that lead to new discoveries [18,20].

Contribution. Our work complements other formal approaches, as we benefit from existing verification techniques (*e.g.* model checking), but provides additional insights that cannot be captured by protocol verifiers. For example, the capability to formally specify user-defined functions in VDM-SL [33] and validate a model, in the protocol specification language *AnB* [36], against them. We also abstract from the underlying cryptographic aspects, assuming specific primitives are made available according to the protocol specification.

We use abstract (uninterpreted) functions in AnB to represent control flow and problem-related state updates, which the declarative nature of the AnB language lacks. Such functions can be formally specified, and are indeed implemented (*i.e.* function for public key of agents pk in AnB is only defined by different tools' implementations). This approach is inspired in their successful use by the CSP model checker FDR, and SMT-Lib decision procedures and predicate solvers. Beyond their implementation in different tools, we formally specify the functions behaviour in VDM, the same language that is being used here for the formal specification of AnB. This is different from other approaches [1,2,5], which compile AnB to different languages (*e.g.* CSP [32], operational strands [31], IF [3]), with a formally specified compilation strategy/set of rules which consider uninterpreted functions only symbolically.

In our case, as with the semantics of AnB, these functions are also specified to be executable, hence enabling symbolic simulation of various protocols of interest. Presence of such functions does not compromise security goals checked, given that the intruder has access to them just like it has to access to symbolic public (non-cryptographic) functions in the abstract model. Therefore, all the intruder can do is to ask the environment to perform the computation and get the result. We think this is important to set the scene and clarify the scope of this methodology.

Outline. In Sect. 2, we present an overview of our methodology, in Sect. 3 we introduce the specification language AnB through a simplified version of the EMV1 Kernel and present the method applied to the full Kernel 3 including key user-defined functions linked to the underlying verification environment in VDM. Section 4 presents our findings, and Sect. 5 summarises our results and discusses future work.

2   Methodology

Working with the payment protocols industry motivated the development of the methodology described here. It is a variation and extension of a successful application of rigorous/formal reasoning [18,21] applied top-down.

Our approach applies model-based techniques for the formal specification and verification of protocol requirements and designs. It focuses on the construction by protocol designers of a declarative description of protocol sequences using the AnB (Alice & Bob) notation [36] (see Sect. 3.1). This model is used to investigate the consistency of requirements, identify descriptive errors, and generate test cases for our POS-terminal emulator capable of performing transactions with both EMV contact and contactless protocols.

This has proved to be effective in both documenting decisions precisely [20, 21,25], and detecting significant protocol flaws early in the development process [18,19], way before deployment or actual implementations. Specifically, it is a variation of a successful industry approach by Praxis (now Altran UK, see www.adacore.com/sparkpro/tokeneer), where formal specifications are used to clarify requirements and then later used to inform its design and implementations. That is, the sound rigour of the formalism does neither hamper the user's experience nor impose unrealistic expertise, yet provides a number of important verification outcomes and challenges (*i.e.* proof obligations) of interest. To illustrate the process, we analysed one of the EMV1 contactless kernels [23]. The process is depicted in Fig. 1, and is explained below.

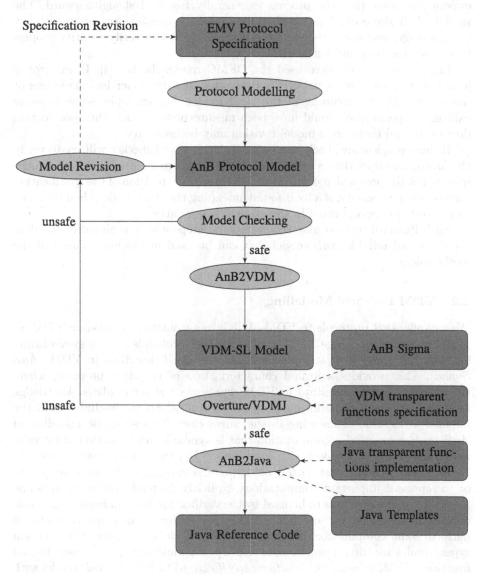

Fig. 1. Methodology

2.1 *AnB* Protocol modelling

Starting from the requirements in natural language (*EMV Protocol Specification*), protocol developers in industry produce flowcharts and UML-sequence diagrams describing protocol message exchanges and information flow. We introduce *AnB* to stake holders in order to systematically capture these exchanges between entities involved in a declarative fashion. Given *AnB*'s simplicity, our experience shows that the process is generally fast and straightforward. The model (*AnB Protocol Model*) is then used to check message-format consistency (*i.e.* messages sent are within agents' knowledge), and to verify security properties such as secrecy and authentication goals.

In our settings, we have used the OFMC model-checker [4]. If an error is found on the message-formats, it is likely that the developer has made one or more errors in the encoding of the *AnB* model. For example, some message exchanges specification could have been misinterpreted, w.r.t. the specification document, and therefore a model revision may be necessary.

If these consistency checks are successful, the model checker will try to verify the protocol against the security goals. If the goals are violated (i.e. the intruder may attack the protocol and the protocol is *unsafe*), a revision of the specification may be again necessary. If a fix is found amending the *AnB* model, then the same will have to be incorporated in the original specification.

Such iterative process may require several steps and it is aimed at building a correct and reliable *AnB* model that can be used in the next phases of the methodology.

2.2 VDM Protocol Modelling

We compile *AnB* protocols to VDM-SL [33] to automatically obtain a *VDM-SL model* of protocols. These VDM models of *AnB* protocols can be symbolically evaluated by the formal language semantics of *AnB* described in VDM (*AnB Sigma*). This provides a formal characterisation of the *AnB* protocol, where the underlying program state in VDM represents the accumulated knowledge accreted as a result of performing a protocol run, which also includes what the intruder is capable of knowing in the worse case. This semantic encoding of *AnB* enables knowledge computation that is symbolic, and a notion of intruder model that is directly linked with (and limited by) the language semantics.

It should be noted that *AnB* is not expressive enough to capture control flow or to represent important computations explicitly. Instead, the user can define abstract function symbols to be used by the verification tools in implementation-dependant manners. For example, if the user defines a new function foo to perform some computation, what most tools will do is to ensure the function types/results are correct and execute as Skip. We make use of these user-defined functions (*VDM transparent functions specification*) to link the *AnB* model with the protocol's underlying required state and specific computations, by formalising their meaning.

Therefore, a protocol/formal-methods expert can write the library, providing executable formal specifications for functions involved in the protocol, and its underlying state once, which can then be reused across a number/family of protocols. For example, EMV1 contactless payment protocols are defined in kernels per issuer-specific implementation (*e.g.* Kernel 3 presented in Sect. 3 is Visa NFC).

The VDM model of the protocol is used for symbolic simulation of protocol runs, as well as test case specification (with the *Overture* and *VDMJ* tools).

2.3 Protocol Implementation and Tool Support

We currently use the *AnBx* Compiler and Code Generator [37] to translate the *AnB* model to Java reference code. The compiler uses template files (*Java Templates*) which are instantiated with the protocol logic and the concrete Java implementation of the transparent functions. The compiler can also apply optimisation techniques in order to minimise the number of cryptographic operations and reduce the execution time [38].

The same tool is also used for translating the *AnB* model to VDM-SL. Moreover, in order to facilitate the adoption by practitioners, we have developed an Eclipse-based IDE [29] supporting many tools used in this methodology.

3   Case Study - EMV1 Kernel 3

In this section, we present the methodology through a case study.

3.1   AnB Language

The *AnB* language [36] is a simple, abstract, and declarative language, where *AnBx* [11,12] is a syntactic extension including various useful patterns of use and a stronger type system for user-defined (abstract) function symbols. Its key feature is the declaration of **Agents** representing protocol actors, **Actions** representing message exchanges between agents, and **Goals** representing desired properties of interest for the messages exchanged to have. Action messages are described in a simple expression language that include user-defined function symbols, some of which are security protocols primitives like private/public keys functions.

A protocol has always five sections: (i) its name; (ii) declaration of agents, types, and user/pre-defined functions; (iii) declaration of initial knowledge for all declared agents, which implicitly include self-awareness (*i.e.*, agent C knows its own identity); (iv) declaration of actions as message exchanges between agents, where various criteria/restrictions (described below) apply; and (v) declaration of desirable security goals, which include messages being kept secret between agents and agents being authenticated by other agents on specific messages. An optional section with reusable (non-recursive) **Definitions** provides local (let-style) abstractions for names.

```
Protocol: emv_visa_k3_simple AnB
Types:
   Agent C,T,iss;
   Number PDOL,Nonce,empty;
   Function [Agent, Number -> SeqNumber] fcnSeqNo;
   Function [Agent -> PublicKey] sk;
   SymmetricKey ShkCiss
Definitions:
   ACPayload:   T,PDOL,fcnSeqNo(C,Nonce);
   AC:          {|ACPayload|}ShkCiss;
   SDAD:        {ACPayload}inv(sk(C))
Knowledge:
   C: C,iss,sk,inv(sk(C)),fcnSeqNo;
   T: T,sk;
   iss: iss,C,sk,empty;
   C,iss agree ShkCiss
Actions:
   T -> C: T, PDOL
   C -> T: SDAD,AC,C
   T -> iss: PDOL,AC,C
Goals:
   T weakly authenticates C on ACPayload
   iss weakly authenticates C on ACPayload
   ShkCiss secret between C,iss
   inv(sk(C)) secret between C
```

Fig. 2. *AnBx* Protocol example

Figure 2 depicts a simplified version of our EMV1 contactless implementation: the simplification is the lack of many user-defined functions, which will appear in Sect. 3. This is a deliberate simplification (EMV1 has other complexities, as illustrated in [15], and elided here): our point is to illustrate that with an abstracted version of the protocol, certain security goals of interest are already breached (see Sect. 4.1).

To complete a payment, a card C needs to endorse the payment information (ACPayload) and this can be verified by both the terminal T and the card issuer iss. The card never exchanges messages directly with issuers, but only using the terminal as an intermediary.

In Types section we define the following identifiers: the Agents (C,T,iis), a component of the payload PDOL which abstracts information about the payment (e.g. amount, date, etc) and a Nonce. The issuer identifier (iis) is a constant (first letter lowercase), therefore, by convention in *AnB*, it is considered trusted. We assume that the issuer systems are uncompromised. Variable identifiers (first letter uppercase) of type Agents can be impersonated by the intruder, while variables of type Number represent abstract values which are different at every run of the protocol.

To illustrate the use of function abstraction, fcnSeqNo is used to represent the capability of agents to generate sequence numbers (used typically in the interaction between the card and the issuer). Public key cryptography is modelled using a function sk, mapping agents to public keys, with the purpose of representing the public keys used for digital signature. Therefore, sk(C) is the public key of agent C, whilst inv(sk(A)) is the corresponding private key. This key is added to the initial knowledge of agent C, while function sk is known by all agents representing the capability of retrieving a certified public key from a keystore or public repository.

Use of cryptographic expressions is shown in section **Definitions**. AC represents the payload (**ACPayload**) encrypted with **ShkCiss**, the symmetric key agreed between the card and the issuer. We assume that the issuer and the card had agreed on a session key (**ShkCiss**) prior to the protocol run. An example of asymmetric encryption is **SDAD**, the digital signature of the payload, obtained encrypting the **ACPayload** with the private key of the card.

The actions are written in order of exchange, for a message from the source to the target agent. The next action must always be a response from the target of the previous action to another agent.

In the first action, the terminal sends its identity and the information about the payment options back to the card. We have shortened the (application selection) EMV1 protocol sequence here for simplicity. Then the card replies with the digital signature of the payload, which is encrypted with their pre-shared key (**ShkCiss**). The digital signature is used by the terminal to authenticate the card, while the ciphertext is forwarded to the card issuer, which uses the pre-shared key to authenticate the card, validate and authorise the payment request.

This description of the protocol actions, describes how knowledge is accreted as a result of the protocol execution. Crucial to this process is the intruder knowledge. It is characterised as what is knowable by a malicious party attempting to interfere with the protocol by either impersonation or passively listening to communication. Different tools will define different knowledge acquisition rules for the intruder, which will determine its threat capability, where a commonly implemented approach follows the Dolev-Yao model [16].

The **Goals** section can specify goals of the following type:

Weak Authentication: B **weakly authenticates** A **on** M and are defined in terms of non-injective agreement [34];

Authentication: B **authenticates** A **on** M and are defined in terms of injective agreement on the runs of the protocol, assessing the freshness of the exchange;

Secrecy: M **secret between** A1,...,An and are intended to specify which agents are entitled to learn the secret message M at the end of a protocol run.

For EMV1, we illustrate goals of interest based on our understanding of the protocol. The first two goals represent the terminal and the issuer authenticating the card on the payment information endorsement (**ACPayload**): payment authorisation request is made by a legitimate card and not by an attacker. Moreover, the protocols would like to achieve freshness, i.e., the same authorisation request cannot be used twice and the issuer is able to link each authorisation with the correct payment request. The two final goals states that various keys must remain secret.

3.2   From Specification to the Model

Following our methodology, after the user writes the *AnB* protocol that is well-formed (*i.e.* no type or name violations, knowledge provisos for message exchange are valid, *etc.*), we translate it to its VDM semantics. For the user-defined functions, VDM library implementations are required. In what follows, we describe the complete *AnB* model for EMV1, including these abstract functions, together with an excerpt of the underlying VDM state and abstract functions module.

EMV1 Visa kernel 3 contactless requirements are given in [23]. The document describes the Visa-specific contactless protocol, which is a variation/simplification of other common kernel features [22].

First, we read and understood these requirements. In the practice we envisage, protocol experts ought to know (or at least have a good idea of) what they are trying to describe. Second, we thought about what security goals would be of interest. Different from other protocols, such as Mondex [28], where security goals were clearly defined from the outset, such goals are not explicitly declared in the EMV1 requirements [22], yet we assume practitioners will know what goals to check; we added some we found relevant below in Sect. 4.1. Finally, before constructing the *AnB* model for EMV, we create UML sequence diagrams to illustrate the key stages/players as described by the requirements.

3.3   EMV1 Kernel 3

Our model of *EMV Visa kernel 3* considers three agents: a card issuer iss, a card C and a terminal (i.e. card reader) T. When the card is issued, it is preloaded with a unique pre-shared asymmetric key that is used to run a key agreement protocol which generates the session key ShkCiss, whose computation is based on the transaction counter. The pre-shared key is known only by the card issuer and the card itself. The session key can be used to ensure that the communication between card and issuer is secure, even though the two agents during a protocol run never exchange messages directly but only through the terminal. The protocol, using the DDA authorisation technology, assumes that the issuer can be trusted. In other words, it is assumed that the issuer systems are not compromised by the intruder, and that for legitimate cards pre-shared keys and session keys with the issuer are stored securely and kept secret.

Along with the ability to encrypt data with the session key, the card is also able to digitally sign messages that can be used to authenticate the card with the terminal. We use a number of abstraction functions in *AnB* actions to represent protocol functionality beyond simple message exchanges between parties through user-defined functions (*e.g.* fcnAgree, fcnCVM, fcnUsage, etc). We also use definitions to name commonly used message expressions (*e.g.* CardVisaCap, TermTransVisaCap, etc). We illustrate here the actions performed during the protocol run, and we will describe the result of the security analysis in Sect. 4.1.

1. T → C: cmdListApps
   The terminal asks the card the list of applications (cmdListApps) (i.e. different EMV Kernels) it is able to run (*e.g.* Visa, MasterCard, etc.).

2. C → T: C,respVisa
   The card replies with its identity and the application it intends to run, in this case Visa - respVisa. A card could store different kernels for different card issuers.
3. T → C: fcnSelect(C,respVisa)
   The terminal tells the card to start running the Visa program, by sending the selection message fcnSelect(C,respVisa). fcnSelect is a function implemented by the EMV kernel, and it abstracts the request as part of the message exchange.
4. C → T: CardVisaPDOL,CardVisaCap
   The card replies with the meta information it requires for engaging in a transaction (i.e. CardVisaPDOL contains transaction date, amount, currency, country, etc.) and what verification methods the card is capable of performing. That is, CardVisaCap contains the card verification methods (CVM) to be used (e.g. online pin number, or offline signature, etc). It is defined as fcnCVM(C,respVisa), where fcnCVM abstracts the card computing its verification method for the requested application.
5. T → C: PDOL,TermTransVisaCap
   The terminal replies with the actual PDOL, a list of values corresponding to the CardVisaPDOL request list (PDOLDate, PDOLAmount, PDOLCountry, PDOLCurrency, etc). It includes the unpredictable number PDOLUPN generated by the terminal and used to identify the transaction. Moreover, the terminal send to the card TermTransVisaCap, which is the intersection between the general terminal capabilities as well as transaction specific capabilities. It is defined by the abstraction function fcnCVM(T,fcnCVM(T,TermUsageValid)), where TermUsageValid is defined as fcnAgree(fcnUsage(C,respVisa),fcnUsage(T,respVisa)). That is, fcnUsage returns the usage scenarios for both card and terminal for the requested Visa Kernel 3 application, whereas fcnAgree ensures that there is an agreeable choice between them. Usage examples include information where the transaction is taking place (e.g. shop, ATM, etc.) as well as kernel-specific limits (e.g. maximum value limit before going online, maximum overall limit per contactless transaction, etc.). The innermost application of fcnCVM to the result of usage agreement between card and terminal determines the transaction-specific capabilities between both parties, whereas the outermost application of fcnCVM ensures this transaction-specific agreement is within what's generally possible for the terminal.
6. C → T: fcnAgree(CardVisaCap,TermTransVisaCap),SDAD,AC
   The card is now ready to start the transaction, provided the capabilities between card and terminal within chosen transaction are agreed (fcnAgree(CardVisaCap,TermTransVisaCap)). The other two components are SDAD and AC. SDAD is a message digitally signed by the card containing the application cryptogram payload (ACPayload), which is composed by the terminal transaction data required by the card (PDOL), the card unique sequence number (CSN) per application, and the card unpredictable number CUPN. The second component is the application cryptogram (AC), which is a

ciphertext of the PDOL and CSN encrypted with the session key ShkCiss, and it serves as an acknowledgement from the card held by the terminal. Since the key is only known to the card and the issuer, only the issuer will be able to decrypt this message.

7. T → iss: PDOL,AC,C

In the last step, the terminal forwards the information to the issuer including the PDOL, AC and the card identity. This represents the terminal "cashing" in its "I owe you"'s given by the card for the transaction.

3.4 EMV1 User-Defined Functions in VDM

The user defined functions for our EMV1 model are interpreted/implemented within our VDM formal semantics of *AnB* abstract functions, which include cryptographic primitives (*i.e.*, the default environment for our *AnB* semantics specify pk, sk, *etc.*). They exist in the context of certain types and a global state.

Listing 1.1 provides the highlights of types defined for our *AnB* abstract functions for EMV1. We abuse the VDM notation slightly here: record fields of the same type are separated by commas to save space; "..." represent types/invariants that may have more fields/predicates. These types (and functions), have been thoroughly investigated in [25] and key findings were presented in [18].

For instance, the Card type models the card identity (*i.e.* its 16-digit number), its card verification methods per application, and if a card has more than one application (*e.g.* Visa Debit, MasterCard Credit). The verification method is defined by choosing the adequate CVM (Cardholder Verification Method) value (*e.g* online pin-verified, offline signature, *etc.*) and usage value (*e.g.* POS-terminal, ATM, *etc.*).

Note this abstracts away underlying cryptographic verification technologies actually employed like CDA, SDA, or DDA. That means we are assuming the *AnB* cryptographic primitives' implementation would be assigned to one of these schemes, which makes them transparent (and orthogonal) to what we are capturing, which is the flow of control and information between protocol entities in order to ensure certain security goals.

```
types Id = seq1 of char;
  Card :: id: Id    cvm: map App to CardCVM ...
    inv mk_Card(-, cvm) == cvm <> {|->};
  CardCVM :: x, y: nat    cap: seq1 of (CVM * Usage)
    inv mk_CardCVM(x, y, cap) == x <= y and
      (forall i in set domain[CVM, Usage] (elems cap) &
        i subset VALID_CVM) and
        range[CVM, Usage] (elems cap) subset VALID_USAGE;
  Terminal ::   id: Id    use: set1 of Usage
    cvm: map App to CVM
    inv mk_Terminal(-, cvm, use) == cvm <> {|->} and
      (forall i in set rng cvm & i subset VALID_CVM) and
      use subset VALID_USAGE;
```

Listing 1.1. VDM types used by EMV1 *AnB* user-defined functions

The *AnB* type system is too weak to represent what we need, hence the need for using VDM types. These types provide an interpretation for the space of possible values for the parameters of *AnB* functions (see Listing 1.2) like fcnSelect, fcnUsage, *etc.* Other details aside, the point of Listing 1.2 is to illustrate how we concretely represent *AnB* abstract functions within our method framework.

This VDM model needs to be written once (most likely by a formal methods expert) for a variety of EMV1 protocols. Given EMV invariants are not mathematically deep, but rather simple if numerous (something common in industrial models), the required expertise is not onerous. We tested this hypothesis by having a good MSc student without formal background develop most of the necessary EMV1 user-defined libraries for another EMV protocol (relay resistance) [35].

```
fcnSelect(a: Agent, app: App) r: App
pre (is_Card(a) => app in set dom a.cvm) and      post r = app;
    (is_Terminal(a) => app in set dom a.cvm)

fcnUsage: (a: Agent, app: App) r: (App * Usage)
pre pre_fcnSelect(a, app)
post r.#1 = app and (is_Card(a) => r.#2 in set (range (elems a.cvm(app).cap))) and
    (is_Terminal(a) => r.#2 in set a.use);
```

Listing 1.2. *AnB* user-defined functions for EMV1 given in VDM

For instance, function fcnSelect insists that the chosen agent application must have cardholder verification methods (CVM) validation criteria in order for it to be selected, and given this test passes, the result is the given application. This illustrates the underlying checking, in this case rather simple, under which conditions the first stage of the protocol can operate.

In general, the precise documentation of various conditions of all EMV protocol stages is at the heart of our methodology. Cumulatively, this forms the compound conditions for every specific successful protocol run. More importantly, it can also be used for further investigation through test case generation that is minimal with accountable coverage, or to have proof obligations about the individual satisfiability of each step (*i.e.* are the given contracts sound?).

For instance, in order to query the expected usage for a chosen agent application (fcnUsage), the input parameters must have passed the conditions for selection (pre_fcnSelect) first. That being the case, the result is the usage present within the corresponding agent type structure. This use of (precondition) referencing makes protocol state dependencies easily accounted for.

Overall, we model these functions and their underlying state (*i.e.* card, terminal, and transaction internal states), hence encoding all necessary invariants, pre/postconditions for the protocol's functional correctness.

This is different from OFMC because we can make claims about the underlying expected protocol specification via the VDM functional correctness model of protocol transparent functions and state. Moreover, when problems are discovered by a VDM simulation or proof, we have to identify whether this is a problem for *AnB* (*i.e.* something about the information flow that OFMC missed), or a problem within the transparent function's behaviour themselves. The former strengthens the verification capability of *AnB* tools, whereas the latter strengthens and precisely documents the underlying assumptions about required transparent functions.

Given the nature of their use, the specification of these transparent functions are a more onerous job. That is because they are capturing the underlying system state and updates, and their verification will require theorem proving, yet these can be done once for a family of *AnB* security protocols. A concrete example of such verification of transparent functions for a family of protocols are the public-key cryptography primitive functions in *AnB* (*e.g.* pk and inv), which must represent an injective relationship between public and private keys.

Because we have a direct formal semantics of *AnB* in VDM as well, a number of further verification and specification opportunities arise, and we are working on integrating those within our methodology in Fig. 1.

4   Results and Extensions

In our simulation environment for the *AnB* language semantics, we have explicit definitions for the pre-defined (cryptographic) and user-defined (EMV1 protocol specific) transparent functions, as well as the other parts of the EMV1 common kernel can perform. This enables us to perform a number of interesting analyses. This model is used to investigate the consistency of requirements, identify descriptive errors, and generate test cases for our POS-terminal emulator capable of performing transactions with both EMV contact and contactless protocols.

The *AnB* protocol semantics, defined in VDM, provides the knowledge accumulated by each agent, including our model of the intruder capabilities, as a result of executing the protocol according to the language semantics. This is a different strategy from other *AnB* tools [4,5]: we explicitly model allowed behaviours by each *AnB* program constructs as defined by the language semantics in VDM, rather than by observing exchanged messages in a translated (IF-notation [4]) format. Arguably, our approach prioritises safety before security. Another way to look at such differences is that we do not encode *AnB* in other languages (*e.g.* CSP [34] or IF-notation) for these languages' tool consumption and limitations. Instead, we represent the underlying *AnB* semantic state and operational semantics transitions using VDM (*i.e.* our approach consists among other things in defining the semantics of *AnB* in VDM-SL).

We derive VDM test cases to exercise key (or if possible all) specification entities (*e.g.,* type invariants, pre and postconditions, *etc.*). We also derive proof obligations that if/when discharged demonstrate the correctness of the model as a whole: without the proofs we have a debugging/testing tool, whereas with such proofs we have a verified functionally correct abstract execution environment for the specific EMV1 protocol of interest.

We have already worked with the Isabelle/HOL theorem prover to discharge VDM proofs, and are currently translating key aspects of EMV's infrastructure to be proved. To ensure proofs in different logics (*i.e.,* VDM's LPF and Isabelle's HOL) can be addressed properly, we follow ideas from [27,41].

Moreover, we can also use other available tools to perform further security analysis (e.g. the *AnBx* compiler translates *AnB* to ProVerif [8]), as well as code generation for a concrete implementation in Java that we plan to deploy to real terminals and run on real cards, all this within our Eclipse-based *AnBx* IDE [29]. Overall, all this gives a valuable exploration and testing platform for protocol experimentation and prototyping. These implementations and their generated test cases can also serve as oracles to real implementations including the myriad complexities involved in an actual EMV1 protocol stack.

4.1 Security Analysis

The security goals we considered in our modelling (Sect. 3.3) are exactly the four goals described in Fig. 2. The only difference is that for the authentication goals we consider SDADPayload, which contains few more components than just ACPayload.

We analysed the protocol with the OFMC model checker. This tool uses the AVISPA Intermediate Format IF [3] as "native" input language, which allows to describe security protocols as an infinite-state transition system using set-rewriting. The major techniques employed by OFMC are the lazy intruder, which is a symbolic representation of the intruder, and constraint differentiation, which is a search-reduction technique that integrates the lazy intruder with ideas from partial-order reduction achieving a reduction of the search space associated without excluding attacks (or introducing new ones).

As the terminal is capable of engaging only in one session at a time, we tested initially the protocol run only for one session. For each goal, our findings were:

- Goal: T authenticates C on SDADPayload
  This goal implies that the terminal is able to authenticate the transaction request endorsed by the card. This goal seems problematic to achieve for two reasons. First, the terminal does not always have an identifier that can be sent by the terminal to the card. Second, the ACPayload that is signed with the private key of C does not include the terminal identity T, therefore it is not possible to prove the injective agreement, i.e. the intention of the card to endorse a message intended for the terminal. A possible fix, if the terminal has an identifier, is simply to add T to the definition of ACPayload. Moreover, at the first step (as in the protocol in Fig. 2) the terminal should send its identifier to the card. This vulnerability can be exploited as shown in attacks, such as [9]: the attacker pre-generates authorisation codes on its own terminal, then goes to a merchant and replies that authorisation code. This will trick the merchant terminal to accept the transaction, hence enabling goods to be taken for free.
- Goal: iss authenticates C on ACPayload
  This goals implies that the card issuer is able to authenticate the transaction request endorsed by the card. We found that this goal is satisfied. Therefore, the asymmetric encryption mechanism (using the session key ShkCiss) seems sufficiently robust.

– Goal: `ShkCiss secret between C,iss`
This goal implies that the session key `ShkCiss` is kept confidential during the
protocol run. This goal is also satisfied, as the key never leaves the card during
the protocol execution. Therefore, as long as the card is uncompromised (*i.e.*
keys are stored securely) this goal is satisfied.
– Goal: `inv(sk(C)) secret between C`
This goal implies that the private asymmetric key of the card used for signature remain secret after the protocol run. Again, this goal is satisfied for the
same reason of the previous goal.

We also tested the protocol for two parallel sessions, and found that the
second goal can be satisfied only for the weak authentication, but not for the
injective agreement. Since a terminal does not engage in parallel session, this is
not a problem for now, but if, in the future, terminals will be able to handle contactless payments in parallel, this might be a matter of concern, as a transaction
authorisation can be used twice, unless mechanisms of prevention are enforced
(e.g. counters).

5   Conclusion and Future Work

In this paper, we presented a new methodology that puts industry-accepted
languages (*AnB*) and state-of-the-art formal reasoning tools (OFMC, ProVerif,
Overture/VDM, Isabelle/HOL, *etc*) to the analysis of payment protocols. In particular, this is motivated by our current work collaborating with EMVCo on the
development of their upcoming EMV®2nd Generation (EMV2) specifications.
Given the current confidentiality of EMV2, we illustrated the methodology with
EMV1 Kernel 3 for contactless payments. Many of the tools and techniques
presented are not new. The key of what is novel is a mixture between how we
put these tools together, what new theories (*e.g.* executable formal semantics of
AnB in VDM), and new tools (*e.g.* formal simulation of EMV1&2 kernels) are
being used by industry.

With the upcoming developments in the "FinTech" industry as a result of
not only EMV2 but also PSD2 and Open Banking APIs, our aim is to enable
the dependable development of payment protocols faster and cheaper, with an
accountable demonstration of why that is the case. This follows in the footsteps
of a proven approach by Altran Praxis: we took considerable inspiration from
their work on Tokeneer, as well as our own work on Mondex [28].

We are currently working on publishing the details of the novel *AnB* semantics, which will enable an extended set of goal verifications automatically beyond
what is possible at the moment. Moreover, we could also work on the automatic
generation of the reference implementation, including the user-defined functions,
from the VDM model rather than directly from the *AnB* model. The workflow
presented in Fig. 1 is currently being applied within the EMV2 protocol. Further
details appear in another paper in these proceedings [26], yet a number of technical details had to be removed until EMV2 becomes public due to non-disclosure
agreement restrictions.

References

1. Almousa, O., Mödersheim, S., Modesti, P., Viganò, L.: Typing and compositionality for security protocols: a generalization to the geometric fragment. In: Pernul, G., Ryan, P.Y.A., Weippl, E. (eds.) ESORICS 2015. LNCS, vol. 9327, pp. 209–229. Springer, Cham (2015). https://doi.org/10.1007/978-3-319-24177-7_11
2. Almousa, O., Mödersheim, S., Viganò, L.: Alice and bob: reconciling formal models and implementation. In: Bodei, C., Ferrari, G.-L., Priami, C. (eds.) Programming Languages with Applications to Biology and Security. LNCS, vol. 9465, pp. 66–85. Springer, Cham (2015). https://doi.org/10.1007/978-3-319-25527-9_7
3. AVISPA: Deliverable 2.3: The Intermediate Format (2003). avispa-project.org
4. Basin, D., Mödersheim, S., Viganò, L.: OFMC: a symbolic model checker for security protocols. Int. J. Inf. Secur. 4(3), 181–208 (2005)
5. Basin, D., Keller, M., Radomirović, S., Sasse, R.: Alice and Bob meet equational theories. In: Martí-Oliet, N., Ölveczky, P.C., Talcott, C. (eds.) Logic, Rewriting, and Concurrency. LNCS, vol. 9200, pp. 160–180. Springer, Cham (2015). https://doi.org/10.1007/978-3-319-23165-5_7
6. Bhargavan, K., Fournet, C., Gordon, A.D., Tse, S.: Verified interoperable implementations of security protocols. In: IEEE Computer Security Foundations Workshop (2006)
7. Blanchet, B.: An efficient cryptographic protocol verifier based on Prolog rules. In: Computer Security Foundations Workshop, IEEE, pp. 0082–0082. IEEE Computer Society (2001)
8. Blanchet, B., Smyth, B., Cheval, V.: ProVerif 2.00: Automatic Cryptographic Protocol Verifier, User Manual and Tutorial (2018)
9. Bond, M., Choudary, O., Murdoch, S.J., Skorobogatov, S., Anderson, R.: Chip and skim: cloning EMV cards with the pre-play attack. In: S&P, pp. 49–64. IEEE (2014)
10. Brzuska, C., Smart, N.P., Warinschi, B., Watson, G.J.: An analysis of the EMV channel establishment protocol. In: CCS, pp. 373–386. ACM (2013)
11. Bugliesi, M., Modesti, P.: AnBx - security protocols design and verification. In: Armando, A., Lowe, G. (eds.) ARSPA-WITS 2010. LNCS, vol. 6186, pp. 164–184. Springer, Heidelberg (2010). https://doi.org/10.1007/978-3-642-16074-5_12
12. Bugliesi, M., Calzavara, S., Mödersheim, S., Modesti, P.: Security protocol specification and verification with AnBx. J. Inf. Secur. Appl. 30, 46–63 (2016)
13. Cortet, M., Rijks, T., Nijland, S.: Psd2: the digital transformation accelerator for banks. J. Paym.S Strat. Syst. 10(1), 13–27 (2016)
14. Cortier, V., Filipiak, A., Florent, J., Gharout, S., Traoré, J.: Designing and proving an EMV-compliant payment protocol for mobile devices. In: EuroS&P, pp. 467–480. IEEE (2017)
15. de Ruiter, J., Poll, E.: Formal analysis of the EMV protocol suite. In: Mödersheim, S., Palamidessi, C. (eds.) TOSCA 2011. LNCS, vol. 6993, pp. 113–129. Springer, Heidelberg (2012). https://doi.org/10.1007/978-3-642-27375-9_7
16. Dolev, D., Yao, A.: On the security of public-key protocols. IEEE Trans. Inf. Theory 2(29), 350–357 (1983)
17. Drimer, S., Murdoch, S.J., et al.: Keep your enemies close: distance bounding against smartcard relay attacks. In: USENIX Security Symposium, vol. 312 (2007)
18. Emms, M., Arief, B., Freitas, L., Hannon, J., van Moorsel, A.: Harvesting high value foreign currency transactions from EMV contactless credit cards without the PIN. In: CCS, pp. 716–726. ACM (2014)

19. Emms, M., Arief, B., Little, N., van Moorsel, A.: Risks of offline verify PIN on contactless cards. In: Sadeghi, A.-R. (ed.) FC 2013. LNCS, vol. 7859, pp. 313–321. Springer, Heidelberg (2013). https://doi.org/10.1007/978-3-642-39884-1_26
20. Emms, M., Freitas, L., van Moorsel, A.: Rigorous design and implementation of an emulator for EMV contactless payments. Technical report, Newcastle University (2014)
21. Emms, M.J.: Contactless payments: usability at the cost of security? Ph.D. thesis, Newcastle University (2016)
22. EMVCo: EMV integrated circuit card specifications for payment systems [books 1 to 4], December 2011. https://www.emvco.com/emv-technologies/contact/
23. EMVCo: EMV contactless specifications for payment systems [books a, b, c-1, c-2, c-3, c-4, c-5, c- 6, c-7 and d], February 2016. https://www.emvco.com/emv-technologies/contactless/
24. Financial Fraud Action: Fraud the fact. the definitive overview of payment industry fraud and measures to prevent it (2017). https://www.financialfraudaction.org.uk/fraudfacts17/
25. Freitas, L., Emms, M.: Formal specification of EMV protocol. Technical report, Newcastle University (2014)
26. Freitas, L.: VDM at large: modelling the EMV(R) 2nd generation kernel. In: Formal Methods: Foundations and Applications - 21st Brazilian Symposium, SBMF 2018, Salvador, Brazil, 28–30 November 2018, Proceedings. Lecture Notes in Computer Science, vol. 11254. Springer (2018)
27. Freitas, L., Jones, C.B., Velykis, A., Whiteside, I.: How to say why (in AI4FM). Technical report, Newcastle University (2013)
28. Freitas, L., Woodcock, J.: Mechanising mondex with Z/Eves. Form. Asp. Comput. **20**(1), 117 (2008)
29. Garcia, R., Modesti, P.: An IDE for the design, verification and implementation of security protocols. In: ISSRE Workshops, pp. 157–163. IEEE (2017)
30. Garrett, D., Ward, M.: Blinded Diffie-Hellman. In: Chen, L., Mitchell, C. (eds.) SSR 2014. LNCS, vol. 8893, pp. 79–92. Springer, Cham (2014). https://doi.org/10.1007/978-3-319-14054-4_6 `
31. Guttman, J.D., Herzog, J.C., Ramsdell, J.D., Sniffen, B.T.: Programming cryptographic protocols. In: De Nicola, R., Sangiorgi, D. (eds.) TGC 2005. LNCS, vol. 3705, pp. 116–145. Springer, Heidelberg (2005). https://doi.org/10.1007/11580850_8
32. Hoare, C.A.R.: CSP - Communicating Sequential Processes. Prentice-Hall (1985)
33. Jones, C.B.: Systematic Software Development Using VDM, vol. 2. Prentice Hall, Englewood Cliffs (1990)
34. Lowe, G.: A hierarchy of authentication specifications. In: CSFW 1997, pp. 31–43. IEEE Computer Society Press (1997)
35. Maiden, J.: EMV's Relay Resistance Protocol in MasterCard Contactless Specification. Master's thesis, School of Computing Science, Newcastle University (2017)
36. Mödersheim, S.: Algebraic properties in Alice and Bob notation. In: International Conference on Availability, Reliability and Security (ARES 2009), pp. 433–440 (2009)
37. Modesti, P.: *AnBx*: Automatic generation and verification of security protocols implementations. In: Garcia-Alfaro, J., Kranakis, E., Bonfante, G. (eds.) FPS 2015. LNCS, vol. 9482, pp. 156–173. Springer, Cham (2016). https://doi.org/10.1007/978-3-319-30303-1_10

38. Modesti, P.: Efficient Java code generation of security protocols specified in *AnB/AnBx*. In: Mauw, S., Jensen, C.D. (eds.) STM 2014. LNCS, vol. 8743, pp. 204–208. Springer, Cham (2014). https://doi.org/10.1007/978-3-319-11851-2_17
39. Murdoch, S.J., Drimer, S., Anderson, R., Bond, M.: Chip and pin is broken. In: S&P, pp. 433–446. IEEE (2010)
40. Schmidt, B., Meier, S., Cremers, C., Basin, D.: Automated analysis of Diffie-Hellman protocols and advanced security properties. In: CSF, pp. 78–94. IEEE (2012)
41. Woodcock, J., Freitas, L.: Linking VDM and Z. In: IEEE International Conference on Engineering of Complex Computer Systems, pp. 143–152. IEEE (2008)

Analysing RoboChart with Probabilities

M. S. Conserva Filho[1]([✉]), R. Marinho[1], A. Mota[1], and J. Woodcock[2]

[1] Centro de Informática, Universidade Federal de Pernambuco, Recife, Brazil
{mscf,rma6,acm}@cin.ufpe.br
[2] Department of Computer Science, University of York, York, UK
jim.woodcock@york.ac.uk

Abstract. Robotic systems have applications in many real-life scenarios, ranging from household cleaning to critical operations. RoboChart is a graphical language for describing robotic controllers designed specifically for autonomous and mobile robots, providing architectural constructs to identify the requirements for a robotic platform. It also provides a formal semantics in CSP. RoboChart has a probabilistic operator ($\mathcal{P}$) but no associated probabilistic CSP semantics. When $\mathcal{P}$ is used, currently a non-deterministic choice ($\sqcap$) is used as semantics; this is a conservative semantics but it does not allow the analysis of stochastic properties. In this paper we define the semantics of the operator $\mathcal{P}$ in terms of the probabilistic CSP operator $\boxplus$. We also show how this augmented CSP semantics for RoboChart can be translated into the PRISM probabilistic language to be able to check stochastic properties.

Keywords: Robotic systems · CSP · Probabilistic analysis · PRISM

1 Introduction

Robotic systems have been used in many real-life scenarios, ranging from simple domestic assistants [26] (household cleaning) to safety-critical activities, such as driverless cars [4] and pilotless aircraft [27]. Despite their complexity, the current practice for implementing such robots applications is performed in an *ad-hoc* manner. These practices are often based on standard state machines, without formal semantics, to describe the robot controller only.

In [20], a domain-specific modelling language, called RoboChart, based on UML, is proposed. It is a graphical language for describing robotic controllers, specifically designed for autonomous and mobile robots. It provides architectural constructs to identify the requirements for a robotic platform. Features of the RoboChart graphical notation allow, for instance, the behavioural description of timed, continuous, and probabilistic properties.

Concerning formal verification, RoboChart has a formal semantics in CSP [22] that can be automatically calculated by RoboTool[1], a tool that supports the use of RoboChart. CSP is a well established process algebra to model

---

[1] www.cs.york.ac.uk/circus/RoboCalc/robotool.

© Springer Nature Switzerland AG 2018
T. Massoni and M. R. Mousavi (Eds.): SBMF 2018, LNCS 11254, pp. 198–214, 2018.
https://doi.org/10.1007/978-3-030-03044-5_13

and verify concurrent systems. It defines the behaviours of a system in terms of events and the interactions of processes. CSP has support for model checking with FDR [24], which provides a high degree of automation for early validation. Using FDR, we can, for instance, establish determinism, and absence of deadlock and divergence.

Besides functional aspects, RoboChart has also a probabilistic operator ($\mathcal{P}$) that can be used to express stochastic behaviours. Currently, however, it has no associated probabilistic CSP semantics. When it is present, for instance, between processes P and Q, a non-deterministic choice ($P \sqcap Q$) is used as semantics.

The work reported in [8] presents a version of FDR supporting the probabilistic operator ⊞. But instead of modifying the FDR algorithm itself to perform probabilistic analysis, the work [8] adds a new algorithm that creates a PRISM specification [14] from a probabilistic CSP specification. This translation was named *WatchDog Transformation*. PRISM is a probabilistic language and model checking tool (both have the same name) which has already been successfully deployed in a wide range of application domains, such as real-time communication protocols, robots applications, and biological signalling pathways.

In this paper we define the semantics of the RoboChart probabilistic operator $\mathcal{P}$ in terms of the CSP probabilistic operator ⊞, preserving all the original CSP semantics of RoboChart. To check for probabilistic properties, we specify a CSP property specification; this is different from the usual way of handling probabilistic model checking, which is based on a temporal logic language to express properties. We reuse the *WatchDog Transformation* provided by [8], which combines the two CSP processes (property and process under analysis), yielding a PRISM specification. With this specification, we just have to check for a specific probabilistic temporal logic formula using the PRISM tool.

The remaining of this paper is structured as follows. The next section provides an overview of RoboChart, and its CSP semantics. Section 3 briefly presents PRISM. The translation from CSP to PRISM is discussed in Sect. 4. Section 5 presents our proposed strategy, and case studies are described in Sect. 6. Finally, we draw our conclusions, and discuss future work in Sect. 7.

2   RoboChart

RoboChart [20] is a UML-like notation designed for modelling autonomous and mobile robots. It provides constructs for capturing the architectural patterns of typical timed and reactive robotic systems, and probabilistic primitives as well. As opposed to other approaches for describing robotic systems, RoboChart has a formal semantics that can be automatically calculated.

We give an overview of RoboChart using a toy model, illustrated in Fig. 1. A robotic system is defined in RoboChart by a module. In our example, it is called CFootBot, and specifies a robot that can move around and detect obstacles. A module contains a robotic platform and one or more controllers that run on this platform. The robotic platform FootBot defines the interface of the system with its environment, via variables, operations, and events. In our example, the operation move(lv,av) captures the movement of the robot with linear speed lv and angular speed av. The event obstacle occurs when the robot gets close to any object in its environment; it is an abstraction of a sensor that detects obstacles. There may be one or more controllers, interacting with the platform via asynchronous events, and between them via synchronous or asynchronous events. Our example has just a single controller Movement. The behaviour of a controller is defined by one or more state machines, specifying threads of execution. Here, the behaviour of Movement is defined by the machine SMovement.

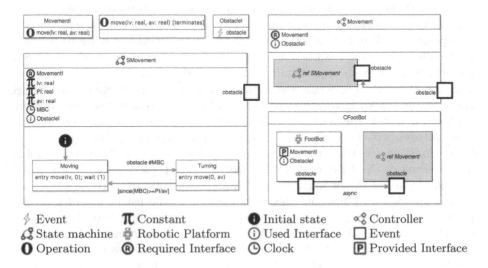

Fig. 1. RoboChart: obstacle detection

Interfaces can group variables, operations, and events. In Fig. 1, the interface MovementI has only the operation move(lv,av), provided by the robotic platform, and required by the controller. ObstacleI has just the event obstacle, which is used in the platform, the controller, and the state machine. In general, different events may be connected, as long as they have the same type, or no type. Types are used when an event communicates an input or output value.

A state machine is the main behavioural construct of RoboChart. It is similar to that in UML, except that they have a well defined action language. In our example, the behaviour of SMovement is as follows: upon entry in the state Moving, after calling the operation move(lv,0), the robot waits for one time unit. The operation call move(lv,0) takes no time; it can be, for example, implemented as a simple assignment to the register of an actuator. The machine, however, is blocked by wait(1) for one time unit (which is a budget for the platform to react to this operation) before it completes entry to Moving.

SMovement declares a clock MBC. In Moving, when an obstacle is detected, MBC is reset (#MBC) and the machine moves to the state Turning. There, a call move(0,av) turns the robot. A transition back to Moving is guarded by since(MBC) >= PI/av. As soon as the guard is satisfied, the transition is taken.

The guard requires that the value of MBC is greater than or equal to that of PI/av, to ensure that the robot waits enough time to turn PI degrees, before going back to Moving, and proceeding in a straight line again.

There may be one or more controllers, interacting with the platform via asynchronous events, and between them via synchronous or asynchronous events. Here, we have just a single controller CForaging. The behaviour of a controller is defined by one or more state machines, specifying threads of execution. In the example, the behaviour of CForaging is defined by the machine SForaging.

Interfaces can group variables, operations, and events. In Fig. 1, the interface IForaging has the events stop, forage and flip, which are used in the platform, the controller, and the state machine. In general, different events may be connected, as long as they have the same type, or no type. Types are used when an event communicates an input or output value.

Further information regarding RoboChart can be found in [19–21].

2.1   Semantics

The semantics of RoboChart is defined using a dialect of CSP called tock-CSP [22]. It is used to describe concurrent reactive systems that are composed by interacting components, which are independent entities called processes, that can be combined using high level operators to create complex concurrent systems. In tock-CSP, a special event tock marks the discrete passage of time.

Before presenting the semantics for our example, we first introduce the required CSP syntax. The process $SKIP$ represents the terminating process, and $STOP$ represents a deadlock process. The prefixing $a \to P$ is initially able to perform only the simple event a, and behaves like process P after that. Events may also be compound. For instance, $b.n$ is composed by the channel b and the value n. The process $P \; \square \; Q$ is an external choice between process P and Q. The process $P; \; Q$ combines the processes P and Q in sequence. The process $if \; b \; then \; P \; else \; Q$ behaves as P if b holds and as Q otherwise. Further information regarding CSP can be found in [22].

We present below a CSP process CFootBot that specifies the behaviour of our example in Fig. 1. The formal semantics of RoboChart is implemented by a tool (RoboTool) that automatically calculates a process that is equivalent to CFootBot below.

$$CFootBot = EMoving; \; Obstacle; \; ETurning; \; wait(PI/av); \; CFootBot$$

CFootBot composes in sequence processes EMoving, Obstacle, ETurning, and wait(PI/av) followed by a recursive call. EMoving is below; it engages in the event moveCall.lv.0, which represents the operation call move(lv,0) in the entry action of the state Moving. In sequence (prefixing operator $\to$), EMoving engages in the moveRet event that marks the return of that operation, and then behaves like the process wait(1).

$$EMoving = moveCall.lv.0 \to moveRet \to wait(1)$$
$$wait(n) = if \; n == 0 \; then \; SKIP \; else \; tock \to wait(n-1)$$

The definition of the parameterised process $wait(n)$ is recursive; it engages in n occurrences of $tock$ to mark the passage of n time units, and after that terminates: $SKIP$. So, $wait(1)$ corresponds directly to the wait(1) primitive of RoboChart. The process $Obstacle$ defined below allows time to pass until an event $obstacle$ occurs, when it then terminates. So, the events $obstacle$ and $tock$ are offered in an external choice ($\square$).

$$Obstacle = obstacle \rightarrow SKIP \ \square \ tock \rightarrow Obstacle$$

Finally, the process $Entry Turning$ models the entry action of Turning.

$$Entry Turning = moveCall.0.av \rightarrow moveRet \rightarrow SKIP$$

3   PRISM

Probabilistic model checking [1] is a complementary form of model checking aiming at analyzing stochastic systems. The specification describes the behaviour of the system in terms of probabilities (or rates) in which a transition can occur.

Probabilistic model checkers can be used to analyze quantitative properties of (non-deterministic) probabilistic systems by applying rigorous mathematics-based techniques to establish the correctness of such properties. The use of probabilistic model checkers reduces the costs during the construction of a real system by verifying in advance that a specific property does not conform to what is expected about it. This is useful to redesign models.

There are some tools that specialize in probabilistic model checking. The most well-known are: PRISM [14], Storm [3], PEPA [25], and MRMC [11].

This work focuses in the syntax of the language PRISM, which can be analyzed by the PRISM tool, the Storm model checker and other probabilistic model checkers as well. The next section gives an overview of PRISM.

The PRISM Language. The PRISM language [14] is a probabilistic specification language designed to model and analyze systems of several application domains, such as multimedia protocols, randomized distributed algorithms, security protocols, and many others.

The PRISM tool uses a specification language also called *PRISM*. It is an ASCII representation of a Markov chain/process, having states, guarded commands and probabilistic temporal logics such as PCTL, CSL, LTL and PCTL*.

PRISM can be used to effectively analyze probabilistic models such as Discrete-Time Markov Chains (DTMCs), Continuous-Time Markov Chains (CTMCs), Markov Decision Processes (MDPs), Probabilistic Automata (PAs), and Probabilistic Timed Automata (PTAs).

To introduce the syntax of the PRISM language, consider the simple probabilistic algorithm due to Knuth and Yao [12] for emulating a 6-sided die with a fair coin (see Fig. 2) that can be found in the PRISM website[2]. The PRISM code corresponding to this algorithm can be seen in what follows.

---

[2] http://www.prismmodelchecker.org/tutorial/die.php.

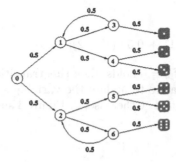

Fig. 2. Graphical illustration of the 6-sided die with a fair coin

dtmc
module die
  $s \; : \; [0..7] \; init \; 4;$
  $d \; : \; [0..6] \; init \; 0;$
  $[] \; s = 0 \rightarrow 0.5 : (s' = 1) + 0.5 : (s' = 2);$
  $[] \; s = 1 \rightarrow 0.5 : (s' = 3) + 0.5 : (s' = 4);$
  $[] \; s = 2 \rightarrow 0.5 : (s' = 5) + 0.5 : (s' = 6);$
  $[] \; s = 3 \rightarrow 0.5 : (s' = 1) + 0.5 : (s' = 7) \& (d' = 1);$
  $[] \; s = 4 \rightarrow 0.5 : (s' = 7) \& (d' = 2) + 0.5 : (s' = 7) \& (d' = 3);$
  $[] \; s = 5 \rightarrow 0.5 : (s' = 7) \& (d' = 4) + 0.5 : (s' = 7) \& (d' = 5);$
  $[] \; s = 6 \rightarrow 0.5 : (s' = 2) + 0.5 : (s' = 7) \& (d' = 6);$
  $[] \; s = 7 \rightarrow (s' = 7);$
endmodule

The first thing to note is the reference to the kind of Markov chain being addressed. In this example, a Discrete-Time Markov Chain (DTMC) was used.

This PRISM specification is composed of a single *module*, but if more than one module is presented an implicit parallel composition of them is considered as semantics [14]. This standard parallel composition can be customised to a new semantics by the use of a *system ... endsystem* section.

Inside a module, we can have local variables such as the s and d of this example. Both are natural numbers, ranging from 0..7 and 0..6, respectively. They need an initialisation. In this case, s is initially set to 4 and d to 0.

The rest of the module's body is basically composed of a sequence of probabilistic transitions, each one starting with a choice ([]) operator. A transition has a guard (expression before the $\rightarrow$ operator), followed by the destination alternatives. The alternatives are identified by the use of + signals. Each alternative has a probability (or rate) before the colon and update rules afterwards. Each update comes inside parentheses and the apostrophe is used to characterise the value of the variable in the next state of the system. The symbol & is used to describe logic conjunction.

Thus the transition

$$[] \; s = 0 \rightarrow 0.5 : (s' = 1) + 0.5 : (s' = 2);$$

may be read as follows: if $s = 0$ holds, then this transition is fired. At this state, we have a 50-50% alternative to update the variable s. In the first alternative, the new value of s is set to 1. Otherwise, 2. Figure 3 shows its Markov chain[3].

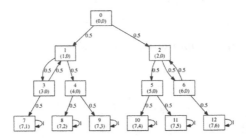

Fig. 3. Markov chain for the 6-sided die

Finally, we can perform probabilistic analysis. For this example, we can calculate the probability of getting one of its 6-sides by writing the following property (standing for "What is the chance of eventually s becomes 7 and d becomes x?")

> *const int* x;
> $P =? \, [F \; s = 7 \; \& \; d = x]$

where the constant x refers to a specific face of the die ($x \in \{1, 2, \ldots, 6\}$). In this example, the probability for each value of x equals 16.67%.

4   WatchDog Transformation

The process algebra CSP was extended to incorporate probabilistic and timed aspects in [16]. The probabilistic operator ⊞ was defined. However, this extension was entirely theoretical; no tool support was available at that time. In the work reported in [8], a version of FDR was implemented to handle the operator ⊞.

Essentially, the standard CSP_M notation (the machine-readable version of CSP used by FDR) was augmented by the following new operator ($[\cdot \sim \cdot]$). Let P and Q be CSP processes. Then

$$P \; {}_{\frac{m}{(m+n)}} \boxplus {}_{\frac{n}{(m+n)}} \; Q \; == \; P \, [m \sim n] \, Q$$

where m and n are natural numbers.

---

[3] To create such a graph, we export the Markov model in the PRISM tool and use the graphviz tool (http://www.graphviz.org/) to create Fig. 3.

The work [8], however, did not change the FDR algorithm to perform probabilistic analysis. Instead, FDR was extended to create a PRISM specification from a refinement assertion. This translation is briefly described as follows.

The *WatchDog Transformation* consists in analysing the probability with which a probabilistic CSP implementation (I) refines a non-probabilistic CSP specification process (S). In this paper it is enough to briefly present the *Watch-Dog Transformation* concerning the traces semantics

$$S \sqsubseteq_T I$$

It consists in mapping a specification process, say S, to a watchdog process that monitors the traces of an implementation process, say I, to indicate whether or not I refines S according to CSP's traces semantics. Precisely, a watchdog process WDT_S is defined such that it can perform a distinguished *fail_* event when I performs a trace not allowed by S.

$$WDT_S(i) = (\square\, e \in \alpha I \cap A(i) \bullet e \to WDT_S(after(i, e)))$$
$$\square$$
$$(\square\, e \in \alpha I \setminus A(i) \bullet e \to fail\_ \to STOP)$$

where $A(i)$ is calculated by FDR as part of the transformation.

The intention is that $WDT_S(i_0)$ can perform any trace tr of I that S can perform, but it can also perform events from the alphabet αI of I not allowed by S/tr (after which it can only perform the event *fail_*). Note that this definition of WDT is expressed in terms of the alphabet of the implementation process I which again must be calculated as part of the transformation. The original refinement check $S \sqsubseteq_T I$ is true precisely when $WDT_S(i_0) \,||_{\alpha I}\, I$ can never perform the event *fail_*.

The previous CSP process in its LTS semantic form is translated into a PRISM specification based on a very few set of variables. The boolean variable *trace_error* matches the event *fail_*. With this, the *WatchDog Transformation* is able to calculate a probability using the following formula[4]

$$Pmax =? [F\ trace\_error]$$

which mathematically corresponds to the following relation

$$S \sqsubseteq_T I \Leftrightarrow Pmax = 0\% [F\ trace\_error]$$

The refinement holds exactly when the maximum probability of *trace_error* becoming *true* is zero (or the event *fail_* never happens). Other interesting probabilities emerge when such a refinement can eventually fail. The interpretation of the above relation is that $Pmax =? [F\ trace\_error]$ gives us the degree on which the refinement $S \sqsubseteq_T I$ may fail.

---

[4] *Pmin* can be used to calculate the minimum probability as well.

Thus, to explore the traces refinement to get useful probabilistic temporal analysis, one has to think of CSP processes as properties in such a way that the traces refinement holds up to a certain point and then fails. From the temporal formula operator F, the traces refinement must resemble a reachability analysis.

By default, the *WatchDog Transformation* creates an MDP PRISM specification. But, if non-determinism may be ignored (for instance, in the 6-sided die example presented in Sect. 3), one can simply change the *mdp* directive to a *dtmc* one in the PRISM specification. In such a case, the PRISM tool can calculate a single probability instead of a min/max probabilistic interval.

4.1 CSP to PRISM

To illustrate that the Markov chain generated by this approach is exactly what we need, we use the same example of Sect. 3. That algorithm written in CSP can be described as follows.

> *channel die* : $\{1..6\}$
> *SixSidedDie* =
>   *let*
> $S0 = S1\ [1 \sim 1]\ S2$
> $S1 = S3\ [1 \sim 1]\ S4$
> $S2 = S5\ [1 \sim 1]\ S6$
> $S3 = S1\ [1 \sim 1]\ DIE(1)$
> $S4 = DIE(2)\ [1 \sim 1]\ DIE(3)$
> $S5 = DIE(4)\ [1 \sim 1]\ DIE(5)$
> $S6 = S2\ [1 \sim 1]\ DIE(6)$
> $DIE(x) = die.x \rightarrow DIE(x)$
>   *within S0*

To obtain the exact Markov chain as depicted in Fig. 3, it suffices to apply the *WatchDog Transformation* on the following refinement

$$RUN(\alpha SixSidedDie) \sqsubseteq_T SixSidedDie$$

The reason is simple. The process $RUN(\alpha SixSidedDie)$ can be refined by any process in the traces model and thus the PRISM variable *trace_error* is always *false* and the formula $Pmax =? [F\ trace\_error]$ will always return 0%.

The generated PRISM code in what follows is naturally different from the one presented in Sect. 3. But its Markov chain is the same of Fig. 3.

```
dtmc
module WATCHDOG
    pc : [0..1] init 0;
    trace_error : bool init false;
    [e2] pc! = 0 → 1 : (trace_error' = true);  // die.1
    [e2] pc = 0 → 1 : (pc' = pc = 0?0 : 1);  // die.1
    [e3] pc! = 0 → 1 : (trace_error' = true);  // die.3
    [e3] pc = 0 → 1 : (pc' = pc = 0?0 : 1);  // die.3
    [e4] pc! = 0 → 1 : (trace_error' = true);  // die.2
    [e4] pc = 0 → 1 : (pc' = pc = 0?0 : 1);  // die.2
    [e5] pc! = 0 → 1 : (trace_error' = true);  // die.4
    [e5] pc = 0 → 1 : (pc' = pc = 0?0 : 1);  // die.4
    [e6] pc! = 0 → 1 : (trace_error' = true);  // die.6
    [e6] pc = 0 → 1 : (pc' = pc = 0?0 : 1);  // die.6
    [e7] pc! = 0 → 1 : (trace_error' = true);  // die.5
    [e7] pc = 0 → 1 : (pc' = pc = 0?0 : 1);  // die.5
endmodule
module P_0
    pc_0 : [0..13] init 0;
    [] pc_0 = 0 → 0.5 : (pc_0' = 1) + 0.5 : (pc_0' = 2);  // _prob.0
    [] pc_0 = 1 → 0.5 : (pc_0' = 3) + 0.5 : (pc_0' = 4);  // _prob.1
    [] pc_0 = 2 → 0.5 : (pc_0' = 5) + 0.5 : (pc_0' = 6);  // _prob.2
    [] pc_0 = 3 → 0.5 : (pc_0' = 1) + 0.5 : (pc_0' = 7);  // _prob.3
    [] pc_0 = 4 → 0.5 : (pc_0' = 8) + 0.5 : (pc_0' = 9);  // _prob.4
    [] pc_0 = 5 → 0.5 : (pc_0' = 10) + 0.5 : (pc_0' = 11);  // _prob.5
    [] pc_0 = 6 → 0.5 : (pc_0' = 2) + 0.5 : (pc_0' = 12);  // _prob.6
    [e2] pc_0 = 7 → 1 : (pc_0' = pc_0 = 7?7 : 13);  // die.1
    [e3] pc_0 = 9 → 1 : (pc_0' = pc_0 = 9?9 : 13);  // die.3
    [e4] pc_0 = 8 → 1 : (pc_0' = pc_0 = 8?8 : 13);  // die.2
    [e5] pc_0 = 10 → 1 : (pc_0' = pc_0 = 10?10 : 13);  // die.4
    [e6] pc_0 = 12 → 1 : (pc_0' = pc_0 = 12?12 : 13);  // die.6
    [e7] pc_0 = 11 → 1 : (pc_0' = pc_0 = 11?11 : 13);  // die.5
endmodule
system
    WATCHDOG || P_0
endsystem
```

Instead of the variables s and d, we have integer variables whose prefix start with pc (resembling the program counter of an assembly code and matching the LTS state) and the *trace_error* boolean variable. Therefore, if one is interested to analyse this generated PRISM code directly, instead of using the formula $P =? [F \, s = 7 \, \& \, d = x]$, it is necessary to use $P =? [F \, pc_0 = y]$ where y must assume one of the values 7, 8, 9, 10, 11, or 12, corresponding to the events $die.1, \ldots, die.6$, which can be detected by simply reading the comments.

Fortunately, we do not need to know anything about the pc variables, nor the above automatically generated PRISM specification. Instead, we just have to formulate the appropriate traces refinement directly in CSP terms and check for $Pmax =? [F \, trace\_error]$. For this example, the CSP refinement could be

Prop $\sqsubseteq_\mathcal{T}$ *SixSidedDie*

where **Prop** $= die.x \to STOP$ and $x \in \{1..6\}$ to check the probability of each face of the die. The property $Pmax =? [F \, trace\_error]$ yields the probability of 83.33%. This means that the refinement *Prop* $\sqsubseteq_\mathcal{T}$ *SixSidedDie* has a 16.67% complementary probability of holding. This corresponds exactly to the calculation in the PRISM website, shown in Sect. 3.

5   Using Probabilities in RoboChart

This section presents our strategy for analysing probabilistic RoboChart models. We first introduce the use of the probabilistic RoboChart operator and then the extended RoboChart probabilistic semantics.

5.1   The RoboChart Probabilistic Operator

To create RoboChart models with probabilistic properties, we have to use a specific operator: Probabilistic Junction ($\mathcal{P}$). To illustrate its usage, we now consider an extension of the state machine of the RoboChart model presented in Sect. 2. We consider that the robot is equally likely to turn to the right and to the left. This new model is shown in Fig. 4.

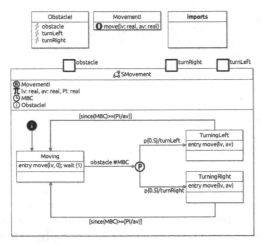

ⓟ Probabilistic Junction

Fig. 4. RoboChart: obstacle detection with probabilities

In this new version, when an obstacle is detected, the control of the model proceeds to a probabilistic junction between two equally likely alternatives. One alternative moves into the TurningLeft state, in which the robot turns to the left. The other alternative moves into the TurningRight state, turning the robot to the right. Afterwards, in both cases, the control goes back to the Moving state.

In the current state of RoboChart, probabilistic properties cannot be automatically analysed, since there is no direct translation from RoboChart to a probabilistic language. Recall from Sect. 2.1 that RoboChart models are automatically translated into CSP. This translation loses probabilistic aspects by using internal choices as semantics. This does not represent the correct meaning of a probabilistic specification; stochastic analyses cannot be done.

5.2   Dealing with Probabilities

To extend the semantics of RoboChart models to deal with probability aspects, we have to consider the CSP probabilistic operator $\boxplus$ to define the semantics of $\mathcal{P}$, instead of internal choices. Let $\langle\!\langle \cdot \rangle\!\rangle$ be this extended semantics.

To be able to analyse probabilistic RoboChart models, it suffices to apply the strategy presented in Sect. 4. That is, take a RoboChart model R, formulate the desired property about R as a CSP specification S, apply the *WatchDog Transformation* on the refinement

$$S \sqsubseteq_T \langle\!\langle R \rangle\!\rangle$$

and use the PRISM model checker using the single LTL formula

$$Pmax =? [F \, trace\_error]$$

Finally, interpret the result of the above formula as it is related to $S \not\sqsubseteq_T \langle\!\langle R \rangle\!\rangle$.

6   Case Study

In this section, we present a RoboChart model with probabilistic primitives. Furthermore, we also illustrate the kind of probabilistic analysis made available for RoboChart models.

6.1   Obstacle Detection

In this section we just illustrate the kind of analysis we can perform on our running example from Sect. 5.1.

We can use as property the following CSP specification.

$$Prop = moveCall \rightarrow moveRet \rightarrow SMovement\_obstacle \rightarrow$$
$$SMovement\_turnRight \rightarrow STOP$$

After performing the refinement

$$Prop \sqsubseteq_T Obstable\_Detection$$

and checking for the probability of $Pmax =? [F \, trace\_error]$ we get 100%, indicating that (by the probabilistic complement) such a refinement does not hold.

6.2   Foraging Robot

This is a more complex example than the previous one. It is a simple foraging robot. It is equipped with an idealised randomising device with two activities that are equally likely to occur; the device generates an outcome in every time step. The robot uses the device to decide whether to terminate or to continue a

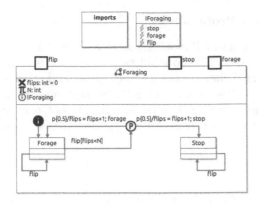

Fig. 5. RoboChart model

particular activity (here, foraging). For reasons of its own, the robot may choose to ignore the outcome of the device. Finally, the robot considers only a limited number of times whether to continue foraging (see Fig. 5).

The initial transition in Foraging leads to state Forage, in which a number of transitions can be taken. If a flip is allowed (represented by the occurrence of the event flip), the robot may ignore the randomising device and remain in the Forage state. Another possible transition from Forage happens when the event flip occurs and the number of choices has not been exhausted, given by (flips < N). The constant N represents the maximum number of choices. In this case, the control proceeds to a probabilistic junction between two equally likely alternatives. One alternative is to move into the Stop state, which it signals with the stop event. The other is to return to the Forage state, signalling this with the forage event. In both cases, the value of flips is incremented (flips = flips+1). This is used by the machine to keep track of the number of choices made.

There is only one transition available in the Stop state: the flip event keeps the controller in Stop; this transition is included to model the fact that flip occurs in every time step, even when the controller has terminated.

The CSP refinement property to check this model can be written as:

$$Prop = (\Box \, e : \{flip, forage\} \bullet e \to Prop)$$
$$\Box \, stop \to STOP$$

By varying the N from 1 to 20 we get the graph depicted in Fig. 6.

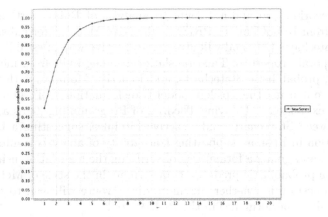

Fig. 6. Graph for Foraging Robot model plotting N from 1 to 20

7   Conclusions

This paper defines the semantics of the RoboChart probabilistic operator $\mathcal{P}$ as the CSP probabilistic operator ⊞, preserving all the original CSP semantics of RoboChart as provided by [20]. We reuse the *WatchDog Transformation* provided by [8], obtaining a PRISM specification corresponding to the analysis of a refinement such as $P \sqsubseteq_T Q$, where Q is the probabilistic CSP specification automatically generated by RoboTool and P is some property of interest.

The strategy reported in this paper has two main advantages over other attempts found in the literature. The first is that it is based on CSP refinement and not in LTL model checking. This allows a more closer analysis style as already present in RoboChart. The second is that all data structures and functional language already available in CSP is inherited by the automatically generated PRISM specification. This is very interesting because it is hard to find rich data structures as well as a readable PRISM specification in the literature.

One drawback of our strategy is that we never get a parameterised PRISM specification. But we can generate several models, each one corresponding to the values of the parameters being analysed. This is what the PRISM tool does directly from a parameterised PRISM specification.

Some works have been proposed for analyzing stochastic properties of robotic systems. In [13], probabilistic analysis are performed focusing on the robotic control software, ignoring the environment. It manually captures probabilistic state machines (using the PRISM language) of swarm systems from [15] in order to check specific properties in PCTL. No formal semantics is reported in this work. Probabilistic properties of swarm robotic models are also verified in [17]. It uses the process algebra Bio-PEPA [2] for modelling such models, which can be mapped to PRISM models by the Bio-PEPA suite of software tools.

We are working on another route to analysis of RoboChart models. This route goes from RoboChart to PRISM's Reactive Modules formalism via probabilistic Statecharts [10], and will give an alternative way of establishing probabilistic temporal properties. This translation is being built from metamodels of RoboChart, probabilistic Statecharts, and Reactive Modules, with the translation carried out using the Epsilon model transformation tool[5]. Our translation can also be expressed in Unifying Theories of Programming [9] as a Galois connection between Statecharts and Reactive Modules, suggesting a bidirectional transformation in Epsilon, supporting traceability of analysis results and counterexamples, and giving a formal way of verifying the translation using a semantics based on probabilistic predicate transformers in the style of McIver [18]. An interesting question is whether this more direct route will lead to models with different analysis performance in the PRISM tool.

Our translations will allow the use of more than just PRISM: the Reactive Modules formalism is also used for input to the MRMC and Storm model checkers, amongst others, and a dialect of probabilistic CSP is used for input to the PAT model checker [23]. We plan to explore the use of these alternatives and compare their performance on benchmarks that we will establish in robotic and autonomous control.

Finally, we plan to verify the results used in this paper, and in particular, the *WatchDog Transformation* as an implementation technique, using the CSP theories in Isabelle/UTP [5-7].

Acknowledgements. This research was partially supported by INES 2.0, CAPES, FACEPE (grants PRONEX APQ 0388-1.03/14 and APQ-0399-1.03/17), and CNPq (grant 465614/ 2014-0). We would like to thank André Didier and Matheus Santana.

References

1. Baier, C., Katoen, J.-P.: Principles of Model Checking (Representation and Mind Series). The MIT Press, Cambridge (2008)
2. Ciocchetta, F., Hillston, J.: Bio-PEPA: A Framework for the Modelling and Analysis of Biological Systems (2008)
3. Dehnert, C., Junges, S., Katoen, J.P., Volk, M.: A storm is coming: a modern probabilistic model checker. In: Majumdar, R., Kunčak, V. (eds.) Computer Aided Verification. CAV 2017. Lecture Notes in Computer Science, vol. 10427. Springer, Cham (2017). https://doi.org/10.1007/978-3-319-63390-9_31
4. Fernandes, L., Custodio, V., Alves, G., Fisher, M.: A rational agent controlling an autonomous vehicle: implementation and formal verification. In: EPTCS, pp. 35–42 (2017)
5. Foster, S., Woodcock, J.: Unifying theories of programming in isabelle. In: Liu, Z., Woodcock, J., Zhu, H. (eds.) Unifying Theories of Programming and Formal Engineering Methods. LNCS, vol. 8050, pp. 109–155. Springer, Heidelberg (2013). https://doi.org/10.1007/978-3-642-39721-9_3

---

[5] www.eclipse.org/epsilon/doc/book/.

6. Foster, S., Woodcock, J.: Mechanised theory engineering in isabelle. In: Dependable Software Systems Engineering, NATO Science for Peace and Security Series, D: Information and Communication Security, vol. 40, pp. 246–287. IOS Press (2015)
7. Foster, S., Zeyda, F., Woodcock, J.: Isabelle/UTP: a mechanised theory engineering framework. In: Naumann, D. (ed.) UTP 2014. LNCS, vol. 8963, pp. 21–41. Springer, Cham (2015). https://doi.org/10.1007/978-3-319-14806-9_2
8. Goldsmith, M.: CSP: the best concurrent-system description language in the world-probably! In: Communicating Process Architectures, pp. 227–232 (2004)
9. Hoare, C.A.R., Jifeng, H.: Unifying Theories of Programming. Prentice Hall, Englewood Cliffs (1998)
10. Jansen, D.N., Hermanns, H., Katoen, J.-P.: A probabilistic extension of UML statecharts. In: Damm, W., Olderog, E.-R. (eds.) FTRTFT 2002. LNCS, vol. 2469, pp. 355–374. Springer, Heidelberg (2002). https://doi.org/10.1007/3-540-45739-9_21
11. Katoen, J.-P., Zapreev, I.S., Hahn, E.M., Hermanns, H., Jansen, D.N.: The ins and outs of the probabilistic model checker MRMC. Perform. Eval. **68**(2), 90–104 (2011)
12. Knuth, D., Yao, A.: Algorithms and complexity: new directions and recent results. Chap. The Complexity of Nonuniform Random Number Generation. Academic Press (1976)
13. Konur, S., Dixon, C., Fisher, M.: Formal verification of probabilistic swarm behaviours. In: Dorigo, M., et al. (eds.) ANTS 2010. LNCS, vol. 6234, pp. 440–447. Springer, Heidelberg (2010). https://doi.org/10.1007/978-3-642-15461-4_42
14. Kwiatkowska, M., Norman, G., Parker, D.: PRISM 4.0: verification of probabilistic real-time systems. In: Gopalakrishnan, G., Qadeer, S. (eds.) CAV 2011. LNCS, vol. 6806, pp. 585–591. Springer, Heidelberg (2011). https://doi.org/10.1007/978-3-642-22110-1_47
15. Liu, W., Winfield, A.F.T., Sa, J.: Modelling swarm robotic systems : a case study in collective foraging. Int. J. Robot. Res. **23**(4–5), 415–436 (2004)
16. Lowe, G.: Probabilistic and prioritized models of timed CSP. Theor. Comput. Sci. **138**(2), 315–352 (1995)
17. Massink, M., Brambilla, M., Latella, D., Dorigo, M., Birattari, M.: On the use of Bio-PEPA for modelling and analysing collective behaviours in swarm robotics. Swarm Intell. **7**, 201–228 (2013)
18. McIver, A.K.: Quantitative refinement *and* model checking for the analysis of probabilistic systems. In: Misra, J., Nipkow, T., Sekerinski, E. (eds.) FM 2006. LNCS, vol. 4085, pp. 131–146. Springer, Heidelberg (2006). https://doi.org/10.1007/11813040_10
19. Miyazawa, A., Cavalcanti, A., Ribeiro, P., Li, W., Woodcock, J., Timmis, J.: RoboChart Reference Manual. University of York (2016). https://www.cs.york.ac.uk/circus/RoboCalc/assets/RoboChart-manual.pdf
20. Miyazawa, A., Ribeiro, P., Li, W., Cavalcanti, A., Timmis, J.: Automatic property checking of robotic applications. In: International Conference on Intelligent Robots and Systems, pp. 3869–3876 (2017)
21. Ribeiro, P., Miyazawa, A., Li, W., Cavalcanti, A., Timmis, J.: Modelling and verification of timed robotic controllers. In: Polikarpova, N., Schneider, S. (eds.) IFM 2017. LNCS, vol. 10510, pp. 18–33. Springer, Cham (2017). https://doi.org/10.1007/978-3-319-66845-1_2
22. Roscoe, A.W.: Understanding Concurrent Systems. Springer, London (2010). https://doi.org/10.1007/978-1-84882-258-0

23. Song, S., Sun, J., Liu, Y., Dong, J.S.: A model checker for hierarchical probabilistic real-time systems. In: Madhusudan, P., Seshia, S.A. (eds.) CAV 2012. LNCS, vol. 7358, pp. 705–711. Springer, Heidelberg (2012). https://doi.org/10.1007/978-3-642-31424-7_53
24. Gibson-Robinson, T., Armstrong, P., Boulgakov, A., Roscoe, A.W.: FDR3 — a modern refinement checker for CSP. In: Ábrahám, E., Havelund, K. (eds.) TACAS 2014. LNCS, vol. 8413, pp. 187–201. Springer, Heidelberg (2014). https://doi.org/10.1007/978-3-642-54862-8_13
25. Tribastone, M.: The PEPA Plug-in Project (2009)
26. Webster, M., et al.: Formal verification of an autonomous personal robotic assistant. In: AAAI Spring Symposium Series, pp. 74–79 (2014)
27. Webster, M., Fisher, M., Cameron, N., Jump, M.: Formal methods for the certification of autonomous unmanned aircraft systems. In: Flammini, F., Bologna, S., Vittorini, V. (eds.) SAFECOMP 2011. LNCS, vol. 6894, pp. 228–242. Springer, Heidelberg (2011). https://doi.org/10.1007/978-3-642-24270-0_17

Timed Scenarios: Consistency, Equivalence and Optimization

Neda Saeedloei[1(✉)] and Feliks Kluźniak[2]

[1] Southern Illinois University, Carbondale, USA
neda@cs.siu.edu
[2] Logic Blox, Atlanta, USA
feliks.kluzniak@logicblox.com

Abstract. We develop a new method for determining the consistency of timed scenarios. If the scenario is consistent, we obtain a canonical representation for the entire class of equivalent scenarios. This allows us to optimise a scenario according to various criteria. In particular, we are able to minimize the largest constant in the scenario's set of constraints: this technique is directly relevant to decreasing the costs of verification for timed automata synthesized from timed scenarios.

1 Introduction

Using scenarios for specification and implementation of complex systems, including real time systems, has been an active area of research for over three decades [8,15,20,21]. Synthesis of formal models of systems from scenarios has also been studied in the past [8,13,15,20,21], and recently there has been renewed interest in this area [4,16,19].

We have recently proposed [19] a form of timed scenarios (called Timed Event Sequences or TES) for specifying partial behaviours of real-time systems. We also developed a synthesis method for constructing a timed automaton from a set of TES. What was not addressed in that work was the question of the consistency of timed scenarios.

We set out to develop, from first principles, a method for detecting whether a scenario is consistent. As a byproduct we obtained a canonical representation for the entire class of scenarios that are equivalent to the given one. This in turn allowed us to *optimise* scenarios (according to various criteria), by replacing a given scenario with an equivalent one that has more desirable properties. The current paper summarizes the results of this study.

Specifically, the main contributions of the paper are as follows:

1. We present a generalized and simplified notion of timed scenarios and their semantics. The new notion is independent of modes and mode graphs [19].
2. We propose a method for determining the consistency of timed scenarios. The method is developed from the fundamental equations and inequations that hold, in general, between the times at which ordered events occur. As a

© Springer Nature Switzerland AG 2018
T. Massoni and M. R. Mousavi (Eds.): SBMF 2018, LNCS 11254, pp. 215–233, 2018.
https://doi.org/10.1007/978-3-030-03044-5_14

byproduct we obtain a canonical representation (a "distance table") for the entire class of scenarios that are equivalent to the given one.

3. We use the distance table to *optimise* scenarios according to various criteria. In particular, given a time distance table corresponding to a scenario we show how to minimize the maximum constant in the scenario. For example, our prototype tool can convert scenario ξ of Fig. 1 to the equivalent scenario η. The maximum constant in η is smaller than that in ξ, so η is better suited for the purpose of synthesizing a timed automaton: the cost of verifying a timed automaton crucially depends on the size of the maximum constant in its time constraints.[1]

4. It turns out that our distance tables are essentially isomorphic to the Difference Bounds Matrices studied by Dill in the context of verification of timed automata [11]. We show how to apply Dill's method to the case of scenarios, both to check consistency and to minimise the maximum constant.

$$
\boxed{
\begin{aligned}
&L_0 : \ a; \\
&L_1 : \ b\,\{L_0 \le 1\}; \\
&L_2 : \ c\,\{L_1 \le 5\}; \\
&L_3 : \ d\,\{L_1 \le 4, L_2 \ge 2\}; \\
&\quad\ e\,\{L_1 \le 11, L_2 \ge 4, L_3 \le 4\}.
\end{aligned}
}
\qquad
\boxed{
\begin{aligned}
&L_0 : \ a; \\
&L_1 : \ b\,\{L_0 \le 1\}; \\
&L_2 : \ c\,\{L_1 \le 2\}; \\
&L_3 : \ d\,\{L_1 \le 4, L_2 \ge 2, L_2 \le 4\}; \\
&\quad\ e\,\{L_2 \ge 4, L_3 \le 4\}.
\end{aligned}
}
$$

Scenario ξ Scenario η

Fig. 1. Two equivalent scenarios

2   Concepts

2.1   Events

Let Σ be a finite set of symbols called *events*. Let Σ^* denote the set of all sequences (finite or infinite) formed from elements of Σ. The subset of Σ^* that contains only all the sequences of length n will be denoted by Σ^n.

The intended interpretation is that $e \in \Sigma$ is the name of a concrete event in the real world, such as "a button is pressed".

Given a sequence $\sigma = e_0 e_1 e_2 \ldots \in \Sigma^*$ we will use the term "event i of σ" (or "the i-th event", etc.) to denote the i-th element of σ, i.e., the i-th occurrence of an event in the sequence. This should not be confused with e_i, which is a symbol in Σ, and which may have many occurrences in σ.

---

[1] Most model-checking tools for timed automata (e.g., UPPAAL [7] and KRONOS [9]) use region-based and zone-based abtraction methods in order to make verification possible in spite of the infinite state spaces of timed automata. It is well-known that both of these abstraction methods depend on the number of clocks and on the size of the constants that appear in constraints. In fact, *the size of the region graph is exponential in the number of clocks and the (encoding of) constants* [3].

2.2   Behaviours

Definition 1. *A* behaviour[2] *over Σ is a sequence $(e_0, t_0)(e_1, t_1)(e_2, t_2) \ldots$, such that $e_i \in \Sigma$, $t_i \in \mathbb{R}^{\geq 0}$, $t_0 = 0$ and $t_{i-1} \leq t_i$ for $i \in \{1, 2 \ldots\}$.*

We will omit the phrase "over Σ" when doing so does not lead to confusion.

A behaviour can be infinite or finite, even empty. In this paper we will discuss mostly finite behaviours.

The intended interpretation of (e_i, t_i) is that the i-th occurrence of an event is an occurrence of event e_i, and takes place t_i time units after the initial occurrence of an event (namely, e_0).

A behaviour can be thought of as a pattern for an infinite number of concrete behaviours that differ only in their starting time. We say that the (abstract) behaviour *represents* all those concrete behaviours.

Given a behaviour $\mathcal{B} = (e_0, t_0)(e_1, t_1)(e_2, t_2) \ldots$ we will use $eseq(\mathcal{B})$ to denote the sequence $e_0 e_1 e_2 \ldots$ and $tseq(\mathcal{B})$ to denote $t_0 t_1 t_2 \ldots$.

We often say "event i of $\mathcal{B}$" (or "the i-th event") to denote event i of $eseq(\mathcal{B})$.

Definition 2. *Let $\mathcal{B} = (e_0, t_0)(e_1, t_1) \ldots (e_{n-1}, t_{n-1})$ be a behaviour of length n. Then, for any $0 \leq i < j < n$, the symbol $t_{ij}^{\mathcal{B}}$ denotes the distance, in time units, of event j from event i in $\mathcal{B}$. That is, $t_{ij}^{\mathcal{B}} = t_j - t_i$.*

We often write simply t_{ij} when this does not lead to ambiguity.

Observation 1. *For any behaviour of length n, and for $0 \leq i < j < k < n$:*

$$t_{ij} + t_{jk} = t_{ik} \tag{1}$$

Proof. Obvious: $t_{ij} + t_{jk} = t_j - t_i + t_k - t_j = t_k - t_i = t_{ik}$. $\square$

We are often interested not in a particular behaviour, but in a set of behaviours that satisfy certain time constraints, e.g., that the door will open sufficiently quickly after the button is pressed. To describe sets of behaviours that satisfy such constraints we use timed scenarios.

2.3   Timed Scenarios

Definition 3. *Given a natural number n, let $\Phi(n)$ denote the set of constraints of the form $d \sim c$, where $\sim \in \{\leq, \geq, =\}$[3] and c is a constant in the set of rational numbers, $\mathbb{Q}$. d is the symbol $\tau_{i,j}$, for some integers $0 \leq i < j < n$.*

---

[2] Behaviours are essentially the "timed words" of Alur [2].

[3] To keep the presentation compact, we do not allow sharp inequalities: allowing them would complicate our definitions and proofs, without affecting the general principles. Notice that sharp inequalities are of mainly theoretical interest: in practice we can measure time only with some finite granularity γ, so $x < c$ is for all practical purposes equivalent to $x \leq c - \gamma$.

218   N. Saeedloei and F. Kluźniak

The intended interpretation is that $\tau_{i,j}$ is the time distance between events i and j in the behaviours described by a timed scenario. This will become clear in Definitions 4 and 5.

Definition 4. *Let n be a natural number and Σ the set of events. A timed scenario of length n over Σ is a pair $(\mathcal{E},\mathcal{C})$, where*

- *$\mathcal{E} = e_0 e_1 \ldots e_{n-1}$ is a sequence of events (i.e., $\mathcal{E} \in \Sigma^n$);*
- *$\mathcal{C} \subset \Phi(n)$ is a finite set of constraints.*

Given a scenario $\xi = (\mathcal{E},\mathcal{C})$, we will use $events(\xi)$ to denote $\mathcal{E}$ and $constraints(\xi)$ to denote $\mathcal{C}$.

In this paper the term "scenario" will always refer to a timed scenario. We will omit the phrase "over Σ" when that does not lead to confusion.

We will use the term "event i of ξ" to denote event i in $events(\xi)$.

External Representation. To make scenarios fit for human consumption, we will usually describe them in a notation that is not unlike a simple programming language. A scenario will be written as a sequence of events, separated by semi-colons and terminated by a period. If the scenario contains a constraint such as $\tau_{i,j} \leq c$, then event i in the sequence will be labelled by a unique symbol L_i, and event j will be annotated with a set of constraints that contains $L_i \leq c$.

In Fig. 2, ξ_2 is a representation of $(abcf, \{\tau_{0,1} \geq 2, \tau_{1,2} \geq 2, \tau_{0,3} \leq 2\})$.

2.4   Scenarios and Behaviours

Definition 5. *Let ξ be a scenario of length n over Σ.*
A behaviour $\mathcal{B} = (e_0,t_0)(e_1,t_1)\ldots(e_{n-1},t_{n-1})$ over Σ is supported by ξ iff

- *$events(\xi) = e_0 \ldots e_{n-1}$ and*
- *every $\tau_{i,j} \sim c$ in $constraints(\xi)$ evaluates to true after $\tau_{i,j}$ is replaced by $t_{ij}^{\mathcal{B}}$.*

For a given scenario ξ, we use $Supp(\xi)$ to denote the set of behaviours that are supported by ξ. (We will often say simply: "the set of behaviours of ξ".)[4]
The set of behaviours of scenario ξ_1 of Fig. 2 is
$Supp(\xi_1) = \{(a,t_0)(b,t_1)(c,t_2)(b,t_3) \mid t_0 = 0 \wedge t_3 \geq t_2 \geq t_1 \geq t_0 \wedge t_1 - t_0 \leq 5 \wedge t_2 - t_0 \leq 4\}$.

Observation 2. *Let ξ be a scenario of length n and let ξ' be the scenario obtained by adding some constraint to $constraints(\xi)$. Then $Supp(\xi') \subset Supp(\xi)$.*

Proof. A behaviour of ξ' must satisfy all the constraints in ξ.   □

Definition 6. *The semantics of scenario ξ, denoted by $[\![\xi]\!]$, is the set of behaviours that are supported by ξ, i.e., $[\![\xi]\!] = Supp(\xi)$.*

---
[4] There is nothing new in the intuition that a scenario describes a set of behaviours: see, e.g., the paper by Somé et al. [20].

Definition 7. *Two scenarios ξ and η are equivalent iff $[\![\xi]\!] = [\![\eta]\!]$.*

Definition 8. *Let $\xi = (\mathcal{E}, \mathcal{C})$ and $\eta = (\mathcal{E}, \mathcal{C}')$ be two scenarios (with the same sequence of events). $\mathcal{C}$ and $\mathcal{C}'$ are equivalent iff ξ and η are equivalent.*

Definition 9. *A scenario ξ is consistent iff $[\![\xi]\!] \neq \emptyset$. A scenario is inconsistent iff it is not consistent.*

For instance, scenario ξ_1 of Fig. 2 is consistent, while ξ_2 is inconsistent, as the constraint that annotates event 3 (f) cannot be satisfied.

Definition 10. *For a consistent scenario ξ of length n, and for $0 \leq i < j < n$, we define*

$$m_{ij}^{\xi} = lmin\{t_{ij}^{\mathcal{B}} \mid \mathcal{B} \in Supp(\xi)\}$$

$$M_{ij}^{\xi} = max\{t_{ij}^{\mathcal{B}} \mid \mathcal{B} \in Supp(\xi)\}$$

The absence of an upper bound for some i and j will be denoted by $M_{ij}^{\xi} = \infty$.

We will often write just m_{ij} and M_{ij} when ξ is understood.

Observation 3. *For any behaviour in $Supp(\xi)$,*

$$0 \leq m_{ij} \leq t_{ij} \leq M_{ij} \leq \infty \qquad (2)$$

Proof. A direct consequence of Definition 10. □

Observation 4. *Let ξ be a scenario of length n, and let $\mathcal{B}$ be a behaviour such that $eseq(\mathcal{B}) = events(\xi)$. If $m_{ij}^{\xi} \leq t_{ij}^{\mathcal{B}} \leq M_{ij}^{\xi}$ for every $0 \leq i < j < n$, then $\mathcal{B} \in Supp(\xi)$.*

Proof. $\mathcal{B}$ obviously satisfies all the constraints of ξ. □

In other words, the set of values from Definition 10 completely characterizes the semantics of a scenario.

Observation 5. *Let ξ and η be two scenarios of length n, such that $events(\xi) = events(\eta)$. Then $[\![\xi]\!] = [\![\eta]\!]$ iff $\forall_{0 \leq i < j < n}(m_{ij}^{\xi} = m_{ij}^{\eta} \wedge M_{ij}^{\xi} = M_{ij}^{\eta})$.*

Proof. A direct consequence of Observations 3 and 4. □

A behaviour of ξ can be viewed as a sequence of discrete timed events in a Cartesian plane, where the x-axis represents event numbers and the y-axis represents time. It might be useful to visualize this as a curve that is obtained by connecting all such timed events. For instance, Fig. 3 shows a consistent scenario along with one of its behaviours (shown with a solid line), namely $(a, 0)(b, 1)(c, 3)(d, 4)(e, 5)$.

The upper and lower curves (in dashed lines) correspond to m_{0j} and M_{0j}, for $0 < j < 5$. Notice that the constraints that annotate the first four events of the scenario seem to indicate that the maximum distance between events

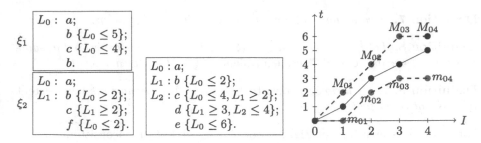

Fig. 2. Two scenarios

Fig. 3. A scenario and one of its behaviours

0 and 3 should be 8, but the constraint associated with event 4 reduces it to 6: the curves must obviously be monotonically non-decreasing.

These two curves can be viewed as the boundaries of the set of all behaviours of the scenario, that is, the plot of every supported behaviour must fit between these two curves.

This is necessary, but not sufficient. For example, the curve of the behaviour $(a,0)(b,2)(c,4)(d,4)(e,6)$ would fit between these boundaries, but the constraint $L_1 \geq 3$ that annotates event 3 (corresponding to $\tau_{1,3} \geq 3$) would be violated.

As noted above, in order to fully characterize the set of all behaviours of a scenario ξ of length n we must determine the minimum and maximum time distances between *every* pair of events in any member of $Supp(\xi)$. That is, we are interested in computing m_{ij}^{ξ} and M_{ij}^{ξ} for every i and j such that $0 \leq i < j < n$.

As an example consider scenario ξ_1 of Fig. 2 once more. The time distance between events 0 and 1 (a and the first b) is constrained to be no greater than 5, event 2 (c) occurs after event 1, but its distance from event 0 is at most 4. Surely, the time distance between events 0 and 1 must be at most 4 in all the behaviours of ξ_1: the constraint $L_0 \leq 5$ on event 1 is not tight. The tightest constraint that can replace it without changing the semantics of ξ_1 is $L_0 \leq 4$. $Supp(\xi_1)$ does, indeed, include a behaviour for which the time distance between events 1 and 2 is exactly 4.

An immediate question is how to determine the various values of m_{ij} and M_{ij} for a given scenario. We begin by elucidating some fundamental relationships between these values.

Observation 6. *Let ξ be a consistent scenario of length n. Then the following inequations hold, for any $0 \leq i < j < k < n$:*

$$m_{ij} + m_{jk} \leq m_{ik} \tag{3}$$

$$m_{ij} + M_{jk} \geq m_{ik} \tag{4}$$

$$m_{ij} + M_{jk} \leq M_{ik} \tag{5}$$

$$M_{ij} + M_{jk} \geq M_{ik} \tag{6}$$

$$M_{ij} + m_{jk} \geq m_{ik} \tag{7}$$

$$M_{ij} + m_{jk} \leq M_{ik} \tag{8}$$

Proof. In equations (3) and (6) are direct consequences of Eq. (1).

For (4), assume $m_{ij} + M_{jk} < m_{ik}$. But then m_{ij} or m_{ik} is not tight enough, or M_{jk} is too tight. That is, $Supp(\xi)$ cannot include a behaviour for which $t_{ij} = m_{ij}$, because then $t_{jk} > M_{jk}$ would have to hold for Eq. (1) and $m_{ik} \leq t_{ik}$ to be satisfied.

For (5), assume $m_{ij} + M_{jk} > M_{ik}$. But then $Supp(\xi)$ cannot include a behaviour for which $t_{jk} = M_{jk}$, because $t_{ij} < m_{ij}$ would have to hold for Eq. (1) and $t_{ik} \leq M_{ik}$ to be satisfied.

The proofs for (7) and (8) are analogous to those for (4) and (5).   □

The inequations of Observation 6 can be presented in compact form:

$$m_{ij} + m_{jk} \leq m_{ik} \leq \left\{ \begin{matrix} m_{ij} + M_{jk} \\ M_{ij} + m_{jk} \end{matrix} \right\} \leq M_{ik} \leq M_{ij} + M_{jk} \qquad (9)$$

It is worth emphasizing that none of the inequations of Observation 6 can be replaced by equations. For instance, consider scenario ξ_3 of Fig. 4. It is easy to see that $m_{01} = 0$ and $m_{12} = 0$, but $m_{02} = 2$. That is, within $Supp(\xi_3)$ there are behaviours for which $t_{01} = m_{01}$ and behaviours for which $t_{12} = m_{12}$, but there is no behaviour for which $t_{01} = m_{01}$ *and* $t_{12} = m_{12}$. Similarly, in scenario ξ_4 of Fig. 4, $M_{01} = 2$, $M_{12} = 3$, but $M_{03} = 4$.

	L_0 : a;
	b;
	c $\{L_0 \geq 2\}$.

ξ_3

	L_0 : a;
	L_1 : b $\{L_0 \leq 2\}$;
	c $\{L_1 \leq 3, L_0 \leq 4\}$.

ξ_4

Fig. 4. Two scenarios

	01	12	02
Min	2	2	4
Max	3	4	7

Fig. 5. The bounds on three events

Inequation (9) can be used to reason about the behaviours of a scenario. For example, consider a scenario ξ of length 3, such that $events(\xi) = aba$, where the minimum and maximum values of t_{ij}, for $0 \leq i < j < 3$, in the behaviours of ξ are summarized in Fig. 5. If we limit our attention to those of the supported behaviours whose time annotations contain only integers, we find a set of six:

$$\{(a,0)(b,2)(a,4), \ (a,0)(b,2)(a,5), \ (a,0)(b,2)(a,6),$$
$$(a,0)(b,3)(a,5), \ (a,0)(b,3)(a,6), \ (a,0)(b,3)(a,7)\}$$

Assume the minimum time distance between 0 and 2, i.e., m_{02}, is increased to 6. The inequation $m_{02} \leq M_{01} + m_{12}$ no longer holds. A way to repair it[5] is to increase m_{12} to 3. As a result, our set will change to:

$$\{(a,0)(b,2)(a,6), \ (a,0)(b,3)(a,6), \ (a,0)(b,3)(a,7)\}$$

---

[5] The other way is to increase M_{01} to 4, but that would introduce new behaviours.

If we increased m_{02} to 7 (instead of 6), m_{01} and m_{12} would change to 3 and 4, respectively. The set would then include only one behaviour: $\{(a,0)(b,3)(a,7)\}$.

We generally have to deal with scenarios that have more than three events, so a tabular representation similar to that of Fig. 5 will be even more useful.

2.5   Distance Tables

Definition 11. *Let $\xi = (\mathcal{E}, \mathcal{C})$ be a scenario of length n.*
$\mathcal{C}$ *is* pruned *iff, for any given integers i and j such that $0 \leq i < j < n$,*

- $\mathcal{C}$ *does not contain a constraint of the form $\tau_{i,j} = c$;*
- $\mathcal{C}$ *contains at most one constraint of the form $\tau_{i,j} \geq c$ and at most one constraint of the form $\tau_{i,j} \leq c$.*

If *constraints*(ξ) is pruned, then we also say that ξ is pruned.

Obviously, given a set of constraints $\mathcal{C}$ it is easy to convert it to a set that is equivalent, but pruned. First, replace every constraint of the form $\tau_{i,j} = c$ with two constraints, $\tau_{i,j} \geq c$ and $\tau_{i,j} \leq c$. Second, for each $0 \leq i < j < n$,

- if $\mathcal{C}$ contains more than one constraint of the form $\tau_{i,j} \geq c$, retain only one with the maximal constant;
- if $\mathcal{C}$ contains more than one constraint of the form $\tau_{i,j} \leq c$, retain only one with the minimal constant.

Definition 12. *Let $\xi = (\mathcal{E}, \mathcal{C})$ be a pruned scenario of length n.*
A distance table for ξ is a triangular matrix $\mathcal{D}^{\xi}$, such that:

- $\mathcal{D}^{\xi}_{ij}$ *is defined iff $0 \leq i < j < n$;*
- *for $0 \leq i < j < n$, $\mathcal{D}^{\xi}_{ij} = (l_{ij}, h_{ij})$, where*
  - l_{ij} *and h_{ij} are rational numbers;*
  - *if $\mathcal{C}$ contains a constraint $\tau_{i,j} \geq c$ then $l_{ij} = c$, otherwise $l_{ij} = 0$;*
  - *if $\mathcal{C}$ contains a constraint $\tau_{i,j} \leq c$ then $h_{ij} = c$, otherwise $h_{ij} = \infty$.*

We will sometimes refer to an l_{ij} as a *low value*, and to an h_{ij} as a *high value*. If ξ is of length n, then we will say that $\mathcal{D}^{\xi}$ is *of size n*.

Obviously, given $\mathcal{D}^{\xi}$ we can construct a set of constraints that is equivalent to *constraints*(ξ). So the distance table for ξ is just another representation for the constraints of ξ.

Figure 6 shows a distance table corresponding to scenario ξ of Fig. 1.

Definition 13. *A distance table of size n is* valid *iff $l_{ij} \leq h_{ij}$, for all $0 \leq i < j < n$. A table that is not valid is* invalid.

Observation 7. *If $\mathcal{D}^{\xi}$ is invalid, then ξ is inconsistent.*

Proof. Obvious from Definition 12.   □

	1	2	3	4
0	(0, 1)	(0, ∞)	(0, ∞)	(0, ∞)
1		(0, 5)	(0, 4)	(0, 11)
2			(2, ∞)	(4, ∞)
3				(0, 4)

	1	2	3	4
0	(0, 1)	(0, 3)	(2, 5)	(4, 9)
1		(0, 2)	(2, 4)	(4, 8)
2			(2, 4)	(4, 8)
3				(0, 4)

Fig. 6. A distance table for ξ of Fig. 1

Fig. 7. A stable version of the same table

Definition 14. *A distance table of size n is* stable *iff it is valid and, for all $0 \leq i < j < k < n$,*

$$l_{ij} + l_{jk} \leq l_{ik} \leq \begin{Bmatrix} l_{ij} + h_{jk} \\ h_{ij} + l_{jk} \end{Bmatrix} \leq h_{ik} \leq h_{ij} + h_{jk} \qquad (9')$$

The distance table of Fig. 6 is not stable. Figure 7 shows its stable version. The distance table for a scenario with no constraints is obviously stable.

Theorem 1. *Let $\mathcal{D}^{\xi}$ be a stable distance table. Then ξ is consistent.*

Proof. Let $events(\xi) = e_0 e_1 \ldots e_{n-1}$. It is enough to show that there exists a behaviour $\mathcal{B} = (e_0, t_0)(e_1, t_1) \ldots (e_{n-1}, t_{n-1})$, such that $\mathcal{B} \in Supp(\xi)$.

That is, we must show a sequence $t_0 t_1 \ldots t_{n-1}$ such that, for $0 \leq j < k < n$, $l_{jk} \leq t_k - t_j \leq h_{jk}$, i.e., t_{jk} satisfies the appropriate constraint in the table.

Let $t_0 = 0$, and for $0 < j < n$ let $t_j = l_{0j}$. Then the constraints in the first row of the table are satisfied: $t_k - t_0 = l_{0k} \leq h_{0k}$.

Let $0 < j < k < n$. The table is stable, so $l_{0j} + l_{jk} \leq l_{0k}$, hence $l_{jk} \leq l_{0k} - l_{0j} = t_k - t_j$. Moreover, $l_{0k} \leq l_{0j} + h_{jk}$, hence $l_{0k} - l_{0j} \leq h_{jk}$. $\square$

Definition 15. *Let $\mathcal{D}$ be a stable distance table, let p and q be integers such that $0 \leq p < q < n$, and let $S = t_p t_{p+1} \ldots t_q$ be a sequence of real numbers. We say that S is* compatible with $\mathcal{D}$ *iff*

- $0 \leq t_p \leq t_{p+1} \leq \ldots \leq t_q$;
- $l_{ij} \leq t_{ij} \leq h_{ij}$ for any two integers i and j such that $p \leq i < j \leq q$.[6]

Of course, if $\mathcal{B} \in Supp(\xi)$, then $tseq(\mathcal{B})$ is compatible with $\mathcal{D}^{\xi}$. And vice versa, a compatible sequence S whose length is the size of $\mathcal{D}^{\xi}$ satisfies all the constraints of ξ, so there is a $\mathcal{B} \in Supp(\xi)$ such that $S = tseq(\mathcal{B})$.

Lemma 1. *Let $\mathcal{D}$ be a stable distance table of size n, let b and c be integers such that $0 \leq b < c < n$, and let $t_b t_{b+1} \ldots t_c$ be compatible with $\mathcal{D}$. Then*

1. *if $0 \neq b$ then the sequence can be extended to the left in such a way that the extended sequence is compatible with $\mathcal{D}$;*
2. *if $c \neq n - 1$ then the sequence can be so extended to the right.*

---

[6] As elsewhere, $t_{ij} = t_j - t_i$.

Proof. We consider here only case 1; case 2 is similar.

Let $a = b - 1$. We must show that there exists a real number t_a, such that $0 \leq t_a \leq t_b$ and $l_{aj} \leq t_{aj} \leq h_{aj}$ for $a < j \leq c$.

For $j = b$, we must have

$$l_{ab} \leq t_{ab} \leq h_{ab} \tag{10}$$

Since $0 \leq l_{ab} \leq h_{ab}$, it is possible to find a t_{ab} that satisfies (10).

For any $j > b$, we must have $l_{aj} \leq t_{aj} \leq h_{aj}$. This is equivalent to $l_{aj} \leq t_{ab} + t_{bj} \leq h_{aj}$, and therefore to

$$l_{aj} - t_{bj} \leq t_{ab} \leq h_{aj} - t_{bj} \tag{11}$$

Obviously, $l_{aj} - t_{bj} \leq h_{aj} - t_{bj}$, because $l_{aj} \leq h_{aj}$. Moreover, $0 \leq h_{aj} - t_{bj}$. This is because, from (9'), $l_{ab} + h_{bj} \leq h_{aj}$, hence $l_{ab} \leq h_{aj} - h_{bj}$. But $h_{aj} - h_{bj} \leq h_{aj} - t_{bj}$ (because $t_{bj} \leq h_{bj}$), so $l_{ab} \leq h_{aj} - t_{bj}$, and of course $0 \leq l_{ab}$.

And so, for any particular $j > b$, it is possible to find a t_{ab} that satisfies (11).

We must now show that a single t_{ab} can satisfy *all* these constraints simultaneously, i.e., first, that the following inequations hold for any j such that $b < j$:

$$l_{ab} \leq h_{aj} - t_{bj} \tag{12}$$

$$l_{aj} - t_{bj} \leq h_{ab} \tag{13}$$

Second, for $b < j_0 < j_1 \leq c$, we must have

$$l_{aj_0} - t_{bj_0} \leq h_{aj_1} - t_{bj_1} \tag{14}$$

$$l_{aj_1} - t_{bj_1} \leq h_{aj_0} - t_{bj_0} \tag{15}$$

If these inequations are satisfied, then the maximum of the low bounds on t_{ab} does not exceed the minimum of the high bounds, therefore it is possible to choose a satisfactory t_{ab}, and hence t_a.

From (9') we have $l_{ab} + h_{bj} \leq h_{aj}$, hence $l_{ab} \leq h_{aj} - h_{bj}$. But $t_{bj} \leq h_{bj}$, so $h_{aj} - h_{bj} \leq h_{aj} - t_{bj}$, and therefore (12) holds.

From (9') we have $l_{aj} \leq h_{ab} + l_{bj}$, hence $l_{aj} - l_{bj} \leq h_{ab}$. But $l_{aj} - t_{bj} \leq l_{aj} - l_{bj}$, because $l_{bj} \leq t_{bj}$, so (13) holds.

From (9'), $l_{aj_0} + h_{j_0j_1} \leq h_{aj_1}$, so $l_{aj_0} \leq h_{aj_1} - h_{j_0j_1}$. But $h_{aj_1} - h_{j_0j_1} \leq h_{aj_1} - t_{j_0j_1}$, hence $l_{aj_0} \leq h_{aj_1} - t_{j_0j_1}$, hence $l_{aj_0} - t_{bj_0} \leq h_{aj_1} - t_{bj_0} - t_{j_0j_1}$. But $t_{bj_0} + t_{j_0j_1} = t_{bj_1}$, so (14) holds.

From (9'), $l_{aj_1} \leq h_{aj_0} + l_{j_0j_1}$, so $l_{aj_1} \leq h_{aj_0} + t_{j_0j_1}$, i.e., $l_{aj_1} - t_{j_0j_1} \leq h_{aj_0}$. Hence $l_{aj_1} - t_{bj_0} - t_{j_0j_1} \leq h_{aj_0} - t_{bj_0}$, i.e., $l_{aj_1} - t_{bj_1} \leq h_{aj_0} - t_{bj_0}$: (15) holds. □

Theorem 2. *Let $\mathcal{D}^\xi$ be a stable distance table of size n. Then each constraint in the table is tight, i.e., for any two integers i and j such that $0 \leq i < j < n$, there exist behaviours $\mathcal{B}_\mathcal{L}, \mathcal{B}^\mathcal{H} \in Supp(\xi)$ such that $t_{ij}^{\mathcal{B}_\mathcal{L}} = l_{ij}$ and $t_{ij}^{\mathcal{B}^\mathcal{H}} = h_{ij}$.*[7]

---

[7] If $h_{ij} = \infty$ then $t_{ij}^{\mathcal{B}^\mathcal{H}}$ can be an arbitrary number not smaller than l_{ij}.

Proof. We consider here only the case of $\mathcal{B}_\mathcal{L}$; for $\mathcal{B}_\mathcal{H}$ the reasoning is similar. Let $t_i = l_{0i}$, and for $i < m \leq j$ let $t_m = t_i + l_{im}$. So $t_{ij} = l_{ij}$. From elementary reasoning (very similar to that in the proof of Theorem 1) we know that $t_i t_{i+1} \ldots t_j$ is compatible with $\mathcal{D}^\xi$.

Lemma 1 shows that we can repeatedly extend the sequence to the left and/or right, while maintaining compatibility with $\mathcal{D}^\xi$ as an invariant. The result will be a sequence of length n, and we can use that as $tseq(\mathcal{B}_\mathcal{L})$.[8]   □

Theorem 3. *Let $\mathcal{D}^\xi$ be a stable distance table of size n. Then, for any $0 \leq i < j < n$, $\mathcal{D}^\xi_{ij} = (m^\xi_{ij}, M^\xi_{ij})$.*

Proof. By Definition 12 ξ has explicit constraints that require supported behaviours to satisfy $l_{ij} \leq t_{ij} \leq h_{ij}$, for all $0 \leq i < j < n$. Moreover, from Theorem 2 we know that each constraint is tight.   □

From Theorem 3 and Observation 5 we immediately see that if we could find an effective way of computing a stable distance table equivalent to the constraints of any consistent scenario ξ, then we would have an effective way of checking whether any other scenario η is equivalent to ξ: they would be equivalent if and only if the stable distance table computed from ξ were identical to that computed from η. A stable distance table could then be treated as a convenient canonical representation of all the equivalent scenarios.

An effective method of computing a stable distance table equivalent to the constraints of a given scenario does in fact exist, and is presented below (Sects. 3.1 and 3.2).

3   Algorithms

3.1   Stabilising a Distance Table

How can we stabilise a distance table without changing the semantics of the associated scenario? If we relax any of the existing constraints, then we are in dire danger of supporting new behaviours. So, if the table is not stable, we must find a way of restoring the validity of (9′) by *increasing* some low values and/or *decreasing* some high values. We must make sure that the modified values are not changed more than is strictly necessary, as we do not want to introduce new constraints that are not implied by the existing ones.

Inspection of in equation (9′) shows that, if it does not hold, it can be restored by applying one or more of six rules (we assume that $0 \leq i < j < k < n$):

$$l_{ij} + l_{jk} > l_{ik} \longrightarrow l_{ik} := l_{ij} + l_{jk} \tag{R1}$$

$$l_{ik} > l_{ij} + h_{jk} \longrightarrow l_{ij} := l_{ik} - h_{jk} \tag{R2}$$

$$l_{ik} > h_{ij} + l_{jk} \longrightarrow l_{jk} := l_{ik} - h_{ij} \tag{R3}$$

---

[8] We are only proving the existence of such a behaviour. A method of actually constructing it is discussed in Sect. 3.3.

$$l_{ij} + h_{jk} > h_{ik} \longrightarrow h_{jk} := h_{ik} - l_{ij} \tag{R4}$$

$$h_{ij} + l_{jk} > h_{ik} \longrightarrow h_{ij} := h_{ik} - l_{jk} \tag{R5}$$

$$h_{ik} > h_{ij} + h_{jk} \longrightarrow h_{ik} := h_{ij} + h_{jk} \tag{R6}$$

For example, if it is not the case that $l_{ij} + h_{jk} \leq h_{ik}$, then the right way to fix it is to decrease the value of h_{jk}, but only enough to make $l_{ij} + h_{jk} = h_{ik}$: this is the function of rule (R4).

Of course, application of a rule may lead to another violation of (9'): if we decrease h_{jk}, then $l_{ik} \leq l_{ij} + h_{jk}$ may cease to be true. So the rules must be applied over and over again, until either the table becomes invalid, or no rule is applicable (i.e., the table satisfies (9') for all values of i, j and k). One of these things must eventually happen, because each application of a rule strictly decreases the difference between a high value and the corresponding low value, and if this difference becomes negative, the table becomes invalid.[9]

Notice that if the various values in the table were integer to begin with, then application of any of the rules keeps them integer. Notice also that if a rule assigns a new high value, then that value is finite.

In our prototype the algorithm is implemented along the following lines:

```
for k := n − 1 downto 2:
 for i := k − 2 downto 0:
  for j := k − 1 downto i + 1:
   while there is an applicable rule R for i, j and k:
    apply R;
    if the table is invalid, stop.
```

It turns out that this triple loop does the job: the table becomes either invalid or stable. The cost of stabilisation is thus of the order of $O(n^3)$. This is not very surprising, since there are clear similarities with the Floyd-Warshall algorithm for computing distances in a graph.

Observation 8 *(Confluence). Let $\mathcal{D}$ be a distance table, and let a valid $\mathcal{D}'$ be the result of applying the stabilisation procedure outlined above to $\mathcal{D}$. Then $\mathcal{D}'$ is determined by $\mathcal{D}$ uniquely, i.e., regardless of the particular order in which the rules R1–R6 are applied.*

Proof. We give an informal outline of a proof.

Consider applying the rules iteratively to a particular instance of inequation (9') (i.e., for some particular choice of i, j and k). There are six rules, and six values that should satisfy six inequalities. Each unsatisfied inequality enables one rule, which modifies one value, and that value can be modified only by that rule. More than one rule can be applicable at the same time, e.g., (R1) and (R6) ($l_{ij} + l_{jk} > l_{ik}$ and $h_{ik} > h_{ij} + h_{jk}$ can hold simultaneously). However,

---

[9] The values in the table are rational numbers, but they have a least common denominator. Adding or subtracting two such values cannot produce a result that does not share that common denominator. So our algorithm cannot decrease the difference between two such values indefinitely without making it negative.

simple inspection shows that it is impossible for an applicable rule to affect either the value set by another applicable rule or its condition of applicability.[10] So the order in which rules are applied for this instance of (9′) cannot affect the outcome.

Consider a particular low value in the table (the argument for a high value is similar). This value may appear in different guises in different instances of (9′): in some of them as l_{ij}, in others as l_{jk} or l_{ik}. Regardless of the order in which the instances are treated, the low value will grow only as much as is needed to satisfy all of them.   □

Theorem 4 *(Equivalence). Let $\mathcal{D}^{\xi}$ be a distance table, and let $\mathcal{D}$ be the result of applying the stabilisation procedure to $\mathcal{D}^{\xi}$. Then $\mathcal{D}$ is equivalent to $\mathcal{D}^{\xi}$.*

Proof. Let η be a scenario such that $events(\eta) = events(\xi)$ and $\mathcal{D}^{\eta} = \mathcal{D}$.

Observation 8 shows that the result of stabilisation is unique. Each low (high) value is increased (decreased) only by as much as is needed to make the table stable. So, for each $i < j$, $l_{ij} \leq m_{ij}^{\xi}$ and $h_{ij} \geq M_{ij}^{\xi}$ (because the various m^{ξ} and M^{ξ} must satisfy (9)). From this and from Observation 4 we have $Supp(\eta) \supset Supp(\xi)$. But the process of stabilisation did not relax any of the constraints, so $Supp(\eta) \subset Supp(\xi)$.   □

3.2   Checking Consistency, Computing a Stable Table

We are now ready to present our method of checking the consistency of a given scenario ξ of length n.

1. We begin by pruning ξ. Its constraints are then arranged in a sequence $\Psi = \psi_0 \psi_1 \ldots \psi_K$.
2. We then iteratively compute a finite sequence of scenarios, $\eta^0, \eta^1, \ldots \eta^k$, such that:
   (a) $k \leq K$;
   (b) $events(\eta^i) = events(\xi)$ (for $0 < i \leq k$);
   (c) $[\![\eta^0]\!] \supset [\![\eta^1]\!] \supset \ldots \supset [\![\eta^k]\!] \supset [\![\xi]\!]$;
   (d) η^0 is a scenario with no constraints and $[\![\eta^k]\!] = [\![\xi]\!]$;
   (e) each η^{i+1} is obtained by adding ψ_i to η^i.
   This is done by iteratively modifying a single table, $\mathcal{D}$. After iteration i the contents of $\mathcal{D}$ represents $\mathcal{D}^{\eta^i}$.
   Each new constraint is added by amending $\mathcal{D}$. If the constraint is not tighter than the one that is already present in the table, then adding it is an empty action. (This is essentially a stronger version of pruning, performed "on the fly". In practice there is no need for the initial pruning in step 1).

---

[10] For example, (R5) depends on h_{ik} and l_{jk}, which can be changed by (R6) and (R3). But if (R5) is applicable, i.e., if $h_{ij} + l_{jk} > h_{ik}$ holds, then (R6) is not applicable: we cannot have $h_{ik} > h_{ij} + h_{jk}$, because $l_{jk} \leq h_{jk}$ (the table is valid); similarly, (R3) is not applicable: $l_{ik} > h_{ij} + l_{jk}$ would imply $l_{ik} > h_{ik}$.

3. After all the constraints in Ψ have been added to the table, $\mathcal{D}$ is stabilised to make explicit those constraints that are only implicitly implied by the constraints in the table (cf. Theorem 4).

The cost of this algorithm is dominated by that of stabilisation, i.e., $O(n^3)$.[11]

If step 3 ended with an invalid $\mathcal{D}^{\eta^k}$, then by Observation 7 η^k is inconsistent, i.e., $[\![\eta^k]\!] = \emptyset$. But $[\![\eta^k]\!] \supset [\![\xi]\!]$, so ξ is inconsistent. If, however, the resulting table is valid, then:

- $[\![\eta^k]\!] = [\![\xi]\!]$, since $[\![\eta^k]\!] \supset [\![\xi]\!]$, and all the constraints of ξ are accounted for in η^k;
- by Theorem 1, η^k (and therefore ξ) is consistent;
- by Theorem 3 for each $0 \leq i < j < n$, $\mathcal{D}^{\eta^k}_{ij} = (m^{\eta^k}_{ij}, M^{\eta^k}_{ij})$, and by Observation 5 this is equal to $(m^{\xi}_{ij}, M^{\xi}_{ij})$, since $[\![\eta^k]\!] = [\![\xi]\!]$.

We will use $\mathcal{D}^{\xi}_s$ to denote the stable table obtained from ξ. Figure 7 shows $\mathcal{D}^{\xi}_s$ for scenario ξ of Fig. 1.

Theorem 5. *Let ξ and η be two consistent scenarios, such that $events(\xi) = events(\eta)$. Then $[\![\xi]\!] = [\![\eta]\!]$ iff $\mathcal{D}^{\xi}_s = \mathcal{D}^{\eta}_s$.*

Proof. A direct consequence of Theorem 3 and Observation 5.

3.3   Using a Distance Table to Find Particular Behaviours

A stable distance table $\mathcal{D}$ equivalent to $\mathcal{D}^{\xi}$ is useful for constructing particular behaviours of scenario ξ. If we are interested in a behaviour that has a particular value t_{ij} for some $i < j$, we must, of course, consult $\mathcal{D}$ to ensure that $l_{ij} \leq t_{ij} \leq h_{ij}$. Once we have chosen t_{ij}, we tighten the constraint by assigning this value to both l_{ij} and h_{ij}, then restabilise the table. This will give us a new set of constraints that will guide us in choosing the value of t_{ij} for some other i and j. We continue to do so, until the complete behaviour is known, i.e., $l_{ij} = h_{ij}$ for $0 \leq i < j < n$.

More generally, we can use a distance table $\mathcal{D}$ to quickly verify whether it is possible for a behaviour to simultaneously satisfy several constraints that are tighter than the ones in the table. We just make those constraints tighter in $\mathcal{D}$, and see whether an attempt to restabilise produces a valid table. In this case our stabilisation method becomes a "poor man's constraint solver".

---

[11] In practice it is often convenient to pinpoint the first "offending" constraint that makes a scenario inconsistent. This is easily done by making sure that the order of constraints in Ψ corresponds to the textual order of constraints in the scenario, and attempting to stabilise the table each time a new constraint is added to it. If the number of constraints is proportional to n, the cost becomes $O(n^4)$.

4   Optimizing Scenarios

Now that we have an effective method of establishing the equivalence of scenarios, it is tempting to convert a scenario to an equivalent one that is "better". For instance, one might want to decrease the number of constraints, or to make them detect an unsupported behaviour as early as possible.

A particularly interesting possibility is that of finding a scenario that is equivalent to the given one, but that has smaller constants in its constraints. As explained in Sect. 1, this has direct consequences for the cost of verifying timed automata that are synthesised from scenarios.

The optimisation is carried out by building the constraints of the new scenario from the distance table in such a way that the constraints with larger constants need not be added if they are implied by constraints with smaller constants.

More specifically, given a scenario ξ of length n we proceed as follows:

1. We use the method of Sect. 3.2 to produce a stable distance table $\mathcal{D}_s^\xi$.[12]
2. We copy all the information from $\mathcal{D}_s^\xi$ into a list L of items with two forms: $m_{ij} = c$ and $M_{ij} = c$.
3. The list is sorted by the constants c, in increasing order.
4. We create a scenario $\eta = (events(\xi), \emptyset)$ and its distance table $\mathcal{D}^\eta$.
5. We now iteratively take consecutive items from L, compare each item with the contents of $\mathcal{D}^\eta$, and modify η and $\mathcal{D}^\eta$ as follows:[13]
   (a) If the item is of the form $m_{ij} = c$ and $l_{ij} < c$ then $l_{ij} := c$; otherwise the item is of the form $M_{ij} = c$, and if $h_{ij} > c$ then $h_{ij} := c$.
   (b) If the table (i.e., $\mathcal{D}^\eta$) was modified in the above step, add the corresponding constraint to η and stabilise the table.

Upon termination $\mathcal{D}^\eta$ is identical to $\mathcal{D}_s^\xi$, so $[\![\eta]\!] = [\![\xi]\!]$. However, if a constraint with a higher constant is implied by constraints with lower constants, then by the time we get to it in step (a) it will already be present in the table, and will not be explicitly added to η in step (b).

Given scenario ξ of Fig. 1 and its stable distance table (shown in Fig. 7), the algorithm described above produces the optimised scenario η shown in Fig. 1.

5   Comparison with Difference Bounds Matrices

Difference Bounds Matrices (DBMs) have been proposed by Dill [11] as an efficient technique for representing clock zones in the context of verification of timed automata. A clock zone is a set of constraints, each of which puts a bound on the difference between the values of two clocks. A consistent DBM has a canonical form that can be obtained by computing all-pairs shortest paths.

---

[12] If the attempt to do so fails because of the inconsistency of ξ, then producing an equivalent scenario with smaller constants is trivial (and probably pointless).

[13] More formally, we create a finite sequence of scenarios, $\eta^0 \eta^1 \ldots$ and a corresponding sequence of tables, $\mathcal{D}^{\eta^0} \mathcal{D}^{\eta^1} \ldots$. We felt that a more pedantic presentation would be harder to follow.

We will now show how Dill's technique can be adapted to address the consistency of scenarios and the minimisation of constants in their constraints.

Given a scenario ξ, one can construct a timed automaton A_ξ, such that the set of timed words over which A_ξ has an accepting run is equivalent to the set of behaviours of ξ. For instance, Fig. 8 shows a scenario, ξ, and its corresponding timed automaton A_ξ. If we make sure that every transition of A_ξ (including the last transition) is annotated with a new clock reset, then, after applying Dill's technique, the DBM that corresponds to the final zone of the augmented A_ξ will contain information that is equivalent to the stable distance table for ξ.

Assume A'_ξ is the automaton obtained by annotating transitions labeled with c and e in A_ξ with two new clocks c_3 and c_5, respectively. Figure 9 shows the stable distance table of ξ and the DBM that represents the final zone of A'_ξ (in Dill's original work the DBM would also contain information about whether the inequalities are sharp). c_0 is a clock whose value is always 0, and an entry a in row c_i and column c_j is interpreted as $c_i - c_j \leq a$. For example, $c_5 - c_2 \leq -4$, i.e., $4 \leq c_2 - c_5$: this corresponds to the minimum in row 1, column 4 of the distance table.

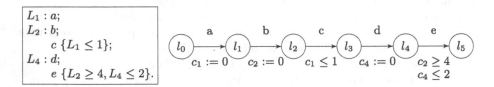

$$
\begin{array}{|l|}
\hline
L_1 : a; \\
L_2 : b; \\
\quad c\,\{L_1 \leq 1\}; \\
L_4 : d; \\
\quad e\,\{L_2 \geq 4, L_4 \leq 2\}. \\
\hline
\end{array}
$$

Fig. 8. Scenario ξ and its corresponding timed automaton A_ξ

	1	2	3	4
0	(0, 1)	(0, 1)	(2, ∞)	(4, ∞)
1		(0, 1)	(2, ∞)	(4, ∞)
2			(1, ∞)	(3, ∞)
3				(0, 2)

	c_0	c_1	c_2	c_3	c_4	c_5
c_0	0	-4	-4	-3	0	0
c_1	∞	0	1	1	∞	∞
c_2	∞	0	0	1	∞	∞
c_3	∞	0	0	0	∞	∞
c_4	2	-2	-2	-1	0	2
c_5	0	-4	-4	-3	0	0

Fig. 9. The distance table of ξ of Fig. 8 and the final DBM of A_ξ (with c_4 and c_5 added)

If $c_i - c_j \leq a$, $c_j - c_i \leq b$ and $a < b$, then the DBM is inconsistent: this corresponds to the minimum becoming larger than the maximum in the corresponding entry of the distance table.

The equivalence of a distance table and a DBM has interesting implications. On the one hand, we can replace the distance table with a DBM in the algorithm of Sect. 4 (the process would be slightly more complicated, because the constraints are encoded in a DBM somewhat less directly than in a distance table). On the other hand, it is possible to take advantage of various techniques for DBMs and apply them to scenarios: for instance, the method of removing redundant constraints from a DBM (as described by Bengtsson [6]) can be used to remove redundant constraints from a distance table, and therefore—as we have shown—from a timed scenario.

The computational cost of applying Dill's original method to a scenario of length n would be $O(n^4)$: we would have to construct n instances of a DBM for n zones, and make each instance canonical at a cost of $O(n^3)$. However, it turns out that there are ways of preserving the canonicality of a DBM while moving to the next zone [6], so the overall cost would be $O(n^3)$, i.e., the same as ours.

In the final analysis, the technique of computing distance tables can be seen as an alternative and more direct approach to dealing with constraints in timed scenarios: in this context we find it simpler and more intuitive.

6   Related Work and Conclusions

For over three decades scenarios (including timed scenarios) have been proposed and used for specification, implementation and also synthesizing formal models of complex systems [4,8,10,21].

For describing scenarios for real-time systems, researchers have proposed extending Message Sequence Charts (MSCs) with time constraints [1,5].

En-Nouaary et al. [12] use timed scenarios for specifying systems, and integrate them to obtain a set of Timed Finite State Machines (TFSMs), a variant of timed automata. Their scenarios are described in a semi-formal language based on structured English or a graphical representation, and are therefore quite different from ours.

Somé et al. [20] propose a method for synthesizing timed automata from a set of scenarios. Our timed scenarios are different from theirs: we do not include "conditions" in our scenarios. These "conditions" are not related to time and assert some facts about the status/mode of the decribed system.

The question of consistency and optimization of scenarios is not considered in any of the references cited above.

Harel et al. [14] study the problem of synthesizing state-based object systems from Live Sequence Charts (LSCs). They perform a consistency check of a set of LSCs to make sure that they are not contradictory with each other, in particular to check that the ordering of the events is correct. This consistency check is different from ours: we consider individual timed scenarios and check their consistency in terms of time.

In our previous work [19] we proposed a form of timed scenarios and developed a method for synthesizing a timed automaton from a set of scenarios: we did not consider checking the consistency of scenarios or optimising them.

In the current paper we propose a notion of timed scenarios and their semantics that is both simpler and more general. We define the semantics of a scenario in terms of the set of behaviours that are supported by the scenario, and propose a method for checking the consistency of scenarios.

Checking the consistency of a set of constraints has already been studied in various contexts [11,17,18]. Our method is different: the consistency check is a simple byproduct of the construction of a "stable distance table". The table can be used as a canonical representation of the constraints of a class of equivalent scenarios, and is thus a good starting point for converting a scenario to an equivalent "optimised" form. Our optimisation minimizes the largest constant that appears in the constraints of a scenario, thus decreasing the maximum constant in the timed automaton synthesized from a set of scenarios.

We also show that the technique developed by Dill for representing clock zones in timed automata [11] can be applied to the domain of timed scenarios, both to check consistency and to minimise constants in constraints.

References

1. Akshay, S., Mukund, M., Kumar, K.N.: Checking coverage for infinite collections of timed scenarios. In: Caires, L., Vasconcelos, V.T. (eds.) CONCUR 2007. LNCS, vol. 4703, pp. 181–196. Springer, Heidelberg (2007). https://doi.org/10.1007/978-3-540-74407-8_13
2. Alur, R., Dill, D.L.: A theory of timed automata. Theor. Comput. Sci. **126**(2), 183–235 (1994)
3. Alur, R., Madhusudan, P.: Decision problems for timed automata: a survey. In: Bernardo, M., Corradini, F. (eds.) SFM-RT 2004. LNCS, vol. 3185, pp. 1–24. Springer, Heidelberg (2004). https://doi.org/10.1007/978-3-540-30080-9_1
4. Alur, R., Martin, M., Raghothaman, M., Stergiou, C., Tripakis, S., Udupa, A.: Synthesizing finite-state protocols from scenarios and requirements. In: Yahav, E. (ed.) HVC 2014. LNCS, vol. 8855, pp. 75–91. Springer, Cham (2014). https://doi.org/10.1007/978-3-319-13338-6_7
5. Ben-Abdallah, H., Leue, S.: Timing constraints in Message Sequence Chart specifications. In: Togashi, A., Mizuno, T., Shiratori, N., Higashino, T. (eds.) FORTE. IFIP Conference Proceedings, vol. 107, pp. 91–106. Chapman & Hall, London (1997)
6. Bengtsson, J.: Clocks, DBMs and states in timed systems. Ph.D. thesis, Uppsala University (2002)
7. Bengtsson, J., Larsen, K., Larsson, F., Pettersson, P., Yi, W.: UPPAAL — a tool suite for automatic verification of real-time systems. In: Alur, R., Henzinger, T.A., Sontag, E.D. (eds.) HS 1995. LNCS, vol. 1066, pp. 232–243. Springer, Heidelberg (1996). https://doi.org/10.1007/BFb0020949
8. Bollig, B., Katoen, J.-P., Kern, C., Leucker, M.: Replaying play in and play out: synthesis of design models from scenarios by learning. In: Grumberg, O., Huth, M. (eds.) TACAS 2007. LNCS, vol. 4424, pp. 435–450. Springer, Heidelberg (2007). https://doi.org/10.1007/978-3-540-71209-1_33
9. Bozga, M., Daws, C., Maler, O., Olivero, A., Tripakis, S., Yovine, S.: Kronos: a model-checking tool for real-time systems. In: Hu, A.J., Vardi, M.Y. (eds.) CAV 1998. LNCS, vol. 1427, pp. 546–550. Springer, Heidelberg (1998). https://doi.org/10.1007/BFb0028779

10. Damas, C., Lambeau, B., Roucoux, F., van Lamsweerde, A.: Analyzing critical process models through behavior model synthesis. In: Proceedings of the 31st International Conference on Software Engineering, pp. 441–451. IEEE Computer Society (2009)
11. Dill, D.L.: Timing assumptions and verification of finite-state concurrent systems. In: Sifakis, J. (ed.) CAV 1989. LNCS, vol. 407, pp. 197–212. Springer, Heidelberg (1990). https://doi.org/10.1007/3-540-52148-8_17
12. En-Nouaary, A., Dssouli, R., Khendek, F.: From timed scenarios to SDL: specification, implementation and testing of real-time systems. In: SDL Forum, p. 67 (1999)
13. Giese, H.: Towards scenario-based synthesis for parametric timed automata. In: Proceedings of the 2nd International Workshop on Scenarios and State Machines: Models, Algorithms, and Tools (SCESM), Portland, USA (2003)
14. Harel, D., Kugler, H.: Synthesizing state-based object systems from LSC specifications. In: Yu, S., Păun, A. (eds.) CIAA 2000. LNCS, vol. 2088, pp. 1–33. Springer, Heidelberg (2001). https://doi.org/10.1007/3-540-44674-5_1
15. Harel, D., Kugler, H., Pnueli, A.: Synthesis revisited: generating statechart models from scenario-based requirements. In: Kreowski, H.-J., Montanari, U., Orejas, F., Rozenberg, G., Taentzer, G. (eds.) Formal Methods in Software and Systems Modeling. LNCS, vol. 3393, pp. 309–324. Springer, Heidelberg (2005). https://doi.org/10.1007/978-3-540-31847-7_18
16. Heitmeyer, C.L., et al.: Building high assurance human-centric decision systems. Autom. Softw. Eng. **22**(2), 159–197 (2015)
17. Mahfoudh, M., Niebert, P., Asarin, E., Maler, O.: A satisfiability checker for difference logic. In: Fifth International Symposium on the Theory and Applications of Satisfiability Testing (2002)
18. Nieuwenhuis, R., Oliveras, A.: DPLL(T) with exhaustive theory propagation and its application to difference logic. In: Etessami, K., Rajamani, S.K. (eds.) CAV 2005. LNCS, vol. 3576, pp. 321–334. Springer, Heidelberg (2005). https://doi.org/10.1007/11513988_33
19. Saeedloei, N., Kluźniak, F.: From scenarios to timed automata. In: Cavalheiro, S., Fiadeiro, J. (eds.) SBMF 2017. LNCS, vol. 10623, pp. 33–51. Springer, Cham (2017). https://doi.org/10.1007/978-3-319-70848-5_4
20. Somé, S., Dssouli, R., Vaucher, J.: From scenarios to timed automata: building specifications from users requirements. In: Proceedings of the Second Asia Pacific Software Engineering Conference, APSEC 1995, pp. 48–57. IEEE Computer Society, Washington, DC, USA (1995)
21. Uchitel, S., Kramer, J., Magee, J.: Synthesis of behavioral models from scenarios. IEEE Trans. Softw. Eng. **29**(2), 99–115 (2003)

Safe and Constructive Design with UML Components

Flávia Falcão[1](✉), Lucas Lima[2](✉), and Augusto Sampaio[1](✉)

[1] Centro de Informática, Universidade Federal de Pernambuco, Recife, Brazil
{fmcf2,acas}@cin.ufpe.br
[2] Departamento de Computação, Universidade Federal Rural de Pernambuco, Recife, Brazil
lucas.albertins@ufrpe.br

Abstract. Component Based Software Development (CBSD) is an established paradigm to build systems from reusable and loosely coupled units. However, it is still a challenge to ensure, in a scalable way, that desired properties hold for component integration. We present a component based model for UML, including a metamodel, well-formedness conditions and a formal semantics via translation into BRIC. We use (our previous work on) BRIC as an underlying (and totally hidden) component development framework so that our approach benefits from all the formal infrastructure developed for BRIC using CSP (Communicating Sequential Processes). Component composition, specified via UML structural diagrams, ensures, by construction, adherence to classical concurrent properties: our focus is on the preservation of deadlock freedom. Partial automated support is developed as a plug-in to the Astah modelling tool. We illustrate our overall approach with two case studies.

Keywords: Component-based development
Correctness by construction · CSP

1 Introduction

Component Based Software Development (CBSD) is a widely disseminated paradigm to build software systems by integrating independent and potentially reusable units called components. One of the motivations for this paradigm is replacing conventional programming with the systematic composition and configuration of components [17].

In some contexts, particularly when there is some criticality involved, a reliable architecture becomes a demand. The architecture is expected to be designed with the goal of verifying the integration of its components in a rigorous and scalable way. However, *a posteriori* verification, can be costly, and is often infeasible.

There are several approaches to CBSD in the literature. For example, in Reo [1], a concurrent system consists of a set of components which are glued

T. Massoni and M. R. Mousavi (Eds.): SBMF 2018, LNCS 11254, pp. 234–251, 2018.
https://doi.org/10.1007/978-3-030-03044-5_15

together by a circuit that enables flow of data between components. Components can perform I/O operations on the boundary nodes of the circuit to which they are connected. There are formal semantics for Reo, based on coalgebras [11] and automata. Another example is [5], which presents component-based refinement that focuses on the separation of interface and functional contracts, supporting different levels of abstraction. The approach in [2] is based on a semantic model encompassing composition of heterogeneous components; the behaviour of a component is described as an automaton or Petri net extended by data and functions given in C++. In [12], the authors introduce a framework for assessing component properties, like completeness and consistency of requirement specifications, using Z [21] and State-charts [10], and an approach to verifying reliability using stochastic modelling formalisms.

In previous work we have proposed a formal component model, together with a rule-based composition strategy, called BRIC [17,18]. BRIC has the process algebra CSP [19] as an underlying semantic model. Given that the argument components are deadlock free, each composition rule ensures that the resulting (composed) component preserves deadlock freedom. By using some metadata and communication patterns, it has been shown that the formal and mechanised verification of component integration, using the FDR tool [8], can scale. In spite of the promising results, in order to use BRIC a developer needs to have a considerable knowledge of CSP and of model checking techniques.

Our aim here is to foster a formal CBSD model for UML [14], motivated by the fact that UML is a widely used notation in industry, and amenable to mechanized analysis. We benefit from the overall formal infrastructure built around BRIC, but this is totally hidden from the developer.

While UML is well-suited for modelling software systems in general, it lacks support for modelling components in the sense of a CBSD approach. The usual design notation to represent a component is a *subsystem*. This is a *package* stereotype with an explicit interface and a set of encapsulated elements (including classes, interfaces and other subsystems). Nevertheless, an appropriate component notion must also include a dynamic behaviour (that can be defined by a state machine) and, considering components as independent units, ports for message passing communication should also be a component design feature. The syntactic (metamodel) definition of a component notion in UML is the first contribution of this work.

In general, UML design elements and diagrams can be used in a very flexible way. However, to tailor the design to a CBSD approach, besides defining a component metamodel, we need additional (context sensitive) conditions to ensure the well-formedness of component systems. In particular, we define how components can be composed to give rise to more elaborate components. This is our second contribution.

Finally, as a third contribution, we define a formal semantics for the proposed component model by translation into BRIC. Components, instances and connections are translated into CSP, and deadlock freedom verifications are conducted in FDR, using the BRIC composition rules. If the verification fails, the problem is traced back to the UML component level, and the problematic composition is exhibited to the developer. Partial automated support is developed as a plug-in to the Astah modelling tool [4].

The next section introduces BRIC. In Sect. 3, we present the proposed UML component model, the well-formedness conditions, the approach to component (instance) composition, and the translation into BRIC. Section 4 is dedicated to tool support and the development of a case study. The final section summarises our results, and discusses related and future work.

2   The BRIC Component Model

BRIC formalises concepts of interfaces, dynamic behaviour, component contracts, and communication protocols with focus on the interaction points of black box components and their runtime behaviour. CSP, as the underlying formal notation, allows modelling system components in terms of synchronous processes that interact through message-passing communication. Process algebraic operators allow specifying elaborate concurrency and distributed process networks. CSP offers rich semantic models that support a wide range of process verification, and comparisons.

A component contract is defined in terms of a component behaviour (CSP process), its ports (CSP channels) and their respective types (interfaces).

Definition 1 *(Component Contract). A component contract $Ctr : \langle B, R, I, C \rangle$ comprises an observational behaviour B, a set of communication channels C, a set of interfaces I, and a total function $R : C \to I$ between channels and interfaces, such that B is an I/O process (see Definition 2).*

Definition 2 *(I/O Process). An I/O process is a CSP process P that satisfies the following properties:*

- *I/O channels Every event in P is either an input or an output, that is:*

$$inputs(c, P) \cup outputs(c, P) \subseteq \{| \, c \, |\} \wedge$$
$$inputs(c, P) \cap outputs(c, P) = \{\}$$

  where $\{| \, c \, |\}$ yields the set of all events on channel c, and $inputs(c,P)$ and $outputs(c,P)$ yield all input and output events on c in process P, respectively.
- *Non-terminating P is a non-terminating process but has a finite state space.*
- *Divergence free P has no livelocks.*
- *Input determinism If a set of input events in P is offered by the environment, none of them are refused by P.*
- *Strong output decisive All choices (if any) among output events on a given channel in P are internal. The process, however, must offer at least one output on that channel.*

In the Dining Philosophers problem, one can model a philosopher and a fork as components. As an example, the behaviour of a fork is described in UML as a state machine *stm_fork*, in Fig. 3. Initially, the fork is available for both philosophers (*available* state); however, two philosophers cannot hold the same fork simultaneously. This is represented in the state machine by two states, *busy*1 and *busy*2, capturing the interactions with the two philosophers that share the fork.

This is given a semantics in CSP for the purpose of formal verification, as explained in detail in Sect. 3. The resulting process *Fork* is parametrised by its *id*, so that several instances for distinct identifiers can be created. It is defined as process *stm_fork* that captures the behaviour of the UML state machine.

$$Fork(id) = stm\_fork(id)$$
$$stm\_fork(id) = available(id)$$

The behaviour of the state machine itself is that of its initial state, which, in this case, is captured by the process *available* that offers two alternative behaviours.

$$available(id) = (port\_fork\_right.id.picksup\_I \rightarrow$$
$$port\_fork\_right.id.picksup\_O \rightarrow busy1(id))$$
$$\Box$$
$$(port\_fork\_left.id.picksup\_I \rightarrow$$
$$port\_fork\_left.id.picksup\_O \rightarrow busy2(id))$$

This choice is denoted as an external choice in CSP ($\Box$). It allows the environment to choose between two processes by communicating an initial event, which resolves the choice. If the first choice of *available* is taken, the philosopher on the right holds the fork, and similarly for the one on the left. Each of these choices is defined as a sequence of events defined using the CSP prefix ($\rightarrow$) operator. For instance, in the first case, the process performs the event *port_fork_right.id.picksup_I*, and then the event *port_fork_right.id.picksup_O* where the former represents the intention to pick the fork, and the latter indicates that it has been performed; finally, it behaves as the process *busy*1. The processes below complete the definition of *FORK*.

$$busy1(id) = port\_fork\_right.id.putsdown\_I \rightarrow$$
$$port\_fork\_right.id.putsdown\_O \rightarrow available(id)$$
$$busy2(id) = port\_fork\_left.id.putsdown\_I \rightarrow$$
$$port\_fork\_left.id.putsdown\_O \rightarrow available(id)$$

The process *busy*1 engages in two events in sequence, capturing the release of a fork, and then behaving again as *available*. The event *putsdown_I* indicates an input operation. Similarly, *putsdown_O* is used as an output operation. The process *busy*2 is analogous, dealing with the second choice. The process *FORK*(*id*) is an example of an I/O process that, as explained previously, has infinite traces, is divergence free, input deterministic and strong output decisive.

Apart from the notation for prefix and external choice, as illustrated in the previous example, CSP offers some basic processes and a rich repertoire of process operators. The processes $SKIP$ and $STOP$ represent successful termination and deadlock, respectively. The sharing parallel composition ($P1 \parallel P2$) synchronises P1 and P2 on the events in the synchronisation set cs; events that are not in cs occur independently. A particular case is when the processes are composed in interleaving, denoted by $P1 \parallel\parallel P2$, in which case $P1$ and $P2$ run independently. For a more detailed introduction to CSP [19].

BRIC provides four composition rules: interleave, communication, feedback and reflexive compositions. Each rule has well defined conditions that ensures a sound composition [18]. The first composition rule is interleave, which aggregates two independent components that will not communicate with each other; the components do not share any channels, so no synchronisation is performed. The second rule is based on the traditional way to compose two components, by connecting two channels, one from each component.

The other two rules provide unary compositions: feedback and reflexive, which enable building systems with cyclic topologies, connecting two channels of the same component. Feedback composition represents the simpler unary composition, where two channels of the same component are assembled, but do not introduce a new cycle. Reflexive composition deals with more complex systems that indeed present cycles of dependencies in the system topology.

In order to connect channels, protocols must be defined. The protocol implemented by a component is given by the abstraction of its behaviour projection over a specific channel. The protocol has the same traces and failures as the projection, but it is divergence-free. We can define one process, $PROT\_FK(ch)$, representing the protocol related to each channel ch from component $FORK$. This process is represented by:

$$PROT\_FK(ch) = ch.picksup\_I \rightarrow ch.picksup\_O \rightarrow$$
$$ch.putsdown\_I \rightarrow ch.putsdown\_O \rightarrow PROT\_FK(ch)$$

Interactions between two component contracts in a composition must be asynchronous, mediated by a bidirectional buffer($BUFF\_IO$). Buffers work as intermediate elements of the composition, copying information from one component channel to another. Information is always accepted, independent of the other component being ready to input. These buffers are not first-class elements; they are implicit to the component model. Buffers are considered infinite [17].

3   Component Model, Design and Verification in UML

Although BRIC provides a sound and systematic development strategy, it is not appealing for practical use, as it requires deep knowledge of CSP. This was the main motivation for our UML based approach. First, in Sect. 3.1, we define a component model in UML, including the relevant well-formedness conditions. Then, in Sect. 3.2, we present the approach to create and compose component instances. Finally, in Sect. 3.3, we define a formal semantics for the proposed component model and composition by translation into BRIC.

3.1   Component Metamodel and Well-Formedness

Although UML has a metamodel for components, this is normally used as a
way to represent concrete artifacts, typically component implementations. We
propose a component metamodel at the design phase, which is closer to the
notion of a subsystem in UML, but we define the necessary elements to form a
detailed component model, including structure and behavioural aspects, as well
as composition rules to produce more elaborate components from basic ones.

In Fig. 1, we define a metamodel that formally captures the structure of the
component model we propose. This metamodel extends constructs from a subset
of UML that are identified as grey filled boxes. The unfilled boxes are the new
elements introduced; these are defined as stereotypes of standard UML design
elements. Next, we explain each element of our component metamodel.

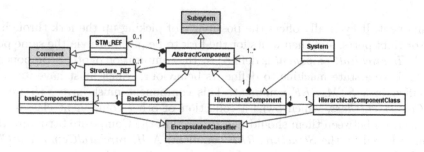

Fig. 1. The component metamodel.

A component is a UML *Subsystem*. A component must be either a *BasicComponent* or a *HierarchicalComponent*. A *BasicComponent* is not defined
in terms of other components. It has one *BasicComponentClass* that describes
the behaviour of the component and its ports. A *BasicComponentClass* is a
UML *EncapsulatedClassifier* element, which, apart from attribute and methods,
includes ports. This is the core class of a component metamodel. Its behaviour
is defined by a state machine that should be referenced in *STM_REF*; this
represents a reference to a State Machine that defines the behaviour of the component. In the model, it is represented by a UML *Comment*, also known as a
Note. The content of this comment must be the State Machine name. The ports
can be defined either in a class diagram or in a composite structure diagram. For
the latter case, the *BasicComponentClass* must be linked to a *Structure_REF*
comment.

In the Dining Philosophers, *FORK* is an example of a *BasicComponent*.
In Fig. 2, it is defined as a *Subsystem* stereotyped *BasicComponent*. It has
a *BasicComponentClass* with two ports, *right* and *left*, both realising the
interface_phil_fork interface. Also, it has a comment stereotyped *STM_REF*
with the name of the state machine of this component. Figure 3 shows the state
machine *STM_FORK*, which represents the reactive behaviour of the *FORK*

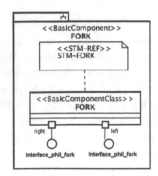

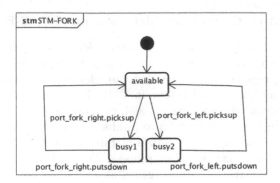

Fig. 2. Class diagram of the FORK component.

Fig. 3. State machine diagram for the FORK component.

component. It cyclically offers the possibility of picking up the fork through its left or right ports, and then waits for the fork to be put down via the same port.

A *HierarchicalComponent* is defined by the composition of other components. It can have a state machine to define its behaviour, which must have its name specified in a *STM_REF* comment. This component must have a *HierarchicalComponentClass*, which owns a collection of other component classes. The connections between them should be expressed in the Composite Structure Diagram referred by the *Structure_REF* comment. A *HierarchicalComponentClass* is a UML *EncapsulatedClassifier* element, hence, it may have ports to interact with other components. Similar to a *STM REF*, *Structure_REF* is represented by a UML comment element. The content of this comment is the name of the Composite Structure Diagram that models the structure of the component. Finally, a *System* is a specialisation of a *HierarchicalComponent* and it can be seen as the root component from where the entire system is specified.

The Dining Philosophers problem is modelled as a *System* element and, therefore, as a *HierarchicalComponent*; see Fig. 4. It has a *HierarchicalComponentClass* that is related to one or more *FORK* and one or more *PHIL* components, using a composition relationship. Also, it has a linked comment specifying the composite structure diagram (*STR-DINING-PHIL*) that details how the parts are connected. The approach to compose component instances is described in the next section.

In addition to the metamodel, we need to define some well-formedness conditions to characterise meaningful models that can be assigned a formal semantics. Furthermore, a precise characterisation of a meaningful model can be seen as a modelling style to guide practitioners during the design of systems. The well-formedness conditions are as follows.

System Element. There must be exactly one *System*, which is the root component. This is a special type of *HierarchicalComponent* that is specified by a class diagram and a composite structure diagram. The former must have a subsystem stereotyped *System* which has composition relationships between its

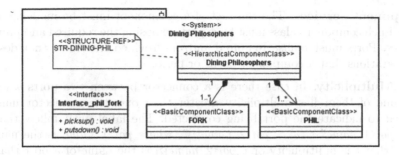

Fig. 4. Class diagram of the Dining Philosophers.

HierarchicalComponentClass (root) and the other component classes. The latter describes the internal structure of its *HierarchicalComponentClass*, that is, how the component instances are connected.

Basic Component. This kind of component is specified by a subsystem stereotyped *BasicComponent* that has one class stereotyped *BasicComponentClass* whose behaviour must be described by a State Machine. The name of the *BasicComponentClass* must be the same as the one for the component. A *BasicComponent* may have an associated structure to describe the ports of the *BasicComponentClass*.

Hierarchical Component. This kind of component is specified by a subsystem stereotyped *HierarchicalComponent* that has one class stereotyped *HierarchicalComponentClass*. Similar to the *BasicComponentClass*, the name of the *HierarchicalComponentClass* should be the same as the one for the component. This class must be the head of a composition relationship with other component classes to express the ownership of other components. The *HierarchicalComponentClass* must have its structure described by a composite structure diagram where the connections between the owned component classes are specified.

Multiplicities. Multiplicities with the * character are not allowed in the composite structure diagram because we are dealing with instances. This is important to make the formal analysis feasible. Also, all parts in a composition relationship must appear in the associated composite structure diagram in numbers compatible with their multiplicities.

Binding Structure and Behaviour to Component. UML Comments (or Notes) are used to bind a state machine or a composite structure to a component. To bind a state machine to a component class the associated comment must be stereotyped *STM_REF* and the content of the note must be the name of the state machine diagram. Likewise, in order to bind a composite structure, the comment must be linked to the component class and be stereotyped *Structure_REF*. The content must be the name of the composite structure diagram.

Component Services. The contract of a component must be modelled using ports. Each component class must have ports exposing the required and provided services. Ports must realise Required and/or Provided Interfaces that describe the operations that a component needs or perform.

Port Multiplicity. In case there is a connector between two ports where at least one of them has multiplicity greater than one, the connector must be labelled to indicate the port being connected. The label must follow the pattern *"port1_name"< − >"port2_name[i]"*, where *port1_name* is the name of a port that has multiplicity one, *port2_name[i]* is the name of a port that has multiplicity greater than one and i is the index of the port of the connection which ranges from one to the number of the multiplicity.

In the next section we explain in detail how component instances can be composed at the UML level and the relationship with the BRIC forms of composition.

3.2   Composition of Component Instances

Composition of component instances is described using a *Hierarchical Component* element. In this section we describe how to compose component instances based on the metamodel detailed in Sect. 3.1.

The simplest form of composition is *Interleave composition*. This is achieved by instantiating components in the composite structure diagram of a hierarchical component. Each instance has a type: a component previously defined. For example, in Fig. 5 we show two instances of *FORK* and two of *PHIL* in a hierarchical component. Before introducing a connection between *phil*1 and *fork*1, the four instances were in interleaving, as the communication of events through the ports can happen without any interference. Therefore, when component instances are created, they are, by default, in interleaving.

Communication composition is performed through the connection of ports from two different components. The same interface must be provided by one component and required by the other one. Figure 5 illustrates in (1) a communication between *fork*1 and *phil*1.

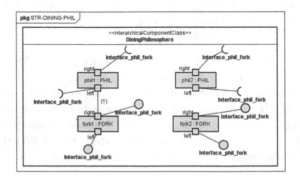

Fig. 5. Inter-component composition UML.

Even when starting with deadlock free components, communication composition can lead to a deadlock if some conditions are not obeyed by the components being connected. It is necessary to verify protocol compatibility of the channels that are to be connected. Broadly, there must always be an output event to be performed, and at least one of the processes must have all enabled outputs accepted by the other process. In our approach, this is verified by translation into BRIC, and using the related verification techniques automated by the FDR tool, completely hidden from the user.

As an illustration, Fig. 6 shows some additional communication compositions in the Dining Philosophers example. While the first three compositions preserved deadlock freedom, the fourth one, labelled (4), introduces a deadlock. This is evidenced by the red line connection, and is displayed to the user by the tool interface, as explained in detail in the next section.

The reason for this well-known deadlock is the symmetry of the design of the philosophers and forks: it allows all the philosophers (two in our example) to pick up, say, the left fork, and then prevents any of the philosophers to pick up the right fork; as a result, the philosophers will starve.

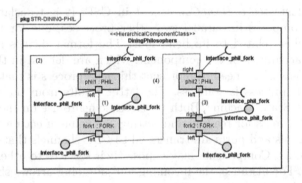

Fig. 6. Component with deadlock.

A possible solution is to break the symmetry and design one of the philosophers to pick up the forks in a different order than the other ones. This fix makes the system deadlock free and the red line is turned into black.

An interesting feature of this step by step composition is that, when a deadlock is found, the developer is warned of the particular connection that is causing the problem. We can identify this connection because, when a deadlock is detected, a counterexample is generated from which we can trace the event related to that particular connection. Also, with the separation of concerns we have adopted in our approach, all the semantic details of the formal verification is totally hidden from the user, who can concentrate on the more appealing graphical UML notation.

As already mentioned, one of the distinguishing features of this work is to verify the properties in background while the UML model is being created to help the user construct a deadlock free model.

3.3   Semantics via Translation into BRIC

In order to perform a mechanised compositional verification during the model construction, we translate, on demand, the UML models to BRIC, which itself uses CSP as the underlying formal notation. We then use tool support for CSP to automatically check properties and trace back any results to the UML level. In this section, we give an intuition on how the UML models are represented as CSP processes according to the BRIC component model.

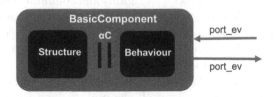

Fig. 7. Illustration of a *BasicComponent* in CSP.

Figure 7 illustrates a *BasicComponent* in CSP. It is translated to a CSP process that composes in parallel two other processes, one for the structural part and another related to its behaviour. The former defines a memory for accessing the attributes of the component, which are defined in the UML *BasicComponentClass*. The need to represent this as a process is that, as a process algebra, a CSP process is stateless. The latter results from the translation of the component State Machine. Both processes synchronise on the set of events αC, which has events for reading and setting the value of each attribute. UML operations, signals and ports are translated to CSP channels that communicate the related events. Components may expose their services to other components through ports. For instance, the incoming and outgoing arrows shown in Fig. 7 communicate these events.

Considering again our running example, the Dining Philosophers, in Sect. 2 we presented the CSP process for the *FORK*, which is a *BasicComponent*. Only the translation of the State Machine depicted in Fig. 3 was presented; its structural part is simply the *SKIP* process, as the component *Fork* has no attributes. The case study presented in the next section considers components with attributes.

The State Machine of the process *Fork* is translated to a CSP process where each state is a process, as shown in Sect. 2. The main process is *stm_fork* from which we can reach the *available* process, and later, the *busy1* or the *busy2* process. Triggers between states are represented by channels; in this case, the trigger *port_fork_right* is a channel that represents the communication through the port named *right* from the *FORK* component. Events are communicated through this channel whose type is a pair: *id.operation*: id (the component identifier) and operations (*putsdown_I*, *putsdown_O*, *picksup_I*, *picksup_O*).

Events that represent operations are derived from the interfaces realised by the component. Each operation from the interface produces two datatypes, both named after the operation, but, the first, suffixed by $\_I$, indicates that this type encodes the operation call and the input parameters; the second, suffixed by $\_O$, indicates that this type encodes the reply to the call together with the output parameters. The *FORK* component provides one interface that has two operations: *picksup* and *putsdown*. Then they are translated to one CSP datatype:

$$datatype \quad operation = picksup\_I \mid picksup\_O \mid putsdown\_I \mid putsdown\_O$$

A *HierarchicalComponent* is specified by the parallelism of its internal components. For instance, consider a *HierarchicalComponent* that has two connected internal components, namely *C1* and *C2*. Wherever two components are connected in UML, such a connection is represented in CSP by the parallel composition of the component processes and a *Buffer* process that orchestrates the communication between the components. Communication in CSP is synchronous while message passing in UML is asynchronous: two events are used to represent the sending and the receiving of a message. Thus, the *Buffer* process simply defines the order in which the events happen through the ports of the components.

The synchronisation alphabet of a component process and the buffer is defined by the events *sent to* and *received from* the ports for that particular connection. For instance, if component *C1* requires a service provided by *C2*, which is represented by the connection between their ports, then $\alpha C1$ has the events of the port of *C1* used in this connection, and $\alpha C2$ has the events of the port of *C2*. The *Buffer* process simply guarantees that the first event comes from the port of *C1* followed by the event related to the port of component *C2*. Finally, a *HierarchicalComponent* can also receive communication from external entities through its ports. These events can be relayed to one of its internal components.

As in the case of basic components, component compositions are also translated to CSP. For instance, the interleave composition of two forks involves no communication and, therefore, no intermediate buffer. This composition is translated to the following process:

$$FORK_{1\_2} = FORK(1) \mid\mid\mid FORK(2)$$

This is checked for deadlock freedom using the BRIC rule for interleaving: it will be deadlock free if one of the components is deadlock free. In this case, both $FORK(1)$ and $FORK(2)$ are deadlock free.

When a connection between two components happens, at the UML level, this entails a communication composition. In BRIC, this can be mapped to feedback or a reflexive composition. As already explained, communication composition in BRIC is used to connect channels of distinct components, whereas feedback and reflexive compositions link two channels of the same component. When a new instance of a component is deployed in the model of *Hierarchical Component*, it is composed in interleaving with existing instances generating a new BRIC component. Therefore, if we connect two instances at the UML level, such a connection can only be represented in BRIC by a feedback or reflexive composition.

For simplicity, we map the instances in a UML composite structure diagram to a single component, and then decide between applying feedback or reflexive composition for deadlock analysis. Then feedback composition is tried first, which requires that the channels being connected are decoupled, meaning that their connection does not establish a cyclic topology [18]. If it fails, then the reflexive composition rule can be applied, as, despite being more expensive, it can handle cyclic networks. The result is then traced back to the UML model.

Figure 5 shows a feedback composition of a communication between *phil*1 and *fork*1 in the process that interleaves two forks and two philosophers. The communication uses the port named *left* from *phil*1 with port *right* from *fork*1.

The Feedback composition represents the simple unary composition case, where two channels of the same component are assembled but do not introduce a new cycle [18]. The process *inter_fork_1_2_phil_1_2* contains all forks and philosophers with no communication. This whole process is now considered a new component. This process interleaves the process for the two forks and two philosophers. For simplicity, we omitted the definition of $FORK_{1\_2}\_PHIL1$, but it simply composes the processes $FORK_{1\_2}$ and $PHIL(1)$ in interleaving.

$$inter\_fork\_1\_2\_phil\_1\_2 = (FORK_{1\_2}\_PHIL1 \;|||\; PHIL2)$$

When we connect two ports of this component, it is considered a Feedback composition, which generates a new component whose process is *feed_inter_fork_1_2_phil_1_2*. This new component is the parallel composition between the process of forks and philosophers (in interleaving) and the buffer, synchronizing on the channels related to the connected ports:

$$feed\_inter\_fork\_1\_2\_phil\_1\_2 = (inter\_fork\_1\_2\_phil\_1\_2)$$
$$\underset{\{|port\_fork\_left.1, port\_phil\_right.1|\}}{||}$$
$$BFIO(port\_fork\_left.1, port\_phil\_right.1)$$

The subsequent connections, as presented in Fig. 6, are all translated to the application of feedback composition, except for the last one, which creates a cycle in the process network; this is translated into a reflexive composition. All these compositions are checked using FDR and, for the symmetric version of philosophers and forks, a deadlock is identified in the final composition, as already explained in the previous subsection.

4   Tool Support and Case Study

To support the proposed CBSD approach, we envision the implementation of a tool with the following features: implementation of the component metamodel and the well-formedness conditions presented in the previous section; editing facilities for model elements and diagrams; creation of component instances and composition of instances by connecting their channels; translation of component models into BRIC; verification of the composition conditions in background (using the FDR tool); and traceability of the verification counterexamples back to the UML component model.

We are currently developing a *plug-in* in the Astah modelling environment [4] to support the above features. Astah has been chosen due to the following reasons: its extension capabilities facilitates the creation of plug-ins; models can be created using several UML elements and diagrams, which allows us to reuse the notation to define our component model, and extend our approach to other model elements in the future; and it has a large community of active users. Also, Astah *plug-ins* allow an easy integration with other tools. In our case, we need to integrate with FDR for the purpose of mechanised verification.

Creating models using Astah is considerably intuitive for UML practitioners. With the plug-in, while the user creates a model, this is incrementally translated into CSP, according to the BRIC metamodel; the BRIC composition rules are used to check deadlock freedom preservation using FDR in background. Given that a deadlock is identified, the user is notified.

Currently, we have a simple prototype of the *plug-in*. Editing facilities are borrowed from Astah, but adherence to the metamodel and well-formedness presented in Sect. 3 is not yet enforced. However, assuming the developer constructs an adherent model, the prototype automatically generates the CSP from the state machines, run FDR in background, and presents a deadlock trace, when a problem is found.

Apart from the Dining Philosopher that we used as a running example, to validate our strategy we developed another case study: a Ring Buffer. It represents a reactive bounded buffer which is composed by a ring of storage cells with a controller and a cache. Each cell is able to store one value. The controller is responsible to intermediate the communication between the environment and the ring, receiving input requests and sending values to be stored inside the cells.

The model of the Ring Buffer system in UML is shown in Fig. 8. It is a *HierarchicalComponent* composed by at least one *Cell* and exactly one *Controller*. We omit the design of these basic components.

In order to allow communication among the controller component and the cells, a common interface is realized by them: *INTERFACE_CONTROL_CELL*. Similarly, *INTERFACE_ENV* is the interface of the *Controller* with the environment.

The connections are captured by the composite structure diagram *STR-RingBuffer*; see Fig. 9. We consider a configuration with three cells. The *Controller* has one port (with multiplicity three), represented by *port_ctr*[3], which is indexed, from 1 to 3, to establish the connections with the three cells. To define which index of *port_ctr* is connected with a port from a *Cell* component, a label is used, for instance: *port_cell* <-> *port_ctr*[1]. The values to be stored to (and recovered from) the Ring Buffer are communicated by *port_env* that interfaces with the environment and realises *INTERFACE_ENV*.

As detailed for the Dining Philosophers, after each connection is performed, BRIC rules are applied to the automatically generated CSP model, and verified using the FDR tool. The complete UML and CSP models for the Dining Philosophers and the Ring Buffer case studies can be found in www.cin.ufpe.br/ ~fmcf2/extendedReport.

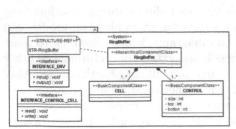

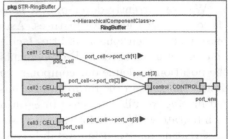

Fig. 8. Ring Buffer system.   **Fig. 9.** Ring Buffer composition.

5 Related Work

There are several approaches to defining component models and verification strategies, based on a variety of formalisms. For instance, in Reo [1], a concurrent system consists of a set of components which are glued together by a circuit that enables flow of data between components. Its formal semantics are based on coalgebras and automata. Another example is rCOS [5], which has a formal semantics based on an extension of the Unifying Theories of Programming (UTP) and automatically generates CSP processes to verify the compatibility between sequence diagrams and the state machine diagram of a contract. A tool for rCOS is introduced in [6], which allows specifying components using operators like parallel composition, hiding, and delegation. However, a process algebraic notation is used as an intermediate specification language, and this has no direct representation in UML.

The Foundational UML Subset (fUML) [16] provides a precise semantic for UML classes, activities and actions. The operational semantics of fUML is an executable model with methods written in Java, with a mapping to UML activity diagrams. The declarative semantics of fUML is specified in first order logic and based on PSL (Process Specification Language) [9]. Despite providing a reliable semantics for a subset of UML, fUML lacks tools for formal reasoning. This could be used to prove the correctness of our transformations, however, as the focus of fUML is on classes and activities, several elements of our strategy, like, state machines, composite structures, among others, would be left out. Therefore, we hope these elements will be covered in the future in order to allow us to prove the correctness of our transformations from UML to CSP.

We use as a basis for our translation from UML to CSP the work presented in [13], which presents a formal semantics for a comprehensive subset of SysML [15] via a mapping into CML [20], a formalism that combines CSP and VDM [7]. The work proposes guidelines that assign some design roles to be played by each of the considered elements in an integrated model. It focuses on state machine, activity, sequence, block definition (class) and internal block (composite structure) diagrams. However, the purpose of [13] is not on component-based design nor on ensuring property preservation by construction.

To our knowledge, there is no work that provides a UML component meta-model and well-formedness conditions that constructively enables the compositional verification of deadlock freedom, including traceability between the underlying formal analysis and the UML model.

6 Conclusion

We propose a UML component model, with associated well-formedness conditions, that supports an incremental design and ensures the preservation of desired properties; we have focused on deadlock freedom. We also define a formal semantics for the proposed component model by translation into BRIC. Components, instances and connections are translated into CSP processes, and deadlock verifications are conducted using the FDR tool, using the BRIC composition rules.

We have also implemented part of the approach as a prototype in the form of a plug-in to the Astah modelling tool. Astah has been chosen due to several facts: its extension capabilities facilitate the creation of modelling plug-ins; UML models can be created using several diagrams that allow us to extend our approach to other model elements in the future; and it has a large community of active users and provide a free edition for students. Using the prototype, the CSP notation and the formal verification is hidden from the user. If the verification fails, the problem is traced back to the UML component level, and the problematic composition is exhibited to the developer who does not need to have CSP knowledge.

To illustrate the overall approach, we developed two case studies (the classical Dining Philosophers and a Ring Buffer) that exemplify the modelling of basic and hierarchical components, with associated state machine and composite structure diagrams with the connection of component instances. We have also described how a UML model, adherent to the proposed metamodel and the well-formedness conditions, is translated to CSP and the BRIC composition rules.

Despite the promising results and the emphasised contributions, our approach has some limitations. The BRIC constraints may reduce the applicability of our approach but they are necessary to ensure the preservation of desired proprieties like deadlock freedom. The Dining Philosophers and the Ring Buffer models, while suitable to illustrate a compositional approach, are not realistic examples in the context of CBSD. We intend to explore more elaborate industrial examples. Concerning automation, the prototype that was developed needs to be significantly improved to support all the features listed in Sect. 4. Particularly, we need to implement adherence to the metamodel and the related well-formedness conditions. Currently, our translation from UML to CSP can be regarded as a semantic definition for the subset of UML involved. In order to establish a notion of correctness for our translation, a formal semantics for UML is necessary; unfortunately, to our knowledge, there is no complete formal semantics for UML in the literature. A possible contribution in this direction is to use the fUML approach as a basis for proving correctness, but this requires extending fUML with a formal semantics for the elements used by our strategy.

As another future direction we plan to adapt the approach proposed in [3] for the construction of heterogeneous collections of components that are defined as patterns using generic (rather than concrete) instances. This allows to parametrise a composite structure diagram by the number of instances involved in a system configuration, rather than being forced to statically determining a particular configuration.

References

1. Arbab, F.: Reo: a channel-based coordination model for component composition. Math. Struct. Comput. Sci. **14**(3), 329–366 (2004)
2. Bonakdarpour, B., Bozga, M., Jaber, M., Quilbeuf, J., Sifakis, J.: A framework for automated distributed implementation of component-based models. Distrib. Comput. **25**(5), 383–409 (2012)
3. Cavalcanti, A., Miyazawa, A., Sampaio, A., Li, W., Ribeiro, P., Timmis, J.: Modelling and verification for swarm robotics. In: Furia, C.A., Winter, K. (eds.) IFM 2018. LNCS, vol. 11023, pp. 1–19. Springer, Cham (2018). https://doi.org/10.1007/978-3-319-98938-9_1
4. Change Vision, Inc.: Astah - software design tools for agile teams with UML, June 2018. http://astah.net/
5. Chen, Z., Liu, Z., Ravn, A.P., Stolz, V., Zhan, N.: Refinement and verification in component-based model-driven design. Sci. Comput. Program. **74**(4), 168–196 (2009)
6. Chen, Z., Morisset, C., Stolz, V.: Specification and validation of behavioural protocols in the rCOS modeler. In: Arbab, F., Sirjani, M. (eds.) FSEN 2009. LNCS, vol. 5961, pp. 387–401. Springer, Heidelberg (2010). https://doi.org/10.1007/978-3-642-11623-0_23
7. Fitzgerald, J., Larsen, P.G.: Modelling Systems: Practical Tools and Techniques in Software Development. Cambridge University Press, New York (2009)
8. Gibson-Robinson, T., Armstrong, P., Boulgakov, A., Roscoe, A.W.: FDR3 — a modern refinement checker for CSP. In: Ábrahám, E., Havelund, K. (eds.) TACAS 2014. LNCS, vol. 8413, pp. 187–201. Springer, Heidelberg (2014). https://doi.org/10.1007/978-3-642-54862-8_13
9. Grüninger, M., Menzel, C.: The process specification language (PSL) theory and applications. AI Mag. **24**, 63–74 (2003)
10. Harel, D.: Statecharts: a visual formalism for complex systems. Sci. Comput. Program. **8**(3), 231–274 (1987)
11. Jacobs, B., Rutten, J.: An introduction to (co) algebra and (co) induction. EATCS Bull. **62**, 222–259 (1997)
12. Kim, H.Y., Jerath, K., Sheldon, F.: Assessment of high integrity software components for completeness, consistency, fault-tolerance, and reliability. In: Cechich, A., Piattini, M., Vallecillo, A. (eds.) Component-Based Software Quality. LNCS, vol. 2693, pp. 259–286. Springer, Heidelberg (2003). https://doi.org/10.1007/978-3-540-45064-1_13
13. Lima, L., et al.: An integrated semantics for reasoning about sysml design models using refinement. Softw. Syst. Model. **16**(3), 875–902 (2017)
14. Object Management Group (OMG): Meta-Object Facility (MOF) Specification, Version 2.5.1. OMG Document Number formal, 01 November 2016. http://www.omg.org/spec/MOF/2.5.1

15. Object Management Group (OMG): OMG System Modeling Language (OMG SysML), Version 1.5. OMG Document Number formal, 01 May 2017. https://www.omg.org/spec/SysML/1.5/
16. Object Management Group (OMG): Semantics of a Foundational Subset for Executable UML Models, Version 1.3. OMG Document Number formal/formal, 02 July 2017. https://www.omg.org/spec/FUML/1.3/
17. Oliveira, M.V.M., Antonino, P., Ramos, R., Sampaio, A., Mota, A., Roscoe, A.W.: Rigorous development of component-based systems using component metadata and patterns. Form. Aspects Comput. **28**(6), 937–1004 (2016)
18. Ramos, R., Sampaio, A., Mota, A.: Systematic development of trustworthy component systems. In: Cavalcanti, A., Dams, D.R. (eds.) FM 2009. LNCS, vol. 5850, pp. 140–156. Springer, Heidelberg (2009). https://doi.org/10.1007/978-3-642-05089-3_10
19. Roscoe, A.W.: The Theory and Practice of Concurrency. Prentice Hall PTR, Upper Saddle River (1997)
20. Woodcock, J., Cavalcanti, A., Fitzgerald, J., Larsen, P., Miyazawa, A., Perry, S.: Features of CML: a formal modelling language for systems of systems. In: 2012 7th International Conference on System of Systems Engineering (SoSE), pp. 1–6, July 2012
21. Woodcock, J., Davies, J.: Using Z: Specification, Refinement, and Proof. Prentice-Hall Inc., Upper Saddle River (1996)

Formal Modelling of Environment Restrictions from Natural-Language Requirements

Tainã Santos[1], Gustavo Carvalho[2(✉)], and Augusto Sampaio[2]

[1] Universidade de Pernambuco - Escola Politécnica de Pernambuco,
Recife 50720-001, Brazil
tms@ecomp.poli.br
[2] Universidade Federal de Pernambuco - Centro de Informática,
Recife 50740-560, Brazil
{ghpc,acas}@cin.ufpe.br

Abstract. When creating system models, further to system behaviour one should take into account properties of the environment in order to achieve more meaningful models. Here, we extend a strategy that formalises data-flow reactive systems as CSP processes to take into account environment restrictions. Initially, these restrictions are written in natural language. Afterwards, with the aid of case-grammar theory, they are formalised by deriving LTL formulae automatically. Finally, these formulae are used to prune infeasible scenarios from the CSP-based system specification, in the light of the environment restrictions. Considering examples from the literature, and from the aerospace (Embraer) and the automotive (Mercedes) industry, we show the efficacy of our proposal in terms of state space reduction, up to 61% in some cases.

Keywords: Natural language · Environment restrictions
Case grammar · Linear temporal logic
Communicating Sequential Processes

1 Introduction

A central element when applying formal methods is capturing the system behaviour precisely, which is typically modelled using some formal notation. Besides modelling the system behaviour, it is also relevant to consider its environment. Although some interactions are possible when only considering the system model, they might not be feasible in practice due to characteristics of the environment. For example, considering a control system operating the car turn lights, in the presence of a turn indicator lever, the control system might not capture a direct change from left flashing to right flashing, since the lever cannot change directly between its extreme positions; it must reside for some moment in the neutral position.

© Springer Nature Switzerland AG 2018
T. Massoni and M. R. Mousavi (Eds.): SBMF 2018, LNCS 11254, pp. 252–270, 2018.
https://doi.org/10.1007/978-3-030-03044-5_16

Here, we consider as environment the collection of entities that interact with the system being modelled. In the aforementioned example, the turn indicator lever would be part of the environment that interacts with the control system operating the car turn lights. Therefore, in order to develop more meaningful models, it is also recommended to take into consideration properties of the environment that, for instance, restrict how the user interacts with the system. In this way, unrealistic interactions are not considered by the models, which tends to reduce the overall system state space. This is more widely beneficial for model checking, simulation, testing and the final system implementation and deployment. For example, when applying model-based testing strategies, infeasible test cases, which cannot be performed due to environment restrictions, are not derived from models.

In this work, we define a controlled natural language (CNL) for specifying restrictions on how a system interacts with its environment. There is a trade-off concerning the adoption of a CNL for requirements specification: one can use a low-constrained CNL to enforce general writing styles, but, typically, formal analysis is not possible by automatic means; on the other extreme, one can adopt a highly-constrained CNL that enables automatic reasoning at the expense of writing naturalness. We seek a compromise between these two extremes: our CNL enforces enough structure to allow for automatic processing of environment restrictions, but aiming at not losing naturalness.

After specifying the restrictions adhering to our CNL, we derive LTL formulae to formalise these restrictions. These formulae are then used to prune, from the specification model, defined using the process algebra CSP (Communicating Sequential Processes) [16], infeasible scenarios in the light of the restrictions. We propose two approaches for restricting CSP models: the first one is based on filtering the inputs, by checking, via a monitor process, which ones satisfy the environment restrictions; the second one involves syntactically modifying the specification so that only valid inputs are selected, but this is done by the process itself, rather than by another process like in the first approach.

Formal modelling of environments is addressed, for instance, in [9,14], where a model is created to capture how the test environment interacts with the system. In our work, the model of the environment restrictions is automatically derived from natural-language descriptions, which are formalised by LTL formulae. Previous works, such as [12], also define ways of generating LTL formulae from natural language, but we differ from them since our formulae are defined over variables and values (not event-based), which enables an easier and more natural way of writing expressions (e.g., one can write $x > 10$, instead of writing $x_{11} \lor x_{12} \lor x_{13}$ to denote the events representing all values x can have that are greater than 10; here, assuming that the greatest possible value of x is 13).

The strategy for modelling environment restrictions presented here is part of a broader research effort for generating test cases from natural-language requirements: the NAT2TEST strategy. In [4], we describe how models of data-flow reactive systems (DFRSs) are automatically derived from controlled natural-language specifications of system requirements. Afterwards, different formal notations can be used to represent models of DFRSs, such as the process algebra CSP, allowing the exploitation of different techniques and tools. In [3] we describe tool support for this strategy: the NAT2TEST tool. A comprehensive explanation of this strategy is presented in [2].

Our strategy for modelling environment restrictions was integrated into the NAT2TEST$_{CSP}$, a version of the NAT2TEST strategy that uses CSP, and, considering examples from the literature, and from the aerospace (Embraer) and the automotive (Mercedes) industry, we show the efficacy of our proposal in terms of state space reduction (up to 61% in some cases). Therefore, the main contributions of this work are the following:

– A CNL for describing environment restrictions;
– A strategy for formalising environment restrictions as LTL formulae;
– Two approaches for imposing environment restrictions on CSP models;
– Integration of this work into the NAT2TEST$_{CSP}$ strategy;
– Empirical analyses concerning examples from the literature and the industry.

This paper is organised as follows. Section 2 briefly introduces background material: linear temporal logic, the process algebra CSP, and modelling data-flow reactive systems as CSP processes. Section 3 presents our CNL for specifying environment restrictions, and explains how LTL formulae are automatically derived from specifications in CNL. Section 4 details the two approaches for imposing environment restrictions on CSP models of the system behaviour. Section 5 gives empirical evidence on the efficacy of our proposal. Finally, Sect. 6 presents our conclusions, and addresses related and future work.

2 Preliminaries

In this section we present an overview of the related background: linear temporal logic (Sect. 2.1), besides the process algebra CSP (Sect. 2.2), which is used to represent the behaviour of data-flow reactive systems (Sect. 2.3).

2.1 Linear Temporal Logic

Linear Temporal Logic (LTL) [15] is a logic for reasoning about linear-time temporal propositions. Given an alphabet Σ of elementary propositions (denoted by lower-case letters), the syntax of LTL is given by the following grammar:

$$\phi ::= false \mid true \mid a \mid \neg\,\phi \mid \phi \wedge \phi \mid \phi \vee \phi \mid \bigcirc \phi \mid \phi\,\mathcal{U}\,\phi \mid \phi\,\mathcal{R}\,\phi$$

Classically, $\bigcirc$ is the next operator (ϕ holds in the next state), $\mathcal{U}$ is the until operator ($\phi\,\mathcal{U}\,\psi$ means that for every execution of the system the formula ψ must eventually become true and the formula ϕ must be true until, not necessarily including, the first point at which ψ becomes true), and $\mathcal{R}$ is the release operator (the dual of $\mathcal{U}$). Two other derived operators are the eventually and the always operators: $\Diamond\phi \equiv true\,\mathcal{U}\,\phi$ and $\Box\phi \equiv \neg\,\Diamond\neg\,\phi$, respectively. The formula $\Diamond\phi$

means that, for every execution of the system, ϕ must hold for some state in the future, whereas $\Box\phi$ means that, for every execution, ϕ holds for all states. In this work, we also consider the weak-until operator: $\phi \; \mathcal{W} \; \psi \equiv (\phi \, \mathcal{U} \, \psi) \vee \Box\phi$, where ψ is not required to occur.

A practical application of LTL is to formalise properties of systems. However, as discussed in [5], it is not always straightforward to define a formula that correctly captures the intended behaviour. In order to make this task easier, a repository[1] was developed to collect patterns that commonly occur in the specification of concurrent and reactive systems. These patterns also have an application scope. Here, our restrictions fit the *absence* and the *universality* patterns, considering the *global*, the *after* and the *after-until* application scopes.

As noted in [11], when considering LTL formulae in the context of CSP specifications, we need to assume an adapted interpretation of the classical LTL operators, since LTL is usually defined for state-based models while the operational semantics of CSP is defined in terms of labelled transition systems (labels are associated to transitions and not states; moreover, some transitions are labelled by the invisible action τ). We follow [11] in this respect.

2.2   Communicating Sequential Processes

CSP is a formal language designed to describe behavioural aspects of systems. The fundamental element of a CSP specification is a process. CSP has two primitive processes: one that represents successful termination ($SKIP$) and another that stands for an abnormal termination ($STOP$), also interpreted as a deadlock. In the simplest semantic model (traces semantics), a process behaviour is described by the set of sequences of events it can perform. To define a process as a sequence of events, we use the prefix operator ($P = ev \rightarrow Q$), where ev is an event, and P and Q are processes.

The sequential composition $P = P1 \; ; \; P2$ states that the behaviour of P is equivalent to the behaviour of $P1$, followed by the behaviour of $P2$, if and when $P1$ terminates successfully. Concerning parallel composition, CSP allows a composition with ($\|$) or without ($\|\|$) synchronisation between the composed processes. CSP processes synchronise between themselves by means of events. For instance, $P \underset{X}{\|} Q$ requires synchronisation on the events in X.

A *channel* can be declared to denote a particular set of events. The term $c!e$, where c is a channel, denotes the event $c.e$ resulting from the evaluation of e, which is any CSP valid expression, whereas the term $c?v$ denotes any event $c.v$ where v is a value of the declared type of c. It is also possible to interpret these symbols ($!$ and $?$) as a process sending or receiving a value through a channel, respectively. Another CSP operator used in this work is hiding ($\backslash$): it encapsulates events within a process and, thus, makes them internal (represented as τ). CSP also has a functional language for manipulating local data.

---

[1] http://patterns.projects.cs.ksu.edu/.

From a CSP specification written in its machine-readable version called CSP_M, the FDR tool[2] [8] can check desirable properties, such as: (1) deadlock-freedom, (2) divergence-freedom, (3) deterministic behaviour, and (4) refinement according to different semantic models (*traces*, *failures*, and *failures-divergences*).

2.3   DFRSs as CSP Processes

The NAT2TEST strategy generates test cases fully automatically from natural-language requirements [3]. The data-flow reactive system (DFRS) model serves as an intermediate formal notation from which it is possible to generate models in several formal target notations, such as CSP. As detailed in [4], any DFRS can be encoded as a Timed Input-Output Transition System (TIOTS), a labelled transition system extended with time, which is widely used to characterise conformance relations for timed reactive systems. However, being more abstract, a DFRS comprises a more concise representation of timed requirements.

Here, we are interested on the CSP-based specialisation of the NAT2TEST strategy (NAT2TEST$_{CSP}$), since it provides us with a sound testing theory. Test generation is mechanised in terms of a high-level strategy by reusing successful techniques and tools: refinement checking (FDR) and SMT solving (Z3[3]). More information is available in [2]. Nevertheless, our results on formal modelling of environment restrictions can also be applied to other strategies, taking as starting point the LTL formulae automatically derived from the textual descriptions.

In what follows, we present a concise explanation of DFRS models, and how they are encoded as CSP processes. A DFRS model represents an embedded system whose inputs and outputs are always available as signals. The input signals can be seen as data provided by sensors, whereas the outputs as data provided to actuators. A DFRS can also have internal timers, which can be used to trigger time-based behaviour.

In the CSP notation, the system behaviour is denoted by the process S, which is defined as $SYSTEM$, hiding all of its internal events (only events related to input, output and time behaviour are visible).

$$S = SYSTEM \setminus \{...\}$$
$$SYSTEM = SPECIFICATION \quad \underset{\{|get,set|\}}{\|} \quad SYSTEM\_MEMORY$$

The process $SYSTEM\_MEMORY$ is defined to allow the parallel components of the system to communicate via shared memory (i.e., global variables, which are not directly supported by CSP). The process $SPECIFICATION$ interacts with the memory reading and writing values via the channels *get* and *set*, respectively; $\{| c |\}$ represents all values that can be communicated over the channel c (e.g., $\{| get, set |\}$ denotes all events communicated over the channels *get* and *set*).

[2] https://www.cs.ox.ac.uk/projects/fdr/.
[3] https://github.com/Z3Prover/z3.

A DFRS model has delay and function transitions. The former occur when the system is in a stable state (no system reaction is enabled, and time might evolve), whereas the latter occur when the state is not stable (system reacts to input stimuli). The process *SPECIFICATION* captures this behaviour.

$$SPECIFICATION =$$
$$... \rightarrow FUN ; ... \rightarrow INPUTS ; DELAY ; SPECIFICATION$$

The first events (not shown) are related to a symbolic encoding of time in CSP, which enables the representation of discrete and continuous time using the standard CSP notation. Since explaining the details of this codification is outside the scope of this paper, we refer to [2] for further details.

After performing these first events, this process behaves as *FUN*, which performs function transitions until the system reaches a stable state, when an output event is performed over the channel *output*. Afterwards, the system performs a delay transition. Basically, time evolves (represented by the *DELAY* process) and new inputs are received (process *INPUTS*) over the channel *input*. In the CSP definition, *INPUTS* takes place before *DELAY* as a consequence of our symbolic time representation – see [2] for more details. Then the process recurses. Therefore, when we analyse a trace of S we observe an alternating sequence of time, input, and output-related events; representing time elapsing, system stimuli and system reaction, respectively.

3   Environment Restrictions

In this section we define a CNL that is convenient to capture restrictions on the environment (Sect. 3.1) and, with the support of case-grammar theory [7] (Sect. 3.2), we devise an automatic translation into LTL formulae (Sect. 3.3). To illustrate our ideas, we consider an adaptation of the vending machine (VM) presented in [9]. We also refer to a Mercedes' turn indicator system (TIS) to illustrate some specific features (explained on demand).

Initially, the VM is in the *idle* state. When it receives a coin, it goes to the *choice* state. When the coffee option is selected, the system goes to the *weak* or *strong* coffee state depending on the time elapsed since the coin insertion. After producing coffee, the system goes back to the *idle* state.

3.1   A CNL for Environment Restrictions

An environment restriction can be seen as the description of an interaction between the environment and the system that is not allowed to happen. It describes input scenarios that are not feasible in practice. The grammar of our CNL for specifying environment restrictions (EnvReq-CNL) is given in Table 1.

The EnvReq-CNL allows for the specification of restrictions that fit the *absence* and *universality* property patterns, considering *global*, *after* and *after-until* application scopes (see [5] for more details on LTL property patterns). The

Table 1. The EnvReq-CNL grammar

```
TestEnvRestriction     ::= (NEVER | ALWAYS) Scope?
                           (StatementClause | ImplicationClause)
Scope                  ::= AFTER AndCondition, (AND UNTIL AndCondition,)?
AndCondition           ::= ...
StatementClause        ::= AndCondition
ImplicationClause      ::= ConditionalClause COMMA THEN ConsequenceClause
ConditionalClause      ::= CONJ AndCondition
ConsequenceClause      ::= RestrictionOrClause
                           | COLON RestrictionOrClause
                           (COMMA AND RestrictionAndClause)+
RestrictionAndClause   ::= RestrictionOrClause
                           | RestrictionAndClause
                           COMMA AND RestrictionOrClause
RestrictionOrClause    ::= RestrictionClause
                           | RestrictionOrClause OR RestrictionClause
RestrictionClause      ::= NounPhrase VerbPhraseRestriction
NounPhrase             ::= ...
VerbPhraseRestriction  ::= VerbRestriction VerbComplement
VerbRestriction        ::= (CNOT | CONLY) VBASE
VerbComplement         ::= ...
```

terminal symbols *NEVER* and *ALWAYS* are mapped to the words "*It is never the case that*" (*absence* pattern) and "*It is always the case that*" (*universality pattern*). After these words, one can specify the application scope (*global* is the default one), followed by the restriction as a statement (*StatementClause*) or as an implication (*ImplicationClause*) clause.

A statement comprises clauses according to a conjunctive normal form (CNF): this structure is ensured by the symbol *AndCondition*. An implication clause is composed by a conditional clause, whose structure is also a CNF preceded by a conjunction, followed by a consequence clause. The consequence clause (also a CNF) describes something that shall be performed (*CONLY*) or cannot be performed (*CNOT*) by the environment. Therefore, this grammar allows for the specification of restrictions in one of the following four templates.

T1 — It is always the case that S, C.
T2 — It is never the case that S, C.
T3 — It is always the case that S, when C_1 then C_2.
T4 — It is never the case that S, when C_1 then C_2.

The symbol S denotes a scope, and if absent it means the global one. The symbol C denotes conditions describing restrictions on the environment. As it can be seen, T2 is the dual of T1; and T3/T4 can be rewritten as T1/T2, respectively, using classical transformations ($C_1 \Rightarrow C_2 \equiv \neg\ C_1 \vee C_2$). Nevertheless, we permit different writing styles aiming at flexibility.

To illustrate our CNL for environment restrictions, consider the VM example. Suppose that a coin can only be inserted when the system is in the idle state: when it is waiting for a coffee request or it is producing a weak (strong) coffee, some mechanical device blocks the hole where the coin should be inserted. The following sentence describes this restriction in accordance to the grammar previously presented. This sentence adheres to T3, considering a global scope.

- VM-RST001: It is always the case that when the system mode is not idle, then the coin sensor cannot be true.

Similarly, suppose that the coffee request button can only be pressed when the system is expecting such an input from the user (the system mode is *choice*). This restriction can be described as follows (template T2 and global scope).

- VM-RST002: It is never the case that the coffee request button is pressed, and the system mode is not choice.

The restrictions can also refer to the previous value of input and output variables. To give a concrete example, consider the following restriction related to the turn indicator system (TIS) of Mercedes vehicles (made available by Daimler; more information in Sect. 5). It is not possible to move the turn indicator lever from the left position directly to the right position. It is necessary to move the lever to the neutral position first. The following sentence (TIS-RST001) specifies this restriction according to the grammar of EnvReq-CNL.

- It is always the case that when the turn indicator lever was in the left position, then the turn indicator lever cannot change to the right position.

The analysis whether the sentences adhere to the EnvReq-CNL is performed by the CNL-Parser, which is part of the NAT2TEST tool [3]. To integrate our work to the NAT2TEST strategy, we modify its CNL (i.e., SysReq-CNL) in order to allow for the specification of both system requirements and environment restrictions. This is achieved by updating the rewriting rule of the start symbol (*Sentence*) as follows. Here, *Sentence* is the start symbol of the NAT2TEST context-free grammar (SysReq-CNL) for specifying system requirements, which can now be rewritten as a system requirement (the non-terminal symbol *SysRequirement*), but also as a restriction on the test environment (the non-terminal symbol *TestEnvRestriction* – see Table 1). More details about the SysReq-CNL are available in [2].

```
Sentence ::= SysRequirement | TestEnvRestriction
```

Before generating the corresponding LTL formulae, we automatically extract requirement frames from the syntax trees of the restrictions. This additional step is performed to decouple the generation of LTL formulae from the structure of the CNL, besides making easier the LTL generation step.

3.2   From Syntax Trees to Requirement Frames

The case-grammar theory [7] is a linguistic theory that can be used to provide semantics to natural-language requirements. In this theory, a sentence is analysed in terms of the thematic roles (TR) played by each word, or group of words in the sentence. The verb is the main element of the sentence, and it determines its possible semantic relations with the other words, that is, the role that each word plays with respect to the action or state described by the verb.

The verb's associated TRs are aggregated into a structure named as case frame (CF). Each verb in a requirement (describing an environment restriction) gives rise to a different CF. All derived CFs are joined afterwards to compose a *Requirement Frame* (RF). Additionally, a RF also has information about the application scope of the restriction. In this work, we consider five thematic roles: the condition action (CAC – the verb related to the condition), the condition patient (CPT – entity who is referred by the condition verb), the condition modifier (CMD – a modification applied to the condition verb), and the condition from/to value (CFV, CTV – values associated to the condition patient). For instance, Table 2 shows the RF obtained from VM-RST001.

Table 2. Requirement frame of VM-RST001

Scope: global			
Condition 1: main verb (CAC): is			
CPT:	the system mode	CFV:	–
CMD:	not	CTV:	idle
Restriction 1: main verb (CAC): be			
CPT:	the coin sensor	CFV:	–
CMD:	cannot	CTV:	true

In order to infer the requirement frame of a given restriction we apply inference rules, which map parts of the CNL structure to thematic roles. The description of these inference rules is outside the scope of this paper.

3.3   From Requirement Frames to LTL

After identifying the requirement frames, we formalise the environment restrictions by generating LTL formulae. First, we identify the core formula (π), which is derived from conditions C or C_1 and C_2 (see Table 3). The symbols ϕ and ψ refer to conditions described by C (or C_1) and C_2, respectively.

Afterwards, we conclude the generation of the LTL formula by considering the application scope (see the correspondence in what follows). The symbol γ refers to the conditions associated to the *after* application scope, and ω to the conditions of the *until* clause (if present). The symbol π denotes the core formula, previously identified.

- Global scope: $\Box(\pi)$
- After scope: $\Box(\gamma \Rightarrow \Box(\pi))$
- After-until scope: $\Box(\gamma \wedge \neg\, \omega \Rightarrow \Box(\pi\ \mathcal{W}\ \omega))$

Table 3. Mapping writing templates to LTL: core formula

Template	Text	Core formula (π)
T1	It is always the case that S, C	ϕ
T2	It is never the case that S, C	$\neg\, \phi$
T3	It is always the case that S, when C_1 then C_2	$\phi \Rightarrow \psi$
T4	It is never the case that S, when C_1 then C_2	$\neg\, (\phi \Rightarrow \psi)$

If the application scope is *global*, the formula is preceded by a single $\square$ operator. When considering an *after* scope, the restriction applies globally only after γ holds. Similarly, regarding the *after-until* scope, the restriction applies globally after γ holds, but until ω holds, which might never occur.

After identifying the general outline of our formulae, we use the thematic roles to generate γ and ω from S, and ϕ and ψ from C (or C_1) and C_2, respectively. The generation of boolean expressions from thematic roles is similar to the one described in [4]. The condition patients (CPT) turn into variables, while their values are extracted from the roles condition from/to value (CFV and CTV). The verbs (CAC) and modifiers (CMD) are used to determine the associated boolean operators. Algorithm 1 summarises the process for generating LTL formulae from requirement frames.

Algorithm 1. *generateLTLFormulae*

> **input**   : *reqFrames*
> **output** : *ltlFormulae*

1 **for** *reqFrame* $\in$ *reqFrames* **do**
2      $\gamma, \omega, \phi, \psi \leftarrow$ *generateBooleanExpressions(reqFrame)*;
3      $\pi \leftarrow$ *mapWritingTemplateToLTL(ϕ, ψ, reqFrame)*;
4   **if** *identifyScope(reqFrame)* = *global* **then**
5   *lflFormulae.add($\square(\pi)$)*;
6   **else if** *identifyScope(reqFrame)* = *after* **then**
7   *lflFormulae.add($\square(\gamma \Rightarrow \square(\pi))$)*;
8   **else**
9   *lflFormulae.add($\square(\gamma \land \neg\, \omega \Rightarrow \square(\pi \;\mathcal{W}\; \omega))$)*;

For instance, considering the roles presented in Table 2 for *Condition 1*, we have that *the_system_mode* (CPT) turns out to be a variable whose value is (CAC) not (CMD) equal to *idle* (CTV) (i.e., *the_system_mode* $\neq$ 1). We note that the value 1 is used to represent the value *idle*. When performing these translations, our tool automatically represents string values as enumeration values. Concerning *Restriction 1*, *the_coin_sensor* is another variable (CPT) whose value cannot (CMD) be (CAC) true (CTV), i.e., *the_coin_sensor* $\neq$ *true*. Filling these expressions into the LTL formula associated to T3 (the template used

in VM-RST001), and considering its global scope, we have the following LTL
formula: $\Box(the\_system\_mode \neq 1 \Rightarrow the\_coin\_sensor \neq true)$.

The LTL formulae derived for the other environment restrictions previously
presented (VM-RST002 and TIS-RST001) are the following, respectively.

$$\Box(\neg\,(the\_coffee\_request\_button = true \wedge the\_system\_mode \neq 0))$$
$$\Box(old\_the\_turn\_indicator\_lever = 1 \Rightarrow the\_turn\_indicator\_lever \neq 2)$$

In the first formula, being pressed is represented as *true* (an optimisation
automatically performed when the possible string values are s and $\neg\ s$ – the
former is treated as *true*, and the latter as *false*). Concerning the system mode,
the value 0 represents the *choice* state.

Regarding the turn indicator system, the positions of the turn indicator lever
(*the neutral position*, *the left position*, and *the right position*) are represented by
the values 0, 1, and 2, respectively. It is also important to note that the *old_*
prefix is used to refer to the previous value of a variable.

The next step of our strategy is to impose the environment restrictions (represented as LTL formulae) to the CSP specification of the system. We do not
translate from the environment restrictions (in natural language) directly to CSP
to make our strategy extensible to other situations when the system behaviour
is not being modelled as CSP processes. In such situations, the effort to apply
our strategy would be to define a translation between LTL formulae and the
adopted formalism to represent the system behaviour.

4   Imposing Restrictions

After obtaining the LTL formulae from the natural-language descriptions of the
environment restrictions, the next step is to consider them to constrain the CSP
model of the system, which is automatically derived from the system requirements by the NAT2TEST$_{CSP}$ strategy; therefore, we emphasise that the CSP
model of the system is also generated from a controlled natural-language specification of the system behaviour (more details in [2]). In the following sections we
propose two different approaches for enforcing the test environment restrictions.

As already mentioned, the first one (Sect. 4.1) imposes the restrictions by
filtering the inputs that obey the environment restrictions; this is captured by
a monitor process. The effect of pruning is achieved by composing the original
system model in CSP in parallel with this monitor. In this way, the original
CSP system specification is totally preserved. Differently, the second approach
(Sect. 4.2) modifies the original CSP model so that only valid inputs are selected.
In addition to reducing the system state space, this approach has the additional
advantage of producing a simpler CSP model that requires less time to compile.
On the other hand, it is not compositional.

4.1   Approach 1: Monitoring Input Generation

In this approach, a monitor process deadlocks (prohibits the system process to
advance) under undesired scenarios. Considering the VM example, part of this

monitoring is performed by the *CHECK_RST* process (shown below); it deadlocks (*STOP*) when at least one of the restrictions is violated. The expressions in the if-clause are derived from the corresponding LTL formulae (see requirements VM-RST001 and VM-RST002 in Sect. 3.

> *CHECK_RST*(*the_coffee_request_button*,
> *the_coin_sensor*, *the_system_mode*) =
> if (not(*the_system_mode* != 1) or *the_coin_sensor* != true) and
>   not(*the_coffee_request_button* == true and *the_system_mode* != 0)
> then ... else *STOP*

Now, we present a detailed explanation of how this monitor process is created for any system. The monitor process (*MONITOR*) interacts synchronously with the system (*S* – see Sect. 2.3) over the channels *input* and *output*.

$$S' = S \quad \underset{\{|input,output|\}}{\|}$$
$$((MONITOR(...) \quad \underset{\{|get,set|\}}{\|} \quad MONITOR\_MEMORY) \setminus \{...\})$$

The process *MONITOR* receives as parameters the initial value (*init_in_val$_i$* and *init_out_val$_k$*) of the system variables (inputs — *in_var$_i$*, and outputs — *out_var$_k$*). Then, it synchronises on the *output* event to record the first output values (*out_val$_k$*). It is necessary to keep track of the current and the previous value of variables since the restrictions might refer to the old value (see Sect. 3.3). Afterwards, *MONITOR* behaves as *MONITOR_LOOP*.

> *MONITOR*(*init_in_val$_1$*, ..., *init_in_val$_n$*,
> *init_out_val$_1$*, ..., *init_out_val$_m$*) =
> *output.out_var$_1$?out_val$_1$...out_var$_m$?out_val$_m$* →
> *MONITOR_LOOP*(*init_in_val$_1$*, ..., *init_in_val$_n$*,
>   *init_in_val$_1$*, ..., *init_in_val$_n$*, *init_out_val$_1$*, ...,
>   *init_out_val$_m$*, *out_val$_1$*, ..., *out_val$_m$*)

The process *MONITOR_LOOP* has the following cyclic behaviour. First, it reads the input values that can be generated (synchronising over *input*). Then, it checks the conditions related to application scopes.

The auxiliary variables *gamma$_i$* and *omega$_i$* are used to keep track of whether γ_i and ω_i (for a given i-th restriction) hold in the current state. It is necessary to perform basic syntactic translations to adhere to the CSP$_M$ syntax (e.g., ¬ becomes *not*(...)). Therefore, Γ_i denotes γ_i in CSP$_M$ (similarly to Ω_i). We note that *gamma$_i$* is only reset to false if the corresponding *until* condition is satisfied.

> *MONITOR_LOOP*(*old_in_val$_1$*, ..., *old_in_val$_n$*, *in_val$_1$*, ..., *in_val$_n$*,
> *old_out_val$_1$*, ..., *out_out_val$_m$*, *out_val$_1$*, ..., *out_val$_m$*) =
> *input.in_var$_1$?in_val'$_1$...in_var$_n$?in_val'$_n$* →
> (if Γ_1 then *set!gamma$_1$!true* → *SKIP* else *SKIP*) ; ...

$$(\text{if } \Omega_1 \text{ then } set!omega_1!true \to set!gamma_1!false \to SKIP$$
$$\text{else } set!omega_1!false \to SKIP) \ ; \ ...$$
$$CHECK\_RST(in\_val_1, ..., in\_val_n, in\_val'_1, ..., in\_val'_n,$$
$$old\_out\_val1, ..., old\_out\_val_m, out\_val_1, ..., out\_val_m)$$

After setting the value of these auxiliary variables, it checks whether each scenario is valid according to the restrictions (auxiliary process $CHECK\_RST$). Being valid means that all environment restrictions (Π_i as the CSP_M version of π_i) are satisfied, if within their application scopes. Since the CSP_M syntax does not support $a \Rightarrow b$, the implications are represented as "not(a) or b". If the application scope is *global*, the values ($v\_$) of $gamma_i$ and $omega_i$ are not considered. If the application scope is *after*, the value of $omega_i$ is not considered.

$$CHECK\_RST(old\_in\_val_1, ..., old\_in\_val_n, in\_val_1, ..., in\_val_n,$$
$$old\_out\_val_1, ..., out\_out\_val_m, out\_val_1, ..., out\_val_m) =$$
$$get!gamma_1?v\_gamma_1 \to ... \to get!gamma_l?v\_gamma_l \to ...$$
$$get!omega_1?v\_omega_1 \to ... \to get!omega_l?v\_omega_l \to ...$$
$$\text{if } (\text{not}(v\_gamma_1 \text{ and not}(v\_omega_1)) \text{ or } \Pi_1) \text{ and } ... \text{ and}$$
$$(\text{not}(v\_gamma_l \text{ and not}(v\_omega_l)) \text{ or } \Pi_l) \text{ then}$$
$$output.out\_var_1?out\_val'_1...out\_var_m?out\_val'_m \to$$
$$MONITOR\_LOOP(old\_in\_val_1, ..., old\_in\_val_n,$$
$$in\_val_1, ..., in\_val_n, out\_val_1, ..., out\_val_m,$$
$$out\_val'_1, ..., out\_val'_m)$$
$$\text{else } STOP$$

If all restrictions are satisfied, the if-condition evaluates to true, and the monitor process allows for system responses (synchronisation over *output*) before behaving as $MONITOR\_LOOP$ again (passing as argument the updated value of variables). However, if this condition is not true, then the monitor process deadlocks. As a consequence, it makes the system process (S) to deadlock as well, since it can only perform input/output events if the monitor process agrees (synchronises) on them.

Deadlock is a desired effect here, since it prohibits the system to advance under undesired scenarios; some traces will not have an output after the inputs that violate the environment restrictions. These traces will not be considered when generating test cases, since we only take into account traces where for each input one can observe the expected system reaction (output).

Although this approach is compositional (it does not require modifications on S) and reduces the final model ($S \ || \ MONITOR$) state space, it does not simplify the original model of the system (S) to consider only valid inputs; consequently, it does not reduce the final model compilation time, which is a relevant aspect when using FDR. The underlying reason is the way FDR deals with the parallel composition. In Sect. 4.3 we discuss in more detail the importance of optimising the compilation of CSP models when using FDR. Nevertheless, this approach might be useful if compositionality is mandatory, when modifying the system model is not possible; for instance, when performing black-box model-based testing.

4.2   Approach 2: Changing Input Generation

Our second approach also imposes the environment restrictions, and the resulting labelled-transition system (LTS) is created in less time. This approach is even simpler to encode than the previous one, but it requires the modification of the CSP process originally created for the system behaviour (S). The idea here is to modify the process *INPUTS* (see Sect. 2.3) to block (deadlock on) the undesired scenarios. Considering the VM example, it suffices to define a process $CHECK\_RST'$ (similar to the one defined in Sect. 4.1), and to compose it sequentially with *INPUTS*: defining a new process $INPUTS' = INPUTS ; CHECK\_RST'$.

In details, let $CHECK\_RST'$ be the following CSP process. After reading the current and previous values of the system variables, along with the values of the auxiliary variables $gamma_i$ and $omega_i$, it checks whether the environment restrictions hold. If so, the process finishes successfully $(SKIP)$. Otherwise, it deadlocks $(STOP)$.

$CHECK\_RST' =$
    $get!old\_in\_var_1?old\_in\_val_1 \to ...$
        $\to get!old\_in\_var_n?old\_in\_val_n \to$
    $get!in\_var_1?in\_val_1 \to ... \to get!in\_var_n?in\_val_n \to$
    $get!old\_out\_var_1?old\_out\_val_1 \to ...$
        $\to get!old\_out\_var_m?old\_out\_val_m \to$
    $get!out\_var_1?out\_val_1 \to ... \to get!out\_var_m?out\_val_m \to$
    $get!gamma_1?v\_gamma_1 \to ... \to get!gamma_l?v\_gamma_l \to ...$
    $get!omega_1?v\_omega_1 \to ... \to get!omega_l?v\_omega_l \to ...$
    if $(not(v\_gamma_1$ and $not(v\_omega_1))$ or $\Pi_1)$ and ... and
        $(not(v\_gamma_l$ and $not(v\_omega_l))$ or $\Pi_l)$ then $SKIP$ else $STOP$

Now, we update the original *SPECIFICATION* process considering a new process for generating inputs $(INPUTS')$. After generating inputs, the scenarios that are not feasible in practice are pruned from the resulting LTS, since $CHECK\_RST'$ deadlocks. S'' denotes the process created using this second approach. This approach yields a faster compilation time, since the environment restrictions are imposed during the creation of the LTS of S''.

$INPUTS' = INPUTS ; CHECK\_RST'$
$SPECIFICATION' =$
    $... \to FUN ; ... \to INPUTS' ; DELAY ; SPECIFICATION'$
$SYSTEM' = SPECIFICATION' \quad \| \quad SYSTEM\_MEMORY$
                          $\{|get,set|\}$
$S'' = SYSTEM' \setminus \{...\}$

It is important to note that our second approach is semantically equivalent to the first one in the CSP trace semantics (Theorem 1). Let $\mathbb{S}$ be the set of all CSP specifications of data-flow reactive systems, S be a given CSP specification, and $appr1$ and $appr2$ functions that yield a CSP specification considering the environment restrictions of S (R_S) according to the first (Sect. 4.1) and the second (Sect. 4.2) approaches, previously described.

Theorem 1. $\forall S : \mathbb{S} \bullet appr1(S, R_S) \sqsubseteq_T appr2(S, R_S) \wedge appr2(S, R_S) \sqsubseteq_T appr1(S, R_S)$

In CSP, the traces refinement relation means trace inclusion. Therefore, if $P \sqsubseteq_T Q \wedge Q \sqsubseteq_T P$ holds, it means that both processes have the same set of traces (i.e., they are equivalent in this semantic model). The proof of Theorem 1 relies on the fact that both approaches create a deadlock on situations where the restrictions are not satisfied. The difference between them is that the first one creates the deadlock via parallel synchronisation, whereas the second one uses the primitive process $STOP$. □

Another important theoretical result of our work is described by Theorem 2.

Theorem 2. $\forall S : \mathbb{S} \bullet S \sqsubseteq_T appr1(S, R_S)$

The CSP specification yielded by $appr1$ (or $appr2$ — see Theorem 1) might deadlock on some (or none) of the traces of S, where undesired input scenarios occur, but it does not produce new traces (new events are not performed). Therefore, the traces of $appr1(S, R_S)$ are a subset of the traces of S. □

Differently, $appr1(S, R_S) \sqsubseteq_T S$ does not hold in general, since we expect the left-hand side process to have less traces than S due to the imposed restrictions.

4.3   Relevance of Compilation Optimisation

Consider the following CSP specification.

channel $input, output : \{0..20000\}$
$A(v) =$ if $v >= 0$ then $output.v \rightarrow A(v-1)$ else $STOP$
$P = input?v \rightarrow A(v)$
$Q = input?v \rightarrow$ if $v == 2$ then $A(v)$ else $STOP$
$R = P \qquad \underset{\{|input,output|\}}{\|} \qquad Q$
$P' = input?v \rightarrow$ if $v == 2$ then $A(v)$ else $STOP$
$R' = P'$

A is an auxiliary process that performs the event $output.i$, with i varying from v to 0. P receives an input value v and then behaves as $A(v)$. Q behaves similarly to the process $MONITOR$: it synchronises on all communications over the input and the output channels, and restricts P to behave as $A(2)$ (suppose that 2 is the only feasible input).

The process R' is equivalent to R (both processes have the same set of traces), but it is defined differently. It follows our second approach (detailed in Sect. 4.2) to restrict the behaviour of P, which involves modifying the definition of P (i.e., defining a new process P'). Considering the channels $input$ and $output$ ranging from 0 to 20,000, more than 60s is necessary to create the LTS of R, whereas the LTS of R' is created within 20s[4].

When constructing (compilation phase) the LTS of R, FDR first expands the LTS of P and Q, and then constructs the resulting LTS via bisimulation. Therefore, although the resulting LTS has less states (reduction of the state space), the time required to construct this LTS tends to be the same or even greater. In other words, in general, the approach described in Sect. 4.1 does not represent performance gains with respect to compilation time, but only regarding analysis time (when the resulting LTS model has already been created).

5   Empirical Analyses

Our evaluation considers examples from four different domains: (i) the vending machine (VM) discussed in Sect. 3; (ii) the control system for safety injection in a nuclear power plant (NPP) presented in [10]; (iii) a priority command function (PC) provided by Embraer[5]; and (iv) part of the turn indicator system (TIS) of Mercedes vehicles[6].

In order to provide an argument to the efficacy of our proposal, we measured the achieved reduction in terms of number of states and transitions. We only consider the approach described in Sect. 4.2, since the other one (Sect. 4.1) does not improve the model compilation time, and, thus, it is does not scale for complex examples such as the TIS (exceeds available RAM memory).

Threats to external validity (the ability to generalise our conclusions) apply to our analyses, since we do not consider a large set of examples. Despite that, the results give some evidence about the efficacy of our proposal. Table 4 summarises our findings; S is the original system model, whereas S'' is the system model constrained by the test environment restrictions (as described in Sect. 4.2).

Table 4. Metrics of the empirical analyses

	VM	NPP	PC	TIS
#restrictions of S''	2	3	1	2
#states of S	4,652	14,681	5,592	215,470
#states of S''	1,814	12,261	2,728	189,644
Reduction (states)	**61.01%**	**16.48%**	**51.22%**	**11.99%**
#transitions of S	4,761	15,617	6,137	228,141
#transitions of S''	1,841	12,975	2,949	200,339
Reduction (trans.)	**61.33%**	**16.92%**	**51.95%**	**12.19%**

A significant reduction in the number of states/transitions was achieved for the VM (61.01%/61.33%) and for the PC (51.22%/51.95%) examples, whereas

---

[4] Considering an i7-5500U @ 2.40 GHz × 4, 8 GB of RAM, with Ubuntu 16.04 LTS.

[5] http://www.embraer.com/en-us/pages/home.aspx.

[6] http://www.informatik.uni-bremen.de/agbs/testingbenchmarks/index_e.html.

it was smaller for the NPP (16.48%/16.92%) and the TIS (11.99%/12.19%). The reduction was smaller for the NPP and TIS examples, since the infeasible scenarios specified by the environment restrictions are less common than the ones considered in the other two examples (VM and PC). Nevertheless, as said before, besides the benefit of reducing the state space, there is a more general benefit of developing more meaningful models, since infeasible scenarios can be ignored by analysis via model checking, simulation and the final implementation.

6   Conclusion

This paper presents a strategy for modelling environment restrictions formally in order to develop more meaningful models of the system behaviour, besides taking advantage of them to reduce the input space of models. The proposed approach integrates different techniques and notations (natural-language processing, linear temporal logic, CSP, and model checking). The restrictions are formalised as LTL formulae, which are automatically generated with the aid of a controlled natural language. Then, these formulae are used to impose the restrictions to a CSP model of the system.

The contribution of this work integrates with the NAT2TEST strategy, which provides means for generating test cases from natural-language requirements, ruling out infeasible test scenarios. The efficacy of our proposal is illustrated considering examples from the literature, and from the aerospace (Embraer) and the automotive (Mercedes) industry. Despite the integration with NAT2TEST, our results can also be applied to other contexts, taking as starting point the LTL formulae automatically derived. For instance, it is possible to take into account these LTL formulae to perform classical model checking [11].

Generating temporal logic formulae from natural-language specifications is not a new research topic. In [6] an action-based branching temporal logic (ACTL) is used to formalise requirements in order to support verification of specification properties. More recently, reference [17] presents another strategy for formal consistency checking of natural-language requirements via the generation of LTL formulae. In [12], similarly to our work, the authors use case-grammar theory to support the generation of LTL formulae. A common aspect between these works and ours is the definition of an underlying structure (via templates or CNL) for writing requirements. However, differently from them, our LTL formulae are defined over variables and values, and not over events.

Formal modelling of the environment has already been addressed too. For instance, in [9] a conformance relation ($i\ rtioco_e\ s$) is proposed to relate implementation (i) and specification (s) models in the light of an environment model (e); all models are defined as timed input-output transition systems. In the RT-Tester tool [14], the system behaviour and the test environment are both modelled as state machines. In [13], considering programmable controllers, the authors propose a strategy for reducing the set of test cases by modelling the plant behaviour, additionally to the system behaviour, as finite state machines. Differently from our work, the user needs to manually and formally model the environment. Here, the formal model of the environment restrictions is automatically generated from high-level descriptions in natural language. However, these other works can model arbitrary properties, which is not our case.

As future work, we intend to: (1) extend our CNL to allow the specification of other types of restrictions, (2) investigate the use of valency grammar [1] in contrast to the case-grammar theory, and (3) conduct further empirical analyses.

Acknowledgements. This work is partially supported by INES (www.ines.org.br), CNPq grant 465614 /2014-0 and FACEPE grants APQ-0399-1.03/17 and PRONEX APQ/0388-1.03 /14. It is also partially supported by the CIn-UFPE and Motorola cooperation project, as well as by the CNPq grants 303022/2012-4 and 132332/2015-9.

References

1. Allerton, D.J.: Valency grammar. In: Brown, K. (ed.) The Encyclopedia of Language and Linguistics, pp. 301–314. Elsevier Science Ltd. (2006)
2. Carvalho, G.: NAT2TEST: generating test cases from natural language requirements based on CSP. Ph.D. thesis, Centro de Informática, UFPE, Brazil (2016)
3. Carvalho, G., Barros, F., Carvalho, A., Cavalcanti, A., Mota, A., Sampaio, A.: NAT2TEST tool: from natural language requirements to test cases based on CSP. In: Calinescu, R., Rumpe, B. (eds.) SEFM 2015. LNCS, vol. 9276, pp. 283–290. Springer, Cham (2015). https://doi.org/10.1007/978-3-319-22969-0_20
4. Carvalho, G., Cavalcanti, A., Sampaio, A.: Modelling timed reactive systems from natural-language requirements. Form. Asp. Comput. **28**(5), 725–765 (2016)
5. Dwyer, M.B., Avrunin, G.S., Corbett, J.C.: Patterns in property specifications for finite-state verification. In: Proceedings of the 21st International Conference on Software Engineering, ICSE 1999, pp. 411–420. ACM, New York (1999)
6. Fantechi, A., Gnesi, S., Ristori, G., Carenini, M., Vanocchi, M., Moreschini, P.: Assisting requirement formalization by means of natural language translation. Form. Methods Syst. Des. **4**(3), 243–263 (1994)
7. Fillmore, C.J.: The case for case. In: Bach, E., Harms, R.T. (eds.) Universals in Linguistic Theory, pp. 1–88. Holt, Rinehart, and Winston, New York (1968)
8. Gibson-Robinson, T., et al.: FDR: from theory to industrial application. In: Gibson-Robinson, T., Hopcroft, P., Lazić, R. (eds.) Concurrency, Security, and Puzzles. LNCS, vol. 10160, pp. 65–87. Springer, Cham (2017). https://doi.org/10.1007/978-3-319-51046-0_4
9. Larsen, K.G., Mikucionis, M., Nielsen, B.: Online testing of real-time systems using UPPAAL. In: Grabowski, J., Nielsen, B. (eds.) FATES 2004. LNCS, vol. 3395, pp. 79–94. Springer, Heidelberg (2005). https://doi.org/10.1007/978-3-540-31848-4_6
10. Leonard, E., Heitmeyer, C.: Program synthesis from formal requirements specifications using APTS. High. Order Symbol. Comput. **16**, 63–92 (2003)
11. Leuschel, M., Currie, A., Massart, T.: How to make FDR spin LTL model checking of CSP by refinement. In: Oliveira, J.N., Zave, P. (eds.) FME 2001. LNCS, vol. 2021, pp. 99–118. Springer, Heidelberg (2001). https://doi.org/10.1007/3-540-45251-6_6
12. Lignos, C., Raman, V., Finucane, C., Marcus, M., Kress-Gazit, H.: Provably correct reactive control from natural language. Auton. Robot. **38**(1), 89–105 (2015)

13. Ma, C., Provost, J.: A model-based testing framework with reduced set of test cases for programmable controllers. In: Proceedings of the IEEE Conference on Automation Science and Engineering, pp. 944–949. IEEE (2017)
14. Peleska, J., Vorobev, E., Lapschies, F., Zahlten, C.: Automated model-based testing with RT-tester. Universität Bremen, Technical report (2011)
15. Pnueli, A.: The temporal semantics of concurrent programs. Theor. Comput. Sci. **13**(1), 45–60 (1981)
16. Roscoe, A.W.: Understanding Concurrent Systems. Springer, London (2010). https://doi.org/10.1007/978-1-84882-258-0
17. Yan, R., Cheng, C.H., Chai, Y.: Formal consistency checking over specifications in natural languages. In: Proceedings of the Design, Automation & Test in Europe Conference & Exhibition, pp. 1677–1682. EDA Consortium (2015)

Author Index

Printed in the United States
By Bookmasters